TO THE LIMIT

TO THE LIMIT

The Untold Story

of the

EAGLES

Marc Eliot

DA CAPO PRESS
A Member of the Perseus Books Group

Cataloging-in-Publication data for this book is available from
the Library of Congress.

First Da Capo Press edition 2005
ISBN 0–306–81398-X

This Da Capo Press paperback edition of *To the Limit* is an unabridged
republication of the edition published in New York by Little, Brown
in 1998, with the addition of a Postscript. It is reprinted by
arrangement with the author.

Published by Da Capo Press
A Member of the Perseus Books Group
http://www.dacapopress.com

Da Capo Press books are available at special discounts for bulk purchases in
the U.S. by corporations, institutions, and other organizations. For more
information, please contact the Special Markets Department at the Perseus
Books Group, 11 Cambridge Center, Cambridge, MA 02142, or call (800)
255–1514 or (617) 252–5298, or email special.markets@perseusbooks.com.

1 2 3 4 5 6 7 8 9—09 08 07 06 05

Dedicated to the memory of
KAREN HUBERT ALLISON

While the sun still spends his fabulous money
For the kingdoms in the eye of a fool,
Let us continue to waste our lives
Declaring beauty to the world.

— Kenneth Patchen

"We're still alive. That must count for something."

— Don Henley

CONTENTS

INTRODUCTION

THE ROOTS OF THE
AVOCADO MAFIA

INTRODUCTION

As American rock and roll staggered toward the end of the sixties, a festival took place on an upstate New York farm to celebrate "Three Days of Peace and Love." Despite the enormous and well-organized hype, Woodstock, as it became known, was in reality less a commemoration of a decade's musical, social, and political achievements than a memorial to what Lionel Trilling would later deplore as the sixties' personality-peculiar "cult of sincerity."

Although festivals remained part of rock's annual summer rituals, nothing quite like Woodstock ever took place again, as the last vestige of hippie flower power washed away during those three days of peace, love, and torrential rain. Most of the seminal acts of the decade, sensing disaster, did not even bother to make an appearance, including a by-now reclusive Bob Dylan, the endgame Beatles, and the strung-out Rolling Stones. Of those who did, almost none carried any musical or cultural influence into the next year, let alone the next decade. The biggest-name performer, Jimi Hendrix, passed away not long after (as did Janis Joplin, who was there, and Jim Morrison, who wasn't), putting an especially bitter coda on the dead-end destiny of the so-called psychedelic sixties.

The single previously heard but still unseen act that emerged triumphant from Woodstock was Crosby, Stills and Nash, joined onstage by Neil Young. Taking their turn at four in the morning, they sat themselves down on stools, reached for their guitars, performed their uniquely structured, lyrically sophisticated, harmonically vivid "Suite: Judy Blue Eyes," and at a generation's wake became superstars.

3

The deliberately dressed-down four had come together during the last years of the sixties, in the legendary clubs along Los Angeles's Sunset Strip, sharpening a sound part folk, part rock, part country, part blues. And all white. It was an amalgam of music at once familiar and surprising, the legacy of the best and brightest of the New York early sixties club scene and the British Invasion, most of the survivors having long since headed west. By the middle of the decade, such former Greenwich Village performers as the Mamas and the Papas, the Byrds, John Sebastian, Tim Hardin, David Crosby, David Blue, and Joni Mitchell had all landed on the night side of Sunset to play a hand in reviving and reenergizing what they still called rock and roll. By combining the fifties-based doo-wop harmonies of L.A.'s Beach Boys with the bouncing rhythms of Liverpool's Beatles, and mixing in a little Nashville-style country to dress the sound in blue-jean blues, dozens of new West Coast groups had flourished. The Byrds, Buffalo Springfield, and the Hollies, three of the Strip's most popular and influential bands, eventually resolved into Crosby (Byrds), Stills (Springfield) and Nash (Hollies), and occasionally Young (Springfield). Having first perfected its act on record, the group then came to Woodstock to stake its claim on the seventies.

Crosby, Stills and Nash's festival success established them with authority. They quickly assumed the position of godfathers of the "new" L.A. sound, the group everyone most respected and wished to emulate. As it turned out, while they pointed the way, C, S and N would not remain atop the rock pile for long. Although they managed to survive through the years in one configuration or another, personal demons, stylistic conflicts, and an idealism too heavily rooted in politics and pot ultimately narrowed their audience and flattened their impact. In retrospect, they were the last great group of the sixties rather than the first great one of the seventies.

Nevertheless, the trail they blazed became rock's latest superhighway. When the next crop of young hopefuls raised their heads in the direction of the music, they too would inevitably look to the West. Indeed, by 1971, L.A. was the unchallenged new mecca of American rock and roll. Like the prospectors of the California gold rush a hundred years earlier, most hopefuls would soon return home in disappointment, their vein of gold records unrecorded. Some would stay a while longer before giving up, and a few would actually get to spend fifteen minutes playing out their fevered dreams.

Fewer still would find glory. Four who did were Don Henley from Texas, Glenn Frey from Michigan, Randy Meisner from Nebraska, and Bernie Leadon from Minnesota. Each came to L.A. not knowing the others, or the city, or the world they wanted so much to be a part of. Each set out simply to make good music, and did, until the day they found themselves onstage together and realized for the first time their combined potential for greatness. Reborn as the Eagles, Henley, Frey, Meisner, and Leadon changed rock and roll again forever.

Their music dominated the seventies and displaced the previous pop-culture power clique of L.A.'s clean-cut, blue-eyed, soulful singer-songwriters. Under the shrewd guidance of David Geffen, the same youthful manager-on-the-make who'd orchestrated Crosby, Stills and Nash's rise to superstardom, the Eagles became point men along the Strip for what was called, variously, the Mellow Mafia, the Southern California Mafia, and the Avocado Mafia, a seventies version of Frank Sinatra's fifties Hollywood Rat Pack. They would be idolized and idealized by the children of the seventies for cutting the self-indulgent psychedelic excess from their big brothers and sisters' music. Taking a vocal cue from the harmony-rich, romantically hip, acoustically countrylike sound of Crosby, Stills and Nash, the Eagles by-passed the more strident echoes of the sixties simply by ignoring them. Instead, in their various incarnations, they reinvigorated rock and roll with pop-heavy doses of rhythm and blues ("Heartache Tonight"), bluegrass ("Twenty-One"), gospel ("The Last Resort"), Motown ("One of These Nights"), surf ("Take It Easy"), reggae ("Hotel California" — listen to it again), blue-eyed soul ("I Can't Tell You Why"), Top 40 ("Witchy Woman"), romantic ballads ("Best of My Love"), classic teenage pop-rock tunes ("New Kid in Town"), bar-band rock ("Chug All Night"), epic album cuts ("The Sad Café"), FM-friendly rock ("Nightingale"), and oh yes, country-rock ("Desperado"). By doing so, they became the quintessential American band, their original configuration (Detroit street-kid, Southern moralist, Midwestern barfly, and country-western banjo player) an apt metaphor for the seventies generational hopes and dreams of a creatively integrated America.

Even so, the songs of the Eagles sound-tracked a time that refused to long nostalgically for the fervor, action, and relevance of the decade just ended. Rather, they reflected the emerging musical style of a seventies postwar America that looked forward to growing up in actual as opposed to imagined peacetime and a better way of living with, if not completely in, the mainstream. To that end, the first truly sexually liberated generation, coming of age in the relatively brief, gloriously guilt-free period of anything goes after the Pill and before AIDS, had no trouble identifying with a band that sang like angels and partied like devils.

Throughout their career, the Eagles rode high with privilege down rock's treacherous fast lane. When the first end finally came, perhaps fittingly at the close of the seventies, they were, perhaps understandably, emotionally road-weary from their increasingly dark journey. It would take fourteen years for Henley and Frey to come into the morning light of their own day-after nineties and reconcile their personal differences. Once they did, they invited their flock to share in the celebration, and for however brief the moment, the world again belonged to them.

In the nineties, the music of the Eagles returned to the charts and minds of the now grown-up children of the seventies, its rebel yell having become more anthemic than moral. Still, even as it remained the best sound track of a collective flight of a generation's youthful fancy, for the Eagles, it all too quickly became the same old story. For what had first made them so great was also what had always driven them so crazy, from their first downshift in the speed zone to the final gassy rev down memory lane. Inevitably, it seemed, no matter how fast they drove, they could never quite lose the reflection that tailed them in the rearview: the image of their own heated youth, already exhausted by their high-speed, chrome-dipped, supercharged, and eternally conflicted souls.

PART ONE

DESPERADOES

ONE

For young Donald Hugh Henley, growing up in the fifties in a five-thousand-dollar brick house on West Houston Street in Linden, Texas, meant that no matter how far you looked in any one direction, all you saw were low roofs, dry crops, and green John Deeres. And those hulking tractors didn't qualify as real vehicles as far as Henley was concerned, just bigger, noisier farm tools. Now hot convertible V-8s, *those* were the chariots of the gods! As a boy, Henley was obsessed with the new breed of sleek, fin-tipped, pedal-heavy American cars. At least part of the attraction came from the isolation and freedom the front seat of a car could provide, a special privacy difficult to get at home or in the crowded confines of the local schoolhouse. "The car is a nice little capsule," Henley once recalled. "Nobody bothers you in there and you have a sense of movement." Every night in his small room, Henley pored over any auto rag he could get his hands on, while the portable picked up the skipwaves of New Orleans's 50,000-watt WNOE-AM. The slicks showed him the latest grilles and dashboards out of Detroit, and the radio turned him on to the sounds of the Delta blues. One offered the vehicles of physical escape, the other the language of creative freedom. As alluring as each was, at the time, neither seemed even remotely within his limited reach.

Linden, Texas, just west of Highway 59, is not far from the border that separates the Lone Star State from Louisiana, Arkansas, and Oklahoma. It is a verdant little farm town with a population of about 2,400, whose inhabitants' primary claim to fame before bragging rights as the birthplace of one of the Eagles was that it had given the world singer-songwriter and pioneering electric blues guitarist Aaron Thibeaux "T-Bone" Walker, and ragtime legend Scott Joplin.

Linden lies forty-two miles from Gilmer, the town where Henley was actually born. They still talk about the night of July 22, 1947, the date of his birth, an unseasonably cold day in July, racked with hail and tornadoes so powerful the entire roof blew off Upshur County's school gymnasium. Henley recalls, "My father and my grandmother always used to tell the story about how they had to turn on the heater in the car when they went to the hospital to see me and my mother."

C. J. Henley, Don's father, was born in a small farming town in Hopkins County, in the northeast of Texas. The family name meant literally "where the hens lay." "It's what is called a 'place name,'" according to Henley. "Some people are named for physical traits, some for places, in this case a field, a meadow, or any nesting place for wild birds. Henley is often spelled with an *S* at the end but we didn't." He adds, jokingly, "My ancestors must have been hatched in a field somewhere."

C. J. worked at various jobs, including at an ice plant and a friend's dry-cleaning establishment until he was drafted into the army. Just before he entered the service, at age thirty-five — relatively late for a Southerner — C. J. married Hughlene McWhorter. Hughlene, like C. J., was native Texan. She was a local schoolteacher until her first and only child was born. After World War II, C. J. went into business for himself, the owner-operator of an auto parts store, where he served as a NAPA jobber.

For every member of the family the waking day began when the sun rose and ended when it set. To Don, as he preferred being called, school offered little relief from the monotony of growing up in a small town buried in Texas farmland. Even at school, many of the day's lessons, like the FFA (Future Farmers of America) elective, were taught with an eye to the business of farming, the profession some of the boys in Linden were likely to go into as soon as they were old enough to work the land.

By the time he entered high school, Henley had developed a strong resistance to that life. He wasn't sure at this point what he wanted to do with his future, but he knew it wasn't following in this burg's fertilizer footprints. Still, opportunities to rebel proved scarce. For the most part, he played the dutiful son and joined the Future Farmers of America. To fulfill the requirements for his senior project, Henley tended an acre and a half of cucumbers, which required getting up at five each morning to tend, harvest, and eventually take them to the pickle processing plant. It was an experience he would later describe as "pure hell."

One way he found to play out the romance of the self-styled rebel was by building his own go-cart from a mail-order kit. When he managed to get it up and running, he loved to gun down the two-lane blacktop from Linden to Marietta, something he often did until he got his first real car, "a forty-eight Dodge that was a hand-me-down from my father. It was like a tank. We slept in it, we threw up in it, we hunted in it. We did everything in that car. I snuck away one summer day and won a drag-racing contest in it, in the lowest horsepower class available, K-stock. I beat a fifty-two Chevy and won a trophy. Which I still have. I didn't tell my parents until a year or two later." Alone behind the wheel, imagining he was starring in his favorite TV show, *Route 66*, Henley proudly wore a "Rat Fink" T-shirt he got from an ad he answered in *Car Craft* magazine.

Somewhere between cucumbers and cars, Henley got the chance to learn to play a musical instrument. "I had piano lessons when I was a kid," Henley says. "My father loved music; my mother loved music. They always had records on in the house. We listened to Glenn Miller, Harry James, Benny Goodman, Guy Lombardo — all the World War II and postwar big band stuff. There was an old black lady who worked for my grandfather who was always singing spirituals, what they called 'negro spirituals' back then. My grandmother was always singing hymns.

"My father also listened to country music on the radio during his half-hour drive to work, back and forth, twice a day. He'd listen to KWKH out of Shreveport, *The Louisiana Hayride*, which, whenever I'd make the drive with him, is how I'd hear a lot of fifties country music: Hank Williams, Ernest Tubb, Red Foley, Patsy Cline, all of it. Later on, of course, there was Elvis, the Everly Brothers, Fats Domino, Jerry Lee Lewis, and Ricky Nelson.

"My mother used to buy me forty-fives. I had one of those little RCA players with the fat red spindle tops. I remember one of my favorite records back then was Bobby Freeman's 'Do You Want to Dance.' Later on, of course, the Beatles came along, and that was it. I was into music before, but after they arrived everything changed. They were a major influence for me. Of course, still later it was the B's — the Byrds, Buffalo Springfield, and the Beach Boys."

Henley set his sights on the trombone after he was assigned the instrument by the high school band. He practiced until he realized he simply lacked the interest and gave it up in favor of something that didn't require the development of a horn lip. Henley's next instrument of expression was the drums. He was encouraged to play at home, especially when he showed some early ability. Because he had already demonstrated a propensity for making noise in a number of ways — one time by blowing up a cast-iron washtub in the backyard — his parents believed the six hundred dollars invested in a drum kit was a small price to keep a safe peace, if not exactly a hushed quiet, in the household.

Hughlene's loving encouragement helped bring mother and child closer together. Their especially close relationship did not go unnoticed by Henley's schoolmates, who took to making fun of the frail youngster. Somewhat shy, he was one of the less popular boys in his class. The redneck ostracism by the other boys fed Henley's insecurities, and the need to display what he considered his "manliness" would continue throughout his life. As a childhood friend later recalled, "In some ways he never did leave [home] and never grew up. I think that's why he was always punishing himself in one way or another, no matter how rich or famous he became. I thought he was tragic in his self-abuse — all the drugs and women, in particular his inability to be faithful. It's not that he didn't love women. He just had to constantly prove he could do whatever it was he wanted. He had to prove he still wasn't that dorky kid."

Henley practiced his drums every day, sometimes for hours, until he became good enough to play with a local group. In the summer of 1962, at the age of fifteen, he joined a pal's Dixieland jazz combo.

Henley's best childhood friend was schoolmate Richard Bowden, whose father was the town insurance salesman. Overweight, loud, known for the intricacy of his practical jokes, and extremely popular at school, young Bowden was in many ways Henley's complete opposite. He found a way to break through Don's loner wall by making him laugh. Henley loved the way Bowden's schemes always played out so perfectly, and they soon became familiar figures around each other's houses.

Henley and Bowden even shared a private language — something they called Bowdenese — a sort of reverse talk, not unlike Cockney, in which words and actions did not match. In Bowdenese, they deferred to an opposite, saying how brightly the sun was shining during a thunderstorm, or smiling when they weren't happy. The two delighted in their articulated privacy, seeing in it some proof that they were in fact hipper and smarter than anyone else in their world.

It didn't take Bowden long to assess his new pal's family situation. "Mrs. Henley was a real fine lady," he later recalled, "but she didn't have control over Don. Not that he didn't respect her; he just didn't always do what she wanted. And then Don's father would have to gently but firmly come down on him."

It was, in fact, with Richard Bowden that Henley had his first real band experience. His friend's dad, Elmer, had formed a Dixieland band with his son, Richie, and one of Richie's school friends, Jerry Surratt. They asked Don to join, and it was that group that became the foundation for the Speeds. Bowden played a pretty good guitar, and when his father left the group, it gradually shifted to an instrumental country bar/club/frat band that played mostly Top 40 covers.

Henley remembers: "We were playing a lot of frat parties and clubs, mostly in Austin, Texas, and Dallas. Later on when I started to sing, rhythm and blues was really popular. The frat boys would all want James Brown, Wilson Pickett, Otis Redding music, which I had to learn. That's how I got hoarse, singing that kind of music four hours a night, trying to sound raspy until my voice blew out. Those singers, and later on John Lennon, were major influences on my singing style."

A local acquaintance remembers, "It was a small town, a limited circuit: high school proms, bars; and everyone wanted a new band every week. In order to keep working, the guys kept changing their name. No one really remembered who they were or what they looked like, and every band played the same basic hit tunes of the day."

Partly out of boredom and partly to separate themselves from the competition, the Speeds started playing their own songs, titles like "I'm Gone" and "God Is Where You Find Him." However, for all the band's intensity and purpose, the plan backfired when the boys realized that audiences were not particularly interested in songs they'd never heard before.

In 1964, the Speeds, or Four Speeds as they were sometimes called, both names an allusion to the road, not the drug, changed their name again, this time to Felicity. "In retrospect," Henley observes, "it's a stupid name, but we thought it was cool then. I've never known anybody named Felicity. We probably changed it in an effort to modernize, because we decided the Speeds, with its hot-rod allusion, was becoming a bit anti-quated." No one quite remembers where the name came from (one former member thinks it might have been the name of another member's girl-friend), but none of them would ever forget the day they managed to snag a contract from a local independent producer and record one of their orig-inal tracks, a Henley composition called "Hurtin.'"

Without question it was the biggest thing that had ever happened to the band. In the early sixties independent record producer–label owner–distributors were rife in the South, bottom-feeders forever looking for the Next Big Thing to sell to the wheels up in New York City. They always made sure to sign the bands' publishing rights as well, so that if any of them ever actually had a hit, the original label would keep a piece of the earnings pie, most often the biggest slice.

The recording contract seemed to elevate Henley's unofficial position as the group's songwriter and leader. Had it been up to him, he would have pre-ferred to stay buried behind his kit. However, in spite of his shyness, it was soon decided by the others that Henley would be Felicity's front man. According to Richard Bowden, "We eventually realized that [lead singers] were where it's at, but nobody wanted to do it. So we put our names in a bowl and drew one out. Don lost and became our lead singer."

Henley remembered the moment this way. "We all tried out for the lead vocalist's job in Richard's living room, and the consensus was that I was it. I was voted lead vocalist by all the other band members, including Elmer. It was as simple as that." Although he may have preferred the anonymity, free-dom, and power of being behind his kit, he accepted this upheaval for the good of the band. His shyness was what may have prevented him from com-ing out from behind the drum kit and standing up front.

After their "breakthrough" record deal, which failed to make any noise at the cash register, Felicity gradually morphed into Shiloh. It was then that Richard Bowden's cousin Michael, whose family had moved from Dallas to Linden, joined the band. Michael recalled how he first met Henley: "When I was fourteen, I became friends with Don. He was in Felicity at that time, with my cousin Richard. I traveled with them on weekends, and when they became Shiloh, my cousin taught me to play bass. Richard had been the original bass player. When he asked me to join, I jumped at the chance."

By now, it was clear to the others that Richard Bowden's humor and Henley's seriousness didn't always go so well together. The jokester was no longer able to make the subject laugh so easily, and the subject found less and less that was funny about the jokester. Bowden didn't understand where Henley's new coolness came from. To Richard, music was about having fun, goofing off, and getting girls. To Don, playing in a band was serious business, requiring focus, rehearsal, and a certain degree of professionalism. In spite of his reluctance, and Bowden's taunts, if the others wanted him to lead, that was exactly what he would do.

The deeper ties that bound them, however, proved stronger than their leader-of-the-band skirmishes. As with most tight small-town friendships formed in childhood, the only-child Henley and symbolic older brother Bowden's relationship was close and meaningful to each of them, protected by an emotional shrink-wrap that allowed the others to look but not to touch. Despite, or perhaps because of, the creative and competitive bond, Richard and Don engaged in what amounted to a powerful, if fragile, sibling rivalry.

In 1965, at the age of eighteen, Henley graduated from high school, moved by himself one hundred miles due south, and enrolled at Stephen F. Austin State University, in Nacogdoches, Texas. Years later, he would reflect upon the reasons he had decided to pursue his education. "[My father] saved twenty-five cents a day from the day I was born so that I could go to college. He had to quit school in the eighth grade, and he wanted me to have a better life than he had. I enjoyed school, or at least the academic part of it. I didn't care for the social scene or even the general campus atmosphere.

"I was going with a beautiful Linden girl, Jana, my high school sweetheart, and we decided to go to the same school. She was gorgeous, and that caused me a lot of problems. I got picked on a lot by these large, macho rednecks who just couldn't stand that a scrawny little guy like me had this really pretty girlfriend. We'd be at the Sonic, the local drive-in, getting a milkshake and a hot dog, and they'd pull up on her side of the car, roll down the window, and start saying stuff. Guys would ask her out all the time. It was one of the things that led me eventually to transfer to another school.

"I did, however, have several good English teachers at Stephen F. Austin. One in particular, Professor Robert Fusillo, was the first real *bohemian* I'd ever seen. He'd hitchhiked all over Europe and seemed completely out of place in what was essentially this Southern redneck campus. He wore big polka-dot shirts with puffy sleeves and had long hair. This was 1965, and you just didn't do that at Stephen F. Austin State University. He and his wife were quite colorful and the talk of the school. He'd come to class in these outrageous clothes and lecture cross-legged on top of his desk. One day he told the class, 'Your parents are asking me what your future career plans are. I know there's a lot of pressure on you to decide.' Then he said something I never forgot. 'Frankly, if it takes you your whole life to find out what it is you want to do, you should take it. It's the *journey* that counts, not the *end* of it. That's when it's all over.'"

These words of encouragement affected Henley deeply, representing an oasis in what was otherwise a seemingly endless desert of beer-soaked redneck hostility.

Drinking helped pass the time between formal inspirations, but what it came down to, as Henley later remembered, was that Stephen F. Austin State, like so much of Texas, was a place where "all you can do is dream. There wasn't anything to do but sit and watch the sun sink in the west."

Whenever he had some free time, Henley liked to drive to Dallas, or east across the Texas border to Shreveport, Louisiana, to check out the music scene. Shreveport, the legendary home of the "Louisiana Hayride" radio broadcast, was the closest city Henley could get to see name bands. It was in Shreveport in 1965 that he first experienced the melded sound of two new white-on-white American folk-influenced country-rock bands, the Byrds and the Dillards.

The music of the Byrds, especially, led by Jim (Roger) McGuinn, was a revelation to Henley. Their unique blend of country, pop, and rock produced a sound that reached out, grabbed Henley by his large ears, and lifted him above the more traditional Delta-based Southern rock and roll on which he'd grown up. "Most of the shows I saw were in Shreveport, because that was the closest city to my hometown where bands would perform. I saw a few shows in Dallas as well. I think, however, this one show was very important to me, a real seminal experience. The funny thing was the odd bill. It had, besides the Byrds and the Dillards, the Barbarians, I think, Herman's Hermits, and Mitch Ryder and the Detroit Wheels, who blew everybody away. They really kicked some ass."

It was a show he would never forget, one that helped clarify his sense of musical direction. He was convinced that now he too could have a place in that world. He wasn't sure quite how to get there from here, but one thing he knew, for him Nacogdoches was nowhere.

That fall, Henley decided to transfer to North Texas State University. "I'd had enough and decided to change schools. There were a lot more longhairs at North Texas and a lot more serious musicians. People there were more interested in politics and art. It was just more of the kind of school I wanted to go to."

It wasn't the only change Henley made. Not long after arriving on campus at North Texas, Henley broke up with Jana. "She wanted to get married, and I didn't. I had plans, I eventually wanted to go to California and give it a shot. The problem for her, a girl growing up in Texas at that time, was if you weren't married by the time you were twenty-one, you were considered to be an old maid. She was great, there was nothing wrong with her, or me. We were just headed in different directions."

At the age of twenty, Don Henley was already the veteran of a local rock band that had somehow failed to change anything, let alone the world, let alone *his* world. The extent of his rebellion had thus far been limited to the length of his hair: considered long, although it barely touched his ears; the amount of beer he could guzzle: pints; and the desire to make music: strong. The summer of 1967, the celebrated "Summer of Love," introduced Henley to two other outside influences. The first was the revolutionary Beatles album *Sgt. Pepper.* The second was the drug of choice for hearing what was between its grooves, LSD. Living off campus in, of all places, the Eagle Apartments in Dallas, Henley remembers, "I bought the album right after it came out. I had some friends in Dallas who were a little more worldly than I was. They were mostly in bands, and one of them gave me the acid. I went into the bedroom, turned on the black light, listened to the album, and watched my face turn into about fifty different people. It was fun, though."

Henley kept up his studies, did well enough to make the dean's list, and along the way compiled a set of literary heroes whose writings would deeply affect him. He was especially drawn to the protagonists of novelist Thomas Hardy *(Jude the Obscure)* and to the ideas of essayist Ralph Waldo Emerson. Years later, Henley would tell an interviewer that it was "Emerson's essay on self-reliance which helped give me the nerve to be a songwriter." Among his favorite passages of Emerson's was one that cautioned, *Beware what you set your heart upon. For it surely shall be yours.*

Kenny Rogers had been born and raised in Texas and played in a number of local bands until 1964, when he joined one of the many touring incarnations of the New Christy Minstrels. Two years later, he quit the group and, with fellow Minstrel Mike Settle, formed the country-rock band the First Edition. The group had a series of soft country hits that managed to cross over to the national pop charts and should have established Rogers as a major star. Instead, he experienced the frustration of finding himself dismissed by rock fans who found him too country (and faux at that) and country fans who found him too pop.

In 1967, Rogers left in favor of a career as a producer. His goal was to develop a stable of crossover groups he could produce and send out on the road. Rogers took his cue from the franchised Christy Minstrels and an old friend, former country singer and present First Edition producer Jimmy Bowen.

Bowen, a one-hit country-singing wonder of the fifties ("I'm Stickin' with You"), had gone on to become a millionaire producing records for Frank Sinatra's Warner-distributed boutique label, Reprise. His work on "Strangers in the Night" and "Everybody Loves Somebody" was credited with reviving the sagging recording careers of Sinatra and Dean Martin. Eventually, Bowen left Reprise to start his own label and cut a deal with Rogers to discover and produce bands that could play the popular hot new sound of country rock. Rogers began listening to unsigned demos and visiting small clubs whenever possible. After one year, hundreds of tapes, and endless visits to the gin mills with live music that dotted the small towns of the Southwest, he believed he had finally found the sound he was look-ing for in a tough little Dallas joint, the Studio Club, that featured a band called Shiloh.

"This was still when long hair was considered to be something wild and outrageous," Henley recalls. "Longhairs were considered by many in Texas to be dirty communists or criminals or some kind of gay perverts. . . . Anyway, it was the sixties, we played Dallas a lot, we were continually perse-cuted for the way we looked, and we had previously been in a couple of encounters where we barely escaped without getting hurt very badly. We became afraid, and justifiably so, when we would go into restaurants after shows, around midnight or one in the morning . . . and it was really rough. We would get a lot of catcalls and whistles. We would be stared at and laughed at the entire time we were eating. There were often threats made. When we would leave the restaurant, people would follow us out to the van sometimes and try to start fights.

"One night, I don't know whose it was, I think it was registered, we brought along a gun in the glove compartment of the fifty-five Chevy that belonged to original band member Jerry Surratt. We were going down Stem-mons Freeway in Dallas; Jerry was speeding and was pulled over. The cops found the gun in the glove compartment and they took us to jail. The Dallas police were quite intimidating, making fun of us. They'd walk by and yell to other cops that they'd brought us to the wrong jail, we should have been put in the women's jail, that kind of thing. Because of some obscure Texas law that was still on the books, the 'saddlebag law' dating back to the eighteen hundreds, we got a break. In essence, if a man rode on horseback from one county to another, he could carry a weapon. They had to let us go."

After completing three semesters at North Texas, Henley went home when his mother told him that C. J. had developed heart disease and arte-riosclerosis and was forced to sell his business. Henley felt the need to give something back by helping to care for and spend as much time with him as he could before his father's health worsened, which it inevitably would. The one good thing that came out of this was the time it allowed for Hen-ley to play more regularly with his band, and to be there the night Rogers first came to check them out.

The way Michael Bowden remembers it, Rogers's visit was the result of a chance meeting. "Jerry Surratt, a member of our band who played the trumpet and keyboards, happened to be out looking for clothes when he met Kenny. Jerry got into a conversation with him about the band, and he seemed interested. Jerry invited him to hear the group play, and he came back that afternoon to hear a sound check. He liked us and came by again that night. We all struck up a friendship, which eventually evolved into our cutting a couple of songs for him in Memphis. One of them eventually became our first single, something I believe was called 'Jennifer,' which Don sang lead on and Jerry played keyboards." Rogers thought "Jennifer," about a Civil War veteran coming home from the front to his girl, was good enough to earn the band a quick recording trip that February to Los Angeles, which led nowhere. When they returned to Linden, a tragic accident broadsided their fate and altered their destiny.

They had been rehearsing in a small vacant building in Linden that had housed various enterprises over the years, including a restaurant, a gas station, and a church. The sessions included a bit of partying and occasional breaks when the boys would get on their dirt bikes and, just for the fun of it, leave a little rubber in the parking lot. One afternoon, Surratt took off on his bike, rode straight into the path of an oncoming car, and was killed instantly.

Henley remembers: "We grew up together in this small town, we were in the high school marching band, the high school stage band, we all won awards and stood out. Surratt was a world-class, brilliant trumpet player. We spent a lot of time together, Bowden, Surratt, and me, riding dirt bikes, driving around in our cars, playing in Shiloh. It was just a freak accident, what happened that day. We could all see that car coming down the road. Before he knew it, it was right there. Surratt was just kind of puttering across the highway. The kid who hit him happened to be a friend of ours. He wasn't looking straight ahead, but over to where we were. He'd seen all these motorcycles and the Kenny Rogers tour bus. Surratt's mom and sister were there and saw the whole thing. The car just picked him up on the hood and threw him over into the bushes.

"That changed everything."

Henley and the rest of the band took Surratt's death hard. Michael Bowden remembers: "Jerry was killed just before 'Jennifer' was released. Two or three months passed, and although it didn't go anywhere, we had to reorganize, to think about if we even wanted to carry on. We all decided it was the best thing to do. Don returned to North Texas State University, where he asked Jim Ed Norman, a keyboard player he was friends with, to audition for the band. Jim came to Linden for a weekend, and we went back to our rehearsal building to try him out. We liked him; he was a good guy, a fine keyboard player, and a good rhythm guitarist."

"After Surratt was killed," Henley says, "I recruited Jim Ed Norman, who'd lived two rooms down from me at school, and another guy named Al Perkins, a pedal steel player. We were really getting into country at that point, heavily influenced by the Burrito Brothers and Poco. We found out about Perkins from some friends of ours in a band in Abilene who played the same circuits we did. One of them was Tommy Nixon, who became a good friend of Glenn and still works for the Eagles. Anyway, it took two talented guys to replace Jerry."

Rogers, meanwhile, who'd remained in California, kept in touch with the band by telephone for another year while the boys continued to work on their music in Texas. According to Jim Ed Norman, "Kenny, after making a deal with Jimmy Bowen, was essentially going to be the group's producer. He took Shiloh's contract to Bowen's newly formed, Los Angeles–based Amos Records. With Bowen's approval, Rogers finally brought Shiloh to Los Angeles."

In June of 1970, they finally got the call to come back to Los Angeles and begin work on an album. Although he was excited about the career break, Henley had mixed emotions over making the actual move. On the one hand, he sensed his vision starting to take shape. He had always wanted to move to L.A., and now he had the opportunity. On the other, he hated leaving his sick father behind. His being an only child meant that the burden of caring for C. J. would fall fully and only on his mother. He struggled between the pull of his dream and the grip of his guilt. In the end, after much agonizing, the dream won.

So it was, then, that early one morning in 1970, the boys packed their few belongings and headed out to find rock and roll glory in the City of Angels. Taking Michael Bowden with him, Henley made the journey west in his '67 SS 396 Chevelle. Richard Bowden followed in his Buick Riviera with his wife, Shane, beside him. Jim Ed Norman manned the Ford van and the U-Haul hooked behind full of the band's equipment.

The others may have seen it as just another gig, with a trip to California added to the mix. For Henley, it meant nothing less than deliverance to the Promised Land, the chance to leave behind forever the Southern-bully rednecks and the Jesus-freak, no-brain crazies, the loneliness and the loonies; to wave a middle-fingered adios to "the Baptists and the Methodists and the Southern purgatory they laid on me when I was a kid and scared the holy fuck out of me so I couldn't sleep at night because I thought I would die and go to hell."

Instead he headed West.

TWO

Even as a kid, Glenn Frey was the ultimate loosey-goosey, a street-smart charmer and proud of it. From the day his hormones kicked in, two things came first to this Detroit-born and -bred boy — girls and more girls, and he soon discovered that music was how to get them. Sports, too, were high on his list. Although he did well in Little League and made his high school wrestling team, he knew he was too small to ever play serious ball and that he didn't have that certain self-denying discipline essential to the serious athlete. That was okay as far as he was concerned, because he learned early on that no one in his neighborhood stood taller than he did whenever he strapped on a guitar.

Born November 6, 1948, Glenn Frey, at the insistence of his mother, started when he was five what would turn into years of dreary piano lessons until, inspired by two Beatles shows at Detroit's Olympia Hall in 1964, he gave up pounding eighty-eight keys in favor of strumming six strings.

To Frey, the Beatles were the very definition of rock and roll, and rock and roll was definitely cool because rock stars got all the glory and with it all the girls. They were the ones who held the necks of their guitars out and proud, as if they were living extensions of themselves. So *tough*! As soon as he learned his first couple of chords, Frey began putting bands together. He knew going in he was definitely big enough to play *this* game.

Frey was cursed or blessed, depending upon who was listening, with a mouth. He loved to spew out long lines of opinion and desires, or four-letter blasts of teen fury. Some thought him to be the most obnoxious smart-ass on the street. Others, like his junior high school teachers, insisted his precocious ways proved he was intelligent enough to be placed in a special program for gifted students. He did well enough but was unmotivated. Academics held no appeal for him. His street smarts told him what really counted was the hip world outside the one where Dick and Jane played. He loved to read but preferred the kind of books they sold for a quarter at the local drugstore, the kind you could stuff into your back pocket and pull out whenever you got the chance. For instance, the novels of Jack Kerouac, who, to Frey, most closely captured in his writing the kind of cool, slouchy arrogance the great James Dean had the *cajones* to put right up there on the big screen.

A quick study when he wanted to be, like when it came to music, Frey soon found himself sitting in with many of the best local bands, the Four of Us, the Subterraneans, and the one that actually got to cut a record, the Mushrooms. This last, psychedelically inspired group's grand score happened because of the sheer relentlessness of Frey's desire to play with his idol, Bob Seger. An Ann Arbor native who had knocked on rock's closed door so long he had no knuckles left and then sung like he couldn't stop the bleeding, Seger had become something of a white-boy legend in Detroit by the midsixties. He drew an increasingly loyal crowd wherever he appeared and was one of the few nonblack acts to freely cross the city's musical and geographical color lines.

For Glenn Frey, Seger was the perfect bridge between the white-bread rock of the Beatles and the black rhythms of Motown. *Dee-troyt! The Motor City, Home of Motown, USA!* In this town, soul music *ruled.* Every white city-boy street tough willingly got down on his knees to worship the silver sidewalks upon which Berry Gordy strode. And it was in Motown where Seger got *down.* He could walk the walk and talk the talk and *mean it,* and that was how Frey wanted to go, what he wanted to say, and how he wanted to say it when he arrived there.

In a Detroit studio in 1967, he got the chance. Everyone tolerated the likable and eager young guy who seemed to always be hanging around, guitar slung over his shoulder, hoping for a chance to sit in with *the man.* During a break one day, Seger let the kid with the guitar talk him up and then listened to him play. Hey, sure, why not? Soon after, he set a mike up and turned the tape machines on.

"Seger was cool," Frey recalled. "I was never in his band, but he liked me and let me come to some sessions when he was recording four-track. He let me play maracas, and on one song he let me play acoustic guitar." Seger always had the good ear, knew talent when he heard it, and heard it when the kid kicked in. By now Frey had developed a nice sense of style on his instrument: a sweet, almost sliding guitar, not totally unlike George Harrison's, with enough of a thumb-pulled bass line to remind everyone he was still homegrown Detroit.

At Seger's urging, his management team, Eddie "Punch" Andrews and Dave Leone, decided to take a chance and tied Frey to a very loose string, promising to get him a few performing gigs and, if things worked out, sign him up full-time as a recording artist at their standard 25 percent fee (and half the publishing). Not long after, Andrews and Leone launched their own local label, Hideout and Punch Records, and signed Frey, along with his sometime backup band, the Mushrooms, to a management and recording contract. Their first single, "Such a Lovely Child," just happened to be written and produced by Bob Seger (whose publishing the two managers also had a piece of).

The song failed to chart, and Frey made no money from it. At this point, Seger took his young friend aside and gave him a piece of advice. He told him that the only way to make it in rock and roll was to write and own your own songs. These were wise words. The business of recording rock's free rebel yell could become quite profitable, at least for those who held the copyrights to that yell.

Frey treated his 45 like a badge of honor and used it to get any and every girl he could lay those magical hands on, a preoccupation he didn't bother to keep from anyone, not even his mother. All of which Nellie Frey found quite amusing. According to her, "I remember telling him once, 'Glenn, if your guitar had tits and an ass, you'd never date another girl.'"

What a concept! Unfortunately, Frey's weak spot for chicks got even weaker when they belonged to someone else. His face was rearranged more than once by a jealous boyfriend who *didn't* think the kid with the guitar was the coolest and most irresistible dude in Detroit. So what, he told friends, if his nose was broken a couple of times? It just made him look badder. And how cool was that?

*   *   *

Glenn Frey graduated from high school in June 1968. On that day he announced he was going to pursue a full-time career in music. Fine, his mother said, as long as you go to college first. Frey laughed. His mother didn't. Nellie Frey had been the head of the house since Glenn's old man had left for good, ultimately preferring a fifth over fatherhood. She was determined to keep her son from following in those footsteps. Never known for her shyness, Nellie got hold of Glenn's managers and threatened to take legal action against them if they didn't agree to stop booking Frey and his band until he quit smoking that awful-smelling pot and enrolled in college full-time. To keep peace at home, Glenn made a deal with his mother that if he went to one of the nearby two-year schools and kept up his grades, she would allow him to continue to play.

That fall, he enrolled as a freshman in college. Bob Seger would occasionally call Frey during that year and ask him to sit in during recording sessions. Out of one of these came Seger's first national hit, the 1968 single "Ramblin' Gamblin' Man," on which Frey sang backup. The record brought him a bit of a local buzz, and soon he was being called to sing and play behind whatever "big" names came through the area. Most older acts that still toured did it mainly for the money, ticket sales being their main source of income. Rock stars like Chuck Berry, Jerry Lee Lewis, and Bo Diddley had all seen their music stolen by shady characters with fat contracts no one ever bothered to read. Now, to pay the bills, they made the rounds, usually alone, playing their old hits the same exact way and hiring local pickups to duplicate the sound of their records. These were usually eager but inexperienced kids who knew the necessary chords and progressions and could get through a set for maybe twenty-five dollars a pop. On that circuit, word spread quickly that no one in Detroit could play better, or came cheaper, than Frey.

Against this kind of action, college classes seemed unbelievably boring. Frey loved to play and party until dawn and sleep until the sun set. His days became his nights, his nights everyone else's days. Like all young, eager musicians, his body clock effortlessly ran counter.

During the heated summer of '68, one of his many girlfriends, Joanie Sliwyn, decided to join her sister Alexandria on a romp to the West Coast, where they wanted to become singers. Frey, feeling what was for him the rare sting of rejection, became convinced this babe was *the* babe. He quit listening to his mother, quit going to classes, quit the Mushrooms, and quit Detroit, choosing instead to take to the open road, find the girl of his dreams, and bring her back home. To prepare for his great journey of rescue and retrieval, Frey read, listened to music, and dropped a tab of acid, the best ways he figured to get to know the new world he was about to explore. "I was from the East," he once observed. "I saw copies of *Surfer* magazine, I got the Beach Boys' albums. I took acid and listened to that first Buffalo Springfield record and got chill bumps and had to lay on the floor and stuff. . . . I got into that whole 'California consciousness.' I saw all the articles in *Post* magazine and *Life* about people taking marijuana and LSD and going to Golden Gate Park and all that stuff . . . and the Grateful Dead and [the Jefferson Airplane's] 'Surrealistic Pillow.' I mean, I was a victim of the media, just the same as everyone else was . . . and I just went out there."

To finance the trip, Frey made a pit stop in Mexico to load his pickup with a hefty supply of cheap Acapulco Gold, after which, in a haze of LSD- and pot-fueled glory, he headed west to reclaim the great lost love of his life. One way or another, he was determined to bring her back where she belonged — worshiping at his feet on the mean streets of Motor City.

THREE

Randy Meisner was born in 1946 in Scottsbluff, Nebraska, the son of share-croppers. His interest in rock and roll began very much like Henley's and Frey's, except his primal influence fell just on the other side of the great generational divide. When Meisner was ten years old, he saw Elvis Presley on *The Ed Sullivan Show* and, like so many children of the fifties, reacted immediately and viscerally. The next day he found a guitar and discovered a natural ability to make music. "Playing was the only thing I really knew how to do," he recalls. "I didn't graduate from high school and never went to college. I was a dropout, and so music was the only thing. My grandfa-ther was a musician, a violinist, so I came from somewhat of a musical family, although I never studied formally. The first time was when I came out [to Los Angeles in the sixties] and I realized I better learn the scales on the bass. I picked it up on my own, from a book of scales. That was it."

At the age of fourteen, Randy Meisner married his childhood sweet-heart. Three years later, he'd become good enough to play in public, which meant for money. He put together a band called the Dynamics, and they gigged at all the local dances. After leaving school, he drifted through the Midwest playing with one group after another for about a year before cut-ting his first record, an EP with the Checkmates, out of Amarillo.

According to Meisner, "One night in 1964, we played a talent contest up in Denver, at the Cow Palace. A group called the Soul Survivors had just lost their bass player to the service. He sang high and played bass. So did I. I sat in with them, and about two weeks later a guy from the band drove over to Nebraska and asked me if I wanted to go out on the road with them to open for an L.A.-based group called the Back Porch Majority, who used to play Denver quite a lot. They convinced the other members of the Soul Survivors and me to come out and try our luck in L.A."

To finance the trip, they played another month of local shows, after which a highly optimistic Meisner threw some clothes in the back of his brand new '64 Barracuda and headed with the band for the West Coast. "Where," he remembers with a smile, "we all nearly starved to death.

"When we first got out there, one of the [Back Porch Majority] had an apartment in Encino, off Ventura Boulevard, behind a Ralph Williams Ford dealership. So we all took apartments there, or rather one apartment, unfurnished, for all of us. We used the mats they left outside the dealership as beds. And it went downhill from there. Eventually, we found a house in Laurel Canyon, Jonathan Winters's brother's house. We lived there for a while. One of the guys in my band, Gene Chalk, finally gave up and went back to Denver."

The rest of the band decided to tough it out in L.A. and eventually managed to land a recording contract with Loma Records, a subsidiary of Atlantic. Loma's offices were in the same building as Atlantic, which was how Randy first met and became friendly with the original members of the Buffalo Springfield — Bruce Palmer, Stephen Stills, Dewey Martin, Richie Furay, and Neil Young. Springfield was signed to Atco, another Atlantic subsidiary, and the members of each band often ran into one other in the corporate hallways and in-house recording studios.

Buffalo Springfield's midsixties breakthrough made it, along with the Byrds, one of L.A.'s most influential new country-folk-rock bands. "After we heard Buffalo Springfield," Meisner recalls, "we kind of shifted away from pure folk rock and into the kind of newer, harder, country thing they were doing."

Still, the Soul Survivors failed to attract the kind of attention Buffalo Springfield had, and not long after Chalk's departure, the living arrangement in Laurel Canyon fell apart. Meisner found a place in the hills, but after a few weeks had to give it up because he couldn't make the rent. The band, desperate for money, began playing small bars for the door. By 1966, Randy was the only original Soul Survivor to have survived, the rest having given up and gone home. The new lineup Meisner put together included guitar player–pianist–vocalist Randy Naylor, Allen Kemp on guitar, Pat Shanahan on drums, and himself, as always, on bass.

To make the changeover official, he decided to rename the band the Poor, an apt description of their financial state. They made frequent pilgrimages to music-friendly Colorado, where the mere fact they came from L.A. gave them an added cachet, along with some much-needed cash. The Poor built up a steady following and usually packed the bars they played, their only serious competition another local Denver band, Boenzee Cryque. Although Cryque never played a gig outside Colorado, it helped move country and rock closer to each other, according to rock chronicler Pete Frame, earning a footnote in pop music history as the first rock band to feature a full-time pedal steel guitar player. And a great one at that. Everyone who heard Rusty Young agreed he "owned that sound."

Despite frequent Rocky Mountain forays, the Poor continued to have money problems. Back in L.A., the band usually stayed at the Tropicana hotel, one of the more notorious L.A. rock residential hangouts of the sixties. Located on Santa Monica just west of La Brea, the Tropicana catered to the decidedly low-rent rock scene, and out-of-work musicians could often be found hanging at Duke's, the hotel's coffee shop, recovering from the social festivities of the night before. Sooner or later, everyone in L.A. who was a player or who wanted to be passed through the Trop. "In those days," Meisner remembers, "John Kay and Steppenwolf stayed there all the time. Oh, man, you talk about parties! It was crazy, all right. A lot of acid was ingested, and weed; it was unbelievable. Everyone was stoned out of their minds. I can remember John Kay sitting still as a statue all day at the pool, wearing his sunglasses, saying and doing nothing for hours.

"I also remember spending one Christmas at the Tropicana by myself, with no money, while everyone else had gone home. It was a truly horrible time for me. On more than one occasion back then, a couple of us would get together and buy eighty pounds of grass, then sell it off in ten-dollar baggies, keeping just enough for ourselves and using the rest to pay for our rooms."

The next summer, the Poor were booked in New York City, at a Greenwich Village spot called the Salvation Club. Meisner believes their managers simply got sick of the band and decided to ship them out of town for a while. He remembers: "When we got down to the club, they were still pounding nails into the walls. We found some guy who told us if we gave him eighty bucks, which just happened to be every cent we had, he'd score us some weed. We gave him the money and never saw or heard from him again. Now we were broke. We were forced to stay up and wait for the early morning dairy deliveries left outside the local stores and steal whatever we could: milk, doughnuts, whatever.

"Finally, the club opened, and the first act was Jimi Hendrix. He'd just come over from England. We were scheduled to play the club that week as the house band. However, we never got on opening night. Of course, no one could follow Jimi. He used to burn his guitar onstage and destroy the PA system. When he finally finished, the manager of the club said to us, 'Hey, good news, you guys don't have to go on at all! Come back tomorrow.' We felt like shit. The whole idea was that we would be the opening act and get some real exposure in New York. We did play a few times the next two weeks, and nothing happened. And then it got worse.

"We ended the gig and couldn't find the guy who was supposed to pay us. We didn't have any money for plane tickets out of there. Nothing. We were all really pissed. Finally, we found out where the manager of the club lived, went there, pounded on his door until he came out, and tried to scare him by telling him simply, 'Either you pay us or we're going to kill you.' He quickly bought us one-way plane tickets back to L.A."

Back at the Trop, Meisner and the boys remained one step above panhandling by selling copies of "the *Freep*," the *Los Angeles Free Press,* an alternative weekly newspaper, on the streets of Sunset Boulevard. A good day might pull in as much as five dollars, enough to buy dinner, usually a box of packaged macaroni and cheese, and maybe a beer to wash it down. The Diggers, a local activist group, collected supermarket discards, vegetables too old to sell, and stale bread, and distributed them to whoever needed food, which, according to Meisner, literally kept him alive.

Meisner and the Poor struggled on the fringe of the L.A. rock scene until May 1968, when Jim Messina, Buffalo Springfield's latest bass player, quit after only six months. A friend of Randy's who knew Richie Furay suggested Meisner might be able to fill the slot. An audition was arranged for him at Furay's house in Laurel Canyon.

On hand to assist with the tryouts were Furay, Messina (there to help choose his own replacement), and a friend of both, Detroit-born John David (J. D.) Souther, a young, good-looking singer-songwriter recently arrived from Amarillo. All agreed Meisner was the best of the dozen or so musicians they heard that day. The only other one who'd even come close was a rail-thin, long-haired, fine-featured bassist with a breathy soprano by the name of Timothy Bruce Schmit. Randy was invited to join Buffalo Springfield on the spot.

Before the reconfigured band ever played a single gig, however, Furay quit to join Messina and Boenzee Cryque pedal steel player Rusty Young in yet another new band, which called itself Poco. Furay and Messina then invited Meisner to join them (along with drummer and vocalist George Grantham).

The deconstruction of Buffalo Springfield signaled to many the subsiding of the first tidal wave of L.A. acoustic-based folk-and-country-flavored rock. Indeed, the clubs along Sunset Strip were already featuring new harder-sounding bands like the Doors, whose musical style and stage theatrics bore little resemblance to anything L.A. had thus far produced. More a beach bum than a Beach Boy, Jim Morrison fronted the Doors with a minimalist, progressive sound somewhere between hot jazz and cool rock. By the end of 1968, Morrison all but owned the Strip, and Furay and Messina thought it wise to find a venue to make their debut away from the frenzied scene that had erupted around the Doors.

They found such a place in the Troubadour, one of L.A.'s first, and for many years neglected, nightspots. The Troub, as it was often called, owned and operated by Doug Weston, opened as a jazz club in the fifties, on La Cienega just east of Doheny. In 1961, Weston relocated a boulevard south of Sunset, to Santa Monica, on the lip of Beverly Hills, and became the first to jump on the emerging acoustic folk movement.

Even as he made the shift from jazz to folk, Weston — tall, stringbean thin, with long hair, sunken cheeks, and a grand way of speaking — deplored the rock scene starting to happen above him on Sunset Strip and adamantly refused to allow any electric instruments on his stage until 1967, after the now-famous incident of police harassment on the Strip.

The great clash between American youth and hard-hatted riot police that took place the night of November 15, 1966, along Hollywood's fabled Sunset Strip — the same unzoned area of watering holes and glamour brothels an earlier generation of movie stars and moguls had used as their personal and privileged after-hours playground — was in some ways more significant than the one that would take place two years later on the streets of Chicago during the Democratic convention. In Lincoln Park the defining mood would be political protest; on Sunset it was a purer, more melody friendly form of adolescent rebellion. Looking to cash in on the surging popularity of L.A. rock and roll, many of the clubs that had suffered as a result of the end of the studio system and Hollywood's golden era of movie star–sized tabs started catering to the new kids on the block. Drinking ages were lowered, liquor licenses overlooked. Before long, the scene had spilled onto the streets, causing traffic jams, difficulties for neighboring merchants, and the growing fear of an impending outbreak of sex, drugs, and violence. Everything came to a head one night outside Gazzarri's, the Whiskey-a-Go-Go, and Pandora's Box, three of the Strip's most popular clubs, when a formal protest against "Police Mistreatment of Youth" was staged. Although nothing more serious than a broken window and a couple of skirmishes took place, the incident marked the arrival of a new So-Cal generation gap.

The net result was a general tightening of the rules of club ownership. A severe, if short-lived, ban on live rock and roll after dark went into effect, along with a sharply increased tension between the officers of the LAPD and the children of the West Hollywood sixties. For the young rockers, it hurt their sense of pride and freedom. For the club owners, it hit them in the cash register. Either way, the social-economic standoff put a definite chill into the hot zone.

Outraged by the incident on Sunset, Doug Weston offered the unzoned and therefore unrestricted Troubadour for free as a showcase for Buffalo Springfield to play out its musical protest to a newly energized and fast-spending crowd. From that night on, the Troubadour became the chief showcase and hippest hangout for L.A.'s music scene. Weston, always with one eye on the bottom line, sought out bands that could fill his club the way Springfield had, and he quickly realized its natural successor was Poco, whose opening night became the hottest ticket in town.

Still, to many, some of the most memorable moments at the club happened at the front bar, away from the main stage. "The Troubadour was everybody's home base," remembers one who was there during the club's heady days of the late sixties. "It was the musicians' favorite hangout. McCabe's [folk club] had a string and pick shop in the front of the Troub, where the bar is now. What was funny about Doug was, in the beginning he fancied himself a folk 'purist.' When he first heard a group rehearse with amplifiers he almost threw them out. He was incensed! That all changed, of course, after Buffalo Springfield played there.

"At the other clubs there were private rooms where the public never had access. The Troub had that too, upstairs in what they used to call the VIP room, but it was used mostly by whoever was performing that night. Otherwise, everyone hung out by the bar. On any given night you'd have the kind of eclectic mix that was pure L.A. You might have Phil Ochs, David Blue, Eric Andersen, Joni Mitchell, the Everly Brothers, Jackson Browne, Elton John, Harry Nilsson, Mick Fleetwood, every established or would-be rock journalist and wanna-be photographer. And always, prodigious amounts of booze."

Randy Meisner recalls, "When I wasn't working, I'd go down to the Troub and just have a blast. You'd go into Doug's office, and everybody would have a pitcher of beer and a shot of tequila before we'd continue. You'd try to chug the whole pitcher. Then go out and practice. Or if you were appearing, then play.

"I can remember stepping inside one night, looking up, and seeing Jimmy Morrison hanging over the railing of the balcony. His very presence was a sign of how hot the club had gotten. He was drunk out of his mind, and he almost fell over. I remember seeing him hanging by one hand, yelling at the top of his lungs. It was kind of the perfect metaphor for Jim and the whole scene."

"Strange combinations came together at the bar," recalled Troubador regular Eve Babitz, "like Gram Parsons and Mike Clarke drinking champagne and Wild Turkey, or Arlo Guthrie falling in love with one of the waitresses. Hoyt Axton and Jack Elliott and David Blue made things seem legit. . . . Janis Joplin would sit in her nightgown with a pink boa, all by herself, drinking. Paul Butterfield would hit the Troubadour the minute he came to L.A., Van Morrison glowered in corners, and Randy Newman was all innocence and myopia. And, of course, there were the most gorgeous women in the world."

A seemingly endless flow, indeed: young, fresh, sweet, not so innocent, and definitely hot. "Like more than one carefully educated young woman watching TV the night the Beatles were on *Ed Sullivan*, I was a groupie," recalled Babitz. "For women like us, hanging out in the Troubadour bar every night was business. . . . The bar was just jammed with record-company people, friends of the bands, the bands themselves, and groupies, beautiful girls with tans and Marlboros and soft hair and clear eyes. . . .

Every journalist and friend and rock and roller got a tab for free drinks and ended up in the bar trying to get laid, get high, or get a deal together."

Poco's November 1968 opening at the Troub shook the town from its denim collars to its silver-tipped boots. The next day the band signed a recording contract with Epic and began working on one of the most highly anticipated albums of the decade.

By this time, Southern California country rock had become a viable force in the musical personality of the sixties. Buffalo Springfield's arrival had restimulated rock's country-western roots. It was the problem of constant personnel shifts that had been the primary industrial as well as cultural reason no single L.A. group had thus far been able to dominate the commercial market. Part of it no doubt was due to poor management. However, a great deal of the blame had to be laid at the feet of the artists themselves, who allowed ego, a general lack of professional discipline, and a tendency to place drinking, girls, and drugs before music, their comrades, and their careers. Prior to Poco, the best chance any band had to make the mainstream leap came in 1968, when a reconfigured Byrds released *Sweethearts of the Rodeo,* a minihistory of American country music. Because of it they became the first rock and roll band to play live at the legendary Grand Ol' Opry. Unfortunately, the group was less than well received in the Southern music capital, where they were looked upon as little more than musical carpetbaggers — Beach Boys in cowboy boots. The disappointing appearance helped break up the latest version of the band and left a commercial gap in West Coast rock and roll that Poco sought to fill. As would others, some from the unlikeliest of places.

As Meisner remembers, "Opening night, who should come down to see us rehearse at the Troubador but Rick Nelson. Man, I was so excited to meet him! He was kind of legendary around the club, as much for the TV show, I think, as for his great hit tunes."

Everyone of a certain age remembers "Ricky" Nelson, the wisecracking son and brother on the long-running *Ozzie and Harriet* television sitcom of the fifties and sixties. His cute face and sly persona endeared him to millions. As he often told the story, in his teens he began dating a girl who was crazy about Elvis. To win her affections he went to a "record your own voice" booth at Wallich's Music City in Hollywood, intending to make a record for the girl as a gift. That part of the story is most likely apocryphal. Ozzie Nelson decided that if his son was going to record, he should do it right, and hired session guitarist Barney Kessel to supervise a professional studio session.

One of the many songs Ricky cut that day was "I'm Walkin'," a cover of the Fats Domino hit. Pleased with the results, Ozzie decided to use it as the tag end for one of the sitcom's episodes. Its airing transformed Ricky Nelson overnight from an awkward teen to a rock and roll star. Lew Chudd, who owned Imperial Records, quickly signed Nelson to a recording deal, and his second release on that label, "Stood Up," shot to number two in the national charts. Its follow-up, "Poor Little Fool," made it to number one. Dozens of singles hits followed, along with an amazing string of twenty-three top-selling albums.

In 1966, *Ozzie and Harriet* went off the air, which for Rick proved a great relief. Free at last to pursue a full-time career in music, he faced a whole new set of obstacles when his record sales fell off, as had those of almost every American rock act, in the wake of the arrival of the Beatles and the subsequent British Invasion. "After the series ended," Rick said years later, "I didn't know what I wanted to do. I didn't have to worry about money or a job, but [without the show] I didn't have a real career. *Ozzie and Harriet* had kept me working steadily for fourteen years on a soundstage."

At the urging of Ozzie, a nonpracticing lawyer who controlled all of his business dealings, Rick left Imperial to sign a new recording deal with Decca, for which he received a million-dollar advance. After several disappointing pop and rock albums, Decca agreed to allow Nelson to record some country songs. They then hired Charles Koppelman and Dan Rubin, two independent producers who had successfully resurrected the career of another fifties crooner, Bobby Darin, by having him record Tim Hardin's Folkish "If I Were a Carpenter." The hit tune returned Darin to the charts and made him viable to a new generation, which was exactly the kind of action Nelson was looking for.

Koppelman and Rubin introduced Nelson to one of their staff writers, an eager recent East Coast college graduate by the name of John Boylan they'd hired to join a growing stable of in-house songwriters that included, among others, Hardin, Lowell George, John Sebastian, and Russ Teitel, all of whom worked at writing hit tunes for a salary of fifty dollars a week.

Nelson recorded an original Boylan tune, "Suzanne on a Sunday

Morning," for inclusion in his 1968 Decca release, *Another Side of Rick*. It did well enough for Nelson to return to the studio later that same year to record another Koppelman-Rubin–produced album, *Perspective*, which contained several Randy Newman songs. Boylan, who by now had more or less taken over producing Nelson, then got into a dispute with Koppelman-Rubin for going outside their stable of writers and using Newman. Before the year was over, Boylan had left the organization.

He did, however, decide to remain in Los Angeles and produced two albums for the Association, at the time one of the biggest pop groups in the country, and one for the Dillards, during which time he continued to hang with Nelson. Boylan, a pretty good guitarist in his own right, liked to jam with Nelson and eventually decided to unofficially return to the studio to help out with a new album (unofficially because Decca, disappointed with Koppelman-Rubin, had disallowed the use of outside producers for any of their roster of artists, Nelson included).

In November 1969, when Poco scheduled its debut at the Troubadour, Boylan went with friends Jim Messina and Richie Furay to the opening. Thinking Nelson might enjoy the scene, he invited him to come along.

For all the excitement Poco generated at the Troubadour that night, by the time the tracks were being mixed for their debut album, internal problems threatened to tear the group apart. Meisner had joined the group believing he was going to be actively involved in the production end, while Furay and Messina considered him nothing more than a hired hand. No matter how talented a bass player and backup singer he was, that was all he was as far as they were concerned. Poco was their baby, and they let Meisner know that nothing was going to change that. When Furay and Messina went into the studio to do the final mix and Randy called to find out when he should join them, everything quickly fell apart.

Meisner says, "I said I wanted to come down and listen to it. 'Oh, no,' Richie said. 'Just Jimmy and I are allowed to hear it.' I said, 'Hey, I played on it too. I'm a musician too.' 'No, no,' they said. 'We never allow anybody in when we're mixing.'

"'Well,' I said, 'if that's the way it is, then I don't feel like being part of the band.' They said okay, and that was it. I was stubborn, I guess, but I felt I had a right to be there. So that was it. That's why, by the way, the dog's picture is on that album's cover and not mine. I didn't talk to any of those guys for nearly twenty years. They even took my voice off the songs I'd sung lead on — I think George Lantham sang on the record — but they left my bass playing in."

Meisner was quickly replaced by Timothy Schmit, the bassist-singer he had originally beaten out at the Buffalo Springfield auditions. Dejected and disillusioned, Meisner began making plans to move back to Colorado when he received a phone call from, of all people, Rick Nelson and John Boylan, both of whom had been blown away that night at the Troubadour by Poco. When Boylan heard that Randy had left the group, he jumped at the chance to get him for the new band he was putting together for Nelson. Randy immediately signed on and suggested to Rick and Boylan that they consider former Poor band members Pat Shanahan and Allen Kemp as well, both of whom Boylan hired. Tom Brumley, a member of Buck Owens's legendary backup band, was added on pedal steel at the last minute when original choice Sneaky Pete Kleinow pulled out. The new group called itself the Stone Canyon Band, suggested by Rick Nelson's fondness for a stretch of land in the hills near Brentwood.

In May 1969, one month after Meisner joined Nelson's group, the Stone Canyon Band made its own landmark debut at the Troubadour. Everyone who saw that show knew it was a career night for Rick and the boys. They sounded great, their choice of material was first rate — Dylan, Tim Hardin, even a couple of John Boylan's better songs — and Nelson was at his naturally charismatic best: a legitimate Hollywood legend who for this moment at least had finally managed to shed the ball and chain of his teen-idol past.

The Buffalo Springfield, Poco, and Stone Canyon Band appearances at the Troubadour helped elevate Weston's club from the hip joint it already was to the cultural epicenter it became. The echoes of those landmark L.A. shows reverberated across the country and around the world, luring the next generation of rock and roll wanna-bes eager to try for center stage even as the last hot rhythm of the sixties began to rattle through the hills and canyons of Southern California.

FOUR

It was unusually cool for Hollywood that evening in June of 1970 when Don Henley's caravan finally arrived in L.A. Just before they exited the 101 freeway, the needlelike top of the Capitol Records building, resembling a stack of records on a gigantic turntable, came briefly into view. Henley's first glimpse of what was then the symbolic pinnacle of the L.A. music scene left him "awestruck." Years later he would recall with religious solemnity his arrival in Los Angeles: "California represented the dream . . . the imagery of the Beach Boys, the Byrds, magazines that I would read, what I saw on TV, it was *the promised land.*" As he was about to discover, it was also the land of broken promises.

The group landed at the Holiday Inn in Encino, where it spent its first night before Kenny Rogers insisted everyone move to his huge Hollywood home. For a number of reasons, not the least of which was Kenny's wife Margo's growing dissatisfaction with having this ragtag group of musicians creeping through the halls all hours of the night, it soon became clear to everyone that this arrangement was not going to work. "After about two weeks," Henley recalled, "they'd had enough of us and put the band up in Howard's Weekly Apartments in Hollywood, where one of the First Edition's roadies was living, a big biker type who was selling grass out of the apartment."

Although Rogers was eager to get the boys into production, a series of delays caused them to wait several more weeks before beginning their album. To pass the time, Henley worked on his lyrics during the day, occasionally dropping by the tiny Amos office on Sunset. It didn't take long for Doug Weston's nightspot to become his favorite watering hole.

As Henley remembered years later, "The Troubadour was the first place I went to when I got to L.A. I had heard about how legendary it was and all the people who were performing there. The first night I walked in I saw Graham Nash and Neil Young, and Linda Ronstadt was standing there in a little Daisy Mae kind of dress. She was barefoot and scratching her ass. I thought, 'I've made it. I'm here. I'm in heaven.'"

One man's heaven, another man's hell.

In this case, two men: the songwriting team of Glenn Frey and J. D. Souther, otherwise known as Longbranch Pennywhistle. It had not taken long for them to start writing and performing together after Frey's arrival on the West Coast. The very first day he showed up in Hollywood, he'd found his ex-girlfriend Joanie living with Alexandria and her new husband, John David Souther.

As Souther recalled, "I'd come here at the age of twenty-two with a bunch of guys in a band called the Kitchen Sink, because we couldn't think of anything else, so we chose a name that sort of followed 'Everything but . . . ' We went to New York for a while because I wanted to experience some of the sixties Village scene. I remember seeing Tim Hardin one night in some club in Greenwich Village and being inspired to want to write songs the way he did. After that, we all went to Florida for a short time, and then I came back out to L.A., where we took an apartment in the valley. It was a very typical rock-and-roll-band kind of thing, five guys, girlfriends, dogs, no money, no car. I think I got around on a motorcycle. I lived in two or three different places before I got married to Alexandria. Shortly thereafter I met Glenn, got a place in Echo Park, and really tried to write songs.

"The girls had more money than either Glenn or me, and some kind of gig or recording contract, which was more than we had. They were beautiful, really, and great girls. However, there was no way Joanie was going to go back with Glenn."

After pleading unsuccessfully with Joanie to take him back, Glenn decided to return to Detroit to lick his wounds and regroup. He was greeted by a bitter Detroit winter and renewed pressure from his mother to go back to school. A month of that was enough to convince him to hasten his return to L.A. and try again to win back the love of his young life. Once there, he discovered Joanie had split. Souther let him crash anyway. "We were both crazy, out of work, looking for a good time, and we both wanted to write songs." They decided to pursue their three common interests, singing, songwriting, and girls, together.

They quickly became part of the front-bar scene at the Troubadour, where J. D. soon had his eye on club regular Linda Ronstadt, whose good looks, sexy outfits, and seductive singing style earned her a following of young gaping-mouthed boys at the lip of the stage, their eyes the same level as her pretty feet. She could break hearts as effortlessly as breakfast eggs and, the word was, liked doing it. For his own part, the kid from Amarillo, as Souther was sometimes referred to around the bar, was said to hold the trophy as the number one cowboy Romeo in town. Irresistible was the way friends most often described his effect on women. He would come to the Troubadour with his green eyes on fire, drinking San Miguels and scoping every babe in the place.

Because both were at the moment unavailable, Souther chose to keep his distance from Ronstadt. "It wasn't so much having her," he once told an interviewer, "but somewhere out there, in one of those gorgeous girls, which somehow look just like all the gorgeous girls you've already had, there might be that one. And whether it's there or not, it provides you with enough excuse to keep chasing. If I ever figured it out completely, I wouldn't have anything else to write about."

Fortunately for J. D., and Frey, he had plenty of material and the good fortune to know how to plug his romantic passions into a certain style of music. It was something Frey had picked up on the first time they'd sat around in the apartment and jammed. "I always thought what I was trying to do at that time was to some degree modern country music," Souther remembers. "It was what I'd been listening to, the Flying Burrito Brothers, the Byrds, Poco, Dillard and Clark. Those guys had listened to Buck Owens and Merle Haggard, and those guys had listened to Hank Williams and George Jones, and those guys had listened to the Louvin Brothers and the Carter Family and Jim and Jessie. It all went back to Celtic folk music. The line has always looked pretty unbroken to me."

Likewise, J. D. had been impressed with Glenn's hard-style Detroit-type guitar rock. It didn't take long before they'd begun writing songs together, intricate, early Everly Brothers–sounding two-part harmonies. As Souther remembered, "We were trying to write songs, and I do mean trying. We were just learning. Glenn played me R&B Detroit-style rock, and I played him Hank Williams. We spent most of our time beatin' on guitars and going around playin' hoots. We got a paying gig, finally, to our amazement, and they asked us what the name of our group was. We didn't have one; we'd just called ourselves John David and Glenn. There was a whole lot of rustic stuff going around, album covers looking like they were carved out of wood, things like that. I'm sure we were smokin' dope, and Glenn suddenly said, 'Longbranch,' and I said, 'Pennywhistle,' and we figured, fine, we'd use them both."

The first job roughly coincided with Alexandria's leaving. By this time, Glenn had found himself a small apartment in Echo Park, and now it was his turn to invite J. D. to crash. Rehearsing night and day, with a half-dozen "simple and deep" tunes under their garrison belts, they managed to land a deal with Amos Records.

Souther says: "I knew two of the guys who worked for Jimmy Bowen, both of whom were from my hometown, Amarillo, Texas. Red Steagal and a guy named Tom Thacker, who'd been a deejay in Amarillo. Thacker wound up producing our album with some of the best if still unknown L.A. studio musicians [including Ry Cooder, Doug Kershaw, and James Burton]." They then managed to get a couple of gigs at the Troubadour, but when it became clear they weren't going to break out, Bowen decided to rethink his priorities.

"Soon after," Frey recalled, "J. D. and I got in a fight with our company and suddenly we couldn't make any more records. Every day we'd go to the office, ask if we could get released, and they'd say no. So we'd go down to the Troubadour bar and get drunk."

Kenny Rogers, meanwhile, having brought Shiloh to L.A., continued to express nothing but confidence and determination about them to Bowen, even though he knew he was facing an increasingly hopeless situation. In truth, his deal with Amos had all but fallen apart in the wake of Longbranch Pennywhistle's failure. Bowen had put everything he had behind the album's launch, but because of independent distribution limitations, it had failed to earn back its production costs. In the months that followed, he became increasingly pessimistic about the chances of even keeping his label afloat. Rogers, meanwhile, kept reassuring him that Shiloh was good enough to turn everything around.

Bowen agreed to hang in, but insisted he was finished with Longbranch Pennywhistle. There was just no point in throwing good money after bad. Souther and Frey were angry at what they felt was Bowen's abandonment of them, and insisted on having the rights to their songs put back in their names and release from their contract, which Bowen refused to do. Even though he no longer believed in the duo's performing abilities, having signed the group to a publishing as well as recording deal, he hoped to make some money selling their songs to other acts on his label.

As J. D. remembered, "The deal from the publishers' point of view was that they would pay us forty or sixty dollars a week and hope we would turn in a few songs every couple of months, mostly for other signed performers' sessions. But they didn't like what we wrote. Meanwhile, Glenn and I were smoking bongs of hash and writing these bizarre, minor-key songs about our 'own experiences' that had nothing to do with these guys." Frey also has bitter memories of Longbranch Pennywhistle. As he recalled years later, "We were playing together for a couple of years as this wacky little folk duo, going nowhere." John Boylan describes the duo's sound as nothing special, little more than "a lot of hair and guitars."

With no real prospects and money increasingly scarce, Glenn and J. D. moved to a smaller, cheaper apartment on Laguna in Echo Park, a sixty-dollar-a-month place they'd heard about from another struggling, street-smart musician from the Troubadour, Jackson Browne. As Souther recalls, "Eventually, Jackson moved out, and I got divorced and moved into his apartment. He lived below us, on the first floor, a little bitty room, which is where he got the name of his publishing company, Open Window Music, because the only breath of fresh air in this tomb was from this one window." Although he too had the sweet baby face of eager innocence as yet untested, unlike Frey and Souther, Browne had already been around the block a few times.

Born in Heidelberg, Germany, Jackson Browne was raised in California, first in Highland Park, then in Orange County, a suburb of Los Angeles where the edge of show business shared a border with teen gangland, USA.

Torn between wanting to be a musician and one of the boys, in the fall of 1965, less than six months out of high school, he signed a publishing deal with Elektra, received a five-hundred-dollar advance, and was busted for pot in the same week.

After using his advance money to pay his fine, Browne decided to drive across country to New York City in search of the celebrated, if fading, Greenwich Village folk-music scene. As he recalled, "Tim Buckley was in New York at the time, and I went to see him play at this place called the Dom. *Dom* was *mod* spelled backward, and there was always this carnival of people around. Andy Warhol with his entourage, a film loop of Lou Reed eating a Hershey bar, Nico sitting at one end of the bar in this Dietrich pose singing these incredible songs, and Tim Buckley as the opening act.

"When I got hired to play, Nico was being accompanied by various members of the Velvet Underground. They'd trade off, Lou Reed would back her one night, John Cale the next, and so on. And she was getting crazy about not having the same guy backing her up every night. So she asked Tim to do it, and he said no. Then she asked me. First thing they asked me was whether I could play an electric guitar. I said yes, but I didn't have one. They said if I could get one, I could have the job. So I borrowed a friend's."

After a brief love affair with Nico, Browne became bored with the scene, seeing a bit too clearly through its Warhol-inspired pretentiousness, and decided to return once more to California. Back in L.A., he formed what he envisioned as a West Coast version of the Velvet Underground. He called the new group the Soft White Underbelly, but when he proved unable to get them to make the kind of music he heard in his head, he simply walked away. He was also, briefly, a member of the Nitty Gritty Dirt Band, but soon enough left that group as well.

On his own again, Browne soon became another of the familiar faces without a big name at the Troubadour. "Jackson was always the kid," recalled one of the club's regulars. "You couldn't help but love him . . . when he stood there with his too-large shirt on and his determined stab at becoming Robert Mitchum by not shaving for three days, which made him look like a Botticelli that needed dusting and not like Robert Mitchum at all, the world came to a complete stop. 'And those cheekbones,' one of the waitresses used to sigh. 'Those eyelashes and those cheekbones. *God!*' "

Although at the Troub most nights, scene-weary Browne, whose cool demeanor toward the women of the club made him all the more appealing, had reservations about hanging out with other unemployed musicians. He'd already had his fill of the faux artiste life in New York City, perceiving it as a substitute for a real community of artists, a place where drinking and carousing were far more important than actual creative expression. As far as he was concerned, the free and loose sex at the Troub far exceeded the level of energy devoted to musicality by the members of the club's bar scene. As he later remembered, "The Troubadour was the big thing then, but I'll tell you something. I don't think there was ever a [real] songwriter's scene around the Troubadour."

Frey felt the same way: "The Troubadour, man, was . . . full of tragic fucking characters. Has-beens and hopefuls. . . . I was always worried about going down there because I thought people would think I had nothing better to do. Which was true."

Browne and Frey weren't the only two who early on sensed the creepiness crawling through the party. There was indeed something not quite right about the place. It was as if the regular nightly players were slightly adrift, orgiastically attending a wake for a time and place that had somehow already passed them by. Gone from the charts were the transient L.A. sixties country-rock groups. Everyone by now had been beached by the mainstream tide of the Doors, led by Jim Morrison, who'd stolen the national commercial spotlight with a dose of sex, onstage theatrical knowhow, and progressive if minimalist rock.

While the rest of the L.A. music scene suffered from the round-robin shift of a group of musicians who banded together, fell apart, and reformed with almost as much regularity as they showed up to party at the Troub, Morrison had managed to catch everyone with *his* pants down. The wild and unexpected commercial success of the Doors had made it clear to the industry executives, if not their stable of artists, that the gap between L.A.'s hip and L.A. hits was beginning to widen. That was what Browne and Frey were sensing in their impatience-with-an-edge reflections on the jaded nightlife of the Troubadour's front bar. Their folk-country style of rock wasn't really dead, they wanted to believe, just in need of something new and vitalizing to relight its fire.

Or some*one*. For if ever there was a need for a miracle worker, that time was now. As it turned out, already in their midst were not one but two such wand-wavers, a pair of saviours-on-the-make from where-else-but New York City. Having followed the flow of music west, Elliot Roberts and David Geffen found themselves in L.A. on a self-styled mission to find and resurrect the soul of sixties rock and roll. For a hefty piece of the action, of course. After all, salvation did not come cheap in this, the City of Angels.

Elliot Roberts was born in 1946 and raised in the Morrisania section of the Bronx, where as a teenager he developed a strong sense of survival combined with a pot-induced appreciation for the music and the meaning of the Temptations. Slight, with reddish-brown hair and a face sunk behind a prominent nose, Elliot always led with his lip. His money card was his streetwise, sarcastic sense of humor, which originally made him want to be a stand-up comic. Sensing early on he might not have the material, let alone the stomach, to take a real shot at it, he opted for the money route, landing a job in the mail room of the William Morris Agency. As with all would-be agents, he started at the bottom, hoping to earn a place in the agency's trainee program.

Everything changed for Elliot one night in 1967, when he happened to catch a late-night performance by Canadian folksinger Roberta Joan Anderson, who was later reborn as Joni Mitchell in Greenwich Village's Café au Go-Go. What Elliot saw blew him away, even if he couldn't exactly put his finger on what the force of her performance was. Folk music? Not exactly. Jazz? Not really. Sixties social protest? Not very. And yet there were elements of all three in the unique combination of Mitchell's singing style, lyrics, and guitar progressions. One thing he was sure of. Up there on that little stage, his future was putting on quite a show.

Before the night was over, Roberts signed Mitchell up, but not as an agent, something she already had. Instead, he convinced her to let him take over the personal management of her career. He quit his job the next day and booked a tour for Mitchell that traveled east to west, winding up in Los Angeles, where he immediately began working to get her a record deal.

It had been one of the established L.A.-based musicians who'd convinced Roberts that Southern California, not New York, was where the real action was. "David Crosby is responsible for my coming to California," Roberts remembered. "When I first met him, he was going with Joni. . . . The day after I first saw her play, we left on tour. She did a month of clubs.

In California I met with Mo Ostin at Warner Brothers to get Joni a record deal. David was going to produce her first album."

By now, Crosby had left the Byrds and was working on his personal sixties rock-star scenario, staying alive and well while living it up in L.A. "Everyone knew David," Roberts recalled, "and David knew everyone. He was sort of a guru to me . . . and just the fact that I was with David gave me a seal of approval. He was the focal point; he was the scene. When we went to the Whiskey, our table was where everyone else wanted to stop and say hello. If we went to the Trip, the seas would part for David. . . . To me this was all incredibly bizarre because he had just been fired [from the Byrds]; he was an unemployed musician. . . . The very first day in the studio [to record Joni's album] at Sunset Sound, about an hour into the session, an engineer comes in and tells David that the Buffalo Springfield were in the room next door."

Crosby took Roberts to meet Neil Young, then with Buffalo Springfield, and the two immediately hit it off. When the singer expressed his desire to leave Buffalo Springfield, Elliot immediately signed him as his second client. He then signed Crosby and formalized Lookout Management, named after the location of the Laurel Canyon house he was living in and working out of.

Elliot's crib quickly became the new hip hangout, a rough, countrified approximation of the midsixties black-lit Village scene fleshed out by a constant mix of musicians, actors, actresses, directors, and hippies. Regular hangers included Peter Fonda, Jack Nicholson, Dennis Hopper, "Mama" Cass Elliott, John Sebastian, Michelle Phillips, David Blue, Tim Hardin, Ned Doheny (the singer-songwriter whose family name graces the street that divided Beverly Hills from West Hollywood), Neil Young, Mark Volman of the Turtles, former Modern Folk Quartet member and resident rock photographer Henry Diltz, and hip FM deejay B. Mitchell Reed. Nearly everyone who hung at Elliot's shared a taste for music, drugs, and sex. The music mostly acoustic guitar and piano, the drugs grass and coke, the sex everywhere. It was, according to David Crosby, "a model environment."

Elliot's place may have seemed the ultimate in laid-back, spontaneous L.A. cool, but he always put together his "swingin' soirees" with one eye, no matter how bleary, to business. By the time Joni was set to make her debut at the Troubadour in the fall of 1968, Elliot had elevated her four-show gig into an "event," one of the most sought-after tickets in town. Combining her talent for performing and his for promotion, both Mitchell and Roberts had arrived at the gates of big time.

At about the same time, David Crosby, Stephen Stills, and Graham Nash began cutting demos in the studio, trying to create a set of workable commercial songs. The group, all veterans of somewhat successful sixties L.A.-based bands, had originally come together under the musical supervision of Paul Rothchild. Rothchild, the Elektra Records producer whose discovery of Jim Morrison and the Doors had changed the direction of the former folk label, was approached by David Crosby to help him put together a new group. Many in the industry blamed Crosby's ego and drug problems for the first breakup of the Byrds, which should have gone on to become the most successful American group of the decade. Now in serious financial trouble, Crosby had met with Rothchild, as had Stills, whose ex-group, Buffalo Springfield, had recently fallen apart; Nash, who'd left the British group the Hollies because of his desire to make music other than the standard three-minute AM pop; and John Sebastian, of the now-defunct Lovin' Spoonful, about the possibility of starting yet another new band.

However, even before the group began to record, it appeared in danger of breaking up when Sebastian decided to pursue a solo career. At the time it seemed the smart move, as the other potential members' legal problems were threatening to prevent them from ever coming together. Each was signed to a different label, with obligations and options on future individual services held over from their previous contracts. Although David Crosby's Byrds label, Columbia, was not enthusiastic about keeping him, Columbia subsidiary Epic, which held the rights to Nash, and Atlantic, which had Stills, insisted on retaining the future rights to their artists.

And with good reason. The strong buzz on the new group was instant once deejay Reed, as a favor to Roberts, began playing the two demos Rothchild had produced for the band, "Long Time Gone" and "49 Bye-Byes," on his highly influential K-MET ("The Mighty Met!") radio program. Because the group still had no name, Reed jokingly dubbed them the Frozen Noses, a thinly veiled reference to what had become the drug of choice among L.A.'s rock and roll hip.

Negotiating the release of each band member from his label ultimately proved too much for Roberts, who, out of desperation, called upon former New Yorker, fellow William Morris mail-room alumnus, and good friend of Crosby, David Geffen to help. By now, Geffen had become a full-fledged agent with unlimited ambition, if little clout. When approached by Elliot, Geffen jumped at the chance to get involved in an increasingly messy situation. Roberts believed Geffen was the only one he knew with enough chutzpah to put the deal together.

Born and raised in Brooklyn, David Geffen attended New Utrecht High School, where he graduated with a sixty-six average, which killed any chance he might have had of becoming a dentist, his first career choice. After a year at Brooklyn College and the University of Texas, Geffen got a job as an usher at CBS. This taste of show business was enough to make him want to try and make a living in it. He applied for a position as an agent at Ashley-Steiner Famous Artists, where he was rejected because he didn't have a college degree.

Turning next to the William Morris Agency, a wised-up Geffen wrote on his application that he had graduated from UCLA and got the job. Assigned to the mail room, he simply waited for the confirmation of references to arrive from the university, steamed it open, and replaced the real letter with one he wrote himself.

According to Roberts, Geffen's work ethics were as much a key to his success as anything else. "The way he [made his move to TV at the agency] was, he would go into the mail room extra early. He taught me this. He'd say, 'When are you coming in?' and I'd say, 'Well, I usually get in at nine,' and he'd go, 'Well, get in at six-thirty. That gives us a good two and half hours to read everybody's memos.' And we would."

By the age of twenty-two, Geffen had worked his way up to the position of junior agent in the television division, under Lou Weiss. Weiss, forty-seven at the time, had been with the agency for thirty years and was considered one of the old-guard big wheels.

Greffen, however, wasn't impressed. Like every other agent, Weiss was twice his age and did not particularly like the brash new kid on the block. Frustrated by the lack of real opportunity in the television division, Geffen instead cozied up to Jerry Brandt, who'd made his agency bones establishing the hot new music division. When he asked Brandt what his secret was, the senior agent turned to the junior agent and said, "*Schmuck!* You think these guys are going to listen to you? They don't care what you've got to say. They're older than you are! Deal with people your own age. Go into the music business, where nobody knows what they're doing, and nobody knows how to do it."

Not long after, in 1968, Brandt left the agency, leaving an opening Geffen sensed he just might be able to grab. Looking around for an act to power his acceleration, Geffen came across an unsold "out-bin" tape of Laura Nyro's performance at the Monterey Pop festival. Nyro, an unknown, overwrought native New Yorker, had dressed in black to play her introverted, minor-key songs hunched over a piano to an audience of California flower-power children. The excitement generated by a then unknown Janis Joplin's dynamic performance helped inflate the largely distorted tales of Nyro's having been "booed" off the sunny stage. In reality, the singer-songwriter was the unfortunate embodiment of a time and place gone by, and her set had left the audience more dazed than dazzled. Nevertheless, Geffen was impressed with a tape of the performance and remained indifferent to the stories of her having flopped at Monterey, hearing something decidedly commercial in Nyro that the crowd at the festival obviously hadn't. He sought out the singer-songwriter, signed her up, took her to Columbia Records' Clive Davis, and talked his way (and hers) into a recording contract. Shortly thereafter, Nyro became a star.

It was the kind of score that makes an agent's reputation, and Geffen suddenly found himself the object of a bidding war for his own talent. Ashley Famous (the newly renamed agency that had originally turned Geffen down for not having a degree) now offered him a job at $1,000 a week, twice his William Morris pay. Geffen jumped, and took Nyro (and half her publishing under his newly formed Tuna Fish Music) with him.

Meanwhile, Elliot Roberts had all he could manage and more with Joni Mitchell, Neil Young, and the problematic Crosby, Stills and Nash. Elliot held out the latter as the client reward if David could put all the pieces of their increasingly difficult deal together. Even as Geffen came on board, the band had decided to get rid of original producer Paul Rothchild. Although many believe Rothchild was forced out by Geffen for wanting too big a wedge of the money pie, according to Geffen, "The band made that decision entirely on their own, before I became involved. Stephen Stills wanted to produce their record with the others, which is exactly what they did." It didn't matter that Rothchild prided himself on having "special" personal relationships with his artists and often spoke of the connection between the integrity of his production work and the importance of loyalty. If the band didn't want him, he was out. Despite his having produced the Doors — who, coincidentally, Geffen repped while still an agent at Ashley Famous in 1968 — the band considered Rothchild too much of a folkie and not enough of a rocker.

When he had carefully assessed the situation, Geffen felt ready to approach Davis. He believed it wouldn't be hard to sell him the group because Crosby, the most famous of the three performers, was already on the label (Epic was a wholly owned subsidiary of Columbia).

After laying out the deal for Davis, Geffen went to work getting Stills's release from Atlantic. He paid a visit to Jerry Wexler, the president of Atlantic Records, who, unimpressed with Geffen's rap, promptly threw him out on his ass. Undaunted, he returned to Atlantic's offices the next day, this time bypassing Wexler and appealing directly to the label's founder and owner, Ahmet Ertegun. Ertegun, far more personable than Wexler, decided it might be wiser to kiss the same part of Geffen's anatomy that he'd landed on the day before. Ertegun listened to what Geffen had to say and decided that he wanted Crosby, Stills, Nash and Young for himself. Geffen realized there might be an opportunity for something bigger than the chance to develop one new act and allowed himself to be charmed into reversing his plan. As close as he was to Davis, he knew neither he nor Columbia wanted or needed any more partners. Ertegun, on the other hand, might even consider an offer to subsidize a new label. Geffen could barely contain his enthusiasm as he agreed to bring C, S and N to Ertegun. As he suspected, getting Columbia to drop Crosby proved easy. Davis personally disliked Crosby for walking out on the Byrds when they were one of the label's biggest acts and was glad to get rid of him. Nash also proved no problem for Geffen, and late in 1968, he formally signed the new group to Atlantic Records.

Geffen followed the Crosby, Stills and Nash coup with an even more spectacular one for himself. Not long after, Clive Davis, perhaps unwilling to let any more of Geffen's clients go, decided to renew Laura Nyro's recording contract and have Columbia-owned subsidiary April-Blackwood purchase her publishing outright, to use as source material for its major acts at the time — Barbra Streisand and Blood, Sweat and Tears. Because he personally owned half of Nyro's publishing, Geffen's end of the deal came to a cool $2 million.

On the way to a party at writer Carl Gottlieb's house one night soon after, according to Roberts, "As we were going across the street, David [Geffen] said to me, 'Listen. This is getting to be too much, and I'm not crazy about being an agent. I'll leave the agency and we'll do Geffen-Roberts,' and I said, 'Gee, I don't know if I want to give up my whole management company and take it apart,' and he said, 'Don't be stupid, I'll make you more money than you make alone,' and I said, 'Yes, David.'" Geffen proposed a fifty-fifty split and guaranteed Roberts that he would soon be a millionaire. They confirmed the deal with a midnight handshake, and the next day the Geffen-Roberts Company was officially in business.

Crosby, Stills and Nash's first album was released in the spring of 1969 and, thanks to the sudden rise of progressive FM radio programming, went on to become one of the biggest albums of the year, selling more than two million copies even before the group's milestone appearance at Woodstock, only the second time they'd ever performed live before a paying audience.

All of which should have made Geffen extremely happy, but in fact had just the opposite effect. By the winter of 1970, according to Geffen, "After a year, I decided I wanted to be an agent again. I didn't like being a manager." Small wonder, having to put up with constant ego clashes, hostile breakups, uneasy reunions, and ever-present drugs. He especially disliked Roberts's good friend David Crosby. Clive Davis had been right about him, Geffen now knew; he was talented, no question about that, and a fun guy, unless you were trying to do business with him. He was simply not worth the time and pampering it took to cater to his particularly distasteful star trip. The breaking point came when Crosby made Geffen his mule, forcing him to transport grass across state lines, which nearly got him busted. That was it, as far as Geffen was concerned. Neither Crosby nor anyone else was ever going to make an ass out of him again.

Geffen remembers "I went back in business with Elliot, rejoined Geffen-Roberts, and that's when I first got the idea to start Asylum Records." Indeed, his involvement with Crosby, Stills and Nash (and Young) had felt more like a drag than a rush, so distasteful to Geffen that it forced him to rethink his essential business. Having done all the work to deliver the group to Atlantic, he then had to sit back and watch the label rake in the big bucks. It seemed more obvious now than ever that the thing to do was start a record label of his own. Well aware of others who had tried the same thing and failed — Jimmy Bowen, for one — Geffen felt his chances were better. First, his pockets were deeper, second, his ear was better, and third, his instincts were sharper. The key to making it all work was finding the right act, with fewer star-trip hassles and all the money kept in the family.

Which is why, that fall of 1969, Geffen took Roberts and went on the prowl, hitting the L.A. club circuit every night, hot to spot the perfect, still-unknown act they could turn into the Next Big Thing.

FIVE

Margo Rogers had taken over the management of Shiloh and booked the group into several clubs in the Los Angeles area, including the San Fernando Valley, one in Hawthorne Beach, and a few others. "Then our two singles and the album came out and flopped," recalled Henley. "As they should have, because it was all crap."

Michael Bowden recalls: "Kenny was at the helm as producer for our album, but in name only. He was around a little bit, but, along with Margo, we were overseeing things ourselves, bungling our way through the recording. I could barely play in two gears, myself. This was all new to us, and we didn't know what we were doing.

"We cut the album at a studio called Larrabee Sound, in Manhattan Beach. Kenny popped in and out from time to time, but we wound up mixing it ourselves. He then released a couple of singles off of it, on Amos. The first was called 'A Simple Little Down-Home Rock & Roll Love Song for Rosie,' with Don singing lead. It was a stiff in every city it was released, except in Bakersfield, California. For some bizarre reason it went to number one there. They wanted us to come play there because of it. We drove up on a Saturday to Bakersfield on a bill to open for Eric Clapton and Delaney and Bonnie, and it was the first time any of us had ever heard ourselves on the radio. I mean they played the record on the local radio station every ten or fifteen minutes, and we thought we had made it. When we got to the show, the only thing the audience wanted to hear was that single. They didn't care about the rest of the album, or us, or anything."

After the release of one more single, Amos Records folded, leaving the band stranded in Los Angeles. Having become part of the front-bar scene at the Troubadour, Henley and the others managed to get themselves booked onto the crowded Monday night open-mike "hoot" session, where they played for the Santa Monica Boulevard crowd for the first time.

The show went well, and the band got to know the others a bit more, including Linda Ronstadt, J. D. Souther, Jackson Browne, Rick Nelson, the Everly Brothers, and David Blue. Surviving in L.A. was a victory all its own, and getting to play the occasional gig was both a break and a breakthrough for Henley's boys. They were determined to make the most of it, until internal problems caused Shiloh to disband.

In 1971, after less than a year back in L.A., Henley had a falling-out with Bowden over the band's leadership and musical direction — Bowden wanted Shiloh to sound more country, while Henley was after a sound less hick and more hip. Although he couldn't quite nail it yet, Henley had picked up a musical vibe coming off the stage from the other Troubadour regulars and wanted to aim the group's arrows a little closer to that bull's-eye. Sure, it all *sounded* like country, but there was something else Henley heard in their minor-keyed chord constructions and lyrical riffs, even beyond the harmony-heavy Top 40 sound Crosby, Stills and Nash were leaning toward, that he found completely irresistible: music harder than country but softer than rock, with a lyric sensibility that turned up the heat.

From the beginning, there had always been a healthy competitive edge to Henley and Bowden's friendship. Bowden, ever the jokester, had continued to use gags and put-down one-liners as a way of asserting himself. He may have been right in the past; this time he came up short. According to band member Jim Ed Norman, when Shiloh's breakup came, it was less about the music than the friendship. "It was more of a personal thing than anything else. Which was too bad. I thought the musicianship was quite good. There was a creativity there, a great vocal sound, a lot of potential."

"I was just frustrated at not getting anywhere," says Henley. "Richard Bowden was and still is one of my dearest friends. He's the reason I'm in the music business. Yes, we had some disagreements, but they weren't large enough to destroy a friendship like ours. He's probably the closest thing to a brother that I have. Still, we were not, in my estimation, a great vocal band, particularly where harmonies were concerned. Our combined talents had gotten us out of Texas, but I didn't see the potential to go much further. It just wasn't happening for Shiloh."

Someone else with the same feeling about her own career was Linda Ronstadt, who'd recently been through some changes herself. Capitol Records had chosen to hype her as a barefoot sex-kitten farmer's daughter, but that game plan ended with the failure of *Silk Purse,* a recording whose cover featured Ronstadt sitting in a pigsty, covered with mud and surrounded by hogs. "I hated that album," Ronstadt recalled. "I couldn't sing then; I didn't know what I was doing. I was working with Nashville musicians, and I don't really play country music — I play very definitely California music." The problem was, in 1970 no one at Capitol seemed to think "California music" meant anything beyond the Beach Boys. At one point they even considered switching her to the label's country division. According to John Boylan, "They just didn't have a clue."

To be sure, these were difficult times for women in rock and roll, especially those who'd chosen the male-dominated L.A. route, where being cute and sexy often guaranteed a rough time understanding that there was one set of anything-goes rules for guys, and another for chicks. It was a conflict that invariably crossed over from the personal to the professional side of the boulevard. At least part of the confusion may have come from Ronstadt herself, whose sexual image had already become the stuff of legend. In spite of it, she was never looked down upon and was always generous and ready to party with and like one of the boys. "I wasn't quite sure how I was supposed to be, if I was supposed to be true-blue and faithful to one man, or if I was supposed to be hanging out at the Troubadour every night. The women, and there were very few of us, were really oddballs. We didn't know how to act, or what to do, or how we were supposed to be. We didn't know whether we were supposed to be real earth mamas like Maria Muldaur, you know, with a baby under her arm and fiddle in her hand . . . or what."

Not that it mattered. The Troubadour boys were having far too much fun being young, freewheeling, and single to ever be caught in something as restrictive as an actual *relationship.* Especially not with another musician, especially *this* musician, who, beautiful and girly as she looked, was a bit on the possessive side and not above getting rough with sloppy drunks if they made too much noise while an act she liked was onstage.

As Ronstadt recalled, "One night I heard Shiloh playing 'Silver Threads and Golden Needles,' using the exact guitar break off my album *Hand Sown*." She might have felt less flattered if she hadn't developed a genuine affection for Henley's group. These boys seemed to understand what her music was about far better than her record company did, which convinced her to make some major changes. First, she decided, she needed a new producer. Ronstadt was particularly impressed with John Boylan, another nightside regular whose work with Rick Nelson and the Stone Canyon Band had made everyone sit up and take notes. One night at the front bar the two started talking, and Ronstadt confided her professional frustrations to Boylan, including her desire to put together a backup group as good as Shiloh or Rick Nelson's. Boylan volunteered to find one for her. As usual, Ronstadt brought a sexual charge to her professional choice. She found her way into his bed.

John Boylan remembers his first encounter with Ronstadt this way: "At the end of 1969, I was called up by Linda, who was so excited about the band I'd put together for Rick that she asked me to put one as good together for her. We hit it off, became involved, and began living together in Laurel Canyon. It didn't last very long, but I continued to work with her because that was the better part of the relationship. At the time, she was being managed by Herb Cohen, who was not musical and couldn't help her form a band the way I could. The group she was working with when I met her was okay, but a little dicey. In January 1970, when her best musician, Chris Darrow, decided to leave, she got rid of Cohen. I then went around the Troubadour looking for guys I thought were good players. The first one I contacted was Glenn Frey."

Boylan "started out to be my boyfriend," Ronstadt said later on, "then he was managing me and was my producer. Then he wasn't my boyfriend, but he was still managing me, and then he wasn't managing me anymore. All those troubles stem from the fact that in our personal relationship, we couldn't resolve things."

Ronstadt did agree with Boylan about Frey. She admired his guitar stylings along with his natural ability to fall into high harmony. Boylan thought he might be able to get Frey to join Ronstadt's upcoming tour and that he might know some other musicians who had some free time and were good enough to play behind her. "I offered him two hundred bucks a week," Boylan says. "I knew his band, Longbranch Pennywhistle, wasn't doing much."

Frey jumped at it. He remembered, "The two hundred a week with Linda was more than I'd seen in about three years in California. I got so excited because I'd never been on the road before — except riding a truck from Detroit to L.A."

The next musician hired by Boylan was Don Henley. "A while back," Boylan recalls, "he'd sent me a record of Shiloh, and now I arranged to see them do a gig at the old Aquarius Theater in Hollywood, where Margo Rogers had booked them. I said, 'Don, look, I'll give you two hundred a week to play with Linda,' and he said, a bit harshly, 'You never listened to the record I sent you!' I told him I did, and he said, 'You actually *listened* to it?' And I said, 'Yeah.'"

According to Henley, "I was initially approached about joining Linda's band by Glenn Frey as we sat drinking beer in the Troubadour one evening. Ronstadt was rehearsing in a little house up in Laurel Canyon. An audition was set up. I went there and ran through several numbers with Glenn, Linda, John Boylan, and the others. I was hired on the spot." Henley signed on.

Henley and Frey had met before, in passing at the offices of Amos Records and at the front bar of the Troubadour. Each was aware of the other's dissatisfaction with Jimmy Bowen, and each admired the other's work. Henley, especially, was impressed with Frey, as much for his charisma as his music. What others often took for unfriendliness on Henley's part was really his intense self-consciousness and shyness. Frey, on the other hand, was the type of guy Henley not only liked but wanted to be more like — outgoing, tough, good-looking, full of self-confidence, great with girls. *Cool!* Plus, he discovered as they talked, he and Frey had the same kind of career goals. Henley recalled, "Glenn was really charming, and he was *going* somewhere. He had this plan: he had this vision."

For Henley, joining Ronstadt meant finally and irrevocably leaving Shiloh. "The thing that made me feel bad, even though we'd technically broken up, was leaving those guys in Shiloh that I'd grown up with. We'd all come out to California together with our hopes and dreams, and I left them for Glenn and Ronstadt. I felt bad about that for a long time, but I had to do something because we weren't really getting anywhere in

California. We had done all right in Texas, but we could only get to a certain level. Richard Bowden was a good musician and a great guy, but we couldn't make it happen. I'd busted my ass in little clubs in Texas for seven years, from 1963 to 1970. Then for another year in L.A. The romance of that life was gone for me."

Michael Bowden remembers the moment as more bittersweet: "There weren't any hard feelings, except Richard, who was the unspoken leader of Shiloh, who may have been upset a little by it, but he knew that Don was more focused and driven, and knew that he was prepared to give it everything to become a successful rock star. Which he did. Still, it wasn't just a snap decision on his part. We talked it over and thought this was really the best thing for him."

The rest of the band consisted of a country-rock lead guitarist by the name of Kenny Bloom and a bass player Boylan had heard in Huntington Beach, Casey Van Beek.

In the spring of 1971, Frey, Henley, Bloom, Van Beek, Boylan (doubling as a guitarist and manager), and Ronstadt went out on the road on a tour that began at the Cellar Door in Washington, D.C. Just prior to leaving L.A., Ronstadt finally became romantically involved with J. D. Souther, whom she now proudly described to friends as the love of her life.

After a couple of gigs, mostly colleges and clubs, the band's sound began to gel, until, as Boylan recalls, "We had a layoff period, and Kenny Bloom couldn't hang. Linda couldn't afford to pay anybody when the band wasn't working. He became the first one I needed to replace. Then Casey went back to his old band. I'd heard Randy Meisner was available, so I decided to call him."

In an effort to save his marriage, Meisner had left the Stone Canyon Band and returned to Nebraska to take a job at a John Deere dealership. Six months later he was back in L.A. working on Nelson's new album, *Rudy the Fifth*. Having finished it, Meisner was trying to decide if there would be enough studio work to keep him on the West Coast, when Boylan tracked him down. Promising his wife he wouldn't stay away long, Meisner agreed to a test gig (with Richard Bowden filling in on lead).

It proved an easy score for Meisner, who, in addition to being able to drop into any style of bass, sang an exceptionally clear high harmony. The other members were impressed that Boylan had managed to get him. To Frey, who'd often stood at the lip of the Troubadour stage to watch him do his thing, Meisner was the closest of any of them to a proven rock star, and he felt privileged to be able to play with him.

"Randy worked great," Boylan says. He then made what would prove to be the band's key personnel change when he persuaded Bernie Leadon to join.

Minnesota native Bernie Leadon was already a veteran of the country-rock scene, having begun his career playing banjo for the Scottsville Squirrel Barkers in 1962. After they broke up, he relocated to Florida and worked with a series of bands until returning to L.A. in 1967 as a replacement member for Hearts and Flowers, a folk-rock band and local club-circuit favorite. Hearts and Flowers led to a stint with the Dillard and Clark Expedition, after which, for two years, until 1971, he was a member of the Flying Burrito Brothers.

Leadon had played with Ronstadt a few times before, and at Boylan's urging agreed to join her new band for a July 1971 date at Disneyland. That gig became the first time Glenn Frey, Don Henley, Randy Meisner, and Bernie Leadon ever played together.

And, as it turned out, the only time on the tour. "Various combinations of musicians played behind Linda," Boylan confirms, "but those four, what I considered the dream configuration for the tour, only played one gig."

Two of the ongoing misconceptions surrounding the origin of the Eagles is that they were conceived as a permanent backup band for Linda Ronstadt and that they played behind her as a fixed unit for her entire 1971 tour. The single gig they did, in Anaheim, went extremely well, and although Leadon reportedly had a little too much "courage juice" before the show, there was something about this combination that no one who heard them that night could miss. While each was a decent enough musician on his own, when they played together on stage, they were terrific. With individual influences as diverse as the Louvin Brothers, the Carter family, the Everly Brothers, the Dillards, the Temptations, the Drifters, the Beatles, the Beach Boys, the O-Jays, and the Byrds, the whole added up to much more than these root components, a sound at once familiar and unique, classic yet original, singularly contemporary as it emerged with raw passion and hot grace from the great collective body of modern American music.

J. D. Souther remembers the first time he heard the four play together: "It's no secret that when they came together they were Glenn's band, although Don could sing anything he wrapped his voice around. We used to call Don 'the Secret Weapon' because he sat back there behind all those drums with his big fuzzy hair. It wasn't that obvious, but that insanely beautiful voice, like four-hundred-grain sandpaper, rough but fine, was incredible to hear, even if you didn't know where it was coming from.

"Glenn was a great natural country singer, as well as a pretty good guitar player. He brought that R&B sensibility to the table with him and kind of learned country along the way. And brilliantly.

"As for Randy, he was a very important component as well. It would never have been the same band without him. His singing on the high end is unlike any other sound. He also helped define a style of songwriter-rooted bass playing, not unlike Paul McCartney. He always managed to make a nice melody under what the others were doing. And he could play light, with the tips of his fingers. The only other person I'd ever heard do that was Stephen Stills.

"And Bernie was one of the best and most overlooked guitar players around. All those great opening guitar riffs, in the beginning, came from Bernie. The great, grand opening of 'Take It Easy,' that's Bernie Leadon.

"Together, well, what can anybody say? When you heard them, you knew. It was just so damn obvious. So gorgeous, in-your-face fabulous.

"It was the combination that worked beautifully. Someone from East Texas, a guy from Detroit, another from the Central Plains, and one from Florida. There was nothing Southern California about that band. They were an all-American rock and roll outfit."

Indeed, it was a band that showed off the individual talents of each member without burying Ronstadt, or perhaps even more important, one another. Frey's urban guitar and sweet voice, Henley's bar-band backbeat and scruffed-up vocals, Leadon's country banjo and guitar, and Meisner's bass and high, soulful singing scored brilliantly beneath, around, and at times in front of the sultry, luscious Ronstadt and her Cupid-cute musical connivings.

One night in the hotel, Frey and Henley confided to Souther that they wanted to start their own band. "And I thought, hey, great idea," says Souther. "Glenn had a couple of really great songs. He wasn't afraid to step out there, he had a definite plan, he was a motivated guy. He'd written a song for Kate Taylor, James's little sister, called 'Get Up Kate.' Linda would occasionally let him do it in the show and sing lead on it. That was really the beginning of the Eagles. It was her generosity that let Glenn step up to the mike during her sets."

On the road, Henley and Frey became closer to each other than the rest of the band. Their private discussions about starting a band, sparked by the Disneyland show, continued throughout the tour, during which the group continued to shuffle personnel. Michael Bowden joined for a brief period, replacing Meisner, and Kenny Bloom came back for one or two dates to spell Leadon. Even J. D. Souther did one show, playing drums for Henley. "I'd never rehearsed with the band," Bowden remembers. "John Boylan brought a tape over to my apartment, and I worked up about ten songs off of it. He thought I sounded good enough, and that was it. Our first gig was at Terminal Island prison, opening for Kris Kristofferson. It was a very spirited, high-energy crowd. Ronstadt sang her tail off that day. I also sat in with Linda and the band for a string of dates at the Troubadour."

After six long months of life on the road with Ronstadt, the rolling mix-master show finally came to an end.

Not included on the tour was Jackson Browne. He was already taken. The first of the front-bar singer-songwriters to get a break, in 1967 he'd managed to snag a publishing deal with Elektra Records, the East Coast–based independent label that had made its reputation as a folkie label. Founder Jac Holzman had recorded such artists as Phil Ochs, Tom Paxton, Tom Rush, Judy Collins, and Odetta before shifting his label's roster to rock and scoring a huge commercial success with the Doors. Paul Rothchild, Holzman's main producer, ever on the lookout for new talent, had caught Jackson's show one night at the Troubadour. While unimpressed with his vocal stylings, Rothchild nevertheless admired his songwriting abilities and wondered aloud "how a seventeen-year-old boy [can] write songs from a seventy-year-old perspective." Not long after, Jackson had his deal. Although Browne never actually recorded for Elektra, Tom Rush covered two of his songs, "These Days" and "Colors of the Sun." "These Days" became something of an early benchmark for the Troubadour singer-songwriters, with its soft melody and melancholy lyrics, so oddly affecting coming from someone not quite twenty-one.

Browne remained the club regulars' favorite-to-make-it, even when, two years later, he was dropped from Elektra for being too folkish for the now solidly rock label. Not long after, he wrote a letter directly to David Geffen, enclosing a tape and an eight-by-ten glossy of himself. "I looked at the glossy," Geffen says, "and thought, 'Would Bob Dylan send an eight-by-ten glossy?' and threw it away. Later that day, my secretary, Leslie Morris, retrieved it from the ash can because she thought he looked cute, listened to the tape, thought it was good, and suggested I listen to it. I did, liked it, and decided to track down Jackson Browne." Geffen wanted to ask Browne to come down to the office for a chat, but by then he was nowhere to be found. Months went by before he finally emerged from yet another wanderlust-driven cross-country journey, arriving in L.A. to find a management contract with Geffen-Roberts waiting for him. Shortly thereafter he was gone again, only this time with Geffen's personal approval and guidance. Jackson Browne, virtually unknown beyond Santa Monica Boulevard, was now the opening act for Laura Nyro on her greatly anticipated world tour.

Geffen was eager to see how audiences reacted to him. The enthusiastic audience response to his performances assured Geffen that he'd made the right decision. Confident he could get him a record deal, upon their return to L.A., Geffen offered Browne to every major label.

And one by one, they all said no. "I went to everybody in the business trying to make a record deal for him," Geffen remembers, "and everybody turned him down. Even Ahmet [Ertegun], and I said, 'I'm telling you, this guy is good. I'm the guy who brought you Crosby, Stills and Nash. I'm doing you a favor.'

"And he said, 'You know what? Don't do me any favors.'

"I said, 'You'll make millions with him.'

"And he said, 'You know what? I got millions. Do you have millions?'

"I said no.

"He said, 'Start a record company and you'll have millions. Then we can all have millions.'

"I thought, 'Fuck him. I *will* start a record company.'"

It was the kind of arrogance Geffen had dealt with his entire professional life. This time he'd decided to do something about it. What was wrong with the industry was the same old story. It was being run by old men who smelled like bad aftershave, smoked big cigars, and heard in the product they sold to the young not the music of rebellion but the sound of jangling coin. They couldn't be the future, Geffen told himself. It had to belong to young guys like him, drawn to a place and a sound that spoke in a language he understood. The music made money because it was great; it wasn't great because it made money. He was convinced that suits like Davis and even Ertegun approached rock through the wrong end of the age-and-idealism scope.

Still, it didn't happen exactly as Geffen had planned. He believed deeply in Browne, and liked him on a personal level so much more than any other musician he'd ever met that if it meant having to finance a new label with his own money to showcase the young singer-songwriter, that's exactly what he would do. Ertegun, impressed as always with Geffen's audacity and sensing he must be on to something to make this deep a personal and professional commitment, made an offer that all but ensured this young man would succeed where so many others had failed. Ertegun arranged for the new label to be distributed through Atlantic.

The name Geffen chose for his venture came straight out of old Hollywood. In the early days of film, the independent United Artists studio was formed by three actors and one director frustrated by what they felt were the financially restrictive and creatively sterile policies of the majors. When Charlie Chaplin, Mary Pickford, Douglas Fairbanks, and D. W. Griffith announced their decision to go against the tide and take back control of their films from the studios, it was considered by everyone in Hollywood to be the height of insanity, a case of the inmates running the asylum.

Now it was rock and roll's rubber room that was about to run amok, as Geffen swung the door to his version of creative freedom wide open.

SIX

David Geffen formally established Asylum Records in 1970. In the next twelve months the Beatles would split up, Bill Graham would close both Fillmores, *Apollo 14* would land on the moon, eighteen year olds in America would win the right to vote, and Jim Morrison would die.

It was a time of consolidation in the increasingly mainstream industry. With disturbing regularity, the major labels continued to absorb the on-the-fringe independents. Not coincidentally, rock and roll's record sales gross for 1971 would exceed $1.7 *billion,* as the music that had once threatened to topple mainstream pop became its biggest product. The power stars of the business were now label executives, less interested in artistic statements than the ones from the bank.

Geffen was well aware of the economic realities of seventies corporate rock and roll and the difficulties he faced trying to start an independent label in that industry. Perhaps his greatest advantage, besides street-smart savvy, was youth. Still in his twenties, he was closer in age and temperament to the musicians he hung with than the suits he dealt with. He believed what was wrong with the business was essentially what had gone wrong with his Crosby, Stills and Nash plan. No matter how brilliant the execution of the supergroup's deal had been, ultimately most of the money went to the label. And in rock and roll, as with all business, whoever had the money called the shots. It was Geffen's dream to keep the money, and therefore creative freedom, in his own hands and those of his artists. He knew that was what would bring the best musicians to Asylum, and that was what would make them *all* rich.

Wanting to demonstrate strong support for Browne, Geffen remained extremely visible during the making of the first album. Even when the process dragged at an agonizingly slow pace, and therefore cost more than he would have liked, he bit his lip and said nothing. This was, he kept reminding himself, the creative freedom he'd promised. Still, anticipating huge start-up expenses, to save front money Geffen had structured Asylum on a split publishing "no advance" system, meaning the label would give the artist nothing upon signing and take half the publishing and pay all production costs, including day-to-day living expenses, in return for a royalty that began with album one. It was the kind of incentive that might make most performers speed up their pace. Unfortunately for Geffen, it had the opposite effect on Browne. Feeling he was being paid to create, he refused to compromise until he achieved exactly what he wanted, no matter how long it took.

Geffen became increasingly anxious for someone to start the cash registers ringing, and he fixed his sights on Linda Ronstadt, whom he'd known from her Stone Poney days as a client at Ashley Famous and whose recently completed tour had been quite successful. So much so that when she went back into the studio that August for Capitol, she'd insisted on taking her favorite version of the road band along. Frey, Henley, Meisner, and Leadon played on every track of *Linda Ronstadt*, including the three "live" performances on the album — Jackson Browne's "Rock Me on the Water," Mooney and Seals's "Crazy Arms," and Smith and Minors's "Rescue Me," all recorded onstage at the Troubadour.

The album proved a striking artistic leap forward for Ronstadt, beginning with the startling opening track, "Rock Me on the Water." Browne's sophisticated lyrics, accompanied by strong rhythmic percussion, ringing acoustic guitars, and great background harmonies, provided the best showcase yet for the singer, the band, the songwriter, and the emerging Los Angeles sound of the early seventies. "Rock Me" was a rock-gospel offering that seemed to come out of the left field of pseudocountry pop. Anyone hearing it for the first time had to wonder whether to dance or pray. Here was a song that sounded uplifting, affirmative, *spiritual,* performed with come-hither sexuality by Ronstadt.

Boylan loved the cut so much he pushed Capitol to release "Rock Me" as the first single off the album. Unfortunately, it proved too far a reach for Ronstadt's audience (and Top 40 programmers), and neither the single nor the album did very well. "Rock Me" reached only as high as number eighty-five in March 1972. Without the engine of a radio-play hit, *Linda Ronstadt* stalled at 163 on the *Billboard* charts.

Still, Boylan defended the album as progressive, a perfect example of the new sound floating in the air. "A lot of people in L.A. were trying to figure out the perfect country-rock sound. We knew that if we could get the combination right and the songs right, we could have something big. And we thought we had."

Browne, meanwhile, finished recording his album, and Geffen quickly moved to release its first single, the infectious "Doctor My Eyes," over Atlantic's inexplicable suggestion to go with Browne's version of "Rock Me." Geffen was convinced "Doctor" was the better choice by Paul Ahern, a onetime promotion executive for Atlantic who knew a hit single when he heard one. For his ability to call the right song, Ahern was brought into the inner circle at Asylum, a company still operating with only three full-time employees. "Doctor" immediately found its way into the top ten. According to Geffen, "Atlantic didn't really disagree about my decision to release 'Doctor' because I had Crosby and Nash singing backup on it. That was one of the reasons the radio stations picked up on it immediately. I actually put their names on the label so no one could miss it." The single, which would be Browne's biggest for the next ten years, was strong enough to push Asylum's first album past the 500,000 sales mark, certified gold.

Thus inspired, Ronstadt was now eager to get back into the studio, although contrary to what has always been assumed, there was never any question as to whether her backup band would remain with her. They wouldn't. Nor was Boylan particularly interested in managing them. He would continue to work with Ronstadt through 1973 and put together several more bands for her, including one with Richard and Mike Bowden. However, for a variety of reasons, his association with Henley, Frey, Leadon, and Meisner was over. He had taken them as far as he could.

According to Henley, "Boylan was a great guy and he helped us enormously, but we envisioned a different style of production and were ready to go looking for it." It wasn't only a matter of vision, however, but a question of legalities as well.

According to Boylan, "Glenn was already beholden to David Geffen. Although Clive Davis, of Columbia, made a very strong pitch for the band to me, in the backseat of a limo outside of the Troubadour, saying if we wanted a deal we had it right then and there, the fact of the matter was, David owned Glenn's recording contract."

It was true. Having been turned on to Glenn Frey early on by Jackson Browne, Geffen sensed now that the former member of Longbranch Pennywhistle had finally found a winning combination. He moved to secure his hold on the group. According to Geffen, "Right after I signed Jackson, he talked me into signing Glenn, which I did as a favor to him. The actual mechanism in my own head was that I had heard a record being played on the radio a lot called 'One Toke Over the Line,' by Brewer and Shipley, who to me sounded a lot like Longbranch. When I was ready to sign Glenn's new group, I simply bought out Longbranch Pennywhistle's recording contract from Jimmy Bowen for $15,000, and Shiloh's, I think, for $12,500. Contrary to what some may have thought at the time, my signing of Ronstadt had nothing to do with trying to get her backup band. Clearly they were never going to be her permanent band, simply because Glenn was already signed to me and eager to put a new group together, which he knew that I would record."

As John Hartmann, Buffalo Springfield's former agent hired by Geffen-Roberts in 1970, recalled later, you had to be deaf and blind not to hear just how good they were. Even this early, "it was nothing," Hartmann recalled, "to believe in what would eventually become the Eagles."

Recalls Geffen: "That was the combination I was looking for. Someone else wanted to add J. D., but I didn't want to mess with what was working, and anyway, the thing I had liked most about John David was his songs rather than his performing abilities. Glenn, I knew, was a born band creature."

Henley believes Geffen wasn't the only one who vetoed Souther's eligibility. "I think there may have been some hard feelings between Glenn and J. D. because of their experience in Longbranch Pennywhistle. Even though it was a group of two, it was still a group, and things happen. I also think there was something that went on between them about a girl. We did talk about it, and J. D. even came and played with us one day, but there was too much water under the bridge between him and Glenn. Whatever wounds there were from being in a group that didn't make it, it was too soon for them to try it again. At that point, it was Glenn's band, and he was calling the shots.

"And I don't think it mattered much to J. D. Like Jackson, he was very much a loner when it came to the group thing. He was signed by Geffen, who had a recording rights claim on him as well from the Longbranch Pennywhistle deal, as a solo act in the first round anyway, so he didn't miss out."

As it turned out, Geffen and Frey weren't the only ones opposed to J. D.'s becoming a member of the group. "At one point," Randy Meisner recalls, "Souther almost joined, but I said no. I felt we had a good thing going with four people who really didn't know each other and that it might work against the group that Glenn and J. D. had been together before." It's possible that everyone in the band was, to a certain extent, intimidated by Souther's talent and charisma. Or, perhaps, as one close to the band observed, it was more of what he lacked that worked against Souther. "The fact of the matter was," this person recalls, "he could have been in the band if he had the discipline and was willing to stick it out, but he didn't. He was a hopeless romantic, more interested in getting laid than in getting recorded."

According to Souther, "I was signed before any of the Eagles. Judy Sill was probably first, or Jackson, then David Blue, and *then* Glen, Henley, and the others. Jackson had taken me up to Geffen's house, I played him some songs, and he said he was going to give me a deal. That's when both Jackson and I said, 'What about Glenn?' He'd already been to Mussel Shoals with Boylan and cut a few R&B tracks with a country music melody overlay that were really good. 'You ought to sign those guys,' meaning Don and Glenn. 'They'll make you more money that the two of us ever will.' We knew what we were talking about. We knew what these guys could do. They wanted to put together a band to do exactly what they did. They were right about me, though. I wasn't a band creature. My report card from school always said the same thing — 'Does not work well with others.' We did consider it. I even rehearsed with them at the Troubadour, but we knew it would never work. I was clearly the fifth wheel. When Glenn and I split, part of the reason was because he wanted to add more players, to put a band together, while I wanted to go home and write songs and be with Linda."

It was naturally assumed by everyone that Frey was the new group's leader. After all, he'd been the one who'd approached Henley about forming their own band, and the one who had convinced the others. The most important thing, he kept insisting, was not to make the same mistakes as groups like Poco — letting individual egos get in the way of the group's primary goal. The idea was for them to make great music together, as a unit, and lots of money doing it.

Henley agreed. "Money," he said, "was a much saner goal than adoration. They'll both drive you crazy, but if I'm gonna blow my brains out for five years, I want something to show for it."

The deal was completed in September 1971. It was a long time coming, and up until the day the band members signed the contract, it looked as if it might not happen. Negotiations over royalties had begun to drag, and Frey was concerned that Geffen might be having a change of heart. He decided to confront him with a take-it-or-leave-it offer. Moments before a hastily called meeting in Asylum's cramped offices on Sunset Boulevard, a suddenly nervous Frey deferred to the calmer, older, tougher, and more experienced Leadon, who, for the purposes of this meeting, was voted the band's spokesman. As the others stood in the office with their arms folded, staring silently at Geffen, Leadon made his pitch. When he finished, the room filled with a tension-heavy silence that seemed to last forever, until, according to Henley, Leadon simply began again. "Bernie says, 'Okay, here we are. Do you want us or don't you?' It was a great moment. Geffen kinda said, 'Well . . . *yeah.*'"

The first order of business was to come up with a name for the group. According to Bernie Leadon, "We all wanted [a name] that was short and concise, with an image, and we were aware that a name is what you make it. I wanted a name with some imagery. Everybody was reading Castaneda then, and we wanted a name that had some mythological connotations. Frey wanted a name that could have been a Detroit street gang and Henley was sort of going along with the Indian vibe and all that, and everybody wanted a name that was just tough, you know, 'Hey! We're the *fuckin'* Eagles, man!' There was definitely a *West Side Story* aspect to it. 'We're the *fuckin' Jets,*' you know. '*We're the fuckin' Eagles; kiss my ass!*'"

Geffen could do without all the mythological horseshit, and being from New York, found the idea of these boys having any *West Side Story* in them laughable. Still, he had to admit that the name they had chosen was inspired. For one thing, it immediately identified them as an American band. For another, an eagle appeared on most American currency. Best of all, though, without question, was the fact that *it sounded like "the Beatles."*

Geffen then decided to temporarily relocate the band to Aspen, Colorado, to try to keep them out of sight and away from L.A.'s three-lane superhighway of women, drugs, and drink so they could focus on their music. Just as important, he didn't want anyone to see them or hear their new songs until they were ready, especially not the gang down at the Troubadour. These days the scene there was made up of as many journalists as musicians — everyone from the *Freep* to *Rolling Stone,* the San Francisco–based rag that had gained the trust and following of the so-called baby boomers. Geffen was not going to give anybody the opportunity to kill his new goose before it had a chance to lay so much as a single golden egg.

According to the terms of the Eagles' contract, which was structured along the same lines as Jackson Browne's, Geffen set up a flow fund of $125,000 to pay all the band's expenses until the album was released, fronted them enough spending money to live on, bought them a van, allowed them to hire a couple of Henley's Linden pals as roadies, and claims to have even arranged to have their teeth fixed, all of which he charged against future sales.

Henley says: "He gave us something like two hundred bucks a week to live on while we rehearsed. I may have had a wisdom tooth out during that period of time. I don't remember a lot of tooth stuff. I don't know if he paid for it or my parents did."

Geffen arranged to have them "woodshed" at the Gallery, a nightspot for Aspen's hippie ski crowd. "He thought we needed more work," Henley recalls. "And he was right. We weren't very tight yet, and he wanted us to get some more time in together. Before we left, we rehearsed at a little place in the valley, on Ventura Boulevard, called Bud's, behind a liquor store called the Spirit Cellar. I remember David and Elliot came to hear us rehearse, and then they packed us off to Aspen."

One night, at a somewhat less fancy joint in Boulder called Tulagi's, the band played a rave-up, holding nothing back and loving every second of the booze, drugs, and all-night rock and roll. At least that's the way Meisner remembers it. The old saw that any guy who played in a band was irresistible to girls had come true for him. He says, "[The women] came out of the fucking woodwork, one hotter, sexier, and more willing than the other, fighting each other to get a chance at us good-looking young boys." Henley, however, recalls a different scene. "It was early September, right after we signed with Geffen. I remember it snowed, and I was flabbergasted. Booze, yes. Babes, maybe [Randy] did better than I did, but there was a lot of drinking going on. Aspen was a wild and woolly town at that time. There was a lot of dope being taken, although we were mostly into grass — that was our only real vice at that point. I don't remember anybody getting girls. In fact, I remember it being pretty lonely 'cause we didn't know anybody. We'd play four sets a night, and we were tired when we got done. People would dance and drink and take acid until they fell down, and then they would leave, and we'd go home, alone, to our little condominium. This was a hard gig."

According to Randy Meisner, "We weren't really a cohesive group as yet, although we did have that special sound. Still, it was more like an extended four-guy jam. We had a couple of songs, not many, that we did every night. 'Witchy Woman' was one of the first, and we did 'Take It Easy,' a Jackson Browne song, more R&B, because that's the way Glenn played it; the recorded version came later. And a couple of Sonny Boy Williamson tunes. 'Pontiac Blues,' I'm sure we did that one every night. And a lot of Chuck Berry. Glenn loved to play Chuck Berry. We'd do four, sometimes five sets every night, and there were times when no one was in the house except maybe a bartender and a waitress or two, and a couple of hungry chicks. It was wild, kind of like what I imagine the Beatles went through in Germany."

While the Eagles did their thing in Colorado, Geffen searched for a producer that the boys felt could capture what they had live on record. At the top of their list was British producer Glyn Johns, one of the prime architects of the sound of the sixties British invasion and subsequent occupation of American rock and roll. (Also on their shortlist was Ted Templeman.) Johns's body of work included what were arguably the best-produced albums of the Rolling Stones, the Who, Led Zeppelin, and the Small Faces. Geffen got in touch with Johns and rather than give him a demo tape, invited the producer to see the band play live in Colorado.

In spite of Geffen's assurance that he would love this band, Johns's first impression was not positive. After catching the band's energetic set at Tulagi's he later recalled, "I personally didn't think they could play rock 'n' roll. When I first saw the Eagles they were doing Chuck Berry stuff and they were blatantly, bloody awful. It was a complete cacophony. You had Glenn Frey, who was a good little rock 'n' roll guitar player, on one side, and Bernie Leadon, a great country picker, on the other, and a rhythm section in the middle being pulled in two directions. There was no cohesion. I thought they were bloody awful. Though I knew they could sing, I turned it down."

Johns's reaction did not sit well with Henley. "He didn't think we could play rock and roll," Henley said later. "I said, 'Glyn, can't you make me sound like [Led Zeppelin drummer] John Bonham?' And he sorta looked down his nose at me and said, 'You don't play like John Bonham.'"

Geffen refused to take no for an answer and kept after Johns until finally the producer agreed to reconsider his decision if he could hear the band in Los Angeles, in a more controlled environment. Geffen promptly set it up.

Johns recalled that "[Geffen] kept after me. I said, 'I won't go to another gig but I'll see them in a rehearsal situation.' The rehearsal was awful. They took a break and somebody picked up an acoustic guitar and they sat down and sang a song in four-part. I said, 'This is what this band is all about.' From then on I had a picture of what the band should be, or could be."

According to Henley, "Now Glyn thought we were a nice country-rock, semi-acoustic band, and every time we wanted to rock and roll, he could name a thousand British bands that could do it better."

Johns wanted to fine-tune the natural harmony that came through when the voices weren't buried behind so much juice and blend it with a strong mix of acoustic guitars, backed by the bluegrassy, Southern twang of Bernie Leadon's banjo pickings. To Johns, the Eagles had the potential to be what he considered a great American country band.

"[Glyn Johns] was the key to our success in a lot of ways," Frey later told *Rolling Stone*. "He'd been working with all these classic English rock & roll bands . . . and didn't want to hear us squashing out Chuck Berry licks. . . . [The problem was,] we just didn't want to make another limp-wristed L.A. country-rock record."

Still, no one in the band was willing to unilaterally veto the chance to work with the already legendary producer. Before leaving America, Johns rehearsed with them extensively. "The same little studio where Rick Nelson had rehearsed with the Stone Canyon Band," Meisner recalls. "Jackson Browne had used it for a place to live for a while when he was between apartments, which seemed to happen to everyone back then. It was located near Tiny Naylor's coffee shop, on Ventura Boulevard, in the valley. The location was great because Tiny's was a real hot spot in those days." Too hot, a nervous Geffen knew. Moving the boys overseas was an even better idea than Colorado. If nothing else, he believed the lack of distractions might finally keep them focused only on their music.

Just before their scheduled departure, the band played one gig at the Ashgrove, in Hollywood, where they showed just how far they'd come. A lot of the songs that would appear on the first album were now a part of their regular set, included "Peaceful Easy Feeling," "Witchy Woman," and "Take It Easy." The band was tight and together, and, according to one who was there, "kicked a little rock and roll ass."

In February 1972, on Geffen and Atlantic's nickel, the Eagles took off for England and the famed Olympic recording studio, Johns's creative laboratory of choice. Although they anticipated a rave similar to what had gone on in Colorado, the Eagles quickly discovered this time it was going to be all work and no play. Geffen had found them a small apartment, and Johns put the band on a strict work schedule that lasted late into the night. By the time they were released, the pubs were all closed. There wasn't even anything to watch on TV. The BBC, then Britain's only station, signed off at eleven. With each day that passed, they felt ever stranger in what to them was a very strange land, and they couldn't wait to get the hell out of it.

In the studio, Frey and Johns continued to clash over the type of music the band should be making. Frey was still looking to put down hard rock and roll, but Johns continued to mix the level of Leadon's banjo and Meisner's bass to approximate what he regarded as the sound of American country music. There was a difference of opinion as to the amount of country-style guitar to be used. Frey and Henley agreed there should be as little as possible, so as not to take away from the tougher rock and roll sound they were looking for. Johns, on the other hand, wanted to emphasize the band's country flavor, and encouraged Leadon to break into his licks on the pedal steel and banjo as often as possible. This stylistic clash became the battle zone between Johns and Henley and Frey, and instigated tensions between band members, most obviously Leadon and the others. Johns's initial refusal to capitulate filled the sessions with a contentiousness that more than once brought a couple of the boys to tears.

Meisner recalls, "Glyn recorded us with three microphones, two overhead and one in the drum pit. He put some baffles up to set us like a live band, and we did those tracks live. He worked on it until he got the sound he wanted. In those days we used Revox machines, where the heads were set to get echoes. They ran constantly; if we were in the studio for twenty-four hours, then he got twenty-four hours' worth of recording. There never seemed any down time, time to cool out."

Further adding to the tension was Johns's rule that during recording sessions there were to be no drugs of any kind in the studio. It wasn't that Johns didn't approve. Anyone who had worked with the legendary abusers he had must have seen plenty. If any of the Eagles did it, however, it fucked them up. Johns imposed his no-dope rule in hopes of improving the quality of the music being played during the sessions, which he still believed was not all that great. All-day rehearsals passed with little music produced that Johns considered good enough for inclusion on an album.

On more than one occasion, Frey openly expressed his growing resentment toward Johns's approach, and like a rebellious adolescent, kept sneaking off with Meisner to get stoned in the men's room. Henley, meanwhile, continued his solitary brooding, harboring a strong resentment of the tactics, taste, and temperament of the band's chosen producer.

Henley remembered, "The sound he was creating for us wasn't powerful. Glyn had this image of us as a ballad group. . . . He was a complete tyrant. We were really young and green and he just lorded it over us. . . . And he had worked with all the heavies, so we really couldn't argue."

After two grueling weeks in the studio, the recording of *Eagles* was finished. This was still a relatively short period of time, even for 1972, when it was no longer considered unusual for a successful group to spend months working on an album. The reasons for the speed were clear — the band members couldn't wait to get out of England, Johns felt he had gone about as far as he could with them, and Geffen wanted to keep his out-of-pocket expenses as low as possible. To that end, the album was brought in for $125,000, which Geffen in turn had gotten Ertegun to advance.

A few weeks after they returned to L.A., the band, along with Glyn Johns, went into a studio and laid down one more track, "Nightingale," by Jackson Browne. "Both Geffen and Elliot listened to the tapes of the album and said that there wasn't enough of me on the album," Henley recalled. "So we went back in and cut that song." "Nightingale" remains the sleeper of the album, a punchy, rough-sounding rocker featuring the unmistakable lyrics of Jackson Browne and a fabulous break done with a nod toward the Drifters' "There Goes My Baby."

The first single released off the album was Jackson Browne's "Take It Easy," followed by "Witchy Woman," by Henley and Leadon, two songs that identify a band. The latter was a catchy Indian tom-tom beat with hooks piled one atop the other and lyrics loosely based on the life of Zelda Fitzgerald. The rest of the album included two Frey songs, "Chug All Night" and "Most of Us Are Sad"; a Gene Clark–Bernie Leadon composition, "Train Leaves Here This Morning"; two songs by Randy Meisner, "Take the Devil" and "Tryin'"; one collaboration by Bernie Leadon and Randy Meisner, "Earlybird"; and "Peaceful Easy Feeling," a song by Jack Tempchin, a Troubadour regular who'd become a good friend of Glenn Frey, which sounded a bit like an alternate take of Browne's "Take It Easy."

For the all-important album cover, the band wanted something that proclaimed "California," a wide-open blue sky at dawn, with maybe a cactus or two, and on the back, a shot of the four Eagles to show off their good looks. To get it, Geffen hired Gary Burden, a former architect whom Mama Cass had once hired to design a house and somewhere along the line decided was the perfect person to shoot her album covers. Burden then hooked up with Henry Diltz, a founding member of the Modern Folk Quartet who had, quite by accident, become one of rock's most sought-after album-cover photographers. For the Eagles shoot, Burden chose the Joshua Tree National Park, a hundred miles east of Los Angeles, an area long considered sacred by Native Americans. It was also a favored drug-taking site of the L.A. rock scene.

Bernie Leadon remembers the session: "We met at the Troubadour at one in the morning, just drank our faces off, all the pot and dope we could find, and went out in my Toyota jeep and somebody else's car and drove off to Joshua Tree. We arrived at four in the morning, before dawn, out to the secret spot of all the old-time dopers, way out in the back overlooking Palm Springs, had this old barber's chair way at the top of the mountain; you could sit there and it was great. We took Henry and Gary and the four of us, carried some guitars and all the camera equipment in the middle of the night, and stumbled up this fucking mountain. We made a fire and a camp and began making peyote tea and trying to eat peyote without throwing up — from, even more, the combination of no sleep, alcohol, and a lot of joints. And the peyote was starting to come on and keep us awake — those pictured are well stoned."

Burden showed the proofs for the album cover and inner sleeve to Geffen, who loved the design, which included a gorgeous Eagles logo hanging above the dawn sky. Geffen scheduled a June 1, 1972, release, and made arrangements to have the band open for a number of major road acts that summer.

To warm up before the tour, the Eagles decided to play their new songs at a party being thrown for Boyd Elder, an artist having a major gallery opening in Venice, California, for his *Chingadōro* ("The Ultimate Thing") exhibit that spring. Elder was well-known on the L.A. music scene and a friend of the individual members of the Eagles from the Troubadour days. "I remember them standing over in the corner," recalls one who was at the opening. "There was beer and broken glass all over the floor. Joni Mitchell was dancing barefoot, oblivious, Mama Cass was there, Geffen was there, Ned Doheny, Jackson Browne, Mark Volman from the Turtles, maybe a hundred people altogether, and the band off in the corner playing in public as the Eagles for the first time. I just remember them real nervous, and playing 'Witchy Woman' over and over, as if it were the only song they felt confident playing live."

After that, the band played its first paying gig of the tour, at the Westlake School for Girls.

On the road that summer, the Eagles opened for several seventies supergroups, including J. Geils, Yes, and Jethro Tull. Each show proved a more bizarre match than the previous, the Tull concerts in particular seeming the ultimate in rock nonsequiturs. On the one hand was a band that represented the new, laid-back L.A. sound: dressed-down jeans, work shirts, rolled-up sleeves, and dirty sneakers, and on the other, Ian Anderson's exotic, elaborately costumed, ultra-British, neo-Rennaissance musical applications.

Predictably, on most nights the still-unknown Eagles were met at best with indifference by crowds waiting impatiently for Tull to come roaring onto the stage. At one point, a frustrated Glenn Frey put down a noisy, impatient Madison Square Garden audience by telling it what he thought of its "hip" hometown and one of its so-called happening groups, the New York Dolls, an ad-lib that did nothing to endear the Eagles to the city's rock fans. Not only were the paying customers offended, but also in the audience that night was the cream of the New York critics, already suspicious of one more West Coast band coming to the Manhattan sidewalk scene with tales of glorious girls and great V8s. Slammed the next day in the press because of Frey's comment, for years after, whenever they played New York City, no band member ever said much onstage beyond "Hello, we're the Eagles *from Los Angeles.*" It's possible to trace a part of the animosity between rock journalists and the Eagles that continues to this day from that show. So offended were the members of the band by the reception the New York papers gave them that they vowed never to cooperate with any writers from that city, refusing to give interviews or even release publicity photos. The feeling among the Eagles was that if New York didn't want them, they didn't want or need New York. In the years that followed, Henley in particular blamed the East Coast rock press for having dismissed the band as "unimportant" in the pantheon of rock and roll and denying it the recognition he felt the Eagles should have received.

Geffen, at the band's urging, had hired a talented, if inexperienced, technical crew to present the band to the public, looking to duplicate onstage the meticulous sound of the band's album. In the early seventies, before MIDI, digitalization, stage enhancement, and other techniques, re-creating recorded music live in front of an arena audience was iffy at best. More than one group had failed trying to compete on tour with the sound of their own records.

Bob Sterne was a member the original Eagles sound crew and did his job so well he remained with the band for nearly a decade, or, as he puts it, "For the whole nightmare." Sterne remembers the Eagles on the first tour as being an upbeat, together group of guys who took that summer's assignment to open for Yes and Tull as a challenge that energized them, as if they were involved in what he called "musical guerrilla warfare," a feeling shared by everyone on the Eagles' production team.

"The band was out to show what it could do, to kick a little ass," Sterne recalls. "We were encouraged by them to make their sound and lighting an art, to try and make them the very definition of great seventies live rock and roll. Part of what we tried to do was to keep the voices as 'front' as possible, to keep the harmonies clear, clean, and distinct. In other words, to attempt to duplicate the sound they had put on record. That was their moneymaker, they knew it, they convinced us, and that's what we gave them."

One of the most difficult things for any new band is to open for a name act. Over the summer, the Eagles, despite Frey's New York temper tantrum, managed to pull it off. Wisely, after the Tull debacle the band decided to let the music do its talking. Often, by the end of their ten-song set, the same songs that made up the first album, they had gained the respect, if not the enthusiasm, of the audience. This was even more of an accomplishment for the Eagles, because while the acts they opened for were among the most theatrical in rock, the Eagles were decidedly not. They hardly moved onstage, Henley as usual sitting behind his kit, the others standing still in front of their mikes. "We didn't go in for glitter or glam rock," Henley comments. "We didn't wear gorilla suits or aqualungs. Ultimately, the music by itself survived and established the band's image."

Lighting specialist Ken Graham was another early member of the Eagles team. As Graham recalled, "The Eagles wanted something simple we could rig quickly and easily. From the beginning they refused any of the visual clichés; no smoke, no gimmicks, no pyro, just straight-ahead lights, blackouts at the end of songs, a couple of color washes here and there to break things up, and follow-spots. The idea was not to create a light show, but to allow the music to come through. The emphasis, always, was on sound over sight."

Eagles, the band's first album, received a rave from *Rolling Stone,* the only review that really counted when it came to sales. "'The Eagles' [sic]," rock critic Bud Scoppa wrote, "is right behind Jackson Browne's record as the best first album of this year, and I could be persuaded to remove the word 'first' from that statement." Geffen had to laugh out loud at the *Rolling Stone* critic's musing over which of his two Asylum artists was better.

Not long after the album's release, "Take It Easy" hit the charts, where it stayed for eight months, steadily rising to the number twelve position in *Billboard*'s singles listing. "Witchy Woman" was even more successful, breaking the band into the top ten and becoming an instant AM staple. In December, "Peaceful Easy Feeling," the album's third single, made it to number twenty-two.

There was no question by the end of 1972 that the Eagles had arrived, all the more dramatically for having come, just as Geffen had wanted it to appear, out of nowhere. Equally impressive was their breakthrough into AM Top 40 radio, where the action and fiercest competition still was. Besides the Eagles' three hits, the hottest singles of 1972 included such great tunes as Roberta Flack's "The First Time Ever I Saw Your Face," Don McLean's classic "American Pie," Harry Nilsson's "Without You," Johnny Nash's "I Can See Clearly Now," Neil Young's "Heart of Gold," the Temptations' "Papa Was a Rolling Stone," the Hollies' "Long Cool Woman (In a Black Dress)," Al Green's "You Ought to Be with Me" and "I'm Still in Love with You," and even an Elvis Presley hit, "Burning Love."

With the exception of Harry Nilsson and the Hollies, noticeably missing from the list was any remnant of the British Invasion, or music that preached the social lessons that had dominated American white protest folk-rock in the first half of the sixties, or psyched-out drug construction, the spine of the second. Don McLean's "American Pie" was a uniquely nostalgic recap of the history of rock and roll overloaded with melancholy and utterly lacking in irony, the former eliminating the drama, the latter the relevance. Nash's pop version of "Clearly" helped introduce Jamaican reggae to America, but his version could hardly be considered political. Neil Young's "Heart of Gold" was too personal to be cool, the Temptations' "Papa Was a Rolling Stone" too danceable to be depressing, and Elvis's "Burning Love" a frightening reminder of just how cruel the punishment was for growing too old to rock and roll.

Among this crop of hitmakers, the Eagles stood out as the only white American rock and roll group, and as such, seemingly lacked anything that even hinted at so-called relevance, social or otherwise. Which is not to say their music was trivial or unimportant. Just the opposite, in fact. The crucial element of the Eagles' breakthrough lay in the essential spirit of their easy, country-flavored rock and roll, the beauty in the sound of their songs rather than the meaning of their lyrics. It was this combination of retro country and innocent rock that shot them to the top. Unlike Crosby, Stills and Nash (and Young), whose twenty-something musical soap-operas mourned over life in the past lane, the Eagles rolled back the age of rock. Their music may have lacked social relevance, but it more than made up for it in emotional significance. They managed to capture in those first songs a primal teen moment, identifiable to every kid in America who ever drank a beer from the bottle while driving around in his convertible trying to get laid. Using a basic backbeat and classic four-part harmony, the Eagles had returned mainstream rock and roll to a context of gorgeous meaninglessness, which meant everything in the world to those young enough to know the music was the message, rather than looking for the message in the music.

What really did it first for the Eagles was their version of Jackson Browne's "Take It Easy," as gloriously refreshing an irreverent song ever to come driving down rock's mythic two-lane. After all the heaviness of the "meaningful" sixties, here at last was a song that said everything *by saying nothing*. No drugs, no protest, no symbols of doom. Nothing more than a tribute to the teenage beauty queens of Winslow, Arizona. No wonder such East Coast, esoteric, sixties-rooted rock critics as the *Village Voice*'s Robert Christgau could only sniff at the Eagles' debut and dismiss it as commercial "product . . . suave and synthetic, brilliant and false. And not always brilliant, either." To New York City kids (and critics) who never owned a car or got the blond girls who wore short shorts all winter, who hardly ever saw the sun, the celebration of the lifestyle the Eagles were singing about might indeed have sounded suave, synthetic, brilliant and false.

In fact, the Eagles were dead-on in their quicksilver reflection of America's 1972 adolescent male spirit. For teenage boys who'd come of age after the first flash of Bob Dylan, the Beatles, Martin Luther King, John and Robert Kennedy, Woodstock, and Kent State — the eighteen-year-olds who that year had seized the lowered voting age to help Richard Nixon win one of the greatest landslide presidential victories in the history of the country — here at last was a band putting out the kind of music they could claim as all their own. "Take It Easy" became the perfect mantra for the decade's arriving studs-to-be, who looked in the mirror and saw a world smiling back that was young, sexy, loose, fun, and free. And best of all, *it belonged only to them.*

To the coming crop of All-American boyhood, nothing was more relevant than that.

SEVEN

By the end of 1972, Eagles music filled the American airwaves. At least one of the group's first three hits was being heavily rotated on every AM and FM rock radio station across the country. A big reason was Geffen's canny and relentless media push of the band, including his choice of Paul Ahern to be in charge of Asylum record promotions. Ahern, like Geffen, was artist friendly; he had been a bass player in college before making the shift to the business end. Once he learned the mechanics of record promotion, he became relentless behind the Eagles. He personally visited every major rock station in all the large markets — KHJ in Los Angeles, KFRC in San Francisco, OR-FM in New York, KTKB in Tulsa, HBQ in Memphis — and did whatever it took — Rolling Stones concert tickets, assorted freebies, and anything else he could think of — to convince the deejays and station managers to get with the product. These were the key stations that the rest followed. It was a methodical, organized campaign, and by pushing these selected buttons, Ahern was effectively able to get the whole country hot-wired to the sound of the Eagles.

For Henley and Frey, success signaled more than acceptance on the part of the record-buying public. It also meant the end of their low-rent Echo Park days. As soon as they hit the charts they hit the road and moved into more spacious houses in oh, those Hollywood Hills, where they celebrated their good fortune the best way they knew, with prodigious amounts of Acapulco Gold, gorgeous girls in their beds, and, of course, Eagles music, the sound track to the never-ending party.

These late-starting days seemed to flow endlessly and effortlessly into well-fueled nights, and back again to morning. "There was a basketball game the guys played every Sunday near Glenn's Kirkwood house," a friend remembers, "that came to be known as the B&B game — for basketball and blow. Everyone always got so fucked up the score at the end of an hour might be ten to four. Nobody really cared about the competitive thing that much. It was really one long stretch of fun, drugs, and camaraderie."

For this tight circle of rock stars, much of the night scene had relocated from the Troubadour's front bar to the more privileged and private one in Glenn Frey's living room. His new hacienda, in Laurel Canyon on the corner of Kirkwood and Ridpath, became affectionately known to those invited to pass through the front gates as "the Kirkwood Casino and Health Club." The party began and often ended with trips into town, either for food, beer, or more drugs. One former member of the club recalls, "At four-thirty or five in the morning, you'd avoid going down Sunset to and from the house because if you were stopped for anything, the shape you were in, or what you were carrying, you'd almost certainly be facing jail time. The ritual was the same every night. Dinner at Dan Tana's [the New York–style Italian restaurant next door to the Troubadour], a quick pit stop at the Troubadour, then up to Glenn's house, where the actual party would begin."

"It was pretty loose and wild," recalled Ahern, Frey's roommate at the time. "You took your life in your hands, no doubt, when you made that late-night run up the canyon.

"We used to have marathon poker games with Dos Equis towers [empty beer bottles] decorating the place. Very bachelor, if you understand my meaning. There'd be hundred of them strewn around the place. The upstairs was one big room with a kitchen area and a poker table, a living room and a stereo, and downstairs were the two bedrooms. When we left it, incidentally, Mick Fleetwood and his wife took it over.

"There were girls, of course, all the time, and drugs. Everyone knew it and did it, but those were the days when no one thought there was anything wrong with it. We were all young, single guys and made the most of it. The games were often 'catered,' I guess you could call it, by a couple of very lovely ladies.

"There was a bunch of regulars who came by for the girls and the games, the poker games that could last three days and three nights continuously. Boyd Elder, who would later create the Eagles logo for a couple of their album covers, Ned Doheny, J. D., roadie John Barrick, later on Irving Azoff, and record executive Bob 'the Boozer' Buziak."

"I lived up the street on Ridpath," Henley recalls, "just a block or two from Glenn. Ahern was living with Glenn, and I lived by myself. Before I had lived a little higher up, on Colecrest, in a house with stilts that Roger McGuinn had lived in before me. That's where we wrote the song 'Desperado.' It was one of those houses that moved when the wind blew. I had to get out of there, so I moved down the hill to Ridpath. Boylan lived just above, on Kirkwood. It was our own little community.

"In 1973 I got to know J. D. from hanging out at Glenn's house. We had some great times there, became friends, and we all wrote 'The Best of My Love.' I still have the couch from that house. There was also a cowboy that played cards with us, Bernie's roommate when Bernie was living in Topanga Canyon. His name was Bill Wild. He did rodeos, trained horses.

"One night former Flying Burrito Brother Rick Roberts came up and played some cards with us, and Bill won several thousand dollars that Rick didn't have. The pots used to get pretty high, thousands of dollars, and if someone was losing we'd sort of let it go, because no one really had any money yet. The games were exciting because we were always playing over our heads. In this one pot, Rick lost seven grand to 'Wild Bill' and couldn't pay him. Bill was a real hard-ass about it. He tracked Rick down, went into his house, and took one of his guitars.

"But mostly it was good camaraderie. I remember we were always sending out for food and booze from Greenblatt's, on Sunset Boulevard, because it was right down the hill. We had a great time. Girls, drugs, booze, cards, and songwriting. We were young and making new friends and having a time. That was it, really, and what more could you want?"

Maybe one thing. His father had passed away two years earlier. "He was sixty-five years old when he died and never really had the opportunity to see what I could do. It was a heartbreaker for me. He was a good man, had worked his whole life to make sure I had a better one."

For all the buddy-boy celebrating, the Eagles were in reality four distinct personalities, with differing tastes in everything from the types of music they liked to listen to and play to the brands of cigarettes they preferred. Except for being in a rock group that made hit records, they probably never would have sought each other's company for any extended period of time. During their early days in the center ring, for all the PR shots of rock band fraternity, none of them could ignore the gnawing, underlying fear that their very success meant having to give up some aspect of private individuality for a new public "whole."

In truth, their music only seemed magical when they played as a group, as *this* group. It made them realize, among other things, that if they didn't now physically stay together as band members, they might not in fact stay together as a band. Camaraderie was the obsessive glue rather than the creative bond that held them together. Among other things, it tended to bring out what passed for humor between them, a constant self-superior mockery wherein each picked at the strengths and laughed at the weakness of the others.

Randy Meisner recalls that early on everyone suddenly had new nicknames indicating how the others saw him. "Mine was Chipmunk, or China Doll, 'cause I always smiled, my teeth would stick out and my eyes would slant up. I was also the Cherry on Top because I had the high, clean voice. The Teflon Throat was another nickname of mine. Henley was Lobster Bat Ears because he got sunburned a lot and his ears really stuck out. Frey was Mandrill Roach, because when he'd have hangovers his eyes would get so dark, or Sportacus, because of his preoccupation with athletics. Bernie, who didn't really do drugs, was Marty Martian, because he was real bright-eyed all the time. We'd always think of him with little antennae sticking out, like *My Favorite Martian*. We used to call Elliot Roberts Alias Robot.

"Geffen got into it as well. He used to call Henley the Man with the Golden Throat because when Don was in Shiloh, the band did a lot of what today you might, if you really stretched it, call hard rock, and he did a lot of lead singing, which affected his voice and made it more raspy. When you play loud in small clubs you usually wind up blowing your throat out. It's how Henley got the sound he's used ever since he was a kid in a bar band.

"I have to say that everyone went along with the nicknames, but Henley, right from the beginning, was always uptight about most things. He and I never really got along well. I remember one time when we had a night off or something, and he and I were down at some bar, I don't remember where, and I decided to get him a little loose. At the time I had some quaaludes and talked him into taking one. We had the best time! He had a few drinks, began laughing, having a really good time, which, even back then for him was very rare. I thought, hey, maybe I broke the ice. But no, the next day he was back to the same old stone face."

Interestingly, at this stage, the tense differences between Henley and Frey had a synergy that gave the band a better, if edgier, creative energy. As Meisner recalls, "Glenn was more of a street-tough type. He and Henley were a real good combination in the beginning because both guys were real intelligent and knew what they wanted, and yet were so completely different, they somehow filled in each other's personalities."

The Henley-Frey partnership played out a familiar pattern in rock and roll in which a siblinglike rivalry at first leads the way to enormous success, before it eventually wrecks the relationship and the band. Henley, an only child, sensed in Frey, as he had with Richard Bowden, the brother he never had. He admired Frey's free-swinging lifestyle. One of the primary reasons the Henley-Frey teaming worked so well in the beginning was that Henley's disciplined dark side tended to give a bit of weight to Frey's airy pop tuneism, while Frey's natural easiness helped lighten up Henley's lyrics.

Another major influence was their geographic difference, which represented strikingly diverse branches of rock. Henley, like virtually every one of the classic white rockers of the fifties, was from the rural South. Elvis Presley, Buddy Holly, Little Richard, and Fats Domino were strong influences on his singing style, and all were bound in one way or another to a Southern religiosity. Frey, meanwhile, was a city boy whose music reflected the witty, more secular rhythms of the weekend street corner. His influences were Bob Seger, the Beatles, Motown, and Mitch Ryder's Detroit Wheels–type frat rock. To him, God was a Corvette.

The creative and emotional tension between the two recalled that of earlier singer-songwriter teams such as the Everly Brothers, whose career was short-circuited by their festering sibling rivalry, Mick Jagger and Keith Richards, whose narcissistic reluctance to share the spotlight ultimately limited their group's musical growth, and John Lennon and Paul McCartney, one a legitimate, cerebral poet-rocker, the other committed to mindless commercial pop. In each instance the conflict first produced great success, followed by long-standing hostilities, as it would between Henley and Frey. Their differences were apparent even in the way they chose to live at this relatively early stage of their careers. Here was Henley, alone, up on a hill, eagerly running to join the endless party at Frey's house. On another level, the mix of Northern athletic good-timer with Southern intellectual introvert gave them the best of both their musical worlds, allowing Frey's loose, citified R&B music to benefit from the classic Texan roots of country-influenced fifties rock and roll. For the life of this band, Frey would forever bring guitar and piano licks to the surface of the Eagles' music, while Henley would hold them in place with the rock-steady, grounded thump of his drumbeat.

"We're the Oakland A's of rock and roll," Frey once remarked, comparing the early Eagles to one of the most successful baseball teams in the history of the sport, known for the players' dislike of each other away from the game. "On the field," Frey said, "we can't be beat. But in the clubhouse, well, that's another story. We're completely different people."

Meisner too had conflicts, although his had less to do with the other members of the band. Even as a teenager he had yearned for a quiet, calm life as a married man but could never give up his desire to play rock and roll and party all night. To push back his troubles, he took too many drugs, washed down by too much drink. Like Henley, Meisner hid behind a self-protective shyness, but he preferred to smile at everyone, using his affable charm and pretty singing voice to mask his own dark demons.

Finally there was Bernie Leadon, whose larger-than-life persona caused him to stand tall, if alone, in his world. A veteran of a number of sixties bands and tours, he no longer had any patience for bloated egos or out-of-control druggies. He preferred life out of the limelight. He had a sharp temper, and the others knew when to back off. They sensed that Leadon was wound particularly tight, with an unpredictable fuse. To them he had the air of someone who could just as soon settle matters with a punch to the face as a kiss to the ass.

Aroused by fame's first wet lick, the boys in the band couldn't wait to return to the structured chaos of the studio. Geffen actually had to hold them back, not wanting new material to cut into the welcome, if unexpected, ongoing chart life of their debut album. To keep their chops (and their sanity), they performed in varying combinations on friends' albums. Leadon sat in on Rita Coolidge's *The Lady's Not for Sale,* and with Henley and Meisner played on Rick Roberts's *Windfalls*. When J. D. Souther went into the studio, Glenn Frey sat in on the sessions. Frey also played and sang harmony on David Blue's *Nice Baby and the Angel*.

David Blue had come to Los Angeles and David Geffen from the Boston and New York circuits of the sixties. Long considered one of the many Dylan look-alikes/sound-alikes, Blue had had his difficulties in the record business until he met Elliot Roberts and David Geffen. Geffen, in particular, recognized in Blue a perfect example of that Asylum artist-first philosophy. "We didn't manage and record people that we thought were necessarily going to be 'successful,'" he comments. "David Blue sold only twenty-five hundred copies of his first album for Asylum after being dropped by two other record companies, but it didn't matter to us. We recorded him because we thought he was a great talent. We had no illusions that he was going to sell as many records as, say, the Eagles. But it made no difference, because we thought of records as documents that we were proud to make."

In a remarkably brief amount of time, Geffen had become a major player in the new L.A. postsixties rock scene. By shrewdly hand-picking a roster of musicians whose acoustically tempered music turned down the volume of the hysterical, out-of-control side of sixties rock, Geffen's label had managed to capture on record the cool, smooth sultriness of the sexy seventies Southern California style.

There seemed no end to the popularity of the Asylum roster, when, suddenly, in the winter of 1972, Geffen's position changed dramatically. Without any advance word, Warner Brothers head Steve Ross announced that his entertainment conglomerate, WCI (Warner Communications, Inc.), had purchased Asylum for $7 million and intended to merge it with Elektra, which he had acquired from founder Jac Holzman two years earlier. As part of the deal, the new company, Warner-Elektra-Asylum, or WEA, would operate as a subsidiary of and be distributed by WCI, with David Geffen at the helm.

The offer could not have come at a better time. Having created one of the most successful independent labels in history, Geffen was, for all his generational devotion to artists, first and always a businessman. Although he'd loved the taste of power Asylum had provided, having learned with C, S and N the unpredictability of the financial return on the high-ride side of rock and roll, after two years he sensed Asylum's early strong run might have made the label as profitable as it would ever be.

Ross's offer also provided Geffen with the opportunity to make yet another major career move. He knew only too well that no matter how many albums a label sold, as far as L.A. was concerned, rock was and always would be kid stuff. The real power in Tinseltown was still the film industry, and Geffen had decided he really wanted to be a player in *that* band. The movie industry was undergoing a revolution of its own, in many ways mirroring what Geffen had helped bring to popular music. A new generation of auteurist filmmakers, including Dennis Hopper, Peter Fonda, Warren Beatty, and Paul Schrader, had brought a rock and roll style to such films as *Easy Rider* and *Bonnie and Clyde,* and for huge profits — the kind of money that made the music business seem like small change. He'd already gotten a first tantalizing taste of it in 1971, when Geffen-Roberts had tried unsuccessfully to put together a combination screenplay–sound track deal for David Crosby with United Artists. The failure of that deal had, for the moment, put a hold on any thoughts on Geffen's part about the movie business.

Everything changed in Geffen's favor when Ross hired Ted Ashley as his new head of studio operations. Ashley had once been Geffen's boss at Ashley Famous, which itself had become a Warner subsidiary in 1970. A native New York City boy, Ashley had always gotten along well with Geffen, appreciating particularly his enthusiasm and knack for hitting the deal. As he restructured the studio into one of the components of the so-called New Hollywood of the seventies, Ashley brought aboard Frank Wells, Don Simpson, John Calley, and former New York club owner Fred Weintraub, all tough, smart up-and-comers, all key components of the studio's rush to power. The "new" Warner's first major hit was the 1970 documentary *Woodstock.* It signaled where the action in Hollywood was coming from and where it was going. Now, eager to join Tinseltown's big boys, Geffen, who enjoyed making the financial killing as much as the creative birthing, sensed the next wave might indeed be in the movies rather than on the record, and, when the opportunity came, he was more than eager to sell out and sign on.

The sale of Asylum also forced his official departure from Geffen-Roberts. While he had supposedly severed his connection to the company when he began Asylum, it was no secret that he had continued to "advise"

Roberts, particularly on decisions involving artists they shared between the label and the agency. Becoming a part of Warner meant Geffen could no longer allow even the most casual link between him and Roberts to suggest anything that might resemble a conflict of interest. To make the break with Elliot as quickly and cleanly as possible, he arranged to have all the company's assets legally transferred to his partner.

Not long after, Roberts, who had never been interested in the agency side of the business, dissolved it and changed the name of the company back to Lookout Management, whose roster now included the cream of L.A.'s, and Geffen's, rock elite — the Eagles, Jackson Browne, Poco, Joni Mitchell, Crosby, Stills, Nash and Young, and a new acquisition, America, a band Geffen believed might be bigger than any other, including the Eagles.

America did have a number of hits but never achieved the kind of excitement (or earned the amount of money) the Eagles did, and became one more in a series of post-Geffen disappointments for Roberts. Some thought the business had gotten too big for one person to handle. Others thought Roberts was emotionally stressed by the split with Geffen. Still others blamed the growing sense of chaos at Lookout on Roberts's most favored preoccupation: getting stoned.

Against the background of their shuffling management, the Eagles returned to the ordered sanctity of the studio, even as they tried to fight the growing feeling among them that in spite of his reassurance that the sale of Asylum was good for both the label and the band, maybe Geffen wasn't merely moving up but had in fact moved on.

Henley, in particular, felt that the sale changed everything. One minute the Eagles were an independent-minded group, recording for an independent label, led by an independent young man. The next they were a corporate band, owned by a team of suits. Perhaps worst of all, it was their success that had been fundamental to Ross's wanting to purchase the label. It also bothered him that while Geffen made millions from the deal, the band received nothing. Henley reflected on the shock he felt when Geffen sold the label without letting anyone, including the Eagles, know ahead of time: "Asylum was an artist-oriented label for about a minute, until the big money showed up, then my, how things changed."

"I remember the exact eureka moment Glenn began to doubt the band's future with Geffen," recalls Paul Ahern, who traveled frequently with the band. While in England, he watched Frey slowly put the pieces of the strange puzzle surrounding the band's lack of overseas sales or promotion together. No one, including Geffen, had had a satisfactory answer for it. "To this point, we had not had an international hit record. EMI had the Eagles overseas and couldn't or wouldn't break them. The reason was, Frey eventually realized, Geffen's much fanfared sale of Asylum to WEA. After that, the EMI guys didn't give a shit. They weren't even making any pretense of doing anything for the band. The reason was, they knew that all the Asylum acts were now lame ducks, and when their contracts were up WEA, which was international, would take them all over. A lightbulb suddenly went off in his head, and he wanted to know why Geffen hadn't told the band any of this."

As a result of the sale, the Eagles — Henley and Frey in particular — felt more strongly the need to affirm their independence. The first step was to expand a new song they'd written together, "Desperado," into a thematic cycle that included indirect references to the merger. As Henley recalled, "Our first album had three hit singles on it, 'Take It Easy,' 'Witchy Woman,' and 'Peaceful Easy Feeling,' and then we freaked out. 'We've sold out!' So [for our next album] we did *Desperado,* which we thought was [going to be] our big artistic commentary on the evils of fame and success, with a cowboy metaphor."

Desperado gradually evolved into an album loosely based on the exploits of the legendary Dalton gang. What appealed to both Henley and Frey was the fact that the Daltons had been peace officers before turning outlaws. The way Henley remembers it: "We were already cynical about the record business and, for that matter, fame in general. We knew that it didn't last, that there was no such thing as a fair shake for the artist. So we came up with this metaphor, which had a part of an idea that had its origins even before I'd gotten to California. J. D. Souther, Jackson, Glenn, and Ned Doheny had already worked on the concept of the Doolin' Daltons. Somebody had given one of them a book about the gang; they thought it was a great story and had tried to write some songs based on it. It eventually got shelved after Jackson wrote the 'Doolin-Dalton' snippet, until Glenn resurrected it when he said he wanted us to try and do a concept album. That, by the way, is when I really started to write. I hadn't written much of anything on the first album, except part of 'Witchy Woman,' my first major commercial song. The stuff I wrote with Shiloh was mostly crap. The music for 'Witchy Woman' was Bernie's, and I tried to give it something of an R&B pulse. *Desperado* was a leap forward for me, but the album was, in retrospect, maybe a bit inconsistent. It was our attempt to be legitimate artists. The metaphor was probably a little bullshit. We weren't outlaws; we weren't living outside the laws of normality. We were in L.A., staying up all night, smoking dope, living the California life, and I suppose we thought it was as radical as cowboys in the old West. We were really rebelling against the music business, not society."

For his part Geffen, either unaware of or unconcerned with Frey and Henley's growing dissatisfaction, was thrilled with the idea of the concept album. As far as he was concerned, *Desperado* was such great music it had every chance of becoming the Eagles' *Sgt. Pepper.* The romance of an album built around a bunch of outlaw American cowboys also appealed to Glyn Johns, enough so that in spite of his battles with Frey the first time around, Johns agreed to return to the studio for another round with the Eagles.

Desperado began to take shape at Frey's house, the band and friends coming together to help formulate "the statement." A record executive for Asylum at the time remembers "Glenn, Ned Doheny, J. D., and Henley gathering around a piano, working out chords, all writing together, eating, breathing, and sleeping music." For inspiration, the band visited an abandoned ranch where film studios had shot Westerns in the thirties and forties. Frey began carrying around the photo album of cowboys J. D. had given him for his birthday, studying the images for inspiration.

As everyone continued to kick ideas around, it became clear that Henley and Frey had decided this one belonged to them. Although the two may have found themselves collaborating as if they were the new American Lennon and McCartney, Leadon and Meisner found nothing funny about being George and Ringo. The real problem was that every member wanted to participate in the writing of songs — and not just because of the need to express himself. It was also where the money was. Songwriting credit guaranteed a writer publishing, airplay, performance, record sale, cover version, and rerelease royalties. In 1973, having a writing credit on a single track of a million-selling album could mean earnings of $40,000 over and above what a singer of that song might earn from performance and sales royalties. Multiply that by twelve tracks and it is not difficult to see why writing (and owning) rock music is, potentially, a highly profitable business.

However, none of that mattered, Henley and Frey insisted. The album was an artistic rather than a business endeavor. Talking to an interviewer during the making of *Desperado,* Henley explained his feelings this way: "Glenn and I wanted every song to be the best that it could be. We didn't want any filler. No stinkers. . . . Glenn is not a great guitar player and I'm not a great drummer. On the other hand, Randy [and] Bernie are incredible on their instruments. We've just taken it upon ourselves that [writing] is our department. We recognize the fact that those guys have got a need to say something and if we can help them say it better, then I think everybody's better off. It's not a matter of credit or money or any of that stuff. We've been splitting the publishing equally from the beginning."

Not exactly. In the beginning, the Eagles' publishing was divided in this way: half went equally to the original four band members and the other half to Geffen's publishing house, Benchmark. After Geffen left Geffen-Roberts, Roberts created a separate publishing unit for each member of the band.

After *Desperado* was released, the band royalties were re-allocated based on who had written which songs. While band members continued to share equally in radio play and stage performance revenues, individual band members now were getting disparate shares of publishing income. All of this was standard practice, but for the Eagles it was the first time everything was no longer equal.

According to Randy Meisner, Henley and Frey railed about the label's corporate shift, but in fact, they followed the band's finances much more closely than the others did. For them, he says, "It was *always* about money. That's what really fucked everything up."

Early in 1973, after months of nonstop touring, Geffen sent the Eagles back to England, where, for the next four weeks, they took over Island Studios and laid down the album tracks for *Desperado.* Although the place was stocked with every type of food and drink, what was missing for the band was nourishment of another sort. The absence of drugs proved intolerable and once again drove some band members to sneaking joints past Johns. There was no way for those who wanted it to get anything harder, which by this time made everything seem more difficult.

It also caused some wacky behavior. At one point during the recording sessions, Randy Meisner, fearing the band was becoming too countrified by both the nature of the new material and Johns's penchant for what he thought American country music sounded like, called for a sit-down with Glyn. "I want to have a serious talk with you," Meisner told the increasingly bemused Johns. "I don't like the way our records sound." Johns asked him what he meant, and Meisner replied that he wanted the band to sound more Motown. Johns said he understood.

Throughout the sessions, Johns couldn't help but notice the growing uneasiness and factionalization among the musicians. Not only were there signs of tension between Leadon and Meisner and the group's songwriting duo, but now Henley and Frey were having loud discussions about Leadon and Meisner and the future direction of the band.

As Johns recalled later, "It was not [in spite of what Henley believed] the Don band with Glenn along! Glenn was far more verbose about being the leader of the band than Don was. My major problem with the Eagles was the desire of Glenn Frey to be the leader of the band. [I did think that as a team] their writing was far stronger than anyone else's. They were quite superior in their attitude to the others' songs. I happen to think that Randy wrote a couple of great songs, and Bernie's written some nice things, but he isn't the songwriter that [Henley and Frey] are.

"I've always seen it as a responsibility of the producer to keep the unit as a unit. Part of that is satisfying everybody's desires without tainting the overall thing. . . . However, Don and Glenn weren't about to have that happen, and they became so insecure about the end result they weren't going to have anything that they didn't think was up to their quality of writing on the record . . . and I could see it cause a hell of a cleft in the band."

Johns's production for "Desperado" caused Henley to ask that former Shiloh member Jim Ed Norman be brought in to help with the string arrangement for one song. Henley wanted someone closer to the sound of Texas than the sound of London.

The final mix of *Desperado* was noticeably thin for a full-length work: eleven songs, with three variations of the musical theme "Doolin-Dalton" — two sung, one instrumental — used to fill out the album. The song was credited to Frey, Henley, J. D. Souther, and Jackson Browne. An Eagles version of David Blue's "Outlaw Man," a song that had appeared on his solo album and that Henley and Frey thought fit the concept of *Desperado,* was also included. Bernie Leadon wrote two songs, "Bitter Creek" and "Twenty-One"; "Certain Kind of Fool" was credited to Meisner, Henley, and Frey, and "Out of Control" to Henley, Frey, and their good friend and roadie Tommy Nixon. However, the two best songs on the album were the Henley-Frey compositions, the title track and the gorgeous "Tequila Sunrise." With these two songs Henley and Frey convincingly proved that they *were* the group's big creative guns.

Geffen funded what would prove to be for him an incredibly expensive album-cover shoot. Once again he called upon the team of Gary Burden and Henry Diltz, who agreed with Bernie Leadon's idea to take the band, dressed as cowboys down to "real" six-shooters loaded with Hollywood blanks, lots of horses, hats, and neckerchiefs, to a Western studio back lot. "We had a great time," Meisner says. "It was out in Agoura, at an old movie ranch there. Everyone was trying to shoot everyone else and play cowboy like in the old movies. Bernie, who was this really burly guy, wanted to do one of those things where he'd run up behind a horse and jump on. He didn't quite make it. He hit the butt and the horse bucked, and Bernie went about five feet straight into the air. After that, he decided he better get on the regular way. The whole shoot was like that: loose, unorganized, crazy, exciting. There was a lot of smoke, all these guns, seeing who could draw the fastest. It was really fun."

"A magical day," recalls one cameraman. "The Eagles really got into it and started acting like they believed they were really gunfighters. They just went out and played cowboys and really got into the mood, like they were actually transformed into these figures from the past. All day long they were shooting each other, falling dead in the street, like little kids. God, it was incredible. Even after dark, they kept it up."

Hoping to justify the expensive shoot, Geffen approved having Burden and Diltz make a promotional film about it for the album: a pre-MTV rock video. According to Glenn Frey, "It was shot in super 8 [-millimeter film] and transferred to sepia [-tinted processing] and from sepia to videotape. We kept losing something [video quality] each generation, and it proved to be fortunate, because it was supposed to be the 1890s in Kansas, and it started to look like cards being flipped, in sepia tones. Each [generation] became more realistic to us. It was a really nice accident."

Clearly visible in the surviving but rarely seen footage are the Eagles, Burden and Diltz, both of whom got into costume, Richie Fernandez, Boyd Elder, Tommy Nixon, J. D. Souther, Glyn Johns, and Jackson Browne. One extraordinary shot from the film graced the back of the album as a framed photo of the day the "Doolin-Daltons" were captured and shot dead. Standing among the posse are Burden, Fernandez, Elder, Nixon, John Hartmann, and, in fancy dude clothes, Johns. On the ground before them lie the "dead" Daltons — Browne, Leadon, Frey, Meisner, Henley, and Souther.

No matter how great it may have looked, sounded, and felt to those there, the public didn't buy it. Nor did the critics, who for the most part seemed to underscore what Henley, Frey, and Meisner had feared from the beginning, that Johns's production of *Desperado* sounded too country for rock and too rock for country. The album's commercial failure helped clarify and intensify the ongoing conflict of style between the band and its producer. What Henley and Frey had instinctively known all along, what had identified and united them as rock and roll songwriters, was their shared sense of the idealism of youth, the passion, hopes, dreams, and desires of first loves, and the illusion that everyone will stay together and remain forever young. Country, on the other hand, was all about disillusionment, the failure of all those hopes and dreams, the bitterness of losing those desires, the inevitability of growing old. This was the reason rock stars had to stay youthful to remain relevant, while country stars' presence improved with age. And, thematically and aurally, the reason the album failed as an artistic statement.

Predictably, it was seen by rock radio programmers as too heavily tilted toward country, and all but completely ignored by country music radio stations. Without airplay or a hit single, *Desperado* failed to break into the Top 40 album chart, peaking at number forty-one. The first single, "Tequila Sunrise," died at number sixty-four, with the follow-up, David Blue's "Outlaw Man," only making it to fifty-nine.

Eventually, the responsibility for the failure of *Desperado* trickled down to Lookout Management and resulted in a further shake-up of its staff. Since 1970, Elliot Roberts had continued to expand, bringing in several new hands, including Young Turk managers John Hartmann and Harlan Goodman, and a new office manager, former Geffen secretary Leslie Morris. Now he added Irving Azoff, a brash, hustling talent manager from the Midwest who'd brought a couple of clients with him to the company, the most popular among them Dan Fogelberg.

Still, the enthusiasm for running the agency just wasn't there for Roberts. "Elliot was really Neil's and Joni's manager," according to Paul Ahern. "He was the Eagles manager too, but in reality no one was really in charge of them anymore. John and Harlan worked with them some, and then Irving Azoff stepped up to the plate.

"Elliot and the management end of the company were all up on the second floor of the Sunset offices, and David was on the first. That was how they had 'separated' the businesses of agenting, management, and the running of the record company. In reality everything was always hopelessly intertwined. When Geffen left, Elliot was in no position to handle it all. The pressure must have been unbelievable as the agency shook out. I remember the day Geffen closed his deal with Warner, he said to me in passing that he had just made Elliot a very rich man. For Elliot, that was enough. His preference was to play golf every day, to start the weekend Thursday morning and end it Tuesday night. That's how he wanted to live, and as long as David was there, he could. In the end, it was just too overwhelming for him, and he didn't want it anymore. He was never going to do the Geffen eighty-hour-week number. He couldn't. So he just walked away from everything and everyone except Joni, Neil, and J. D., everyone including the Eagles."

Early in 1974, while out on the road with one of his acts, Roberts developed a tic in his left eye. When the tour ended, he consulted a doctor, who told him his nerves were effectively shot. "That day," he remembered, "I called a meeting of all our clients and I dropped everybody but Neil and Joni and I split up the management company [among the other managers in the office]. Hartmann and Goodman took America and Poco. I talked to Crosby and Nash [Stills had already left the company] and said that I really wanted to scale down. The Eagles wound up going with Irving Azoff."

It was a very quick end to one era and a startling beginning to a new one. In April 1974, Front Line Management was formed, after which its owner wasted no time letting everyone in shouting distance know that *from now on, all bets were Azoff!*

EIGHT

Irving Azoff grew up in Danville, Illinois, intending to study medicine until one night in 1965, still in high school, he attended a Yardbirds concert that he would later insist changed the direction of his life. The power of the band and the size of the crowd convinced him his true calling was rock and roll. Unlike most of the others there that night, however, Azoff had no interest in being the next Jimmy Page. What he really wanted to do was manage him. Although he had no talent as a musician, Azoff could play all sorts of money numbers in his head, and everything that night added up to big bucks.

He began booking gigs for a local band called the Shades of Blue. By the age of sixteen, he was handling promotion for a dozen local bands and after graduating, landed a booking job for a chain of small college-crowd clubs in the Midwest. Azoff soon found himself juggling dates for eighty-six acts in five states, including such up-and-coming bands as the Buckinghams, the Cryin' Shames, and the James Gang.

His next move came in 1972, when he relocated to Los Angeles to check out for himself the so-called new Southern California music scene. In L.A. for less than a week, Azoff happened to run into Joe Walsh, whom he had known and admired from the James Gang, playing a solo gig to a near-empty room at the Whiskey-a-Go-Go on the Sunset Strip.

Native New Yorker Walsh was still in his teens when he'd seen the Beatles on *Ed Sullivan* that now-famous Sunday night in 1964. The first thing Monday morning, like a million other fevered teenagers (including Glenn Frey and Randy Meisner), he decided to devote his life to rock and roll, and not long after was playing guitar for a local Jersey group called the Nomads.

When Walsh graduated from high school in 1965, his parents insisted he follow through on the family plan and enroll in college to learn a real profession. Reluctantly, Walsh quit the band and matriculated at Kent State, described that year by *Playboy* magazine as something of a country club.

Shortly after starting classes, and far enough away from home not to have to worry about mom and dad, Walsh ignored his studies, resumed playing, and was soon the lead guitarist-vocalist for the Cleveland-based James Gang. One night, in 1969, they were approached by producer Bill Szymczyk, who felt they were good enough to take into the studio. Szymczyk, a New York staff producer who'd made B.B. King's "The Thrill Is Gone," was there scouting talent for ABC Dunhill Records. The resulting tracks landed the group a Dunhill recording contract and a management deal with regional promoter Mike Belkin. He arranged for them to open in Ohio on the Who's American summer tour. The gig went so well that the British supergroup invited the James Gang to continue on with them in Europe. For Walsh, the opportunity to travel and share a stage with the legendary group became a critical turning point in his understanding of what it meant to perform, rather than merely play, for audiences.

When the tour ended, Walsh, who'd been in no hurry to finish school, returned to classes at Kent State, where, on May 4, 1970, four participants in a demonstration against Nixon's continued bombing of Cambodia were shot dead by the National Guard. Disgusted, Walsh left the campus and never went back. Soon after, he decided to leave the James Gang, having become frustrated with what he now felt were the group's limited abilities. Still in Cleveland, he briefly considered an offer from Dee Anthony, manager of Humble Pie, a happening British band, to join it, but was legally prevented from recording with another band by the James Gang, and so chose instead to check out the scene in Colorado.

There he signed a separate management deal with Belkin and recorded *Barnstorm,* a solo album for Dunhill that Szymczyk produced. It went nowhere, Walsh left for the West Coast, and by the summer of 1972 was playing weeknight gigs to near-empty houses at the Whiskey, where, one night, Irving Azoff happened to drop in. Having gotten reacquainted, they went for a drink after the show and wound up talking into the night. During the conversation, Walsh confessed to Azoff just how bad things had gotten. Azoff told Walsh the problem was not his playing but his management, and confidently predicted that with proper handling he could be a star. The next day Azoff signed to manage Walsh, promising to devote every waking hour to taking over his affairs and getting him released from all existing contracts.

At the time, Azoff was sharing a small Hollywood apartment with his one other client, Dan Fogelberg, whom Azoff had met in Illinois and, as he had now done with Walsh, also guaranteed to take to the top. One year later, in 1973, both Fogelberg's album (on Epic) and Walsh's (on MCA) went gold, the latter on the strength of the enormous hit single "Rocky Mountain Way." Each expressed his newfound L.A. rock-star status in rather eccentric fashion. Fogelberg insisted on being interviewed in the dark, while Walsh set about perfecting the fine art of hotel-room deconstruction.

Not long after, twenty-two-year-old Azoff confidently marched into the hot 9126 Sunset Boulevard headquarters of Geffen-Roberts, went right up to Geffen, and asked what the chances were of getting a job there. Remembers Geffen, "I hired Irving for a salary; I don't remember for how much. The deal was, his clients were now ours. One of his major functions was to book a club on Sunset Boulevard [the Roxy] Elliot and I owned a piece of."

The next day, Azoff set up shop in a corner, sharing phones, secretaries, executives, and agents. He fit in seamlessly, as if he'd been working there for years. "And I knew," Geffen adds, "he was going to be trouble from day one. I could just tell."

Although he had gradually come to know the members on a nod-to-nod basis in the office, the first time Azoff came into direct professional contact with the Eagles happened because of a mix-up by a Geffen-Roberts staffer. No one had arranged for limos to take the band to the airport. The increasingly frazzled Roberts, not up to taking the call from an irate Glenn Frey, asked Azoff if he would mind handling it. "Tell them to get a hippie in a cab," Roberts said. Azoff relayed the message and then held the phone from his ear while Frey unloaded on him: "Yeah, that's good. America records for Warners. They get limos. We record for Asylum; we get hippies in taxis." After fifteen minutes of listening to Frey's complaints, Azoff assured him that everything would be taken care of, hung up, and quickly straightened out the situation, making sure a limo got to the airport and drove the boys home. From that day on, with increasing frequency, Roberts called upon Azoff to help handle the Eagles.

Gradually, Azoff began to think that it might actually be possible for him to take over full-time management of the band. Surely, he felt, if he could get his hands on the Eagles he could take them straight to the top of the rock pile. It had become increasingly obvious to Azoff just how disappointed the band was with the relative failure of *Desperado* and the problems they were having in the time leading up to the recording of their next album.

Late in 1973, the Eagles returned to England to begin work on their third album with Glyn Johns. Halfway through the allotted recording time, only two tracks that anyone thought usable had been put down — "The Best of My Love" (Henley-Frey-Souther) and "You Never Cry Like a Lover" (Souther-Henley). Frustrated and fed up, the Eagles packed it in and flew back to Los Angeles.

"We couldn't think over there," Henley remembers. "We couldn't create." Randy Meisner adds, "You can't settle things out if you're not alone in your own home."

"The six weeks in the studio were a disaster area," Johns readily agreed, adding, "but I will tell you that it had nothing at all to do with me. I certainly got frustrated on some occasions and pissed because they wouldn't grab the situation by the balls and get on with it, though. I don't believe in kid-gloving artists. There were a lot of hang-ups, individually and with each other. But what it boils down to is they weren't ready to make another record."

What Johns perceived as a lack of readiness was in fact a crucial aspect of the Eagles' creative process. The chaos that drove Johns to distraction was precisely what worked for the band. The creative tension between Henley and Frey always tightened in the confines of the studio and would invariably lead them to produce their finest, if hardest-won, collaborative work.

Richie Fernandez, the band's new road manager, was there during the aborted recording sessions and remembers, "Glyn recorded them very live and was still trying to capture a certain kind of country sound. He loved what Bernie could do with a banjo and guitar, almost a pure bluegrass sound. Glyn had recently worked with Waylon Jennings and had tried to get some of that Southern twang sound on 'Wild Horses' with the Stones. What appealed to him now about the Eagles was that they were four guys who could sing country and play it in tune."

Frey and Henley continued to pressure Johns to give the band a more basic rock sound. To let out some of his frustration, away from the studio Frey turned to his other favorite obsession, girls. Remembers Fernandez, "Glenn, the self-proclaimed Teen King, had girlfriends all over the place."

Henley, meanwhile, spent one night with a beautiful young Latin girl named Juliet, who, to his great relief, spoke very little English.

Fernandez remembers: "Work on the album dragged on, and to kill the dead hours the band took to playing a lot of cards. That's about the time Henley and Frey came up with the game of Eagle poker, a draw game in which the winner takes a pot and everybody who's stayed in has to match it. The game can have some pretty high stakes. We were in the middle of trying to lay down a track, had taken a break, and an intense game began. Elliot [Roberts] and Neil [Young] happened to stop by. Neil was in England for the *Tonight's the Night* tour. Elliot suggested the Eagles take a break and open for Neil for a week. They agreed, and so we rented a bus and traveled around the U.K. Our last night, in Birmingham, Neil's bus broke down. He and his entourage rode with us. Because we opened, we usually played cards during Neil's set.

"That night, Ben Keith, a member of Neil's band, and David Briggs, Neil's sometime producer, were all drinking quite a bit, and when Briggs saw us playing cards began bragging about what a good player he was. Henley and Frey looked at each other; Glenn came over to me and said to make sure the bus was stocked with a lot of booze, and then invited the producer to join the game. Pretty soon the stakes got real high; this guy was getting drunker and drunker and really bummed out because he was losing. He started making these weird comments aimed at Henley, 'You're never going to make it anyhow,' things like that. Don's eyes narrowed, his jaw tightened, he kept very calm and continued to play. By the time we got to London, the guy owed Henley seven thousand dollars."

Eventually, it fell to Azoff to deal with the problem of getting the new album finished. As a possible replacement for Johns, Azoff suggested Bill

Szymczyk. He'd intended to use Szymczyk for REO Speedwagon but instead decided to put him together with the Eagles. He played the band Szymczyk's masters for Joe Walsh's just completed, as yet unreleased *The Smoker You Drink, the Player You Get* and arranged for the band members to meet him. They liked what they heard and saw. Satisfied that they had found someone they could work with, they returned to the studio to complete working on the stalled album.

As soon as the first tracks were laid down, Azoff held a series of meetings with Henley and Frey about the possibility of their leaving Lookout so he could devote his life to them.

According to Frey, "The first night we met with Irving, Henley and I and him got in a room together. There was something about it. We started telling him our problems with the band, how we wanted our records not to be so clean and glassy and how we were getting the royal fuckin' screw job. He told us he had come in with Walsh and Fogelberg and didn't know anything himself. It was perfect from the start. Here was a guy our own age, going through exactly the same thing, catching his rising star the same time we were. We decided that night that Irving could manage us."

The opportunity to make the actual switch came in the winter of 1974, when Elliot Roberts officially downsized his agency. It didn't happen as smoothly as the Eagles or Azoff had hoped. Roberts's action caused a rush of confusion and several aborted power plays that resulted in a house coup, leaving the diminutive Irving Azoff standing tallest when the smoke finally cleared. The feeding frenzy had actually begun several months earlier, when Lookout manager John Hartmann urged Geffen to use his influence with Roberts to let him take several of the agency's biggest discarded acts to Premier, a relatively new and powerful rock agency. Geffen made a counteroffer. He told Hartmann that if he remained with Roberts at Lookout, he, his friend and partner Harlan Goodman, and Irving Azoff could have the management side of the entire operation — as long as it was understood that Geffen could still have what he referred to as "input" into the direction of the groups. It remains unclear if Hartmann and Goodman left or were fired. Either way, they set up their own agency and took America and Poco with them.

This poker chipping infuriated the Eagles, none more than Don Henley, who still blamed Geffen's sell-out of Asylum and the group (along with the lack of any breakout single) as the reason *Desperado* had flopped. Henley remained convinced Geffen's deal with Warner and his subsequent focus on a film career had interfered with his promise to let nothing get in the way of his making the Eagles bigger than Crosby, Stills and Nash. As the agency dissolved and the numbers came forth, the Eagles realized how little money they had actually earned. Most of the profits from their work, they now realized, had gone in one way or another to Geffen (and Asylum), in the form of publishing, production reimbursements, fees (to Lookout), and advances. Moreover, the fact that the band's business managers also happened to be Geffen's made any challenge to the financial records impractical at best.

The Eagles had then decided to call a meeting with Roberts to see if a new and more favorable deal between them could be worked out. Geffen decided to sit in and, when the band finished verbally unloading, agreed with every point they made and wished them the best of luck as Roberts released them from all further obligations to Lookout. Frey and Henley then approached Azoff and informed him they were definitely leaving Lookout and wanted to know if he was committed to coming with them. Azoff, who had been complaining about what he felt were unfulfilled compensation promises to the Eagles, used that as his reason for leaving with them. The past Christmas, the band had gone out on the road to make some badly needed holiday money. However, every cent they earned was kept by the agency to pay back commissions and advances, leaving the boys with nothing.

According to Azoff, "Jerry Rubenstein, the agency's accountant, gave Lookout all the profits instead of giving it to the band. A lot of screaming went on over that."

"The fact is," Henley adds, "both Roberts and Geffen, with their combination management/record company, had a huge conflict of interest, and we decided to call them on it. Suddenly, the management company was downsized, and we were out on the street. We could have sued both of them right then, because there were conflicts all up and down the line, but we were young and we didn't know the ropes well enough. We just wanted to find a new manager and get on with our primary mission, which was music. Fortunately for us, Irving was there."

With Azoff behind them, the band felt much more confident about making its big move. Geffen, perhaps fearful of the PR as well as the legal consequences of his dealings, effectively handed his prize act over to Azoff in what amounted to a bloodless coup. As part of the deal, Azoff took back the two acts he'd brought to Lookout, Fogelberg and Walsh, and a new group he believed in more than Roberts did, REO Speedwagon. He declined an offer from Hartmann and Goodman to join forces with them and instead formed Front Line Management. He named his new agency after something Graham Nash had said to him one night: that he, Azoff, seemed to always be "in the front lines."

According to Geffen, "When Irving took over the management of the band, I was more concerned with conflicts of interest between the record company and the management company than anything else. That's why I okayed Elliot to release the Eagles to Irving." Still, it seemed to many that he had indeed written the Eagles off.

Glenn Frey could remember a time not so long ago when he, Jackson, J. D., and Ned Doheny had all been naked in Geffen's sauna as their mentor solemnly swore he would always keep Asylum small, that he would never sign more artists than could fit in the sauna that night. Now, Frey thought, Geffen was sitting on top of the hottest recording conglomerate in the world, his ascent due in no small way to the music of the Eagles.

While Geffen wished the Eagles and Azoff well, privately, he wondered why anyone would want to be associated with the small (five foot two) manager who'd quickly gained a reputation as a supremely unlikable fellow. What benefit could there possibly be in allowing such a combative personality to become involved with a high-strung band like the Eagles? Hadn't they flourished, Geffen wondered, precisely because of his personal brand of "benevolent protectionism"? As he recalled, "I knew he [Azoff] had talent, and I recognized even from the beginning that there's something lovable about Irving, as there is always about the devil, otherwise why would you invite him in? But in the end he's still Irving."

"Make that the luckiest Irving who ever lived," adds Bob Buziak. "He was at the right time and the right place; it's as simple as that. Boz Scaggs, for instance, came to Irving as a client before *Silk Degrees*. Then he got Steely Dan before *Aja*. When he took over the Eagles, they had sold a respectable number of albums, and even though *Desperado* was something of a stiff, they were still perfectly positioned for superstardom.

"Either way, Geffen had handed him the golden goose on a beautiful platter, and Irving ran with it as if he were the one who'd sat on the egg all that time waiting for the Eagles to hatch. The acquisition legitimatized an essentially small-time manager's entrée into the first rank, an opportunity he seized with a vengeance unlike any I've ever seen before. He was the nastiest fuck in town, and no one ever really understood why. But it worked for him, there's no question about that. And for the Eagles too."

Indeed, unlike Elliot Roberts, Azoff had a boisterous, in-your-face style of doing business, what Paul Ahern described as "bunker mentality, as in 'Let's go get 'em.'" His manner caused some to fear, others to mock him. Still others found his manner unbearably petulant, a grown man the size of a child who was nouveau power crazy, insensitive, annoying, and manipulative. He seemed to embody the worst of the so-called new breed of rock managers, inexperienced hustlers attracted to the big money and self-aggrandizement that coexisted so neatly under the guise of youthful exuberance. As one record executive described Azoff at the time he took over the Eagles, "He was like so many in the long tradition of rock and roll, from the Colonel on down, just one more motherfucker to have to deal with."

Another had this to say: "Irving Azoff was the type who always wanted to be one of the boys, the shortest kid in school who dreams of making the basketball team, the girl in the wheelchair who wants to be a ballerina."

"Permission," still another observer noted, was Azoff's real talent. "That was Irving's great gift to the Eagles. Permission to do everything they did anyway."

One person who really appreciated the way Azoff handled himself was Don Henley. Azoff's style of roughhouse permissiveness pushed all the right psychological buttons for Henley. Finally, here was a father figure who behaved like a mother, someone who would not only never say no to him, but go to the mat against anyone who did. According to Henley, "I believed, and still believe, that Irving had his own concept of fairness and it didn't mesh with the corporate mentality that then governed and still governs the music business. Irving had a David-and-Goliath mentality, perhaps due in part to his physical stature." Not surprisingly, Henley and Azoff were tight from the start. While for Geffen, money and power had come first, and Roberts's true devotion seemed locked in the good times, with Azoff it was clearly Eagles first, oxygen second. As he used to tell the Eagles, "Everyone on that side of the line is the enemy, everyone on this side of the line I'll kill for."

Whenever Azoff's manner was attacked in print, Henley was always quick to jump to the manager's defense. If he was a Napoleon type, as one journalist claimed, Henley said he was "Napoleon with a heart. I'm always awed because he's screaming at some guy twice his size and never gets his face crushed for it. I think it helps that people are shocked at this short, deceptively *cute*-looking guy who goes to the top floor of a building and just *explodes* on some guy for his incompetence. Irving has always been one of my best friends. He may have been a bit of a terrorist, but so are a lot of the other guys in the business. They're just more genteel about it. He just sort of lays his cards on the table. If he's ruthless, he learned at Geffen's feet. He's just more flamboyant, if such a thing is possible. He did a good job for this band, he protected us and is the reason we're one of the few groups that actually made some money for itself, rather than everybody else."

Azoff loved to flex his well-toned power-trip muscle but was always careful never to kick sand into the faces of any of the Eagles, particularly Henley, whose friendship he especially coveted.

Azoff quickly got the chance to prove to the band just how far he was willing to go for them. In the middle of a tour, they decided to travel to the Bahamas for two days of one of the Eagles' favorite recreations, a high-stakes card game. At customs, the group was stopped when Azoff was found to be carrying a stash of Valium in one of his boots, Frey a half ounce of marijuana, and Henley's girlfriend rolling papers in her bag. Somehow, because Henley was clean, Azoff was able to convince the Bahamian customs officials (who were notoriously unbribable and reportedly resisted $5,000 cash from Azoff) to look the other way. Not only were the Eagles and their entourage let go, they were given a special escort through the rest of customs.

Like many in L.A. who had to do business with him, Geffen was quickly put off by Azoff's abrasive manner. Still, it was in his best interest to keep the relationship between WCI and Front Line Management a good one. Indeed, with the newly signed Bob Dylan proving to be more difficult and his first album for Asylum less successful than Geffen had hoped, Linda Ronstadt's first Asylum album not the success he had wanted, and J. D. Souther's newly formed Souther-Hillman-Furay Band debut disc a commercial disappointment, the Eagles were more valuable than ever to the label. Therefore, Geffen knew, so was Azoff.

With their new management in place, the Eagles got down to the business of finishing their long-delayed third album by choosing the final set of songs they were sure no one could mistake for anything but rock and roll. Once Szymczyk began to lay down his tracks, though, it became clear something was still not quite right about the way the band sounded. They simply didn't have enough musical heft to play the kind of rock they wanted to. Szymczyk suggested adding another guitar, and Frey said he knew the perfect guy — Don Felder. Felder, a veteran session-and-touring player, had just returned to L.A. after being on the road with Asylum recording artist David Blue and was ready to step in and help kick the band up a notch. Henley and Frey also knew Felder from his days touring with David Crosby and Graham Nash, and okayed a tryout.

Because Leadon was the one Eagle who had always gotten along with Glyn Johns, it came as something of a surprise to the others that he was so enthusiastic about adding Felder. As the banjo player and pedal steel guitarist, Leadon had provided the most easily identifiable elements of the band's style on the first two albums. The addition of Felder meant, for all practical purposes, eliminating most of the country instrumentations in favor of four rock guitars, five if you counted the couple of acoustic chords Henley occasionally added to the mix.

As one close to the band at the time reflected, it was clear the moment Johns was gone that Leadon was going to be the next odd man out, something he may have been more than ready for. "Bernie was always having problems with the band of one sort or another. The other guys just wouldn't respect the fact that he was tired of what their life was becoming, or had in fact become. For instance, he really didn't do drugs anymore. He didn't drink. He didn't eat the same kind of special salad the others insisted on being served in restaurants, and believe it or not, that became an issue between them. It's not that he was a Goody Two-shoes or anything like that. Leadon had done it all in his pre-Eagle days and then managed to give up most of his self-destructive indulgences, to the point where healthy living had become the major nonmusical issue in his life. The other guys could have said, 'Good for you, Bernie,' but instead, in their mocking way they so loved, said, 'Hey, what's wrong with you?' It was almost as if he was held in suspicion for not doing drugs. You have to wonder what kind of mind-set that was, but I'll tell you this: Don and Glenn took it as a personal indictment by him of their own lifestyles."

Felder noticed the tension among the group's members as soon as he stepped foot in the studio: "When I first walked in," he recalled, "everything seemed crazy. Bernie was quitting, and Randy was talking about quitting. Everyone was yelling at each other and fighting. They had just fired their manager and their producer. I thought I had joined a band that had just broken up. 'Oh,' I said to myself, 'smart move.'"

According to Richie Fernandez, Leadon was no angel and probably hurt his own cause by refusing to go along with the realities of life in a rock band. "Bernie was such a character; he was a unique individual all to himself and, to be fair, at times a little tough for the others to take. When you're on the road, it's living together twenty-four hours a day. We would go into a hotel, and I would walk up and get the keys, and Bernie would always be the first one out of the car; he's got the door open, he's out, he's up at the front desk saying, 'I'm Bernie, where's my key?' and expecting them to just give it to him.

"I think in the end, Bernie Leadon floated by on genius, and because of it, there were always everyday things that didn't make any sense to him and eventually drove him and the other members of the band crazy. If they couldn't make eggs for him in a restaurant the way he liked them, unlike the other members of the band, who'd start complaining, he'd simply walk into the hotel kitchen and start making them himself."

Regarding the change of producer and the addition of Don Felder, both of which he saw as commercially calculated steps to widen the mainstream appeal of the Eagles, Frey commented at the time: "We had more freedom in the studio with Bill [Szymczyk]. We learned tons and tons from Glyn. How to cut through a lot of bullshit in arranging songs and how to shape them up real fast in the studio. He helped us take professional attitudes and mold them into professional recording artistry. He also taught me a lot about myself.

"[The real problem was] no country-rock band had gone big time. Poco had done okay. They could play maybe three-thousand-seaters in L.A. and a couple of other cities. Loggins and Messina had had a couple of hits, but they weren't really a concert draw like bands like Yes, Jethro Tull, or Edgar Winter, which were some of the bands we opened for. We ultimately realized we needed to toughen up our sound and add a guitar player to be able to perform in those bigger venues. . . .

"I'd been a Don Felder fan for about a year and a half, ever since I heard him playing in a dressing room in Boston one night. I saw him in concert in L.A. and asked if he'd come down and put some slide on 'Good Day in Hell.' With every take he just blew us all away. If he isn't Duane Allman reincarnate, I don't know who the fuck is. I feel better than ever [about the Eagles] since he joined."

Frey took the moment of change to reflect on the then-current status of the band. "Bernie and Felder are proud guitar players, and to me, I don't mean to make their work comparative, but respectively they're carrying on the work of Clarence White and Duane Allman. Don Henley is like a rock, besides the fact that he's the best singer I've ever worked with. He's brilliant. Randy is the perfect ribbon for the package. He adds all the top and all the bottom, singing like a lark and giving that growly Nebraska R&B-orientated bass feel to the country stuff."

According to Henley at the time, "Frey adds the grease. He's all action, and he moves more than any of us trying to get people off. Maybe *that's* why he's called the 'Teen King.' Glenn's got a real positive ego and he's not afraid to do things even though sometimes he does them wrong. He pulls us all through because he's the catalyst of the Eagles."

On the Border, the Eagles' third album, was finally released in March 1974 and quickly became their fastest selling, reaching gold status in less than two months. It hit number seventeen on the U.S. charts and became the album that broke the Eagles internationally. *On the Border* proved so strong that sales of *Desperado* surged, and as a result, all three Eagles albums went certified gold.

The first track, "Already Gone," was a Jack Tempchin–Bob Strandlund out-and-out rocker, an effective Eagles kiss-off to Johns. Musically it sounded like a fuel-injected rave-up, with melodic echoes of both "Peaceful Easy Feeling" and "Take It Easy." Szymczyk had correctly pushed Frey's vocals to the front, along with his sneering guitar, and created a sound that once and for all declared the Eagles an all-American rock and roll band. The heat and fire that had been missing from the first two albums now came roaring out of car radios and living-room stereos all over the world.

"Already Gone," which peaked at number thirty-two, was followed up by the release of a Souther-Henley-Browne-Frey tune, "James Dean," written at the Troubadour front bar and Dan Tana's, a reverential bow to the dead film idol the band loved for his fast cars, idealized image of teenage rebellion, and head-on embrace of unpredictable fame. It never achieved hit-single status, but, surprisingly, remains among the most requested (and least played) Eagles tunes on classic-rock radio stations.

The remainder of *On the Border* was made up of a tune by Bernie Leadon ("My Man"); the title song, credited to Leadon, Frey, and Henley; a smart-sounding version of Tom Waits's "Ol' 55"; a Henley-Frey collaboration, "Good Day in Hell"; one song by Randy Meisner, "Is It True?"; "Midnight Flyer," by P. Craft; and two songs left over from the Glyn Johns sessions, remixed by Bill Szymczyk, "You Never Cry Like a Lover" and "The Best of My Love." The last, ironically, would prove the band's biggest hit yet.

For nine months, Frey, perhaps concerned that the cut sounded too much like the *Desperado* Eagles, insisted "Best" not be released as a single. When it finally was, it became the group's first number one. What should have been the band's finest moment, however, became a nightmare when, at Henley's insistence, the 45 was almost pulled from record stores when he realized that forty seconds from the album version were missing. While the band was on tour, an executive at Asylum had made a unilateral edit to keep the cut a radio-friendly three and a half minutes long. Amazingly, it was made without the knowledge or approval of the band members, and they were furious. The label's promotion people defended the move, claiming they had asked for the record to be reedited because they couldn't get the song on the radio in its original long form.

When the single passed the million sales mark, Azoff sent a gold record with a piece cut out of it to the label, mounted with the caption "The Golden Hacksaw Award." Someone hung it on the front door of Asylum. Frey then threatened to take a chainsaw and do some in-house editing of his own.

And, as might be expected, Glyn Johns was delighted at the surprising turn of events. "I must say it put a large grin on my face when 'Best of My Love' hit a year later. That was the record that really put them on the map . . . [after] they [had] turned themselves into what they thought was a rock 'n' roll band. A pretty lame one, in my view."

After announcing to the world that Don Felder was now the official fifth Eagle ("A late arrival," according to *On the Border*'s liner notes), the band set out on a world tour. Remembering the nightmare of being an opening act, the Eagles were careful to choose someone they liked, whose music and style would fit in well with theirs and serve as a proper audience warmer, with no threat of stealing the spotlight. They found what they believed was just such a performer in the then unknown Jimmy Buffet and his Coral Reefer Band. "Oh, yes," a band member recalled, "he was right there at the trough."

As always, Irving Azoff was in the trenches for every date. And loved it. While most managers dreaded the physical toll the endless hours on the road took, the constant waiting around, the cheap, fatty food, the mind-warping repetition of sound check, performance, press conference, all-night party, and heavy morning after, Azoff actually thrived on it. He became more energized as the weeks rolled on. To him, the road was where the action was, the closest he ever came to really being "one of the boys," and he made the most of it. He particularly loved the band's mocking humor and used it as the basis for an ongoing and increasingly bizarre series of practical jokes.

Someone along for the ride that summer remembers the night Irving tore down the walls of a hotel room the band was staying in because he wanted to see what was behind the plaster. Then there was the night a promoter wouldn't pay up, and Irving, the story goes, took the fellow up in a helicopter and threatened to have him thrown out of it. He made good as soon as they touched ground.

There was supposedly the time J. D. Souther, Irving, and Don were in a Lear jet in the middle of winter, and Irving had the pilot land at some obscure airport. One of them got out, Azoff slammed the door, and the plane suddenly took off. After a while it came back. And then left again without stopping. Twice. An expensive practical joke, as each landing and takeoff came with an airport fee, but it didn't matter to Azoff. If it was going to be funny, it was worth it — to the same guy who, according to one associate, would scream bloody murder if he thought someone was screwing him out of a dime.

There were the inevitable ultimate room trashings. Even here, Azoff was determined that the Eagles outdo every other band and always had road manager Fernandez or the band's new accountant, Bob Hurwitz, standing by with a stack of hundred-dollar bills, ready to start peeling them off to placate whomever he had to, to make any problems go away.

Joe Berry, one of the Eagles' longtime road techies, remembers that "no matter what Irving or the band did, no matter how destructive it got, he knew there was a price that could fix it. He actually encouraged the guys to be as wild and crazy as they wanted to be. For Irving, that was the whole funny point, that they could do anything and get away with it."

Bob Sterne recalls how Irving taught him to "quarter jam" a hotel-room door so the person inside couldn't get out. "It's simple. You take quarters and start putting them under the door, stacked, until you lift it just a little, which makes it impossible to throw the dead bolt open. Irving used to love to do it to someone he was pissed at. Or hot-glue them. One time, I remember, there was an accountant along with us, and he was really getting on Irving's nerves. So Irving got hold of a hot-glue gun and simply glued the guy's door shut, imprisoning him in his room. It caused a great deal of trouble for the hotel, and they were really angry until Irving started peeling off the hundreds. When they were paid enough, they simply broke the door down with an ax, let the guy out, and the next day replaced the door."

Upset with the service in a restaurant one time, rather than complaining, Azoff set the menu on fire.

In 1978, at his own wedding, in what he later insisted was an act of endearment, Azoff smashed his mother-in-law in the face with a piece of wedding cake.

Not all the road games were for fun. One night Azoff grabbed a walkie-talkie and had the road crew remove all the equipment from the stage an hour before a scheduled show in New Orleans because promoter Barry Mendelsohn was slow in paying the band's guarantee.

However, "The quintessential Irving Azoff story," according to one reporter, involved [rock] manager Michael Lippman. It was Lippman's fortieth birthday, and he was being feted on the tennis court of his Beverly

Hills home. Once among Lippman's closest friends but lately an adversary, Azoff was invited but didn't show. Instead, he hired a delivery man to present a gift-wrapped box to Lippman. Inside was a live boa constrictor Azoff had borrowed from Alice Cooper. This was Azoff's idea of a joke.

And, as with all rock and roll tours, women played a crucial, hot part. For Henley and Frey, especially, it became a world of endless opportunity. If the band went for an afternoon swim at a hotel pool, girls would immediately appear: gorgeous, bikinied, young, nubile, and willing. *Very* willing. More than once a young beauty appeared with the first names of band members temporarily tattooed on her chest. At a Holiday Inn, a young-looking mother showed up with her teenage daughter, offering both to one member of the band as a family-that-plays-together-style treat. Before long, the Eagles had joined the elite ranks of sex-obsessed bands, sharing top groupie chart position with the Band, the Allman Brothers, and the Rolling Stones.

When the *Border* tour ended, the weary but energized Eagles returned to L.A. and almost without a break, sometimes together, sometimes individually, began to play on their friends' new albums. Henley, Frey, and Leadon all sang on Randy Newman's *Good Old Boys;* Frey and Meisner on Dan Fogelberg's new album (produced by Joe Walsh); Frey, Henley, and Meisner on Joe Walsh's *So What?* Henley played drums and Frey acoustic guitar on "You Can Close Your Eyes" for Linda Ronstadt's *Heart Like a Wheel,* and Henley and Souther sang on Jackson Browne's crucial and classic 1974 release, *Late for the Sky.*

Without question, the sound, lyrical force, and interior shadings of *Sky* influenced every seventies L.A. rock and roll album that followed, none more than those of the Eagles. The power of Browne's lyrics inspired Henley to try to fine-tune his writing style, to take more risks. *Sky* also remains the best argument for why Jackson Browne could never have been a member of any group, *especially* the Eagles. His was a singular focus that became a stylistic force, as individually expressive and uniquely evocative as any in rock, and impossible to incorporate without diffusing and dissipating the fragile beauty of its presentation. *Late for the Sky* remained on the charts for nearly a year, its enduring presence increasing the already heavy pressure on the Eagles from Asylum to produce a follow-up to *On the Border* that was as good as, if not better than, anything out there, including the masterwork of one of their best friends.

Or at the very least, one that would outsell him.

The Eagles returned to the studio late in 1974, ready to begin work on their fourth album, *One of These Nights*. Once again, Henley and Frey's song-writing dominated, as they cowrote five out of the album's nine tracks. Leadon was given three songs, none of which was released as a single, and Meisner only two, on one of which he shared cowriting credit with Felder. Production stretched into the winter of 1975. "One of these nights we might actually finish this thing" became a running joke in the studio.

At least part of the delay could be blamed on the unavailability of the "sixth and seventh Eagles." Jackson Browne was still out touring behind *Late for the Sky*, and J. D. Souther was also on the road with the Souther-Hillman-Furay Band. Nor did it help matters any that Szymczyk, Henley, and Frey were snail-paced perfectionists, in no hurry to turn out anything they didn't consider first-rate. Responding to the daily requests from the label for a solid delivery date, Frey grumbled to friends that the Eagles' first three albums had been the product of twenty years of living, and now that they were riding high, the suits upstairs expected the next one in twenty minutes.

Henley claimed all the pressure from the record company was affecting his creative process. Long days in the studio dissolved into weeks, with, for the most part, nothing salvageable to show for them. Every so often, Henley and Frey would simply throw their hands up, escape to Aspen, and cool out for a while before returning to the discipline of the recording studio. If they didn't leave town, they'd spend most nights hanging out at Dan Tana's. One time while J. D. was in town on a break between tour dates, they had piled into one of the restaurant's horseshoe-shaped red leather banquettes with a couple of other friends and were passing the night scoring the seemingly end-less parade of vavoom babes, when, as Bob Buziak remembers, "Someone looked up and saw an older man with an absolutely gorgeous young blond across the room. Frey laughed, turned to us, and said, 'Look at those lyin' eyes!' Everyone knew it as soon as he said it. Pens and napkins flew." The moment became the basis for the Henley-Frey tune "Lyin' Eyes," which many consider among the best L.A. rock and roll songs ever written. Its portrait of a beautiful cheating girlfriend framed one of the band's favorite themes: that men were victims of scheming, sneaking women.

And "that," said one of the Eagles' ex-girlfriends, "was exactly what made them so appealing, and so ludicrous. Let's face it. These were the horniest boys in town, living life without rules or limits. They had it all, fame, money, drugs, women throwing themselves at them, at a time when no one was worried about anything, overdoses, AIDS, I mean anything. And still, they loved to portray themselves in their music as the underdogs, the taken-advantage-of victims of all those women they fucked over. We used to call that song 'Lyin' Guys.'"

Midway through the making of the album, tensions twisted a turn tighter when Bernie Leadon insisted his new girlfriend, Patti Davis, the daughter of highly conservative governor of California Ronald Reagan, be allowed to sit with him in the studio.

Henley was livid. It didn't matter that like him, Davis was liberal leaning, an environmentalist, and publicly at odds with her Republican father. Henley simply couldn't stand having her around, anywhere, but especially in the studio, clinging to Leadon in Yoko-like fashion. What made the situation worse was Leadon's stubborn insistence that Davis be given cowriting credit on "I Wish You Peace."

When asked about it some time later, Henley told a reporter, "Nobody else wanted [the song]. We didn't feel it was up to the band's standards, but we put it on anyway as a gesture to keep the band together." A hollow gesture at best, as from that point on both Henley and Frey made it clear that as far as they were concerned, the band had progressed beyond the level and sophistication of Leadon's idiosyncrasies, as well as his style of playing.

And Leadon seemed to know it. After the songwriting flap, he appeared to lose interest in the making of the album, at one point walking out during a long session in the studio just as everyone was about to sit down and decide what to include in the final mix. Nor was it the first time he had left without warning. Once before, during a critical recording of a particularly complex track, Leadon had simply disappeared for three days. While it was apparently all right for Henley and Frey to take spontaneous Aspen breaks, as far as Henley was concerned, Leadon's walkouts were inexcusable.

In fact, his actions were meant to send a message about the way he felt he and Meisner were being treated. Besides the royalty situation, Leadon particularly resented that often during the making of the album, Henley and Frey would take the rough mixes to a hotel room or the separate rental up on Briarcrest, above Sunset. There they would share a glass or two of tequila and listen to the tapes over and over again, making decisions about what should stay in and what had to go.

This was arguably Frey's creative peak. To help his focus (and decrease the intensity and relentlessness of his partying) he gave up the "Kirkwood Casino," moved to Briarcrest with Henley, rented a separate place for his now displaced roommate, Paul Ahern, and began listening to a lot of rhythm and blues, most notably the music of the Spinners and Bobbie "Blue" Bland (the latter whose "I Wouldn't Treat a Dog" sounds quite a bit like "One of These Nights" in both chord structure and melody).

Three months and several hundred thousand dollars in production costs later, Frey and Henley finally pronounced the project complete. Once again, they delivered in spectacular fashion. *One of These Nights* became the Eagles' first number one album.

The record-buying public couldn't get enough. As soon as *One of These Nights* hit the charts, every other Eagles album again took a huge jump in sales. The first single, "One of These Nights," entered the top ten as the Eagles began a worldwide fifty-nine-city sold-out stadium tour. "Lyin' Eyes," the next cut to be released, went to number two on the pop charts and number eight in the country listing, a notable achievement at a time when few rock groups were able to make that kind of crossover. "Take It to the Limit," a perfect showcase for Randy Meisner's beautiful high-end vocals, was the third single off the album, rising to number four on the national charts. It was the Eagles' fourth consecutive top five single.

In June 1975, the band made a triumphant return to London, where they performed before a friendly and receptive audience on a bill that included Elton John, the Beach Boys, and Joe Walsh, before continuing on to Europe. A month later, they returned to the States and played to a massive crowd at an outdoor concert in Oakland, California.

In August, they were officially deemed by *Time* "the top U.S. rock band." The magazine made mention of how "some 850,000 people will pay $5 million to see them on their current tour." The article went on to profile the individual members in unusually glowing, uncritical terms. It described Frey as a charming, harmless ladies' man ("a nocturnal playboy"), Henley as a card-carrying intellectual ("he reads Rimbaud"), Meisner as a happily married family man, and noted that "Leadon and Felder are almost recluses. An eight-mile-long dirt road separates Felder's rustic ridgeline house from the Pacific Coast Highway far below. On tour, Leadon is a loner who prowls music stores to discover new instruments for his $80,000 collection." The magazine's then-notorious antirock stance was temporarily shelved in its depiction of the Eagles as innocent American Beatle–type popsters, a welcome editorial endorsement of their not very public faces.

In September, the Eagles were awarded the prestigious and highly coveted cover of *Rolling Stone* magazine. They appeared aboard a boat, shirts either open or off, shoeless, except for Henley (in rubber sandals), beer cans in hand, all looking posed and uncomfortably out of place. Henley sported what appeared to be a bubble perm, Frey and Felder wore aviator sunglasses, and while everyone tried to smile, as in most of their posed photos, nobody looked happy.

The majority of the profile focused on Henley and Frey and lauded Azoff. The piece was blessed with a leadoff quote from no less a seventies superstar than Neil Young, in which he declared the Eagles the one band that perfectly captured the new musical feeling coming out of L.A.

At the end of a summer of stadiums and celebrations, benefits and barn burners, the Eagles joined Jackson Browne and Linda Ronstadt in Los Angeles for what was to be the crowning achievement not only for them but for the entire Southern California rock scene. On September 30, 1975, the twentieth anniversary of the death of James Dean, a gorgeous Sunday afternoon layered in warm Santa Ana winds and good vibrations, fifty-five thousand young people showed up at Anaheim Stadium to witness the most anticipated concert of the year.

When the sun began to recede and the sky shifted slowly to purple and orange, Toots and the Maytals kicked things off with a spirited reggae set, followed by Jackson Browne, who then introduced Linda Ronstadt to the now roaring crowd. It was dark by the time she finished and, under the bright blue-white of the overhead spots, the five Eagles, joined by J. D. Souther, finally took the stage. The infield lay covered with blankets and picnic baskets, an ocean of California kids come to see their idols. Endless waves of clean-cut, open-mouthed boys and bikini-clad girls screamed as the band began with a ripping "Lyin' Eyes." The foundation of the stage literally shook from the stomping, cheering force that came up from the now standing crowd. They followed with "Take It Easy," "Good Day in Hell," and "On the Border," a set from *Desperado,* including the title track and "Doolin-Dalton," Bernie Leadon's "Train Leaves Here This Morning," and two new tunes, "You Never Cry Like a Lover," and Tom Waits's "Ol' 55," before ending the set with a rousing version of "Peaceful Easy Feeling." The next series of songs was presented to underscore the new rocking energy of the band. They kicked in with "Midnight Flyer," "James Dean," and the song that brought the crowd back to its feet, "Already Gone."

They were up in the strato-air, young, privileged, and powerful, the first American rock and roll heroes of the seventies. They were superstars, their time was now, and to them, now felt like forever. At the top of their world, they were determined that no one would ever be able to take any of it away.

No one, that is, except themselves.

The Early Years

Crosby, Stills and
Nash. The last great
group of the sixties
and the spiritual god-
fathers of the so-called
Avocado Mafia.
(Henry Diltz/Rebel
Road)

First "official" Eagles publicity photo, taken at Joshua Tree in California.
L to R: Don Henley, Bernie Leadon, Randy Meisner, Glenn Frey.
(Henry Diltz/Rebel Road)

Jackson Browne. The first artist David Geffen signed to Asylum, and the coauthor of several Eagles hits, including "Take It Easy."
(Henry Diltz/Rebel Road)

J. D. Souther, who wrote several Eagles hits, including "New Kid in Town."
(Henry Diltz/Rebel Road)

Linda Ronstadt and J. D. Souther. The Eagles came together as her backup band. Both Ronstadt and Souther had their greatest success on Geffen's Asylum label.
(Henry Diltz/Rebel Road)

Doug Weston outside his legendary Troubadour club.
(Henry Diltz/Rebel Road)

David Geffen among his flock at Boyd Elder's *Chingadōro* ("The Ultimate Thing") art show opening in Venice, California, 1971. L to R: Bernie Leadon, Jackson Browne, John Barrick, unknown, Joni Mitchell, David Geffen, Ned Doheny. (Barrick's early death would be memorialized years later by the Eagles in "The Sad Café.")
(Henry Diltz/Rebel Road)

Simulating a historical photo for the *Desperado* album cover shoot, Agoura, California, 1972. L to R (standing): Gary Burden, Larry Penny, Richard Fernandez, Boyd Elder, Tommy Nixon, John Hartmann, Glyn Johns. L to R (foreground, as the dead Dalton brothers): Jackson Browne, Bernie Leadon, Glenn Frey, Randy Meisner, Don Henley, J. D. Souther.
(Henry Diltz/Rebel Road)

The Glory Years

Don Henley
(Laurens Van Houten/Star File)

Glenn Frey
(Jeff Mayer/Star File)

Bernie Leadon
(Laurens Van Houten/Star File)

Randy Meisner
(Laurens Van Houten/Star File)

Don Henley on rhythm guitar.
(Laurens Van Houten/Star File)

Irving Azoff backstage at Wembley
Stadium, London, England, 1975.
(Andrew Kent)

Don Henley and Glenn Frey
aboard the band's private tour jet.
(Henry Diltz/Rebel Road)

The Teen King, on tour with the
band in Holland, 1975.
(Laurens Van Houten/Star File)

The Eagles'-eye view, Wembley Stadium, London, England, 1975.
(Andrew Kent)

PART TWO

LIFE IN THE FAST LANE

NINE

In the fall of 1974, Don Henley became seriously involved with the stunning, provocative twenty-two-year-old Loree Rodkin, a native of Chicago who'd moved to Southern California in 1971 and fallen in with the Troubadour's front-bar circle of musicians. Soon she had relocated again, this time to study film at New York's New School for Social Research. She returned to L.A. a year later, eager to use her social connections to kick start a career in interior design. She was soon working for some of the bigger names in show business. What separated her from the competition was her combination (rare among Hollywood fame babes) of dark-haired beauty and first-class mind.

Not long after an emotionally draining breakup with actress Suzannah Martin (partially inspiring "The Best of My Love"), Henley met and fell hard for Rodkin, who at first refused to go out with him. Henley, never one to take rejection in anything resembling stride, pursued her that much harder. Rodkin, however, was emotionally unavailable, still nursing a bruised heart over her broken engagement to Bernie Taupin, Elton John's good-looking songwriting partner, and had no desire to date anyone, especially another raunchy rock boy. It wasn't until she discovered through friends that Henley had actually gone to college, majored in English lit, and could hold a conversation, that she relented and agreed to go on a date with him. And then only after having dinner with Glenn Frey.

She hadn't been sexually interested in Frey either, and had only gone out with him on a strictly defined friendship basis. Still, when he showed up at her door in a pair of dirty, ripped jeans, his long hair parted down the middle, which accentuated his heavy nose and long face, resembling what

Rodkin would later describe as a witch, she was physically repulsed. Frey picked up on her smart vibe and pegged her as more the type Henley might go for. Frey may in fact originally have dated her only to play matchmaker. When she did finally give in and date Henley and confessed she didn't know what instrument he played, he patiently gave her a set of his albums.

Not long after, they were buying sheets and pillowcases together. Rodkin moved in so quickly that Henley's housemates, J. D. Souther and his current girlfriend, were caught completely off guard. As far as Henley was concerned, J. D.'s presence was no problem. Rodkin, however, saw things differently. Early in 1975, Henley signed the lease to a new weekend beach house just for the two of them in Malibu.

Once the exclusive province of movie stars and heads of studios, the area had lately been taken over by the hot new stars of the music business. Neil Young kept a beach place nearby, Carole King lived a few houses away, Cheech Marin had a beach pad, so did Elton John, Linda Ronstadt, Harry Nilsson, Bob Dylan, and several members of the Monkees and Fleetwood Mac.

Among the few new people Henley felt comfortable socializing with were Peter and Betsy Asher. Betsy was a onetime Greenwich Village coffeehouse waitress who'd quit the cream-and-sugar circuit to work for the Rolling Stones' New York office before moving west to follow the flow, with friends Alice Ochs (Phil Ochs's ex-wife) and David Blue. Not long after her arrival in L.A., she met and married Peter Asher, and became close to Linda Ronstadt and Loree Rodkin. To Betsy, and others, the somewhat extroverted, spontaneous, energetic Rodkin and the usually quiet, shy, often sullen Henley made for the oddest of couples. It was not only his moodiness but the way Henley treated Rodkin that Asher couldn't quite figure out. For one thing, there were the "Henley household rules" that had to be followed. Like when it came to cleanliness. After "KP," Henley would stand with a sponge in his hand and inspect the countertops. If he found so much as a spot of orange juice or the tiniest crumb of toast, he would insist it could not be his, and Rodkin had to clean up immediately.

Other issues surfaced as Henley experienced domestic life with a female for the first time. One problem was that he remained far too interested in chasing other women. Several times a week, Henley and Souther liked to go out together for a night on the town. They were, after all, two of the best-looking and most successful single men in L.A. They had their choice of the most beautiful babes in Hollywood, and they knew it. According to one friend, the two were quite full of themselves, and with good reason. "They could make any woman feel lucky to be in the running. J. D. was the love of everyone's life. He had this fantastic ability to make every girl feel like she was the only one for him and forever, when what he really meant was for however long it lasted. He often dated the hottest looking and most successful Hollywood actresses, including Marcia Strassman and the absolutely gorgeous video queen Kay Lenz. Both were really happening at the time, and both were really crazy about J. D." It was, if anything, to be expected, all part of the process that dictated so much of how these boys lived their lives. Another friend recalled with a smile how they'd phone their girlfriends to say they were going to be stuck in the studio, good night dear, while some other young woman was lying naked next to them in a hotel room.

At first, Rodkin tolerated Henley's womanizing, rationalizing it by viewing it as an essential part of his creative process: muses to his ears, that sort of thing. Nor was Henley the only one in his circle whose rock was "inspired" by the adventures of romance. One night Jackson Browne punched an unemployed actor "defending a woman's dignity" at a local bar and wound up getting the shit beaten out of him. He got the girl too. The unemployed actor was Dylan's pal Bobby Neuwirth. The girl became Jackson's wife. The song was called "Sooner or Later." It was how the process worked.

According to Henley, "A lot of times a girl one of us had gone out with liked to think the songs we wrote were about her. All the songs are composites, really. There's some of every girl that I've ever been with in all my songs; they're combinations of characters, like fiction. Some of the more derogatory parts of 'Hotel California,' however, are definitely about Loree Rodkin — *Her mind is Tiffany twisted, she got the Mercedes bends; she got a lot of pretty pretty boys that she calls friends* — that's about her, and I wouldn't be crowing if I were Ms. Rodkin. As far as I'm concerned, she's the Norma Desmond of her generation."

The everyday rules of the studio became a bigger problem for Rodkin, as the Eagles' post–Patti Davis edict dictated that no girlfriends were allowed inside. To her, this meant she was expected to assume the position of sweet little woman waiting with dinner on the table when Henley got home from a hard day at the office. Definitely not her style. Nor was catering to Henley's at-home work habits. Writing was often an agonizing process for Henley. It could take months for him to write a song. He could spend days lying around, sitting on a chair, staring off into space, then scrawling lyrics on a yellow legal pad. He might come up with one or two lines he liked, maybe a verse, leave them, and go back months later. Henley had a great ear and was constantly trying to work phrases he overheard into songs, things like this guy is "brutally handsome," or that girl "terminally pretty." Sometimes, when nothing came, Henley might disappear for days, to Frey's house or to a hotel where there were no distractions to his concentration.

Or pressure from the record company, which was constantly pushing the band for new product. Feeling it from all sides, early in 1976, Henley developed a serious stomach disorder. According to one friend, during those days, "Tagamet was his best friend, and that other crap he always drank right out of the bottle, Mylanta. Sometimes he'd have this little white mustache, like a kid with a glass of milk, from it."

It all finally became too much for Rodkin. No longer willing to tolerate Henley's relentless womanizing, moodiness, and what one close to the scene described as the "need to argue and win every time as a nervous tic the relationship couldn't resist," one morning she woke up, decided it was over, and left. According to someone close to the relationship, "Rodkin did teach Henley a great deal about 'things'—which sheets to buy, what art nouveau lamps were cool—but at the end of the day they had very little in common. The relationship was basically about sex, but that wasn't enough to keep it together. She was trying to turn him into something he was not, and he grew increasingly unhappy with the lifestyle she had chosen for them."

Henley waited nearly a month before contacting her, using as the reason his excitement about a new song he'd written called "Wasted Time." By all reports, Rodkin was not amused, even after Henley went to great lengths to explain the song: that it was not about wasting time (with her), but *wasted* time, a difference a bit too subtle for even the most discerning critic. It was a kind of farewell song, he insisted. Then he told her that the real reason he'd called was that he wanted to get back together. Not possible,

Rodkin said. She was already involved. So quickly? Yes. With who? A very successful man. *Who?* Her former fiancé, Bernie Taupin. *Click.*

The pain of this breakup stayed with Henley for a long time. He left the beach and moved in again with Frey, now living high in Dorothy Lamour's former house, built in 1942 atop Trousdale, with a 360-degree view, in the Hollywood Hills. After settling in, Henley tried to focus on songs for the new album. In between sessions, to let off steam and recharge their batteries, Henley and Frey liked to get stoned and go out looking for women. "Glenn and I would go through a series of moving in together and then moving out," Henley recalled years later. "We'd have girlfriends and live with them for a while, and then we'd get ready to do an album and we'd move back in together. Dudes on a rampage . . . [We were] the odd couple. I was sort of the housekeeper, the tidy one. He was the lovable slob. All around the house he'd leave these little Century Cities of cigarette butts standing on end. Burns all over the furniture and carpet, coffee cups all over the place. We would get up every Sunday, watch football together, scream and yell, and spill things."

"Or we'd have a little coffee, maybe a beer, and start writing songs. We'd work in the mornings, sometimes all afternoon. There was a room in the house that had originally been built as a rehearsal studio for singers. We soundproofed it and made a little recording studio for ourselves.

"On our first albums, Glenn did a lot of composing on guitar. Around this time he started writing on the piano a lot more. Sometimes we'd start with a lyric, other times a melody. There was no set pattern to it. We'd come up with a title a lot of times and then go from there. With 'Lyin' Eyes,' he had the lyric, then the hook, then some chords, and I helped write the verses. Sometimes I'd come in with an idea, and he'd sit down at the piano and just start playing. I'd sit on the couch and smoke cigarettes and listen to him play piano. When I heard something that I thought would fit, I'd come in.

"At night, when we'd finish, we'd go down to the Troubadour, or maybe Dan Tana's, and hang together. These were really wonderful days.

"After that he moved to Coldwater Canyon, into James Cagney's old house. It was small, almost like a guest house that Cagney had built. The estate was bigger than that at one point, and this was the little piece that was left. Cagney was still alive when Glenn rented it. I remember the day

Glenn walked in to look at it, and Cagney was sitting there playing the piano. He got up, put his arm around Glenn, and started walking him around the room, talking about all the parties he'd had there, if-these-walls-could-talk kind of thing. We wrote a lot of songs in that house too."

Late in 1975, Henley became involved with Stevie Nicks of Fleetwood Mac, a relationship that made headlines.

Nicks had begun her singing career in San Francisco in the late sixties, met guitarist Lindsey Buckingham, and moved with him to Los Angeles, where they tried to break into the new spawning ground for mainstream rock. In 1975, they met drummer Mick Fleetwood, shortly thereafter joined him in the tenth configuration of his group, and recorded the groundbreaking *Fleetwood Mac*. Released on Warner/Reprise in August of 1975, it charted for over a year and sent the band on the road for an extended tour.

One night, Henley, long an admirer and aware of the competition between the two bands for best-selling album of the year, decided to pick up the phone and call Nicks, even though they'd never met or talked to each other before. The two hit it off, and a series of intense wherever-you-are-I'll-find-you phone calls ensued, during which they commiserated on the loneliness of the long-distance rock-star lifestyle. Henley, still full of Rodkin, found a sympathetic soul in Nicks, who'd recently split from Buckingham. How much worse off was she, Nicks asked Henley, having to perform with her ex every night?

Inevitably, the two groups played the same cities. Knowing Henley was planning to make an appearance backstage one night, Mick Fleetwood and John and Christine McVie of the Mac decided to play a little joke on Nicks by sending her a bouquet of flowers with a card "signed" by Henley that read, "The Best of My Love . . . Tonight? Don . . ." A highly offended Nicks fumed over what she considered Henley's arrogance, until he convinced her he had nothing to do with the prank. The two then began a serious two-year affair.

Nicks remembered it this way. "When Lindsey and I broke up during *Rumours*, I started going out with Don. . . . He was *really* cute, and he was elegant. Don taught me how to spend money. I just watched him, that's how. He didn't visibly set out to do that. I just watched him. He was okay with, say, buying a house [just] like that, or sending a Lear jet to pick you up.

"He is sexy. He's such an interesting guy. Here's one thing that Don did that freaked my band out so much. We were all in Miami, Fleetwood Mac and the Eagles. They're recording at this gorgeous house they'd rented on the water. It's totally romantic, like Mar-a-Lago. Anyway, he sends a limousine driver over to our hotel with a box of presents for me, and they delivered it right into the breakfast room where everyone's eating. There's a stereo, a bunch of fabulous records. There's incredible flowers and fruits, beautiful . . . The limousine driver is taking all this out onto the table, and I'm going 'Oh, please, please, this is not going to go down well.' And they want to know who it's from. And Lindsey is not happy. . . . So I went out with Don for a while. I went out with J. D. Souther for a while [as well]. We had an incredible time. Those Eagles were an interesting group of guys."

She became pregnant, and neither doubted Henley was the father. The "situation" was resolved quickly and quietly when Nicks, between tour dates, had an abortion. Although Henley did not try to force the issue, according to friends, she was deeply upset about what she considered his fast and easy consent to her decision. Nicks took it as Henley's way of saying he wasn't interested in any type of serious long-term commitment. As had become his pattern, in the beginning Henley played the ultimate Southern-charm gentleman — flowers, phone calls, words of love, Lear jets to Paris for romantic dinners. In the end he was distant, unreachable, brooding, argumentative, and elusive. It was a pattern by now so familiar to the Eagles crew it had become a running joke. Henley's favored method of seduction came to be known as "Love 'em and Lear 'em."

Years later, Henley had this to say about his affair with Nicks: "[Stevie had] named the unborn kid Sara, and she had an abortion." She then wrote the song of the same name (which became a huge hit for her) and, according to Henley, dedicated it "to the spirit of the aborted baby."

Frey, on the other hand, had no such romantic complications. He simply believed he loved them all, and they loved him. That is, until Janey Beggs, a Fort Worth debutante whose family wealth and influence made it seem to Frey as if he were dating an American princess.

They had met in July 1975 at a dinner party, and by all accounts, Frey was immediately smitten. He pursued her for months, an astonishing time for him to remain interested in one woman, and late that fall they began living together in Santa Fe. Having recently played a gig there with the Eagles, Frey had been won over by the town's desertlike terrain and large number of resident artists.

And something else. Although he was still reluctant to admit it, he was now doing incredible amounts of coke, and the more he did, the more people seemed to want to give him. He needed a physical escape from temptation and thought he'd found it in Santa Fe. He felt safe among the communities of musicians and painters, away from the pressures of rock superstardom. He hoped to be accepted as just one more artist in town, even if he was the one with seven gold records (three albums, four singles). He and Beggs went out of their way to be accessible to Santa Fe's colony of artists, took an active part in the town's affairs, and often entertained friends at their adobe-style home.

Until somebody set it on fire.

Twice.

Not long after, it was broken into, and Frey's checkbook was stolen. Frey paper began showing up everywhere. Glenn's initial reaction to these events was to get high. After the fires and the break-in, he found himself doing more coke than ever, often an eight-ball (eighth of a gram) at a time, laid out in one fat, curvy line for a swift roundhouse snort. This wreaked havoc on his relationship with Beggs, who'd come from a background that frowned upon such anti-Christian vices as drinking. It also eventually destroyed the lining of Frey's nose, which he had to have surgically repaired twice, the second time with Teflon to replace the mucous membranes. It complicated his stomach problems as well. Like Henley (and Meisner), Frey had developed a burning stomach.

Friends of the band suspected coke fueled the ongoing and increasingly tense battles between Henley and Frey, which were mostly over one issue: who was the group's creative leader. Both Henley and Frey were by now heavy coke users, but it seemed to give Henley the control advantage because he appeared to function in the studio better when he was on it. In spite of the others' objections, he gradually came to dominate the focus and direction of the group's music.

After the success of *One of These Nights,* it was hard for anybody to argue against the obvious: that Henley had moved to the front and become the Eagles' major creative force. Indeed, he had gone from the shy drummer upstage behind the kit (like the shy boy alone and safe behind the wheel of his car) to a self-styled singer of distinction and a sharp, if dark, lyricist to be reckoned with. Frey had sung only one solo lead on *One of These Nights*, although "Lyin' Eyes" was arguably the record's best track. From that point on, Frey would never again share equal singing or writing time on any Eagles album with Henley.

Years later, Henley tried to explain Frey's acquiescence. "[Glenn] was generous in that respect. He would push another guy up to the front and say, 'You carry the ball for a while and I'll just sit back here and block.' He was a good team player that way, a good captain."

"In many ways we were equal," he says. "If I began to do more than he did, it was because if someone had a strong suit he would play that card. 'You sing this, you sing it better,' that kind of thing. He certainly remained an integral part of the production of all the albums. Arranging was always his strong suit. We used to call him 'the Lone Arranger' because he was so good at it."

In truth, Frey may have chosen to step back, or he may have been pushed. Or he may have come to prefer coke to chords, or simply not have been strong enough to hold onto the reins of power.

All of which may have proved the breaking point for Leadon, who felt the ongoing internal struggle for creative control was the main reason for the band's losing whatever was left of its, meaning his, original country sound. He also had to have been dissatisfied with the resulting diminishing share of publishing money, having received sole credit on only one song from *One of These Nights*, "Journey of the Sorcerer," and cowriting credit on only two others, "Hollywood Waltz" (with his brother Tom, Henley, and Frey) and "I Wish You Peace" (with Patti Davis). None was released as a single.

According to Randy Meisner, one night during a preproduction meeting in a hotel room in Cincinnati, while Henley and Frey were arguing over who was going to tell the other what to do and what the other thought of that idea, Leadon told Frey to cool down, poured a beer on his head, and walked out. Henley recalls: "Yeah, that happened, but it only marked the end of it. One reason Leadon didn't last in the band was that he was so contrary. Success freaked him out a little; he was always 'worried' about our success, about coming from a 'pure' bluegrass background and making it in rock and roll. He thought we were selling out from the very beginning. To me, the point was to reach as many people as possible. To Bernie, I think he saw that as meaning we had to soften our sound, to commercialize, which wasn't the case at all. If you want to be a cult band, or marginal, fine, go do it. Glenn and I wanted to make it all the way, and also to make some money, because we didn't think it was going to last that long. To me, it wasn't just an art or entertainment. It was a job. I looked at it like being in football. After a while, your knees go and you have to start selling insurance. He didn't see it that way, and it made him angry and frustrated." After months of repeated denials, on December 20, 1975, Front Line released a brief statement confirming the rumors that Bernie Leadon was no longer an Eagle.

His replacement came faster than a deejay could cut to a commercial. Even as he continued to publicly deny Leadon's imminent departure, Irving Azoff put together a deal to make Joe Walsh the newest Eagle. The official announcement about Walsh came immediately after the one confirming Leadon's departure.

Walsh's joining the Eagles was one of the more unusual moves in rock, particularly during the seventies, when it was common for record labels, managers, and lead singers to break up groups to develop the strongest individual component parts as solo acts. It was relatively rare for a successful solo act, which Walsh had become, to retreat from the spotlight into another band, especially as a high-profile replacement.

By all accounts, including Walsh's, it was indeed Azoff who first came up with the idea. "I believed in him," Walsh said. "I'd be with him whatever he did. . . . Anyway, [being part of an established group] took a whole lot of weight off my shoulders."

Still, he was not immediately accepted by the other members of the band, more than one of whom wondered if "Rocky Mountain Way" belonged on the same stage as "Peaceful Easy Feeling." Walsh was only allowed in after Azoff managed to convince a reluctant Don Henley that it was the best move for the band. Henley's hesitation wasn't hard to understand. Leadon's departure had not left a musical gap. If anything, it helped sharpen the band's harder edge. Moreover, it had taken years for Henley to complete his symbolic move to the front. Walsh, Henley knew, was his own man, and easily the hardest rocker among them, Frey included. He was also a great stage performer, a real crowd pleaser with a high-caliber star quality all his own. Henley didn't want Walsh to come on like an American Pete Townshend and upset the component balance of the band.

It had to have been a masterful selling job by Azoff. It was clear by now to everyone in the group that as Frey had been Geffen's boy, Henley was Azoff's. This surrogate dad loved everything about his favorite son, and it appeared that Henley thrived on that level of devotion, even if it meant letting another sibling into the family. Perhaps to maintain his idea of the status quo, early on Henley told Walsh in no uncertain terms that the Eagles did not "perform" onstage. This "Henley doctrine" insisted any movement, theatrics, or fancy lights distracted from the sound of a show, that it was the music, after all, that audiences came to hear. Walsh, one of the best stage performers in rock, had to agree to a certain amount of handcuffing in order to get past Henley, who resented what he considered to be Walsh's star trip. It was as if it were the guitarist helping the band out and not the other way around. "When we brought Joe in he definitely helped the band," Henley said later on, "but I think Joe had the attitude that he was doing us a favor. In fact, his career was in really bad shape at that time. He wasn't getting anywhere. It was a shot in the arm for him, certainly, and I think he was ashamed of it for a while."

Walsh, coming off a string of solo hit singles and albums and definitely not into shame, was from the beginning put off by what he saw as Henley's self-centered pomposity, and early on considered leaving the group altogether. At one point he went to Henley's oldest friend, Richard Bowden, for advice. "Joe Walsh came to me just after he joined the Eagles and said, 'You've known [Henley] the longest. Tell him to relax,' " Bowden told a journalist years later. "I told him to just let Don be tense. He's always been that way. When he solves one situation, he just moves on to something else to worry about." Assured that the problem really was Henley's, Walsh permanently committed himself to the group.

According to Henley, "Joe did have some run-ins with Glenn and me regarding other matters, one being Joe's campaign to add his longtime drummer, Joe Vitale, to the band as an equal partner. The Eagles had hired Vitale as an additional tour drummer, and the two Joes decided, during an all-night drug-and-booze marathon somewhere on the tour, that Vitale should be an official band member with full equity. Needless to say, Glenn and I—after six years of busting our assess—did not have warm and fuzzy feelings for that idea."

The Eagles began 1976 with another world tour, which also meant the start of production on the new album would have to be postponed. Part of the stated reason for touring was to test one or two of the new songs, the other, unspoken, was to make sure Joe Walsh fit in.

Walsh became the most popular live Eagle. His slightest gyration, grimace, or stylistic wrist-bending flourish never failed to bring roars from the sold-out stadium crowds, and he milked it for all it was worth. Walsh's playing was so good that Don Felder could now share lead guitar duties, something that made him less than thrilled with the newest Eagle. Frey, meanwhile, took the opportunity presented by Walsh's arrival to express his approval and shoot this verbal jab at Leadon: "Well," he told an interviewer, "[Walsh's addition is] as good as we thought it would be; the guitar playing in the band, and the musical platforms, are much more to my liking now."

In some ways, Walsh was a natural-born Eagle. Along with his collection of guitars, he took a chain saw on tour, which he liked to use on hotel-room furniture, usually tossing the pieces out the window. The saw had been a welcome gift from Larry Solters, whom Azoff had chosen to handle the group's public relations. Solters had learned the profession working with his father, one of the partners in Solters, Roskin, Friedman, whose wide range of clients included Frank Sinatra, Barbra Streisand, Carol Channing, and Barbi Benton. With his father's blessing, Solters left the firm in 1976 to join Front Line Management. His first day at 9126 Sunset, he asked Azoff where his desk was. "No desk," Azoff said, pointing to an empty corner. Solters blended in and soon learned about the special requirements of working with the Eagles, the band Azoff assigned to him. The Eagles were in desperate need of someone to handle the press. They ignored nearly every request for interviews, were rude to anybody from the media, liked to raise hell, and didn't care who knew. It became one of Solters's primary objectives to keep the band out of the newspapers, where coverage was usually negative, due to the Eagles' lack of PR savvy and offstage propensities.

Joe Walsh, meanwhile, wasted no time in sharpening his sawing skills during a night in Indianapolis when he had adjoining rooms with Azoff.

Walsh objected to the adjoining rooms and used the chain saw to turn the separate quarters into one grand suite. A little later on, at the Astor Towers, he did $35,000 worth of damage with the saw and then decided to try to cut the wallpaper off the bedroom walls. Another time the band stayed in a hotel in Washington that was undergoing renovations, refurbishing the odd floors. Walsh decided to help them out with the even ones.

Even when he was the victim of the joke, Azoff could get into it. One time Walsh snuck into Azoff's room and cut the legs off all the furniture so everything would seem smaller than it really was to the manager. In retaliation, Azoff nailed all of Walsh's furniture to the ceiling. Another time, a hotel manager had to close the pool after Walsh decided to carve up a painting of a sixteenth-century nobleman hanging alongside. Using a penknife, he defaced the work by carving "Party Til Ya Puke" in the canvas.

Walsh's favorable critical reception further unsettled Henley, especially when, after seeing the latest configuration of the band, rock critic Robert Hilburn wrote in the *Los Angeles Times,* "The good news this morning for Eagles fans is that the band may be more appealing than ever. It retains — both musically and conceptually — the basic Eagles sound, but Walsh brings the potential for a slightly tougher, more forceful edge to the music."

While Walsh assumed the role of the latest golden Eagle, Azoff continued to manipulate the band's every offstage move, his actions intended to put the word out to promoters that the Eagles were not a band to mess with. During the tour, he committed the band to appear at the New England Folk Festival, only to cancel prior to their scheduled appearance because part of the band's guarantee hadn't been paid on time. Not long after, Azoff attended a conference entitled "Working Together: Overcoming Obstacles to Cooperation in the Talent Business." After pontificating on the subject, he turned the floor over to New England Folk Festival producer Richard Romanello and started to walk away. Taking the microphone, Romanello pointed to Azoff and shouted, "Turn around, Irv, because I'm suing you for a million dollars!"

The next day, Azoff countersued for $7 million, charging, among other things, slander and mental anguish. A few weeks later, both suits were dropped.

Whereas Geffen had tried to elevate the band's importance by creating a mystique around them, Azoff traveled a far simpler and more tangible route. His singular goal was to make the Eagles the most profitable band in the business. According to Steve Wax, then executive vice president of WEA, Azoff could "drive us all a little crazy" with his intense focus on promoting the Eagles. "When they were still at the middle-growth stage he'd rush them into cities as soon as their records hit the charts. Two weeks after 'One of These Nights' hit in Chicago, the Eagles were playing there."

If Geffen didn't exactly approve of Azoff's tactics, he was careful not to say so in public. He wisely chose to keep a respectful distance between himself and the band until, in December 1975, he was promoted to the position of vice president of Warner Brothers Pictures. As part of that deal, Geffen was required to sell his remaining passive financial interests in Asylum to Steve Ross's Warner Communications, Inc.

To Geffen, the leap into film was at once the realization of his most sought-after professional goal and the beginning of his worst personal nightmare. In less than a decade, having started in the mail-room obscurity of the William Morris Agency, he had become one of the most powerful men in Hollywood. It was the challenge of making it in the movies that made him want in to that world.

It was cancer that took him out.

Or rather, a cancer scare. At the age of thirty-two, rich and powerful, David Geffen walked out of his doctor's office one day early in 1976 with the news that he had a tumor on his bladder that would have to be removed. Frightened and confused, Geffen, who had earlier that year handed in his resignation to Steve Ross, the chairman of Warner, over, among other things, a disagreement as to the fluctuating value of his stock and option deal, decided the time had come to move back to New York City.

Geffen's meteoric rise had lately fallen behind a cloud of disappointment and disinterest. No sooner had he left, or been legally forced out of, his partnership with Roberts and given up control of the Eagles than the group's revenues skyrocketed. The $7 million Geffen received for Asylum was now thought by some to have been far too low in comparison to what the label's acts, led by the Eagles, were currently grossing. Geffen shrugged off those who thought he'd come out on the wrong end of that deal. He'd been reaching for something higher, something most wouldn't have had the nerve to even think about. Then there was the Roxy, the Sunset club he'd owned a piece of. Here too, he'd fallen out of love with the business of the business of music. He'd quickly discovered that owning a club was like running a restaurant; the work and the hours were never justified by how good the meal you prepared for others tasted in their mouths. Any whispers that followed the financial folly of the Roxy only confirmed for Geffen that he was no Doug Weston. Small potatoes, in the end, were not Geffen's favorite cash crop.

He briefly considered a run as an independent film producer after his resignation, but decided instead to read the handwriting on Hollywood's Walk of Fame and retrace his own footsteps to success. As Geffen recalls, "I had already left Warner Brothers at the time of the diagnosis, basically because they were unhappy with me and me with them. Quite frankly, I wasn't well suited to the job. I was young and rich; who needed all the stress and tension? I'd had a good scare and wanted to enjoy myself now by heading east and having a good time."

At least one former client believes Geffen used the excuse of a "questionable" tumor as a way to get out of a series of embarrasing deals. "He had worn out his welcome, and nothing was working for him. The sale of Asylum was a joke — the Eagles alone grossed more in one year than he got paid for it. He was, to say the least, not suited to cater to the public, and his film career was nonexistent. If he didn't have a tumor, he could have invented one, because it provided the perfect excuse to crawl out of town with his tail between his legs — done, of course, in the patented Geffen style of poor, poor, pitiful and very rich me."

Geffen's departure prompted Azoff to immediately file a ten-million-dollar suit against Warner Communications for the return of all outstanding Eagles copyrights. Azoff's position, and the Eagles', was that Warner had no right to the ownership of any Eagles music, because Geffen had acquired it through an allegedly illegal conflict of interest when he was still the Eagles' manager, publisher, and owner of the label for which they recorded. Azoff insisted that all outstanding rights, including those that had passed from Geffen and Asylum to WCI, be immediately returned to the band.

"Bullshit," according to Geffen. "It was bullshit then and it's bullshit now. After I left the company, [Henley, Frey, and Azoff] sued to get back half the publishing I owned, claiming that I had cheated [them] out of it, when in fact *I gave Henley* the half he owned in the first place. He didn't own any of it in the beginning. Because of the nature of his first deal, it had all been owned by Jimmy Bowen. The whole issue was really created by Irving Azoff to try to get a settlement out of Warners."

As might be expected, Azoff's actions infuriated everyone in a position of power at Warner, no one more than Joe Smith, who, upon Geffen's departure, had taken over as head of the music division. It was a delicate situation, because the Eagles were the most profitable band on the label. Smith wished he had ten Eagles albums a year instead of one, a slender enough output now thrown into jeopardy by Azoff's assault. "There's no question," Smith recalled, "the engine that was powering the Warner music machine was the Eagles, because they sold in such incredible numbers. Jackson [Browne] broke loose too in that period, and Linda Ronstadt had her greatest success, but the Eagles were by far the biggest act we had."

It was true. At the time of Smith's taking over the reins of power at Warner, the Eagles were selling a million albums a month and responsible for 57 percent of the label's gross. And Azoff knew it: "Whenever I'd call Smith, I'd tell the receptionist it was 'fifty-seven percent' calling."

Smith, like Geffen, knew that Azoff was going to have to be dealt with, and carefully. He came with the Eagles, and if you wanted the band, you had to take Azoff. Smith recalled, "When I first took over from Geffen, Irving took over Chasen's for lunch and had all his artists come to greet me, which was a terrific thing to do. Twenty minutes after lunch he insisted on renegotiating the Eagles deal."

It would prove to be a long and complex renegotiation. As was his style, once Azoff saw his opening, he pounced. He not only wanted those copyrights returned, but now demanded an increase in royalties as well, *retroactive to the Eagles' first album.* Smith, hoping to work a deal, looked over the band's contracts and found a little room to maneuver. The truth was, the Eagles, for all their success, were among the lower-paid supergroups at the time. The Rolling Stones, for example, had a deal in the 20 percent range, while the Eagles were still hovering around 12.

Dealing with Azoff, Smith soon learned, was especially difficult due to what he described as Irving's short attention span, cut with an especially mean-spirited sense of practical joking. "He has the concentration time of a flea. One time during negotiations, I took off my shoes, and Irving hid them. He put them in a refrigerator. Another time I was dealing with a lawyer for another group, and suddenly I said to this lawyer, who wanted a fifty-thousand-dollar advance for greatest hits rights, 'I'll tell you what. I'll flip you. . . . If I win, you get nothing; if you win, I'll give you a hundred thousand for it.' The lawyer didn't go for it, but Irving, who happened to be there, did. And convinced the other guy. 'That's it, yeah, yeah, let's go. . . .'

"It was so odd, seeing him willing to flip for a hundred thousand dollars of an artist's money! I remember the lawyer turning to Azoff and saying, 'You must never, never say anything,' Irving's cue to rush out the door and get on the phone.

"He had all these little tricks that he'd pull to get more money out of the company. Whenever the Eagles had an album coming out, he would send every bill that ever came to his office to us to be paid, whether it was the electric bill, Don Henley's car lease, anything, assuming most of it would get through, because if any of the kids in accounting or the other departments bucked it back to him, he'd scream, 'I'll kill that Smith!' So I had to get everybody together before we had an album and say, 'We've been soft; we have not known terror for a while. Now, terror will be visiting us.'"

Azoff's tactics may have been a visitation of terror on Joe Smith or something, if less dramatic, more calculated. Smith believed that at least partly, the band's delay in going back into the studio was Azoff's way of pressuring the label into settling the copyright issue before it went to court. At this point, a new Eagles album could balance the label's books for the entire year. As Smith recalled, "Every time [the Eagles] put out a record, Irving renegotiated their royalties. Holding back a record might represent thirty-five million, forty million lost in billing. The Beatles used to knock off three albums a year. Three Eagles albums could take ten years . . . and Jackson Browne, our other huge artist at the time, would make a record every time Halley's Comet came around."

Azoff may, as Smith and others believed, have been keeping the band on the road and out of the studio until all their differences with the company were settled, or he may simply have been buying time for the boys, who might not have had enough material in place for a new album.

In March 1976, having succeeded in getting their royalties adjusted, Azoff allowed the Eagles to return to the studio. The copyright issue was resolved in principle, as one party put it, before a single deposition was taken (although it would take years to be officially settled). However, it was not soon enough to prevent a flood of bad press for Geffen. Once that of the golden-boy, artist-friendly genius of rock, his image took a beating when court papers revealed the extent of his early conflict-of-interest machinations, which did not seem to bother Azoff at all. Geffen, however, felt the wound deeply and carried hard feelings over it toward the band, Henley, and Azoff for years.

Exhilarated, if exhausted, by what had developed into a three-month around-the-world tour, no sooner did the Eagles return to L.A. than they learned they had to leave again. Bill Szymczyk was now insisting on recording the new album in Miami, at that city's famed Criteria Studios. The Eagles preferred being closer to home, on the more familiar professional turf of the Record Plant in L.A., but Szymczyk insisted his position was nonnegotiable. His reason, he explained, was completely logical, a morbid fear of earthquakes, which would prevent him from ever working in Los Angeles again. Eventually a compromise was reached, and at least half the album was laid down at the Record Plant.

The Eagles' purposeful delay in recording had prompted Smith, looking for a way to boost the label's revenue, to follow through on one of Geffen's final acts before leaving the company and issue an Eagles "best of" compilation album. Greatest hits albums are always moneymakers for everybody because there are almost no production costs or advances, usually the two largest up-front expenses. Smith's move paid off when the album proved a monster, the band's, and rock and roll's, biggest selling album of all time. Released on February 17, 1976, *Eagles — Their Greatest Hits 1971–1975* was certified platinum (one million sales) its first week in stores and in its initial release remained on *Billboard*'s top 200 for two and a half years.

Despite this enormous financial windfall, more than one Eagle grumbled within earshot of the label his displeasure at the compilation, claiming it was nothing more than a ploy by the record company to sell product without having to pay additional production costs. An amused Smith noted in response that the members of the band benefited as well from the additional sales of prerecorded songs without having to spend any more time writing or in the studio. Not the point, Henley told those who would listen. It was about the *integrity* of the original music. In this post–*Sgt. Pepper* era, bands like the Eagles prided themselves on the concepts binding albums like *Desperado*. Henley felt that the use of "Desperado" and "Tequila Sunrise," lifted out of their original album context, was detrimental to the nature, quality, and meaning of the music.

Henley says: "It's that typical corporate thinking. All the record company was worried about were their quarterly reports. They didn't give a shit whether the greatest hits album was good or not, they just wanted product. It's what was so frustrating, the forced and hideous marriage of art and commerce. They didn't make good bedfellows, as far as we were concerned. Yes, Joe Smith was always pushing us to work faster, but we worked as hard and fast as we could without killing ourselves, and we almost killed ourselves anyway. Some things can't be rushed. Quarterly projections and stockholders and board members were their problem, not ours. I refused then and still do to have my music dictated by that."

Whatever in-house complaints the band had were effectively muted by Smith's being able to point to the enormous success of *Eagles — Their Greatest Hits*. However, in part because of it, Henley and Frey were convinced the band still wasn't being taken seriously by the label or the critics, and they became more determined than ever that the next album would be the one to erase any lingering doubts that this was a great rock and roll band. Maybe the greatest.

They already had the concept and a working title. The concept had to do with taking a look at all that the band had gone through, personally and professionally, while it was still happening to them. "We were getting an extensive education," Henley says, "in life, in love, in business. Beverly Hills was still a mythical place to us. In that sense, it became something of a symbol, and the 'Hotel' the locus of all that L.A. had come to mean for us. In a sentence, I'd sum it up as the end of the innocence, round one."

The working title was "Hotel California."

TEN

By 1975, the worldwide demand was so great that manufacturing plants worked around the clock turning out Eagles albums and tapes. On tour, everyone in the group and its manager traveled by a private jet (referred to as the "party plane"), often having breakfast in one city and lunch in another. They stayed in the finest hotels (*all right*), and band members built homes in California, Santa Fe, and Aspen. They were American rock royalty, with all the material privileges accorded to those who ascend via talent rather than birthright.

The high-flying Eagles may have believed the world now and forever belonged to them, but the suits knew better. They understood that the biggest rock stars rarely stayed on the charts for more than seven years, the rough equivalent of the peak teenage-to-early-twenties record-buying days. Such was the mind-set of Joe Smith when he looked at his roster of stars and realized his most important group was into its fifth contract year. No matter how he looked at it, sociologically, culturally, politically, or economically, the band was doing a hundred and twenty toward the great brick wall of obsolescence waiting just over the hill.

And then, on an ultracool October night in a small packed club on the Sunset Strip, the wall got a little closer.

If the Eagles functioned off the dialectic between Henley's icy intellect and Frey's emotional heat, Bruce Springsteen's front was the ultimate solo. He was literally and figuratively "the Boss." The Eagles idealized the Southern California sound of white middle-class teens of the seventies; Springsteen celebrated the ethos of the East Coast urban working kid. The Eagles hardly moved onstage; Springsteen was the ultimate live performer. The Eagles were "laid back." Bruce . . . *wasn't*. And finally, the Eagles were for the most part dismissed by reviewers and loved by their record-buying fans, while Springsteen was the greatest critic's darling since Bob Dylan, even if before *Born to Run* he'd sold so few records Columbia had considered dropping him.

As late as 1975, Jackson Browne was still the only one of the Eagles-Souther-Ronstadt axis who "got" Bruce Springsteen, and only because they had both spent part of their early years in Greenwich Village, where Browne often ran into Springsteen on the coffeehouse circuit. When advance word that Bruce was coming to town hit L.A. the summer of '75, it was met by a largely indifferent rock crowd, both in the business and on the street, an indifference that came to an end the night Springsteen played the Roxy and blasted onto the scene and into the psyche of the seventies Sunset Boulevard generation.

Rock and roll's shifting cycles can be landmarked by the arrival of a handful of icons. In 1956, Elvis Presley unquestionably defined the primal image of rock and roll and in doing so altered the face, look, and sexual mores of the white teens of the fifties. In 1962, Bob Dylan reinvented the root poetics of rock, sharpening its musical focus while expanding its lyrical and ethnic landscape. Two years later, the Beatles commercialized the essence of R&B and pop and in doing so helped channel Dylan's cool countercultural tidal wave into the warmer waters of the mainstream.

Nineteen seventy-one marked both the rise of corporate rock as personified by Clive Davis at Columbia and the emergence of a new and powerful independent artist movement in the form of David Geffen's Asylum. While Davis sought to exploit the politics of the sixties for commercial purposes, Geffen meant to bring rock back (and therefore move it forward) to the place he thought it belonged — corporately headquartered but emotionally located in the hearts and minds of a new generation. By 1975, the Eagles' West Coast sound that was the progressive (if by now solidly corporate) foundation of Asylum had come to dominate American music.

However, a year later, Bruce Springsteen's breakthrough on (post-Davis) Columbia revitalized the East Coast sound of the city's soulful streets and in doing so once more revamped pop culture's heroic iconography. After *Born to Run,* the essential image of rock was recast once more in the persona of a charismatic solo artist with backup band rather than the faceless fraternal equanimity of a group.

Rock and roll has always jumped rather than drifted onto youth's latest cultural pose. The moves are easier to recognize in retrospect — the repressive fifties convulsing with Elvis, the intellectual first half of the sixties articulated by Dylan. The sixties' migration of the music from Greenwich Village to the West Coast was a microcosm of the cultural direction of youth's free spirit, a creative pilgrimage, as well as a rejection of the European-dominated environment of the boomers' parents. Despite the internal struggles, the Eagles' presentation as a group represented the abstract of the faceless Vietnam army troop, the barracks mentality, the subversion of the individual. The rise of Springsteen perfectly followed the end-of-the-war resurrection of the individual, especially to the generation that had to go and fight it.

There was all that, and something else. In 1975, the first boomers were approaching thirty. The record-buying curve of the children of the late sixties and early seventies was about to take a precipitous drop. The last vestige of adolescent male bonding was all but gone, the corner pals replaced by wives and babies. The economy didn't help either, as an American recession clarified the rock-or-butter realities of the day.

By contrast, Springsteen's rise from obscurity signaled the awakening of the first post-Vietnam generation rediscovering its own urban roots. The fallout of the American loss in Southeast Asia gave rise once more to what had always been the heart of American rock: the singular voice of its ethnic underbelly. This time, youth's ever-ticking bomb found its ignition in the street poetics of a singular, rock-volatile kid from New Jersey with the narcissistic swagger of Elvis, the intellectual intensity of Dylan, and the romantic rage of the American working class. And, by 1975, everyone within Geiger range knew it.

Almost everyone, that is.

While the rest of L.A.'s rock stars were wiping the debris from their faces after the explosion that was Springsteen, the Eagles seemed merely to shrug their shoulders. One who was there for the changing of the generational guard recalled, "The Eagles thought rock and roll was about them and *only* them. They couldn't see what was happening right before their eyes, but everyone else knew that Bruce Springsteen took something away from the Eagles that night he played the Roxy in L.A." Although the band's commercial success would continue for the next five years, the Eagles had come to a cultural and creative watershed.

While Springsteen was professionally hamstrung by legal problems that would keep him out of the studio for the next two years, the sheer force of his 1975 breakthrough blew open the floodgates for the next wave of edgy, lyrically sophisticated postwar singer-songwriters who, prior to Bruce's breakthrough, were considered too fringy for the majors. Among them, Warren Zevon, Elvis Costello, David Byrne and Talking Heads, Deborah Harry and Blondie, and Graham Parker. No less a rock historian than Greil Marcus acknowledged the arrival of this next wave by pointedly comparing one of the stars of the second half of the seventies to the reigning stars of the first: "Zevon is on Asylum, a famous home for self-pitying narcissists; [including] Don Henley and Glenn Frey of the Eagles. The people who inhabit the commercial context in which Zevon makes his music aren't merely integrated into the system [they were] out to fuck up, they *are* the system."

In Henley's opinion, "Greil Marcus is bizarre. He's a West Coast academic with an East Coast soul. He's never been a fan of mine or the Eagles, and really, it has nothing to do with the band. It's more a factor of a cultural war — East Coast–style pseudo-intellectualism versus L.A. hedonism, or what he perceived to be that. We were supposed to have represented everything that was wrong with Los Angeles, as if New York didn't have hedonism, drugs, booze, or women."

Either way, it would soon be impossible to ignore rock's newest commercial topsy-turvy. The emergent sound of New York's lower East Side, led by the cerebral CBGB set, helped stretch the limits of the acceptable and even helped make possible — necessary, in fact — the antithetical explosion of mindless disco from the uptown crowd of Studio 54. The biggest-selling album in the seventies would not be an Eagles album, or a Springsteen album, but the disco-dominated sound track to a movie starring John Travolta, *Saturday Night Fever*.

Perhaps inevitably, in the wake of these new waves, the music of the Eagles began to sound less timeless than dated. Without question, their songs about freedom and driving and girls had inspired a generation's temperament. However, that generation had grown up and moved on.

As early as 1976, the increasing shadows of twilight had begun to darken the horizon line of the Eagles' endless highway. They knew enough to understand that the only way to prove they were still players was to go back into the studio and kick more musical ass. Henley in particular roller-coastered through a series of relationships, as if to load up on some emotional high-octane. Once more on the make for his muse, he split with a woman he was seeing in favor of reuniting with his one true passion — madam music. As one close to the band recalled, "His method was simple, really. Women. Love 'em, leave 'em, break a heart or be heartbroken, then write a song about it."

In March 1976, when the Eagles returned to the studio, in deference to Bill Szymczyk they agreed once again to work in Miami. During the recording of the album the band rented a house in Miami. While Henley felt uncomfortable recording out of L.A., it didn't take long for Frey to discover the coming South Beach scene.

Azoff, meanwhile, to enable them to better handle the charitable requests for money and appearances that now poured in daily, okayed the creation of an annual tennis festival. Henley had taken up tennis at his doctor's urging. After he developed an ulcer, his doctor had recommended a sport in which he could hit something. The group's popularity was reflected by the impressive roster of celebrities who agreed to play, among them Mick Jagger, Jeff Beck, the Captain and Tenille, Peter Cetera of Chicago, Alice Cooper, Flo and Eddie, and Davy Jones.

Although the October 1976 tournament proved a huge financial success, it disappeared after a brief run — less for the difficulties in organizing, according to one closely involved, than the approach by Azoff, whose tactics involved more arm twisting than back patting and in the end were not all that conducive to charitable cooperation.

Moreover, in spite of the public show they put on at the tournament, the struggle between Henley and Frey regarding the leadership and direction of the band continued to intensify, in direct proportion, it seemed, to the amount of coke they consumed. Drugs made their differences ever more difficult to deal with, while providing some respite, however temporary, from the emotional war zone. Even before the Eagles returned to the

Miami studio, the tension between Henley and Frey exploded in a full-tilt blast-out at Frey's L.A. house, resulting in Henley's angrily moving out and dropping anchor at sympathetic surrogate-parent Irving Azoff's place, where he would live for the next year and a half.

For Henley, Frey was not the only problem. His dislike for Joe Walsh also seemed to have intensified, made worse by Walsh and Frey's growing friendship. Frey, on the other hand, personally disliked Felder, while Henley considered him a vast improvement over Leadon and crucial to the band's harder-edged sound. Frey and Henley had grown tired of "baby-sitting" Meisner, and he in turn was growing less fond of Frey and Henley, primarily because of their having put him on the band's creative (and therefore economic) back burner.

As Meisner remembers it, "We were [all] real close, more or less, up until the year of *Hotel California*. I just didn't feel like I was part of the group at that point. Man, [Henley and Frey] had their share of arguments. . . . Success changed everything. When we first started, we were really close, like brothers. We'd sit around, smoke a doob together, drink beer, and have a good time. By 1976, it just wasn't the same. We couldn't sit down like the guys anymore. It was all business. The friendships were kind of gone at that point."

After seven difficult, increasingly acrimonious months in Miami, the Eagles returned to L.A., finally ready to throw open the doors to the Hotel California.

The Eagles had arrived at the peak of their popularity, that moment of glory when the celebration of reaching the highest of highs also began the slide toward the lowest of lows. For Henley, it became the metaphorical point of departure for his Grand Guignol. The Beatles had *Sgt. Pepper,* the Rolling Stones *Sticky Fingers,* for Dylan it was *Blood on the Tracks,* and for Henley and the Eagles it was *Hotel California,* a meditative summation of a time and a place shared by his band and a generation yet fine-tuned to the complexities of this most singular artist.

At once vibrant and vicious, heroic and victimized, rhythmic and ruminative, masculine and feminine, *Hotel California,* sung in the stylish first person, was the bold explication of Henley's artistic soul.

A lone car drives down a dark desert highway. The wind is redolent with the smell of home-grown Tex-Mex. Up ahead a "shimmering light" comes into

view. The weary, lonesome traveler stops for some much-needed rest at what
appears to be a hotel. At the entrance, he is greeted by an unidentified woman
whose sexual allure proves irresistible, even as mission bells ring with an omi-
nous warning. She lights a candle and leads the traveler down a long, mysterious
corridor, while voices from unseen figures welcome him to the Hotel California.

But is this really a hotel at all? Or is it a mission of some sort? Or perhaps a
brothel? Is She saint or slut? The holiest of holy, or the hottest of hot?

Such are the ambiguous events described in the opening track of Don
Henley's moody meditation on the moral consequences of privilege and
excess, a Sunday morning sermon on the emotional price one pays for living in the fast lane. The song "Hotel California" opens and closes with one
of the most immediately recognizable signatures in popular music: the
clanging twin guitar riffs of Don Felder and Joe Walsh. "All that music was
written by Felder," Henley says. "He had a little studio in his house. He'd
been an engineer at one point, before he began to play full-time, so he was
really good at it. He created the music track, and although we rerecorded it,
basically all the parts were there. I put the melody on top of it while driving
around in my car. I write a lot of my songs in the car, still the only time and
place in my life I can get some privacy. When it came time to record it, I
spent so much time in the studio I did a lot of *Hotel California* in a
bathrobe, singing, playing drums, and drinking gin." The interior of the
song conforms to a more traditional verse, chorus, verse, chorus structure,
if an unusually long one at six and a half minutes. Its grandiose lyrical
cacophony suggests a world hopelessly fractured, a musical journey of
physical disorientation and spiritual dissipation.

Through the eyes of Don Henley, one of rock's great moralizers, "Hotel
California" is a fire-and-brimstone, unholier-than-thou autobiographical
masterpiece in which he deals with the failure and the success of his
unending search for the elusive muse. Delirious, obsessional, and provocative, "Hotel California" remains one of the most luxuriously haunting personally ambivalent spiritual excursions in the history of rock and roll.

"A lot of the best lines in 'Hotel California' are quite specifically about
Don's relationship with Loree," recalled one who knew Rodkin and Henley as a couple. "And when you listen to that song with the understanding
that on one level it's about what Henley went through after the breakup
with Loree, it takes on a different, more personal edge. The whole album,

in fact, is on one level a kind of description of their relationship, which is one of the reasons why it works so well. It's specific, real, yet expansive, without losing any of the individual detail or the fabulously implosive emotion."

The second cut on the album is J. D. Souther's marvelously redemptive "New Kid in Town." It returns the Eagles to the more specific and accessible turf of teenage boyland, capturing a precise and spectacular moment immediately familiar to any guy who's ever felt the pain, jealousy, insecurity, rage, and heartbreak of the moment he discovers his girlfriend likes someone else better and has moved on. This is the kind of adolescent angst rock and roll does best and no one did better than the Eagles. There were those who heard in the song something else as well, in keeping with the grander, if more personal themes of the album, a suggestion of the fickle nature of both the muse and the masses. After all, there *was* a new kid in town, Springsteen, and he did seem to steal the band's "girl." The lead, sung by Glenn Frey, complete with inspired, tortured echo, "I don't want to hear it," remains an unforgettable track, capturing a moment as perfectly precise as the mood of "Hotel California" was necessarily ambiguous.

The third cut, "Life in the Fast Lane," is a variation of the album's first two meditations on the price of fame, a further reflection on the alluring, pleasurable evils and so-called privileges of rock and roll. "Life in the Fast Lane" was written while Henley was using coke with increasing frequency. "Everybody's got cocaine now, no matter how shitty it is," he would say about those days later on. "I could hardly listen to ["Life in the Fast Lane"] when we were recording it because I was getting high a lot at the time and the song made me ill. We were trying to paint a picture that cocaine wasn't that great. It turns on you. It messed up my back muscles, it messed up my nerves, it messed up my stomach, and made me paranoid." It also inspired one of the best tracks the Eagles ever laid down.

Cut four, the bittersweet ballad "Wasted Time," was the first song Henley had written with Frey for the album and was partially inspired by his breakup with Loree Rodkin. It is, more or less, Henley's reaction to the end of their affair, a visceral elegy for this sad morning after and a metaphorical description of the moral price of fleeting romance.

After a brief musical reprise comes "Victim of Love." Henley, credited with coauthorship (along with Felder, Souther, and Frey), continues as the album's narrator, once more struggling to distinguish between himself as user (of women, of drugs, of the privileges of excess) and as victim.

Cut seven belongs to Joe Walsh. "Pretty Maids All in a Row" twists the screw one turn tighter in its description of the sexual corruption and victimization of and by young girls. A musically dense piece, overproduced and lyrically simplistic, it was a reach by Walsh beyond his usual comfort zone.

The album soars once more with "Try and Love Again," the only song on *Hotel California* sung and written by Randy Meisner. Meisner, in the midst of divorce, was sensing his days with the band coming to a close. His minor-key mourning of the end of one life while looking toward another with the hope of getting beyond, if not over, the disappointment and disillusionment of love lost is gorgeously rendered. Accompanied by Glenn Frey's superb lead guitar, the song is full of classic American rock heartbreak. In many ways, it is the sleeper gem of the album.

Meisner's and Walsh's tracks reveal the second-level depth of the individual Eagles, a peeling back, as it were, of the layers of the vocal harmonics and textured instrumentals of the group's two star players.

Finally, *Hotel California* ends as it began, on the long, lone, and metaphorical road. In "The Last Resort," or, as the band members referred to it, "The Vast Report," once more the unnamed "She" appears, called upon by Henley in both melancholy flashback and bitter prophecy of a journey to a place where the future of the creative spirit of a symbolic America hangs in precarious balance. It is the story of a nation's moral self-destruction and physical decay told as a metaphor for personal creative burnout, itself a symbol of the inevitable end of youth. "People tend to think the album about California," Henley told one interviewer, "but I think it was about the dark underbelly of American culture at large."

It was perhaps this dark underbelly that, somewhat perversely, saw and heard things in the album that even Henley could not have foreseen. The inside cover art of the record album depicted a shadowy figure leaning over a balcony with arms spread like wings, giving rise to persistent rumors that the figure was the devil and that the album took place in hell, damnation its message. Another rumor claimed "Hotel California" was a code name for cocaine, both song and album a description of a journey into addiction.

Others heard embedded in the album's loose-fitting imagery and shadowy references to "She" a reflection of Henley's and Frey's own troubled "marriage," the Hotel California a symbol of their mutual creative entrapment.

Finally, one may perceive "She" as Henley's own maternally nurtured creative soul, its personification as evil seductress–angelic savior a result and expression of the conflict Henley felt between his masculine, controlling side—the legacy of his father — and his creative side, the redemptive gift of his loving mother. The resultant guilt over his own complex relationships with women, his confusion over whether he was the victim or the victimizer, and the remnant of his Southern roots cranking up the guilt over his excessive, privileged West Coast lifestyle — where he came from, who he was, and why — was what made *Hotel California* as close to genuine personal revelation as Henley would ever allow.

Hotel California, released Christmas Day, 1976, was a commercial and artistic triumph and became the band's undisputed masterpiece, one of rock and roll's few legitimately great theme albums. It debuted at number one on the charts and in its first months sold five hundred thousand albums *a week*, more than fourteen million copies (in all formats) to become the eighth-highest-selling album of all time. (The single "Hotel California" almost didn't get released at all because the record company asked the Eagles to shorten it. "They had no respect for the integrity of the song," says Henley. "They were worried about the length rather than what it had to say. We'd always cite these other songs to them, like Dylan's 'Like a Rolling Stone,' to show them it was possible. We thought by now we had enough clout. 'Lyin' Eyes' was six minutes long, although it doesn't seem like it, and had gone to number two in September 1975. We took a stand and refused to have 'Hotel California' released in any version but the one we'd recorded. We felt quite vindicated when it went to number one in March 1977.")

Although the album put the Eagles right back on top, at the time, *Rolling Stone* magazine seemed to think it less important than *The Pretender* and chose to put Jackson Browne, rather than the Eagles, on the cover of its December 1976 issue. "We felt like we'd been mistreated by the press from the beginning," Henley says on the subject. "*Rolling Stone* and some of the other publications and critics. People like Lester Bangs, Robert Christgau, who is such a cynic and has no business writing about rock and roll. All in all, we'd been abused by the press, so we developed a 'fuck you' attitude toward them, which pissed off guys like Jann Wenner all the more. We were cocky too, and that didn't help either. We had this attitude that we didn't need the press, we could make it without them. They didn't like Led Zeppelin, either, and somehow they did all right. So we just clammed up. Part of it was because we hated the press, and part of it was because we wanted to preserve 'the mystique.' We felt that overexposure was a bad thing and if we could be mysterious and quiet and out of the public eye, our career would last longer. That's why we were faceless. No one knew what we looked like, and we cultivated that. We looked different in every photograph. We'd grow beards, mustaches, we'd shave them off, we'd have long hair, then short hair, to look different every year. That was a calculated effort on our part. Glenn and I became very choosy about who we would talk to, or if we would talk to anybody. We dictated band policy on the press. It pissed a lot of people off, but we didn't care. And when they did write about us it was always the same stuff — California, country rock, what they perceived our lifestyles to be, the hedonism. No one ever mentioned that no matter how much booze or women or drugs or running around [we did], Glenn, Walsh, Felder, and I had a real ironclad work ethic. We rehearsed a lot, several hours a day, every day. It was a mission to us, and that was never addressed."

The Eagles felt they were unfairly tagged with being the band that most represented the so-called sound of L.A. and worse, the prototypical seventies country-rock band. "We did all types of rock and roll in our albums," Henley says. "After Leadon, there was very little country left in our music, but we could never shake the critical pigeonhole that we were the 'Los Angeles country-rock' band."

Souther agrees. "All of us got tagged with that L.A. thing. It was like being tagged the Ellis Island guys. Los Angeles was where we came *to*, not where we came *from*."

True enough, except that for Henley and the Eagles, Los Angeles was not only a locale but a continual theme in their work. From the frontier rebellion of *Desperado* to the gothic excess of *Hotel California* (and eventually to the dark edginess of *The Long Run*), they not only wrote out of, but *about,* Los Angeles as a metaphor for the excesses of American culture. It was as much their tar baby as they were its, and became as grand and singular a subject for them as it had for such other modern-day artists as Raymond Chandler, Nathanael West, and Charlie Chaplin.

When *Rolling Stone* did finally review the album in January, the increasingly influential journal gave it a mixed reception, stating in part that while " 'Hotel California' showcases both the best and worst tendencies of Los Angeles–situation rock . . . its lyrics present a convincing and unflattering portrait of the milieu itself."

Henley reacted angrily to what he felt was a sniffing dismissal by granting an interview to *Crawdaddy!* magazine, at the time *Rolling Stone*'s only major competition, in which he pointedly compared his own writing to *Rolling Stone* coverboy Jackson Browne's and that of the new critical darling of the day, Bruce Springsteen. "Our songs just don't get enough attention," he said. "That's the fast lane for us, working on the songs. People talk about Jackson's lyrics, but they don't seem to talk about ours. It's not that they don't look at us as good songwriters, but they just seem to emphasize the songs that were hits rather than the ones that weren't. They don't seem to think you can write a catchy tune that's a hit that means something. . . . I think our songs have more to do with the streets than Bruce Springsteen's."

Whether it rivaled Springsteen or not, with its powerful linear story of lost love and multiple metaphors for the creative struggle and the resultant loss of innocence, its great aural productions, and fabulous dueling Felder-Walsh guitar runs, *Hotel California* proved as irresistible to the public as its mysterious eponymous dwelling did to the narrator. In the end, those seduced and those who did the seducing all willingly shared a room at the inn of decadent redemption. *And that,* Henley seemed to be saying, in this, the year of our Lord nineteen hundred and seventy-Springsteen, *was the whole point.*

ELEVEN

The Eagles kicked off their *Hotel California* world tour on January 14, 1977, in one of American rock and roll's original hometowns, Cleveland, Ohio. Despite months of advance work, it wasn't until the last minute that lighting designer Ken Graham came up with the dramatic new stage plan for the tour. It included a giant backdrop reproduction of the gorgeous twilight-hour David Alexander photograph of the Beverly Hills Hotel that graced the album's cover. The revised effects proved nothing short of magical from the opening moment, when the houselights went down and the Eagles appeared in dramatic silhouette.

Only five days before the tour began, Graham received a call from Richie Fernandez, telling him to hop on a plane to L.A. for a meeting with Henley, Frey, and Azoff. If all went well, Fernandez told Graham, he should be prepared to join the tour as the Eagles' new production manager, replacing Jimmy Johnson, a former lighting man who'd been with the band for years and was being promoted. That was the spin Fernandez used. The truth was, Henley had been dissatisfied with Johnson's execution of the new and highly complex lighting scheme and had decided to replace him. Fernandez suggested the man who had designed it was probably best suited to run the whole show.

"I was flown to L.A.," Ken Graham recalls, "sat in Irving's office for a good long talk with Glenn and Tommy Nixon, one of Don's friends, who'd hung with the band forever, and Irving and Richard Fernandez. Richie picked me up at the airport and coached me as to what to say and what not to say, how much money to accept, what the offer would be, and to expect a raise a little down the line, so if the initial offer was not as much as I thought it should be, I'd get more once I proved myself.

"When I arrived at Irving's office, I sat down and listened to them tell me what they wanted to do. They asked me if I thought I could handle it. I said yes, and everyone seemed in agreement. Except for one thing. I had to wait for Don. He was going to have the final say. 'It's a threesome,' Irving said. 'Glenn, Don, and me.'

"I felt comfortable but nervous, and shook hands with everybody, and now I'm waiting in the outer room while Irving continued to go about his business. Meaning his usual yelling and screaming. It was an amazing thing to see. Now Don comes walking in, and Richie, who's been sitting with me, gets up and says enthusiastically, 'Hey Don, remember Ken Graham?'

"'Yeah, sure,' he said. 'I remember Ken. He'll be fine.' And with that, he walked right out, and I had the job."

In some ways, the *Hotel California* tour proved to be unlike any the band had done before, both on and off the stage. Once again, the Eagles turned to Jimmy Buffett as their opening act. Everyone liked the young Floridian, who was as party hearty as anyone out there on rock's rough road. To Buffett, party time was anytime and anytime was party time. He helped Frey refine his approach to women until the rap was as smooth as the opening lick of "Take It Easy." "Hi girls, we're the Eagles from Los Angeles" became his sexual mantra. It usually didn't take much more than that for Frey to be seen leaving a rehearsal or a sound check with one or more of the hottest cuties who'd somehow gained access to the most restricted parts of the show's venues.

As for Henley, he became known as "Nikon Don" because of his propensity for carrying around a super-8 movie camera and making a series of home movies starring the prettiest and most willing young girls who made themselves available to the band. Viewing these films became one of the most sought-after recreational events among band members and crew on the tour.

This time around, however, to many veterans of the Eagles' road crew, the extent of the band's self-indulgence seemed worse than ever. Moreover, the competitive friction between Henley and Frey not only hadn't let up, it became more intense on the road, where the two were constantly in each other's faces, their conflicts over the band's leadership fueled by ever-increasing amounts of cocaine.

Things became worse when each developed factions of support within the crew and nobody from one faction was allowed to communicate directly with anyone from the other. Each now occupied his own section of the band's jet, with only his friends allowed there. Each suffered a variety of ailments, Frey ongoing nasal problems, Henley constant back pain that necessitated a full-time masseuse to provide nightly spine manipulation. And each still had stomach problems.

On past tours, the crew had been encouraged to feel as if it were part of one big family. They'd hung easily with the band, joining in the all-night card games and weekend softball choose ups. They had been encouraged to talk about anything they wanted, at any time and with anyone. Some had openly shared their problems with the Eagles as easily as they had shared their drugs. This time out, however, things were different. There were, one recalls, endless restrictions on the divided crew, many of whom began referring to the tour as "the Prison California."

Joe Berry, a lighting technician for Northwest Sound and head electrician for the Eagles' tours, remembers, "We rehearsed intensely for ten days before opening night, about fifty of us altogether, and nobody could miss 'The Glenn and Don Show.' By now, what went on between them was sometimes more entertaining than the actual performance. They'd shout at each other, argue over the slightest thing, threaten to kick each other's ass, and sooner or later one or the other would storm off the stage.

"We called Henley Massa Don because he was such a perfectionist and wanted everything done his way. For this tour, he insisted on having a king-size bed and mattress available at all times, which the crew had to drag around everywhere. The tour seamstress made a special cover for it, with handles, to make it easier to pack it in the truck every night. It was Don's bed, it went everywhere and never once got used, because no hotel would allow us to bring it in."

On a stop in Canada, after an all-night flight, the hotel Henley was staying in had screwed up the reservations. In a fury, he chewed Richie Fernandez out for bungling the situation, and wanted him fired. However, it was Azoff who, fed up with what he considered to be Fernandez's out-of-control drug intake, "gave him his walking papers. It happened after a night flight into Montreal during which Fernandez got so stoned on pot he nearly got busted going through Canadian customs," Azoff remembers. Henley backed Azoff, and Fernandez was out.

"Richard's a good guy, but I did have him fired," Henley says. "He was a pothead. I wanted somebody I could depend on, and Richie wasn't that guy. He would get up and smoke a joint for breakfast. He was stoned all the time, which made him less than the most efficient road manager. I got tired of it. Getting stoned was the band's job. As for the mattress, this was during a period when my back was in so much pain from drumming and stress, and drugs, too, [that] one of my shoulders was literally an inch and a half higher than the other one. I was in excruciating pain and couldn't sleep at night. Hotel mattresses are usually awful, the worst goddamn thing in a room. So I bought my own mattress and had it trucked around with the equipment. And then he fucked up. At that point I told Irving, 'Either Richard goes or I do.'"

"One time in Japan," Berry recalls, "Don for some reason bought fifty kimonos. Now we had to figure out how to lug them around. During load-out, someone got the bright idea of rolling them in between the stage rugs. So there was the whole crew, rolling kimonos. No one understood why they were doing this, but no one asked any questions either.

"There was a general kind of paranoia that developed, maybe because of all the drugs that were around. Almost everybody was using coke, and during some point in the middle of each day someone would give a signal and we'd run off, do a quick pump, and come back. The running joke was, you had to sleep four hours a week, whether you wanted to or not. We'd get so stoned we'd play bumper cars in traffic using real rental cars. And if someone got tired during a particularly rough grind, someone always had this bag of little yellow pills. If you were starting to nod off, he'd give you one or two, and you'd come right back to life.

"There were still some good times, though, like what we used to call the Third Encore. We'd give out these buttons during the show to the prettiest girls in the audience, which served as their invitation to the nightly party. Often, arrangements were made ahead of time with the managers of local hotels, who were paid enough so they would kind of look the other way and not bother us. The girls had to come alone, no boyfriends, and I don't remember anyone ever saying no.

"But even that was spoiled by Richie's being fired. After that, the jokes and the parties stopped, and everyone's mood dropped into the deepest part of the darkest ocean."

According to Randy Meisner, "At some point, the feeling of being on tour went from something like a game show to a soap opera. There was discontent among the two factions of the band over everything, from accommodations to salaries, because Henley and Frey both wanted to make sure their people were getting paid at least as much as the other one's. And then things got worse after Richie left, when someone decided for the first time ever that the band would stay in different, better hotels than the crew. A couple of guys who had been with us years, seen us through some really tough times, considered themselves our friends, just couldn't handle watching our little family turn into a cold business.

"All decisions concerning the operation of the tour were now being made by the triumvirate of Irving, Glenn, and Don. The only problem was, Glenn and Don were no longer speaking directly to one another. If you needed to get something resolved, even other members of the band, you had to go through their individual roadie captains. Glenn had Jimmy Collins, Don had Tony Taibi. What it came down to was that if someone needed to talk to Don, he had to speak first to Tony, and he would then convey the message. And if Don then had to ask Glenn about it, he would ask through Tony, who would then go to Jimmy, who would ask Glenn, who would tell Jimmy his answer, who would convey it to Tony, who would tell Don, who would then tell Tony, who would then get back to whoever asked the question.

"It got real difficult, especially when something went wrong during the show. There was very little tolerance for mistakes. One night at the Capital Theater in New Jersey, the stage was shaking, and Don got really upset because he was trying to play the drums and sing. His mike, which was on a big boom, kept hitting him on the lip. He was real angry about it."

Henley decided Bob Sterne, one of the most long-standing and loyal Eagles techies, had fallen down on the job and could destroy the tour. Henley was also bothered by Sterne's creation of an independent company —

Northwest — that designed lights, sound, and stages for other rock tours. To meet the growing demand for his services while he went on the road with the Eagles, Sterne trained and sent out other teams. One night during the *Hotel California* tour, the band did a single-night stopover, and Sterne decided to send a subordinate in his place so he could help prep a crew for another band. The Eagles show went on without incident. A week later, when Sterne rejoined the band for their next rollout, he was summoned by Henley, "like a king from his throne," as he remembers it, to come to the band's private plane for a talk.

Once aboard, he was instructed to sit in the main lounge area until Henley, in his own quarters, was ready to see him. For three days, Sterne spent all his travel time in the same seat, alone and ignored, until he was finally sent for. With Azoff seated next to him, Henley asked Sterne if he was still interested in working with the band. Of course, Sterne replied. Henley then lectured him on the nature of priorities, telling him how important it was to be where he was supposed to be and when, and that he was not getting paid to send someone in his place. If being with the Eagles wasn't important enough to him, Henley said, he didn't have to stay with the tour.

Sterne apologized, said it wouldn't happen again, and Henley told him he could go. From that day on, Sterne never missed another show, even if there was absolutely nothing for him to do, even if it meant giving up other bookings for his company. And he never complained.

The next to feel Henley's wrath was Randy Meisner, whose presence on the tour had become increasingly problematic, for himself as well as the other members of the group.

Meisner recalled, "Toward the end, Henley was clearly trying to run everything. Both Joe Walsh and I were into R&B, and great fans of Chuck Berry, so sometimes we'd do his famous duck walk during the show, and that used to really burn Don's ass, and he'd let the both of us know. Joe would just laugh it off, but I couldn't. I was there from the beginning and didn't appreciate the star trip Don was on.

"So one night a couple of the guys wanted to go to the Coconut Grove. I decided not to join them. I had some things on my mind, and anyway, I was no longer into hanging out with them. Later that night, Walsh and Felder dropped by, and they were kind of buzzed. We sat around and talked for a while, and they began complaining about Don and Glenn. 'They're ruining everything; they've taken over, and I don't want my song done that way,' that kind of thing. I said, 'Hey, I feel kind of left out too. Why don't we just start a little trio or something, our own group?'

" 'Yeah, yeah,' they said.

"That conversation was on my mind the night I got sick a few weeks later in Knoxville, Tennessee, during the second domestic swing of the tour. We had been out for a total of eleven months, and everybody was starting to feel the strain. My ulcer was acting up, and [I had] a bad case of the flu as well. Still, we all sounded great onstage, the audience loved the show, and we were being called back for another encore. 'No way,' I said. I was too sick, and generally fed up. I decided I wasn't going back out.

" 'You pussy,' Glenn said to me, in my face. So I took a swing at him. We started going at it, and the security police were backstage like that. They grabbed the both of us, and after a few minutes let go of Glenn but continued holding me. He grabbed a towel, wiped the sweat off his face, walked right up and threw it in mine."

When push came to shove, Meisner found out, no one in the group was going to back him up. The notion of starting a band with Walsh and Felder evaporated, if it had ever existed at all, replaced by accusations from the others that he was trying to break up the Eagles. After his fight with Frey, no one on the tour spoke to Meisner. He knew it was over for good when, a few days later, back in L.A., the band was attending a record industry affair in Beverly Hills. "I took the opportunity to take Glenn aside and said, 'Look, I apologize for what happened. I was sick, and I'm really sorry.' Glenn told me he wouldn't accept my apology."

With good reason, according to Irving Azoff. "The Eagles' show was musically very carefully constructed. The first part of the show was filled with a lot of their early country-rock stuff, the middle with individual performances, the romantic ballads, and the last third the band rocked out. It was during the second section that Randy gave the boys the most trouble. It always ended with his 'moment,' 'Take It to the Limit.' No question, it was a real showstopper every night. And it made him crazy every night. It also turned him into some kind of reverse prima donna.

"Randy was extremely uncomfortable with so-called superstardom. He was, after all, a veteran of bar bands and would have much preferred playing small rooms to a couple of dozen people every night of the week. He liked the Eagles much more when they were an unknown, struggling bar band. That's what he came out of, and that's where I think he would like to have stayed. His life was one of constant turmoil. He drank, took too many drugs, always had problems with wives and girlfriends, was used to being broke, those kind of things. Dealing with fame was a problem for him, especially when he had to move to the front every night and reach for that fabulous high part at the end. For him, the whole concert came down to that one final note. There was a spotlight set up for him that he was supposed to stay in. Things got worse when he began to intentionally move out of it. He literally did not want to be in the limelight.

"And then he began complaining between shows about having to do the song. Increasingly, he'd piss and moan about one thing or another, mostly having a sore throat, and suggested a couple of times that maybe they ought to drop the song or have someone else sing it. His constant complaining began to drive the others crazy. This was a band that had very little spontaneity in its show. They were out there to re-create their hits and were meticulous about the precision of their performance.

"The night of the fight between him and Frey began with Randy complaining, as usual, about his throat. And he was drinking. After they finished the show, while the audience was cheering for an encore, Randy was guzzling from a bottle of booze and then said he simply wasn't going to go back out. That's when a very fed-up Glenn called him on it. In truth, Randy had become a major pain in the ass, and I think he knew it. He was probably looking for a way to leave. That night he found it."

Henley summed up the Meisner affair this way: "He didn't want to do ["Take It to the Limit"] because he'd been up all night doing drugs with two chicks in a hotel room. There was a reason for how he was. . . . He was a hypersensitive guy. That's why his health was always a wreck. He was always sick, his marriage was always breaking up, he was always quitting the band, every two or three weeks. 'We're touring too much. . . . I've got to go home to my wife. . . . I can't take this life on the road. . . . We're doing this, we're doing that. . . .' There was always something wrong for him.

"And then on days when he felt good and everything was right in the world, he could be a really great guy and fun to hang out with, and he could sing, but he would always descend into this dark, paranoid vision. He's the reason I have an ulcer.

"Glenn had much more patience with him than I did. Glenn tried to help him write his songs and get performances out of him. The night in Knoxville, that was the biggest song in the set. Because he was strung out, he didn't want to sing it. It's that self-destructive thing that rises up in all of us. *'I'll show me!'* The truth of the matter is, he was afraid he couldn't hit the notes. The audience didn't give a shit whether he could hit them or not. They just wanted to hear the song. When he refused to sing it, Glenn calmly went over and tried to console him and said, 'Randy, it's going to be okay, you can sing it, let's just go back out and do it.' Meanwhile, the audience is out there cheering. *'No, man, I'm not gonna sing the fucking song,'* Randy said, snapping at Glenn. Glenn backed up a couple of steps and said, *'Well, fuck you then!'* That's when he threw the towel, Meisner took the swing, and everything escalated."

Meisner says: "When the tour ended, I left the band. Those last days on the road were the worst. Nobody was talking to me, or would hang after the shows, or do anything. I was made an outcast of the band I'd helped start."

After their final performance of the *Hotel* tour, a brief public announcement was issued by Azoff's office stating that Randy Meisner had quit the Eagles due to exhaustion. He was immediately replaced by the long-haired, rail-thin Timothy Schmit, the musician he'd successfully competed with in 1970 for the bassist slot in Buffalo Springfield, and who'd replaced him once before, in Poco. It was J. D. Souther, who had originally auditioned Schmit for Poco, who urged the Eagles to bring him aboard. Everyone agreed on Schmit, a seasoned musician whose breathier vocal quality and expertise on the bass fit in quite well. His mellow peace-and-love personality also made him easy for everyone to get along with, which, for this band, was a welcome relief. The only member of any of the configurations of the Eagles actually born in California, Schmit had been one half of the sixties folkie duo Tim and Ron, which first evolved into a surf band that called itself the Contenders. When the Beatles hit, the Contenders once again switched styles, grew long hair, and enjoyed a brief run at success before breaking up for good. Schmit opted for college and majored in psychology at Sacramento State, supporting himself doing weekend gigs with New Breed, which became Glad sometime in the sixties and landed a recording deal with ABC

Records. Schmit left New Breed to join Poco when Meisner left the band to join Rick Nelson's Stone Canyon Band. Schmit stayed with Poco for seven years, until he received the call from Glenn Frey inviting him to join the Eagles.

According to Meisner, "Irving agreed to continue managing me after I left the group. I released my first solo album [*Randy Meisner*], and he was eventually able to get one of my songs on a movie sound track. However, I wasn't getting much in the way of live bookings, which is the lifeblood of any new band.

"So I went up to his office one day and said, 'Hey, how come my boys aren't getting any dates?' Now, I have to say that I thought I already knew the answer and was trying to see if there was any truth to it. What I'd heard on the street was that Glenn and Don kind of threatened Irving that if he continued to manage me they would find themselves someone else. Anyway, I guess I caught him on a bad day or something, because until then, he'd been up and funny, the 'good' Irving. All of a sudden he said to me, 'Come out here for a minute, in the hallway.' I stepped into the hallway with him, and he backed me up against one of the cement walls, I think so that when he started screaming at me, the echo would really hit my ears hard. *'You get out of here and never come back!'*

"I never did. To this day I believe they blackballed me in the industry, to the point where I couldn't get a record deal or a decent date or anything."

According to Azoff, "He couldn't get a deal or a play date because he couldn't sell a record or put asses in seats. He was unbookable. I may not have been the most diplomatic guy in the world, but I did try to help Randy at first, until his self-destructiveness became too much. I was running a business and wasn't interested in helping Randy run himself, his career, and Front Line into the ground."

The *Hotel California* tour lasted more than a year and left the Eagles emotionally and physically exhausted. When it ended early in 1978, the band members and road crew crawled back to the comfort of the City of Angels.

Later that year, on a cool spring afternoon, Henley was walking by himself on Rodeo Drive in Beverly Hills when he happened to run into Boyd Elder, the artist who'd designed the famous skull logos for the band's album covers and at whose exhibit seven years earlier the band had made its first official appearance as the Eagles. They hadn't seen each other in a long time, not since Elder had fallen out with Azoff over the fee for the logos. Now, as the two walked, they reminisced about the days and nights they'd spent years ago hanging out at the Troubadour, when the whole gang used to pool its pocket change to afford a single pitcher of beer and the Eagles had promised each other that if any band member left, they would immediately disband the whole group. The conversation gradually faded, and they continued on in silence until Henley, staring straight ahead, quietly said, "Everything's changed."

TWELVE

Henley was right. Everything had. Randy Meisner's going and Timothy Schmit's coming meant Henley and Frey were now the only original Eagles left in the group. Internal affairs, however, were not all that was different. The City of Angels itself, that landscape of romance and redemption that had inspired the music of the Eagles, was hardly recognizable.

The Troubadour, for instance, headquarters of the holy hip in the early years of the decade, now sat mostly empty at night, more like the ghost town the Eagles had sung about in *Desperado* than the hot nest of action it had once been. The club's negative vibe began a specific night in 1974, during John Lennon's infamous lost weekend, which culminated in his ejection from the Troubadour while wearing a tampon taped to his forehead. It was the beginning of the decline of L.A.'s once most celebrated club. As had happened a decade earlier in New York City, once the musicians who had first gained recognition in the club moved on, the autographed "With thanks for everything" photos on the wall were no longer enough to keep the scene or the cash register alive.

In truth, there was little love lost between many of the artists who'd gotten their break at the Santa Monica Boulevard club and its eccentric and increasingly reclusive owner. Always more businessman than patron of the arts, Doug Weston knew that loyalty was a low priority among the crowd he employed. It was always the same; as soon as his regulars made it, he could kiss their profitable appearances good-bye. He therefore initiated a complex contractual arrangement to insure that any act that played the club was obligated to return as many times as he could negotiate. A necessary fact of nightclub life, it was also the kind of economics that limited the influence and in some cases ended the existence of a venue that had given these performers their big break. Whether the club had played a crucial part in the explosion of the L.A. sound or the class of musicians it offered had given the place an aura by association, the economic incompatibility of stardom and a small stage helped kill the Troubadour's golden era.

After the Lennon debacle, most name acts tied to Weston's multiple-appearance contracts simply opted to buy their way out, the most famous being Elton John, whose first American appearance at the club while still unknown had catapulted him to international fame and fortune. He gladly paid $25,000 to get out of any further obligations to the Troubadour. Things had gotten so bad that loyalist Jackson Browne organized a benefit to help owner Doug Weston resist an Arab cartel rumored to want to buy the place and turn it into a souvlaki stand. These days playing the Troubadour was the surest way an artist could make it look as if he or she were professionally on the way down.

The decline of the club was one more clear indication of just how much had changed since the Eagles had been point men for the postsixties revival of independent rock and independent labels. They were the biggest money-makers for the largest corporate conglomerate, even as a new record-buying generation had now arrived that knew the Eagles as nothing more than the ultimate example of corporate-driven rock and roll, and instead looked east, to New York and England again, for newer waves. Three chords and less had once more become the purest definition of rock, played by a new set of nihilists determined to eliminate any of the sugar that had sweetened the music of the Linda Ronstadts, Jackson Brownes, and Eagles.

Suddenly, it seemed, punk, new wave, and disco were everywhere. The hottest clubs in L.A. were no longer the ones that had the latest bands and an audience of openmouthed teens watching their every move. The main action now took place in neon dives where no bands played at all. Deejays spun records, while the people on the dance floor did the performing. Because of this, the hottest club supergroup was the Bee Gees, a band that had gotten its start in the sixties with a harmonious blend of folk-country rock not that different from the music of the early Eagles, faded, and made a major comeback by adapting its studio sound to disco.

Two things Henley and Frey could agree on were their utter loathing for the new music, especially disco, and their belief that no matter who thought what or why, the Eagles were still relevant to rock and roll. As if to underscore this, in response to a question from an interviewer, Henley emphasized the band's ongoing commitment to social issues. "Because of our stature," he said, "and our power and our money or whatever, we got involved in some political things this year. We got involved with Jerry Brown, the governor of California, who was running for president, and we also got involved with the initiative to try to stop the building of nuclear power plants. I've always been an environmentalist, I've always thought of myself as one and I have always cared about the planet, but this year we really went out and did something. We did benefits [during the *Hotel California* tour] and tried to do some good work — tried to use our power in a good way. So, in some ways, we all grew up a lot and don't just write *silly little love songs* now because there's more than that happening, you know."

Henley continued his explication of the Eagles' social conscience, integrity, and broad-based appeal during a rare radio interview with L.A. rock deejay Jim Ladd, then considered one of the most knowledgeable and authentic of FM-esoteric hosts. To a question about how the line in "Hotel California" that plays off the lost "spirit" of 1969 related to what was happening in music, Henley replied, "People seem to be lost. There seems to be this apathy, and all the magic seems to be missing. People seem to need something. . . . Los Angeles was always an archetypal place to me, watching the sun set in the west, it seemed like paradise and happiness had something to do with geography. That's something I've learned is not true."

Even as they felt the need to culturally retrench and emotionally recharge, their record label came looking for one more Eagles album. Henley in particular felt drained — creatively as well as physically — and sent a reply through Irving Azoff to Joe Smith that the company was going to have wait until he was good and ready to start working again. And he wasn't going to be until *he said* he was.

Among the more pressing matters for Henley was his on again, off again romance with a well-known actress. His relationship with the beautiful, if high-strung, movie star seemed over for good at this point. Henley had really liked her, but one close to the situation believed that what ruined everything was that she insisted on an all-or-nothing commitment, forcing a clean break.

"When I met her, I was a mess and she was too," Henley observes. "It was just the wrong time in both of our lives."

What may have made it harder for Henley to deal with this time around was that Glenn *was* very involved with a cute little debutante from Texas. Henley's sibling rivalry alarm went on twenty-four-hour alert.

Henley knew he needed to reload his creative engine. He searched for inspiration in new women, of course, and according to reports, younger and in ever-varying combinations. A couple of friends began referring to him as "old velvet cuffs" after his preference for securing girls to his bed with a binding that wouldn't leave marks. It didn't exactly solve his creative problems, but, one friend joked, it probably was not that bad a way for him to pass the time while fighting off the stomach-chewing fear that his band had become insignificant to the younger generation of the decade it had helped define.

It was a feeling that couldn't have been helped when *Rolling Stone* published the results of its second Annual Readers' Poll, and the Artist of the Year award went to the Eagles' chief competitors, Fleetwood Mac. Runners-up included Linda Ronstadt, Jackson Browne, Peter Frampton, and Stevie Wonder. Male Vocalist went to James Taylor, who beat out Jackson Browne. Female Vocalist went to Linda Ronstadt, with Stevie Nicks coming in second. "Dreams," Fleetwood Mac's hit single off their *Rumours* album, beat out "Hotel California" (second) for Best Single of the Year. Band of the Year also went to Mac, the Eagles again coming in second. *Rolling Stone*'s poll accurately reflected the difference between the popularity of the Eagles and Fleetwood Mac. The British-American group would always have a broader if less intense following. Quite simply, the presence of Stevie Nicks and Christine McVie was what separated the men from the boys. The Eagles' primary audience ranged across the board, if more single male adolescent than boomer couples. If Mac also "aged" more gracefully, it was because the music it made came from the real-life drama of its romantic relationships, while the songs of the Eagles seemed by comparison to come from loners, not-so-young men acting like teenage boys still on the sexual make.

Also in January 1978, the Eagles were nominated for several Grammy Awards, including the all-important Record of the Year for the single "Hotel California." With the band still smarting over what it felt was the unfair snubbing it had received in *Rolling Stone,* Azoff decided he needed to protect it from any further humiliation. Pierre Cossette, the Grammys' television broadcast producer, had approached Azoff about having the Eagles appear on the telecast, and he went into manic overdrive. He saw Cossette's invitation as the perfect opportunity to restore a bit of enthusiasm, if not total unity, to the boys. But only if they won. Azoff told Cossette that the Eagles would be happy to perform at the twentieth annual awards ceremony if Cossette *guaranteed* that the Eagles would win Record of the Year.

Cossette swallowed hard and asked Azoff how he thought they could possibly get away with rigging the Grammys. Azoff, without missing a beat, suggested the band simply be given a secret dressing room. If they won, they would emerge in dramatic fashion and blow everybody away by their presence. If they lost, no one would know they were even there in the first place. Shocked, Cossette nevertheless assured Azoff his suggestion would be brought to the table.

A few days later, Cossette called Azoff to tell him that the board had turned his request down. Fine, Azoff told him, he'd talked it over with the boys and they wanted to know if it would be okay to send someone to accept for them, like, say, Jackson Brown or Linda Ronstadt. No, Cossette said, the rules were clear; only the host could accept for the band. Good news, Azoff said, the Eagles would show anyway. Cossette was overjoyed and thanked Azoff profusely for his great work in pulling off the seemingly impossible.

However, much to Cossette's dismay, as the awards were being handed out during a live telecast before six thousand attendees and a worldwide television audience of millions, the Eagles were nowhere to be found. Nor was the promotional clip Azoff had assured would be provided for the reading of the nominations. Cossette had given the Eagles the prestigious final slot of the show, and as time ticked by and it became clear the Eagles were not going to show, he was forced to hastily reshuffle the remainder of his broadcast.

When "Hotel California" won Record of the Year, an angry Cossette insisted the presenter announce that the Eagles had not shown up to accept it. At a press conference the next day, Azoff explained that the band couldn't attend because they were holed up in Malibu "tightening up some tracks for the next album." That might have actually worked, except this was Irving Azoff, who couldn't resist adding, "That's the future; this [the Grammys] is the past." In fact, the Eagles and Azoff watched the ceremonies from home and thought the sight of Andy Williams accepting a Grammy for them was, according to Azoff, "One of the great moments of rock and roll."

Cossette tried for the final word; he publicly replied to Azoff's comments in a hastily called news conference during which he revealed that Azoff had tried to guarantee that the Eagles would win the Grammy as a condition of their appearing. That spurred the Eagles on. Henley told the *Los Angeles Times*, "The whole idea of a contest to see who is 'best' just doesn't appeal to us." Azoff took it one step further and, while failing to respond to Cossette's claims about the band's insistence on a guaranteed win, officially denied he had ever promised Cossette that the Eagles would appear in the first place. "I never indicated," he insisted, "ever, that we'd be there."

Glenn Frey added his two cents when he told a *Rolling Stone* reporter, "There's a credibility gap. Debby Boone wins Best New Artist, and Warren Zevon and Karla Bonoff aren't nominated." Nor, Frey said, had he been pleased to see David Crosby and Stephen Stills dressed in black tie and tails. "Rock and roll does not belong in a tuxedo," he told *Rolling Stone*. "When we saw [Crosby and Stills] walk out there, my fuckin' heart sank. It was like the end of an era."

One week after the awards ceremony, the Bee Gees' *Saturday Night Fever* sound track displaced Fleetwood Mac's *Rumours*, which had been the number one top-selling album in the country for thirty-three weeks.

Although it was possible to see the Eagles' attitude and behavior toward the Grammys as a hip gesture criticizing an industry that seemed out of touch with rock and roll, both the band and Azoff came off as childish and petty when, three months later, they collided with Jann Wenner, founder and publisher of *Rolling Stone*.

By 1978, Wenner, like Azoff, found himself the singular power behind a fantastic pop-cultural moneymaking machine. The original concept for the magazine had come out of San Francisco's fabled 1967 "summer of love," and it went on to become the journal of record for the sixties. In the seventies, the Bay Area–based magazine, under Wenner's tight editorial supervision, proved increasingly idiosyncratic in its selection of entrants into the pop-music pantheon, particularly when it came to the new rock royalty out of Los Angeles. Jackson Browne, with his Dylanesque lyrics, cover-boy looks, political awareness, and accessible manner, became a *Rolling Stone* favorite, while the Eagles and their style of music seemed to Wenner's stable of writers a rejection of everything sixties rock had stood for. As a result, the band rarely got mentioned in the pages of the magazine, and when it did, as was the case with *Hotel California*, it was treated as little more than a marginal entry in the official history of rock and roll.

According to journalist Robert Draper in his book on Wenner's magazine, "The *Rolling Stone* critics loathed the Eagles. Where Dylan had been rock and roll's mind, the Beatles its heart and the Stones its loins, the Eagles represented a new and almost parasitic entity — spongelike, it seemed to the critics, sopping up the genre's very blood. Greil Marcus, Dave Marsh, Peter Herbst and [Charles] Young had each taken swipes at the band."

Nor was the magazine particularly fond of Irving Azoff. According to Draper, "As a short, brash, brilliant upstart in the record business, Eagles manager . . . Irving Azoff served as a natural rival to Jann Wenner. Each seldom missed an opportunity to take the other to task. When Jann attended a party for the Eagles in Hawaii, he telephoned the office, demanding that the next 'Random Notes' include the fact that the Eagles served cheap vodka."

In May 1978, *Rolling Stone* ran an item in its "Random Notes" section about the Eagles' having been "trounced" in a softball game by rock impresario Bill Graham's team. What was unusual about the piece was not what it said, but how many times the magazine said it. Over the next several issues, the item kept reappearing in various forms, as if the magazine was not only poking fun at the band, but goading them into making some kind of printable response.

Henley failed to see the humor in any of this and decided to throw the gauntlet back into *Rolling Stone*'s yard. He challenged the magazine to a duel, as it were, to be played out on the dirt of a softball field.

The band and the magazine agreed to play a game for the following stakes: If *Rolling Stone* won, the Eagles would give the magazine an interview. This was something they had vowed never to do again given that several members of the band remained unhappy with the magazine. And the results of the second Annual Readers' Poll didn't help matters. Finally, the Eagles were upset by ongoing critical dismissal of their friends and colleagues, including J. D. Souther and Karla Bonoff. If the Eagles won, the band members could each write a story for *RS* about the game. Wenner sensed an "event" and insisted that a charitable donation be made by the loser. Peter Herbst, an editor at the magazine, suggested a $5,000 donation be added to the gate and given to the UNICEF World Nutrition Program. Everyone agreed, and the game was set for May 6, 1978. To make things truly interesting, Wenner and Azoff made a sizable side bet that had nothing to do with charity.

Wenner was determined to win. Aware of the Eagles' interest in sports and their relatively good physical condition — especially when compared to *Rolling Stone*'s team of rock critics, editors, and ad-space sales personnel — he all but abandoned the upcoming issue of the magazine and relocated his team to L.A. for a week of practice. There, it was rumored, several staffers broke into the homes of the Eagles and left telltale markers, such as notes calling the Eagles "beach bums" and "sissies" and threatening to mess up one of Frey's prized collection of souped-up cars. The rivalry had taken on the proportion and cultural significance of a summer camp "color war."

The game was held at the University of Southern California's Dedeaux Field. *Rolling Stone* hoped for the best, having padded its team with advertising director Claeys Bahrenburg, a former hockey player, and chief financial officer Jim Dunning, who had once been recruited by the Baltimore Orioles.

The Eagles came to play as well, with determination in their hearts and spikes on their shoes. Just before game time, Wenner quietly reminded Azoff that it was, after all, only a game and that someone could actually get hurt by those spikes, to which Azoff replied, "How exciting."

The event began with "Life in the Fast Lane" played over the loudspeakers as a substitute for the national anthem and ended in a lopsided victory for the Eagles, who outscored the Gonzos, as the *Rolling Stone* team called itself, 15–8. Azoff couldn't resist a final dig, telling writer Charles Young after the game that the Eagles could have played a lot better, suggesting the band had beaten *Rolling Stone* with one hand tied behind its back. Henley seized the moment of victory to tell a reporter from the *Los Angeles Herald-Examiner* that the writer he had most enjoyed beating, because he was the one he "most despised [at *Rolling Stone*]," was "probably Peter

Herbst. No, Dave Marsh. Maybe Chuck Young. Oh, I know . . . Greil Marcus — he's the one. Marcus [who had failed to turn out for the game], he's too chicken to come out and play."

The animosity between *Rolling Stone* and its target seventies band, the Eagles, remained at Def-Con 3. As a result, to this day the band has never received what it considers the proper amount of coverage or acknowledgment of achievement from Wenner and his magazine. (It should be noted that Wenner was a founder of the Rock and Roll Hall of Fame, into which the Eagles were inducted in 1998.)

Also in 1978, Irving Azoff turned the heat up a few degrees in his fevered desire to make the leap from manager to mogul. Having turned Front Line's office into his personal fortress, from which he ruled his musical fiefdom with a combination of bullying tactics, exaggeration, and lies, now he became determined to make the big move from rock and roll to movies. Like his predecessor David Geffen, Azoff had come to the realization that the biggest game in Hollywood was still film. To that end he began networking past the invisible screen that divides those who operate in Hollywood with real power from those who don't and want it.

He became shoulder-rub friendly with some of the film industry's more influential figures, including Universal Pictures vice president and legendary film editor Verna Fields, who'd just won an Oscar for her work on Steven Spielberg's *Jaws.* Through Fields, Azoff gained access to the high ranks of the Burbank-based studio, and before long, he had a deal to executive produce *FM,* a relatively low-budget film light on plot and heavy on music. *FM* dealt with the adventures of an FM deejay (played by Martin Mull) who decides to lead a revolt to take back creative control of his overly commercialized station.

While not exactly *Citizen Kane,* the film had something *Kane* didn't — concert sequences by Linda Ronstadt and Jimmy Buffett, and a sound track to kill for, including cuts by the Eagles, Ronstadt, Buffett, Warren Zevon, Jackson Browne, Joe Walsh, Randy Meisner, and Steely Dan. However, before the film was released, Azoff exercised his contractual right to remove his name from the credits because, in his view, Universal had failed to make the picture he had envisioned. It was a move that baffled everyone in the business. "No one except maybe a self-styled rock and roll mogul" would have done such a thing, according to one familiar with the deal. "It's usually the other way around — people fighting to keep their name *on* a film."

When it was finally released later that year, *FM* proved a box-office disaster, but, as Universal had correctly figured when it had given Azoff the green light, it yielded a successful two-record sound track that sold more than a million units.

Azoff then decided his next venture would be a feature-length film based on "Hotel California." It seemed a no-brainer to him. As early as *Desperado*, everyone in the band had always talked about how "visual" their music was, and there had even been one brief, quickly aborted attempt by David Obst to develop that album into a movie.

At this point Julia Phillips entered the mix. Phillips, the talented if controversial Oscar-winning producer of such seventies movie classics as *The Sting, Taxi Driver,* and *Close Encounters of the Third Kind,* was riding high. One day she happened to hear an Eagles song on the radio, which reminded her how much she loved their music. Always looking for a new project, she believed "Hotel California" had the necessary ingredients to make a terrific movie. She decided to get in touch with Azoff and set up a meeting. As she soon discovered, the would-be mogul jumped through no one's hoops, real or imagined. Merely nailing him down to a time and place took weeks. When they finally did meet, Irving, in full deal drive, "confessed" to Julia among other revelations that he "hated music." Phillips, whose bullshit detector had its own satellite, yanked him a little. "You don't hate music; you hate the music business."

"No, no," Irving explained. "I *love* the business," in response to which Julia nodded her head slowly up and down.

Before the meeting was over, she managed to effect something resembling a predevelopment deal to explore the possibilities of an agreement. Later, after Azoff had left, she went over the credits on the back of the *Hotel California* album and noticed something in the small print: *"Copyright in dispute."*

Phillips called an attorney friend familiar with the situation. He explained that it was the only way Warner could release the album because the copyright lawsuit the Eagles had instituted against Geffen and Warner was still not fully resolved at the time of its completion. Normally, he told her, a copyright dispute would be enough to prevent an album from getting made, but because the Eagles were so important in terms of cash flow, the company had decided to go ahead and release *Hotel California* anyway, believing that whatever it wound up with in the end would be worth the risk.

Phillips then called Frank Wells, a friend high in the executive pyramid at Warner Pictures, to find out how potentially damaging the situation was. After speaking with Wells, she called Azoff, who sounded far less charming this time around. He refused to discuss the details of the copyright dispute except to say it had been settled in principle, and when Phillips suggested they meet again in person, he insisted both Henley and Frey be present.

If Phillips thought she could handle Azoff, she was less certain about the two Eagles who showed up with him. They were scruffy and sullen, acting, in her opinion, amateurishly arrogant, as if they were determined to prove that what everyone in film thought about rock stars was true. They came off smug, studiedly casual, and talked of protecting their "purity" even as, according to Phillips, they snorted an ounce of coke off the table. As Henley talked on, she began to imagine what he would be like onscreen, got hung up on his funny ears, and determined that Henley could never make it as a movie star.

According to Henley, "She's a liar. Both Glenn and I remember that day quite vividly. We had gone to her house reluctantly. We'd already had some bad experiences with movie people. Movie pukes, we called them. Ray Stark had tried to get us to let him make a movie out of *Desperado*, which went badly. They always thought we should be excited or flattered because they wanted to make movies out of our songs. In fact, we really didn't want anything to do with it. We were pretty sure they'd take our songs and ruin them. We knew enough about the film business to know you'd have to relinquish all control and that it's somebody else's vision, just like rock videos are today.

"We went to take the meeting, to hear what she had to say. It was midday, or early afternoon, during a period of time when coke was at the peak of its popularity in Hollywood, and Phillips was in the process of flaming out her career on it. We sat there, polite but not terribly friendly. We were too wary to be friendly. In an effort to loosen us up, and to create some kind of camaraderie, she dragged out this huge ashtray filled with a mound of coke. One of her writers was there. She offered us some, and we said no; we didn't know her that well, and it was a business meeting. It was a little early in the day for us. She looked nonplussed at that. I don't remember if she went ahead and did some or not, but I know for certain we didn't. She wants to remember it that way for her own reasons. She's bitter about everything that's happened to her, but I don't know why she feels it's necessary to say that we did drugs with her. We were doing lots of coke in those days, every day, but not with her. I guess it made her first book more interesting. I ran into her in a sushi bar after it came out, and I reminded her that we didn't do drugs together. I followed her back to her table, called her a liar, and that freaked her out. The last thing I said to her was, 'Sleep well.' So she decided to take another shot at me in her next book."

When the meeting ended, Frey decided to leave immediately for Colorado to cool out. Not long after, Henley was felled by another episode of stomach problems. Azoff then called Phillips and told her that anything having to do with an Eagles movie was going to have to be indefinitely postponed.

No problem, Phillips told him, and hung up. Even before the meeting, she had known the copyright problem meant the deal was dead, and anyway, as far as she was concerned, *Hotel California* would never be *A Hard Day's Night* because, no matter what the buzz, Henley and Frey were no Lennon and McCartney.

According to one close friend, neither Eagle was very upset about the collapse of the deal. "They really didn't want to see 'Hotel California' made into a movie. They were suspicious of the film business. After all, that was what 'Hotel California' was all about. I remember from the first day, Henley seemed really reluctant about it. Being the control freak that he is, he sensed he'd never be able to control the making of the film and was afraid of seeing what he considered his finest, most personal work reduced to the level of a sitcom."

With no movie deal and the Eagles in no hurry to make another album, Azoff decided it was a good time to marry his longtime girlfriend, Rochelle (Sheli) Cumsky. The move surprised the Eagles, especially Henley, still very single, still very demanding of Azoff's total devotion. "Henley and Irving had a real love-hate relationship," remembered a close friend of both. "Don loved the pit-bull quality about Irving, but there was a bit of childish jealousy when Irving branched out to other acts and then got married. Henley's attitude became 'What do you mean, you're not thinking about me for every single part of the day?' "

Another friend added, "Then, of course, the marriage left Henley the odd man out. Here was Glenn, seriously involved with a debutante, and Irving, *even Irving,* able to find himself a wife. If he'd wanted, Henley could have found a lot of reasons to be pissed at Irving. There was the fuckup with the Grammys and the failure to break the group into the movies. And then this weird kind of abandonment. Yet Henley, even if a little pissed, swore by Irving, and remained close to him. No question, Irving made Don a ton of money, and money was important to these boys, but it wasn't everything. There was always a certain amount of mystery about Don's allegiance to Azoff. Maybe it was the father-son thing, maybe it was a good guy–bad manager thing, who knows, but however uneasy it made other people, he stood by Irving. I don't think in the end it was based on any rational or explainable reason. It was simply a very powerful, purely emotional thing."

According to still another friend, Henley had nothing to worry about. "Irving soon made it clear that Henley was still his shining prince. He teased Don that he had a better royalty deal than most newlyweds' prenups."

One warm winter day in L.A., Glenn Frey was bombing around with the top down and Linda Ronstadt by his side. She loved to drive with him, anywhere and anytime, but especially on warm afternoons like this one. As usual, he was feeding the tape deck with custom-made cassettes of great rock and roll. Ronstadt recalled, "Glenn Frey is the best single source of material for singers. He's got stacks and stacks of cassettes he's made of all these different things. That afternoon I looked at him and went, 'Remember when we used to sit around the Troubadour bar and go, Oh, it's so horrible and I can't get a record deal? We were so broke and so miserable and we'd feel sorry for ourselves and we were so precious about it.' Then, all of a sudden I looked at him and I went, 'Boy, life's really tough. We're going off to ski [in Colorado] with all this money in our pockets, we're going to have a good time, and we've got great music on the tape player.' Just then 'Back in the USA' came on and I went, 'God, that would be a great song to sing. I think I'll do that one.'"

The difference in the way each responded to primal rock and roll pointed out the essence of the dilemma in which Frey found himself. While Ronstadt could take easy inspiration in the music of artists like Chuck Berry, Frey bathed his head in it as a kind of mean-spirited self-taunt. He believed, as Henley did, that in order to continue to move forward, the Eagles needed to produce nothing less than original music — something that each successful album made ever more difficult. The last had left everyone wondering how the Eagles could possibly top — or was it escape from? — *Hotel California*. Or, exactly how *did* you check out if you could never leave?

THIRTEEN

The only new release the band had in 1978 was a great out-of-nowhere single cover of Charles Brown's "Please Come Home for Christmas," which Henley had chosen to record. He'd heard it on the radio as a child and now, with every other group recording holiday songs, thought the Eagles should do one too. It was as good a way as any to stay on the radio between album releases. It must have been extremely gratifying to the band that the public was so eager for anything Eagles that the 45 shot onto the charts, reaching number eighteen. No matter what was happening in the rest of the music world, clearly the Eagles could record the phone book and their audience would buy it. The fact that they didn't was enough to make Joe Smith stop believing in Santa Claus.

Ironically, while as the Eagles they could not seem to produce anything like a new album together in the studio, as individuals they couldn't stay away, appearing separately on many of their friends' albums.

Joe Walsh, with nothing much to do but wait around for Henley and Frey to get their act together, released a solo album entitled *But Seriously Folks . . .* and then decided to run for president of the United States. *Seriously.* He appointed Larry Solters his campaign manager, had buttons made up, stumped along the campaign trail, and generally goofed his way into the hearts and minds of his fellow Americans. He decided to quit the race when he started to think there was a possibility he might win. Henley, as might be expected, was not at all amused by what he considered Walsh's clownish behavior.

In March 1978, Azoff managed to convince the members of the band to reconvene in Miami and at least try to begin work on a new album (an accomplishment Bill Szymczyk described as "the Impossible Dream"). Joe Smith was delighted when he heard the news. In the wake of sound tracks, disco, and remixes, he needed something to help balance an otherwise off year for the label and knew of no one who could do the job more reliably than his favorite in-house desperadoes. So eager was Smith for an Eagles album that he offered the band a cash bonus of a million dollars if they delivered it in time for the Christmas rush.

The Eagles, via Irving Azoff, told Smith that wasn't going to happen, as they hadn't even finished writing their new songs. In response, Smith sent them a rhyming dictionary. In a more serious attempt to demonstrate the label's good faith, Smith had helped to convince Geffen and Warner to finally and completely settle the last few remaining unresolved details of the copyright lawsuit. While Azoff could proudly claim a total victory for the band, in truth Smith had played his money card and could fairly take his share of the stakes. What it came down to was simply that as valuable as the copyrights were, their worth depended upon the ongoing activity of the band. It was one of the peculiar truths of American pop culture that the more successful an act was, the more successful it had to continue to be. Inactivity usually brought about downward reevaluation, along with a very quick pass of the catalog to the cutout bin. Besides, it hadn't really been Warner's or Smith's battle. It was Geffen who'd laid the original claim to the copyrights, and he was for all intents and purposes out of the picture. When it came down to making a decision, the Eagles' future meant far more to Smith and Warner than Geffen did. Now he agreed to a raise in royalties, once again retroactive, knowing full well — as Azoff and the band did — that with a new release, the Eagles' entire back catalog would jump back onto the charts.

"Our motto," Azoff boasted after winning the copyright and royalty battles, "is pay now, pay more later. Figure out a fair price, add a third, and that's what we get in our contracts. We only hear from [the record company] about ten times a month. When they project a $116 million year because Linda Ronstadt and the Eagles are going to release albums, and then come up $40 million short from not having an Eagles album, they hurt."

In truth, both Smith and Azoff could claim a measure of success in what amounted to one more skirmish in their continuing battle of wits. Each had an agenda, and each defended it with considerable expertise. Smith's function was to get as much product as he could from his most profitable act. Azoff's was to make him pay as much as possible for it. Although they were necessarily business adversaries, Smith and Azoff forged a close friendship.

Having settled this latest round with Azoff, Smith believed the Eagles would now do the right thing and deliver a new album, ideally before the end of the year. He was wrong.

"I Can't Tell You Why" was the first new idea for a song the Eagles took into the studio, a contribution by Randy Meisner's replacement, the bassist and vocalist who now wished to be referred to as Timothy B. Schmit.

Schmit's "I Can't Tell You Why" also became the new album's first completed track. A moody, meditative song, gorgeously rendered by Schmit's high vocals, Frey's sliding guitar solos, and an organ and rhythm section borrowed from Al Green, it resonates with the unspeakably pure emotion that brings some lovers together and keeps others from drifting apart.

As good as the song was, it signaled the creative bankruptcy of both the Henley-Frey collaboration and its individual components. Whereas in the past, each had fought for creative control, now, significantly, both seemed more than willing to concede the album's crucial opening track to the band's newest member.

With "I Can't Tell You Why" finished, the band spent another couple of weeks in the studio, but nothing more came out of it. Everything had come to a creative dead end. Henley and Frey reverted to their familiar bickering. No longer about who was in charge, their disputes now seemed minor and meaningless, an obvious substitute for their missing creative energy. Before the band finally gave up and left the studio and Miami, several near-fistfights had broken out: two between Henley and Frey, and one between Frey and Felder. Over nothing specific anybody could remember, although hostility toward one another continued.

"Our friendship really started to break down during the making of the album," Henley recalls. "We were stuck. We just weren't coming up with a lot of great material. We were physically and emotionally spent, doing way too many drugs, and creating more pressure than there already was on ourselves. Although there was plenty coming from outside as well. After the success of *Hotel California*, the powers that be wanted more, and they wanted it quick. Here we were having made something like a quarter of a billion dollars for Warner Brothers, and they still kept the pressure up for another album. When you're bringing in that much cash, everyone at the company turns into a yes-man. That's when Glenn and I started to come apart. We got into arguments about creativity, lyrics, and some angry words were exchanged. The crux of it was about whether or not everybody was carrying his fair share of the burden. There were the usual problems that all bands have with ego. A couple of the band members felt they were being underrepresented as far as the songwriting was concerned. This had always been a problem for us, going back to Meisner and Leadon, and it continued on with Walsh and Felder. Everyone wanted to do everything. Everybody wanted to be a lead singer, to write the songs, and it just can't work that way. Somebody's got to take charge, and somehow it had shifted to me, and I felt enormous pressure to come up with all the lyrics, since Glenn had sort of backed off. In essence, we were all just too strung out. Everything was a drama. All kinds of little wars were going on within the various factions of the group, little mutinies and games being played. It was just ridiculous. We needed what Aerosmith has now, a group psychiatrist."

Meanwhile, the other band members were forced to sit, wait, and wonder when they were going to get around to making music. According to Joe Walsh, part of the problem was the pressure Henley and Frey still felt about having to top *Hotel California,* which produced a level of anxiety and frustration that proved too much for either of them to deal with. "When we finished 'Hotel California,' people started saying things like 'You guys are amazing' and the album became this huge seller. It made us very paranoid. People started asking us, 'What are you going to do now?' and we didn't know. We ended up on the next album in Miami with the tapes running, but nobody knowing what was going on. We lost perspective. We just kinda sat around in a daze for three months."

Azoff thought the Eagles might rekindle their creative spark if they played before live audiences, and arranged for them to go back on tour. For the rest of 1978, the band stayed out of the studio and on the road, where, even as the lines of communication continued to break down among them, they struggled to come up with new material for the album.

It took another *year* before they felt ready to return to Miami and begin to record. However, no sooner did they enter the studio than the creative logjam resumed. A pattern of noisy outbreaks separated by long stretches of silence set in, until the summer of 1979, when something resembling an album slowly began to come together. Joe Walsh later told an interviewer from the *Los Angeles Times* that Glenn Frey's vocals for "Heartache Tonight" were the album's turning point. "The creative stalemate was broken the night the band recorded 'Heartache.' Glenn went out and sung his ass off on that track. We knew then that we were off the hook a little. We had a single. The next break came when we recorded 'The Long Run.' When Henley sang those words, we knew we had the beginning of a concept. The next step was 'Sad Café.' Again it was the words. That's when we were finally able to say to ourselves, 'Hey, this is going to be OK.'"

Of the ten new songs that made the final mix, nine were partially credited to Frey and Henley with one or more collaborators. Only two new tracks, "King of Hollywood" and "The Greeks Don't Want No Freaks," were listed as Henley-Frey collaborations.

The opening cut, "The Long Run," was credited to Schmit, Frey, and Henley, which made it difficult to figure just who'd written what. The lyrics are purposefully vague. "We can handle some resistance, if our love is a strong one" sounded like it might be about trouble in a relationship. The question was, which relationship? Was it the one between Frey and his wife, rumored to be on the rocks? *"Those debutantes down in Houston, baby, who couldn't hold a candle to you."* Or was it the one between Henley and Frey? *"Did you do it for love? Did you do it for money?"*

The second track was Schmit's "I Can't Tell You Why," followed by Joe Walsh and Barry De Vorzon's "In the City," an unusual-sounding, out-of-thematic-context song for any Eagles album, understandable since it had in fact appeared the year before on the sound track of Walter Hill's feature film *The Warriors*. Like the movie, the song is harsh, tough, loud, and somewhat crude, salvaged only by Walsh's superior guitar work. Its inclusion on *The Long Run* seemed to reflect nothing so much as Henley and Frey's paucity of new material.

Cut four, "Disco Strangler," represented a new low for the band. The Felder, Henley, and Frey composition, with lead vocal by Henley, was a nasty attack on the disco craze, done without a lot of humor, charm, irony, or musicality.

The final track on side one (of the original vinyl release), "King of Hollywood" (Henley-Frey), was another angry-sounding song, filled with the rocking clash of conflicting egos. Self-congratulatory and self-mocking, it chronicled the conquests of an L.A. lothario. Although close in theme and tone to the songs of *Hotel California,* it lacked that work's ironic distance, moral ambivalence, and lyrical sophistication.

Side two began with "Heartache Tonight," arguably the best song on the album. Although it was listed in the credits as a collaboration by Henley, Frey, Bob Seger, and the always reliable J. D. Souther, the fact that Frey sang the lead, plus the presence of his mentor Bob Seger on background vocals, suggests that it was much more Frey's song than Henley's. Enriched with Joe Walsh's slide-guitar playing and a hand-clapping rhythm section, "Heartache Tonight" was first-rate Eagles and rightly became the first single to be released from the album. Souther recalls: "Glenn and I were walking around my living room just clapping our hands, without any instruments, which is pretty much how we recorded it. I always thought 'Heartache' would have been a perfect song for Sam Cooke. Bob Seger, by the way, gave us the title."

"Those Shoes" was next, a Felder-Henley-Frey composition with lead vocal by Henley and tube-in-the-mouth "talk box" guitars by Walsh and Felder, along with an inspired solo by Walsh. Lyrically reminiscent of "Lyin' Eyes," it is the depiction of a hot young woman getting ready to go out on the town and, presumably, on the make. However, it lacked lyrical brilliance and was overproduced. This time around, the layers of imperious morality came off sounding cranky and cynical, with nothing new, interesting, or inspired.

"Teenage Jail" was even worse. Henley, Frey, and Souther collaborated on this oddly irritating song about no one seemed quite sure what. Teenage life is a prison? Teenage prison life? *Life in prison after being with a teen?* Its musical and thematic confusion make it completely forgettable in the canon of Eagles music.

"The Greeks Don't Want No Freaks" followed, with its fuzz-tone guitar opening sounding like the Beatles' "Birthday" and a vaguely doo-woppish background vocal featuring Jimmy Buffett and the Monstertones (Eagles techies and roadies). Another Henley-Frey composition, this was also not one of the songs for which they would be remembered.

Years later, Henley said of these last two, "I heard 'Teenage Jail' on the radio the other day and I laughed out loud in the car. At that point we were just saying to hell with it. We were so miserable making that album that it actually got funny at one point. Our humor got very dark and very sick and that's how 'Teenage Jail' and 'The Greeks Don't Want No Freaks' ended up on the record. I heard 'The Greeks Don't Want No Freaks' the other day, too, and I thought it was funny."

The album's final cut, "The Sad Café," one of the most elegiac tunes the band ever recorded, was set in a metaphorical café reminiscent of the early days at the Troubadour. Henley explains: "The song is about the demise of the club, the passing of the glory years, the fact that the city took up the railroad tracks from the middle of Santa Monica Boulevard. That's what the reference in the song to the tracks being gone is about. Steve Martin used to perform at the Troubadour when he was still a stand-up comedy banjo act, and he occasionally led the entire audience out of the club and onto those slow trains passing by. Everyone would pile onto a flatcar and ride to La Cienega Boulevard and then walk back.

"Those were truly great times, like when Doug Dillard's girlfriend tried to run him over in front of the club. He was with another woman, or had been, or something, and she drove right into the front window of the Troubadour trying to hit him.

"It had been everyone's favorite hangout. The Dillards, during the revival of bluegrass, would stand up at the front bar and sing a hymn, and everyone would join in. Harry Dean Stanton would hang out, Jackson, J. D., Graham Nash, Kris Kristofferson, Joni Mitchell, Linda, the Everly Brothers, Jack Nicholson would stop by. . . . It was the place to be, the center of the universe, as far as I was concerned.

"And it's about Dan Tana's, the restaurant next door, the other half of the craziness. If things got a little too crowded or crazy, we'd just go over to Tana's, get a booth, have a drink and eat some spaghetti. We wrote a lot of songs in there, fell in love, got in fights, snorted drugs in the wine room or the restroom. At the Troub, I saw Elton John's debut on the American stage, just him and a piano, very unflamboyant. Janis Joplin in there just a few days before she died, sitting at a table looking very unhappy, a kind of premonitional vision. We wrote the song as an acknowledgment that those glory days were definitely over."

It was dedicated in the album's liner notes to the memory of John Barrick, the onetime road manager for the group who died in the early seventies before the Eagles' glory days. Still, for all its good intentions, the song wallowed sentimentally in memories of irretrievable innocence. And it sounded a little too much like "The Last Resort," using a similar chord pattern and rhythmic structure. This time, however, despite David Sanborn's beautiful, mournful saxophone solo, the effort felt self-conscious, a dramatic denouement less forceful than forced.

The Long Run offered a clear demonstration that the band, whose members were all in their thirties now, had taken their adventure about as far into rock (and out of country) as they could. They had begun to repeat their style and themes without extending the range of their music. *The Long Run* sounded more self-imitative than innovative, a studio-created echo of their younger, faster, more melodically exciting days.

According to Henley, "By and large I don't think [*The Long Run* is] a very good record. We needed a vacation. We needed to take some time off and away from each other and we didn't do it. We just kept going until we burned out. There was always that pressure from record companies and ourselves to follow up 'Hotel California': 'Give us another one of those!' You can't do that again. I think we realized we had peaked. I think in the back of our minds we knew we had reached that zenith that all groups reach. We had seen our finest hour. We were spiritually exhausted and really had nothing more to say."

The album ("The Long One," as it had come to be known in Warner's executive halls) was finally ready for release on September 24, 1979. The first new collection of original Eagles songs in nearly three years, *The Long Run* proved an immediate hit. Driven by the release of the first single, "Heartache Tonight," which shot to number one, the album also entered the charts at the top position, where it remained for nine weeks, longer than any other album that year. The single "The Long Run" also made the top ten (number eight), as did "I Can't Tell You Why" (number eight). By the first week in February, the album was certified gold.

The demand for any new Eagles product proved just how strong the group's popularity with the public continued to be, a fact that wasn't lost on *Rolling Stone*. When the album came out, Wenner's magazine gave it the coveted lead record review slot and a surprisingly positive nod. Timothy White, in a piece entitled "Last Tycoons in a Lost Lotusland" called *The Long Run* "A chilling and altogether brilliant evocation of Hollywood's nightly Witching Hour. . . . Not a collection of hot car-radio singles, *The Long Run* is a raw synthesis of previous macabre Eagles motifs, with cynical new insights that are underlined by slashing rock & roll."

White's and *Rolling Stone's* would not be the prevailing critical view. Writing in the *Los Angeles Times*, Robert Hilburn, from the beginning one of the band's most enthusiastic supporters, panned the album. He was disappointed by its many weaknesses, especially the lack of subjective first-person emotion that had marked so many of the Eagles' greatest songs in the past.

Others found the album's message confused and ultimately disappointing, the music too downbeat, the lyrics overly self-absorbed and underarticulated. In the end, the Eagles had proved that looking back was simply not a particularly compelling subject for rock and roll, particularly when it came from the other side of the great generational divide.

Ultimately, despite its early surge, *The Long Run* was no *Hotel California*, either in content or sales. (It eventually sold seven million copies in the U.S.A.) With strong Christmas release competition for chart position from Pink Floyd (*The Wall*) and Fleetwood Mac (*Tusk*), one thing became clear. To keep the album on the charts through the new year, the band was going to have to sell it, which meant one more long run down the concert trail.

The Eagles returned to their early practice of breaking in material by traveling as far away from their home turf as they could get. The choice this time was Japan, where their audiences always proved far less critical than those in America. They returned to the States in January 1980, just in time to appear at a benefit for Governor Jerry Brown held in San Diego's Sports Arena. The event took on an air of unexpected nostalgia, as the Eagles, J. D. Souther, and Linda Ronstadt (now dating the governor) appeared onstage together. Ronstadt sang her version of "Alison," written by Elvis Costello.

Backstage, the bickering among the group erupted again, this time when Henley, apparently having second thoughts, expressed his unease to the others about the Eagles, the great nonpolitical band of the seventies, appearing at too many of these fund-raisers. Recently, Henley reminded the others, they had turned down appearance requests from such luminaries as Ted Kennedy in his run for president. When asked about it, Frey joked to reporters, "We did [the benefit for Brown] because Linda was going out with Jerry."

Henley, out of loyalty to and respect for Ronstadt, agreed to do the show. However, in a rare *Rolling Stone* interview (to promote the album), he made it known that he thought "it really was not a very good idea to do benefit concerts for individual politicians. Jackson . . . kind of influenced us to get involved in the antinuclear movement and some more political things. But we always had to be careful. Politics is a dirty game and being involved on any level could have hurt us or the people or movement we were trying to support." Henley was also acutely aware that taking sides, especially in an election year, could alienate half the band's audience, the kind of alienation that could cost a lot of record sales.

The benefit kicked off the American leg of the *Long Run* tour. J. D. Souther joined the band on several dates, helping out on background vocals and providing an additional acoustic guitar. He also gave the others a breather in the middle of the set when he sang a couple of songs off his recent solo album, *You're Only Lonely.*

Throughout the tour, the tension between the Eagles remained high. On a set with thirty-five standing guitars, something as simple as entering and exiting the stage became a problem. More than one shoulder brushed against another, and heads turned a little too quickly. Backstage, tempers flared and fingers pointed in faces. When band members left a venue, they tried to avoid each other as much as possible. Each had a suite in a different hotel. During sound checks, messages between Frey and Henley continued to be passed through an ever-increasing number of go-betweens. Still, when the lights came up, the boys were always in place, the band's tough professionalism, rather than artistic inspiration, pulling it through. On those occasions when a backstage journalist happened to catch one member of the band arguing with another, Azoff was always ready with spin. After one particularly exhilarating show when the band members came off stage and disappeared without saying a word to anyone, Azoff, for the first time willing to acknowledge the obvious, that the band might be approaching the endgame, told Robert Hilburn of the *L.A. Times:* "The recording of 'Long Run' could have broken 'em. The longer you're in a band, if you don't let the standards slip, the harder it is. The first album was recorded in two, three weeks. The second in four weeks and so forth. 'Hotel California' took nine months. 'Long Run' took 1½ years. They're 32,

33 years old now. They've built houses. They've made tons of money, but they haven't had time off to really enjoy it. So, there are lots of reasons to back off from all the pressure. The thing that keeps them together is they enjoy the music. If that music doesn't continue to hold them, it could all disintegrate in a second."

Henley added to the feeling that things were coming to a close for the Eagles when, later that night, he told Hilburn, "What I think I'd like to do is make a really great studio album — maybe even a double album — to go out on. I'd like to see us go out gracefully, like the Band did, rather than wait until it starts going down." Away from the press, Henley was more direct about his intentions. He confided to one friend that he couldn't see ever again putting himself through anything like the difficult, tension-filled process of the making of *The Long Run*. "It just isn't worth it," he said.

In February 1980, the Eagles won the Grammy for Best Rock Vocal Performance for a Duo or Group for the single "Heartache Tonight." This time, Pierre Cossette, the show's producer, didn't bother to go through the motions of asking Azoff if the group would appear or perform. His instincts were correct. Because the Eagles' feelings about the hypocrisy of the awards hadn't changed, they would have declined the invitation to play.

In March, the Eagles returned to Los Angeles for their first live non-benefit performances there in more than three years, five sold-out shows at the Forum. On opening night, Elton John joined the group onstage for a medley of Chuck Berry songs. That show, like the four that followed, was greeted ecstatically by the band's hometown audience. The *Los Angeles Times* called these performances the Eagles' best since the *Desperado* tour. On closing night, during the final encore, the band's opening act, country-rock legend Roy Orbison, made a surprise appearance. Still, for many, the highlight of the tour was the moment during every performance when the band would come down to the front of the stage, sit on stools set up in front of mikes, and reach back into the past to perform a beautiful, nostalgically tinged acoustic version of their unrecorded country-playlist perennial, Steve Young's "Seven Bridges," a tribute to the Southern California seventies that had delivered them to fame, wealth, and glory.

The tour proved so successful that one night in Canada, the Eagles, for the first time in their history, broke through the magic barrier of a million-dollar gate for a single show. Not long after, Joe Smith, looking ahead to the 1980 Christmas season, once again began to press the Eagles for new product to boost the label's year-end numbers. Like everyone else, Smith sensed the end was near but still hoped to get one last album from the band — if not a collection of new songs, perhaps a live collection.

"I spent a year trying to convince the Eagles to do a live album," Smith recalled. "I knew they were going to break up, and I needed that last one. I made the pitch to them that at one point in every artist's career if they've done a lot of appearances, the audience always wants to relive that moment, and they seemed to go along.

"I figured on a two-record set, which would make the wholesale price six or seven dollars, and knew I could easily sell five, six, even seven million albums around the world. They were scheduled to do a special weeklong set of intimate shows at the Santa Monica Civic Auditorium, starting on a Monday and ending on a Friday, which would give us plenty of performances and material to choose from.

"Then, just before the shows were to take place, I got a call from Irving. 'I think we have a problem with the guys,' he said.

"'What are you talking about?' I said. 'What problem?'

"'Well,' he said, 'Let Glenn talk to you.'

"So Glenn gets on the phone and says, 'Joe, Don and I just don't want to be spending any time together. We don't get along, it's stale, you want us to do a new song in this, we said we'd do it, that means we have to sit and edit it, and you know how we are. We'll be hours in there, and we're just going to get into a fistfight every night over something or other, and we can make more money going out and playing three dates fast and doing that . . .'

"'I can't believe I'm hearing this,' I said.

"'But,' he said, 'we promised you, so we'll give you a chance here. If you can answer a question, we will do the album.'

"I said, 'Hey, this isn't *Let's Make a Deal*! This is serious!' Well, we used to play a lot of baseball trivia, particularly Glenn and I. So now he says, 'In 1971, the Baltimore Orioles had four pitchers that each won more than twenty games. Can you name them?'

"They claim that if you see your child under the wheels of a truck, you have the superhuman power to lift that truck. I saw forty million dollars, and every chip in my brain starting whirring, processing 1971 pitchers, and I named all four of them. Dave McNally, Jim Palmer, Mike Cuellar, and Pat Dobson. 'So guys,' I said. 'What do you think?'

" 'We'll see you Monday night,' Glenn said. Later on, I asked them separately what they would have done if I hadn't come up with the right answer, and both swore they would have skipped the live album and gone back out on the road.

"You couldn't hardball guys like the Eagles. What else could I do?"

Not much. Smith, who remained one of the band's strongest supporters at the label, knew the live album was almost certainly the group's last. Even if he were somehow able to suddenly solve all the band's internal problems, the hard truth was that the Eagles were in the seventh and final year of their contract. Keeping them would cost Warner a fortune, and there was a growing feeling among the other suits that the "boys" had simply gotten too old. The hard but obvious truth was that their core audience, which continued to support the band, the kids who'd grown up with the Eagles, was long past the demographic peak and didn't buy nearly as many records as the eighteen to twenty-fives did.

Still, when word got out in L.A. that the Eagles were going to do a week of concerts that fall at the legendary 3,000-seat Santa Monica Civic Auditorium to record a tour-ending "live" album, the tickets became the hottest in town. According to Ken Graham, "They wanted to do a very special show in their hometown. We hung two columns of sound per side, so we could keep the volume low and yet very fat. And we had more lights than we ever had on any show before, indoors or out, including the big stadiums. We brought everything into that little theater. We had sidelights, we had side follow-spots suspended, every backdrop we had, all the way back to *Desperado*, we found a way to rig, so we could fly them out for the different songs. We really went over the top."

Just before the week of scheduled shows was to begin, Henley found time to help out a struggling Randy Meisner on his second solo album, *One More Song*. Meisner, back in L.A. looking to take another shot at a solo career, had called Henley to ask if he'd consider playing on the album, and he agreed. Meisner caught a real moment with the great "Deep Inside My Heart" (with Kim Carnes), and the single went to number twenty-two on the charts. Two other songs from the album, "Hearts on Fire" and

"Gotta Get Away," also did well. The album rose to the number fifty position on *Billboard*'s chart before fading away.

Following the tremendous success of the Santa Monica Civic Auditorium shows, the Eagles agreed to do a benefit in Long Beach to raise money for California senator Alan Cranston's reelection campaign fund. The band had recently done a fair amount of fund-raising, including several benefits for Native Americans, particularly the California-based Chumash tribe. The stunning success of the recent MUSE (Musicians United for Safe Energy) concerts in New York City may have weighed in the decision to do one more. The cover of the issue of *Rolling Stone* that had given them the lead review for *The Long Run* featured a group shot of the stars of MUSE. There they were — Bonnie Raitt, Bruce Springsteen, James Taylor, Carly Simon, Graham Nash, John Hall (of Orleans), and Jackson Browne — looking out from every newsstand in America. MUSE had been the brainchild of artists Hall, Browne, Raitt, and Nash and activists Sam Lovejoy, Howard Kohn, Tom Campbell, and David Fenton, founded to raise awareness in America of the danger of atomic energy and to honor the memory of antinuclear activist Karen Silkwood, who'd been found dead in her car, a Jackson Browne tape engaged in the cassette player.

The MUSE shows proved a smashing success. They packed Madison Square Garden and drew enormous crowds at outdoor rallies held around the city. A double album was released and quickly went platinum. A film was made that scored heavily at the box office. As well as raising money for a good cause, every performer connected to the show benefited from a terrific image boost, the kind that the best PR campaigns in the world couldn't buy.

With all that in mind, Frey especially was eager to affiliate the Eagles with a newsworthy political event, and a benefit for the liberal senator seemed perfect. According to Henley, "The decision to do a benefit concert had absolutely nothing to do with the MUSE shows at Madison Square Garden, nor did it have anything to do with an attempt to get an 'image boost' (as if we needed one). The decision to help Alan Cranston in his reelection campaign was the direct result of a visit the Eagles made to his office in Washington, D.C., while the band was in the area. Band members and Irving Azoff talked with the senator at length and were very impressed with his record on several matters that concerned the band, including Native American issues, environment, and the proliferation of nuclear power plants and nuclear weapons."

The decision, however, was not a unanimous one among the band members. Walsh said fine. So did Schmit. Felder, however, voted against it, saying he was suspicious of all politicians. "Bull," said one close to the band at the time, "He wanted the money. He didn't like to play for free, no matter what the cause." Either way, he wasn't about to do any favors for Frey, whom he'd never gotten along with and blamed for limiting him to only two songs on *The Long Run*. Henley also had his reservations but agreed to go along with whatever the majority of the band decided. With Azoff's blessing, after much acrimonious debate, they decided to do the benefit.

The afternoon of the performance, the Eagles agreed to sit for what was for them a rare event — a live press conference. Most of the questions revolved around what Cranston represented to the Eagles and why they had agreed to do this. In response to a question directed at him regarding the band's politics, Felder shrugged his shoulders and said Cranston was not that important to him, that as far as he was concerned this was just another show. He shot a pointed glance at Frey and then looked away.

Frey was furious, and continued to burn backstage before the concerts. There had been from the beginning a layer of animosity between the two. Some of it was musical. Felder had always wanted to be considered a lead singer in the band as much as a guitar player, which he was not capable of being, at least not in this band. He had also wanted to write more songs than there was room for. There were also complaints from Felder about money. He insisted on knowing where every penny was going, often going into the other band members' rooms on the road to make sure his was as big as theirs. One close to the band thought it became a pathological thing: "Am I getting my fair share of the money, am I getting my fair share of the glory, am I getting my fair share of the chicks, am I getting my fair share of the dope, is my limo as big as his limo?"

Eventually his pushing and shoving brought a measure of reward when he became, along with Henley and Frey, one of the three corporate owners of "The Eagles." For all he had gotten, especially having joined the band after its first, and hardest, incarnation, Frey felt Felder was profoundly ungrateful. Even as a full business partner, he remained unsatisfied, feeling that no one gave him due credit for his musical contributions to the band. It was a short leap to his not wanting to do benefits for anybody, no matter who or what the cause was.

Still, both Frey and Felder had allowed it to turn personal, and at this show, the heat turned a few degrees hotter.

Henley told Frey to stop making a big deal out of it, but as they took their places behind the stage curtain, according to one backstage observer, "If looks could kill, Felder would have been dead. Frey stared at him through the backstage darkness, never taking his eyes off him for a second."

When the curtain went up, the band kicked in, and even as they sang and played, Frey began riding Felder. "When this show is done," he said at one point, "I'm going to kick your ass." Up in the sound booth the two techies running the board dove for the dials, pulling Frey's mike back to zero except when he sang to prevent the audience from hearing what he was saying to Felder. Frey kept it up, after each song walking up to Felder and letting him know how many were left before he was going to get his ass kicked.

"That's three more, pal, get ready."

"No sweat," Felder replied, getting an adrenaline rush as the band slipped into the delicate harmonies of "The Best of My Love" and brought the crowd to its feet.

When the curtain came down, Felder, perhaps feeling as if he might actually be about to get his ass kicked, quickly left the stage. The exit route for the band was a staircase that led behind the columns holding up the Long Beach Arena. As Felder started down the stairway, Frey rushed toward him. Felder whirled around and began swinging an acoustic guitar over his head like Davy Crockett at the Alamo. Frey stopped short, and the two shouted threats at each other until Felder smashed the guitar into one of the columns, sending a crazy, loud clang echoing through the arena as splintered wood flew everywhere.

As if on cue, blistering arguments broke out between some members of the band. They all got into each other's faces, screaming and shoving, until a dozen roadies decided to step in before somebody got hurt. Felder jumped into his limo and took off, with Frey shouting after him, *You cheap asshole, you would break the cheapest guitar!*

When things finally calmed down, a still-angry Frey left the arena without saying a word to anyone. The next day he placed a direct call to Azoff to say he was getting involved in some other projects and would not be available for the remainder of the tour.

Azoff wasn't concerned. This kind of thing happened in one way or another at the end of every Eagles tour. There was always one member of the band saying he was quitting and never coming back.

A few weeks later, in mid-October, Henley received a call from Frey. "We started the conversation as usual, talking about football. Then he said he wanted out and to do his own thing. Not forever, he said, but for a while. He said he had some ideas for an album. I knew what he was telling me. He may have been trying to low-key it, but the message was clear. I knew during the making of *The Long Run* he felt that maybe he had taken a backseat to me, and maybe I'd been taking up too much of the oxygen in the room. For the sake of the band he had sacrificed a lot of things he'd wanted to do, to make it go, to push me up to the front and write the lyrics and maybe sing more songs, at his expense. He was feeling creatively and artistically short-changed.

"I understood that. I wished him luck and hung up. And that was it. The Eagles were history. After a couple of days, as reality sunk in, everything else in my life fell apart, and I began seriously freaking out."

Azoff tried everything he could think of to effect a truce among the boys, but nothing worked. They even traveled individually and at different times to Florida to supervise their parts for the final mixes for the *Eagles Live* album. Sometimes they didn't even bother with that and simply sent their edits in by mail. According to Bill Szymczyk, "When we were doing fixes on the album, I had my assistant in Los Angeles with Glenn, and I had the rest of the band [fly to] Miami. We were fixing three-part harmonies courtesy of Federal Express."

Joe Smith, who'd hoped to have at least one new song on the album to increase its "sell" potential, offered the group a million dollars *a song* for two new ones. He got nothing.

Eagles Live was released on November 7, 1980, reached number six on the charts, went platinum, and even yielded a single hit. The group's version of "Seven Bridges Road," the only performance song they had never previously recorded, went to number twenty-seven on the singles charts. "Jesus," one record executive noted. "How bad could things get? These guys could sing a chorus of 'shit stinks on shinola' and sell a million copies!"

And Irving Azoff knew it, which made the breakup of his gorgeous flock of golden birds that much worse. As far as he was concerned, this was a truly lousy way to open the eighties.

PART THREE

THE END OF
THE INNOCENCE

FOURTEEN

Don Henley was having a bad day. Four months after the breakup of the band, he was still mourning the end of the Eagles. Hungover and exhausted from yet another marathon jag of drinking and nose candy, he stood in the center of the small neat garden behind his house in the hills, squinting from the bright morning sun. The grass was perfectly manicured, as always, the huge trees smartly pruned. Although modest by superstar standards, for Henley this little hacienda was perfect: spacious, yet small and easy to manage. He'd taken a personal interest in its design and was quite proud of the way it had turned out. From where he stood, he could see the entire city spread out before him, just like on one of those quarter postcards they sold at the liquor stores down on Sunset.

He hadn't gone out much lately. For the last couple of weeks, since the plane crash, the thought of even venturing down to the Strip seemed a bit too dangerous for him. It felt like a different century there, a hundred years from those heady days when the entire town seemed his personal playground. Before the Eagles had flown the coop and gone their separate ways. Before *"Glenn Frey"* became the chant from the crowd he couldn't ignore during the band's last show in Japan. Before he began to conduct business at home.

Here in his own words is Henley's account of what he went through during the harrowing days, weeks, and months following the breakup of the Eagles: "The group's splitting really sent me over the edge. At the time I thought my life was over. My God, what am I going to do now? On the one hand it lasted a lot longer than I ever expected it to. I had had more of a career than I'd ever anticipated in my wildest dreams, but on the other hand I felt like I wasn't done yet, I still had a lot to offer, I was relatively young, and then I met Maren Jensen.

"I was in Miami trying to finish the live album while Glenn was in L.A. Fed Exing tapes back and forth. I was down there trying to pull all that together. Maren, an actress, was going to the same exercise class I was, and our teacher sort of introduced us. I called her up, she met me for dinner one night, and we started dating. This was just after I'd gotten back with Lois Chiles, whom I'd been dating on and off, when I realized that was over for good. These were my first romantic experiences with working actresses, and it's when I first realized what a cruel, hideous meat market the film industry is, how it chews women up and spits them out. I wasn't ready for it. It hurt me having to deal with women like Lois and then Maren coming home every day telling me what some guy had tried to do to them. I couldn't handle it. I'd want to march down to the studio, or the producer's office, or the director's house and shoot them in the head.

"Lois was a bit stronger than Maren, who was relatively fragile. She was doing her TV series, *Battlestar Gallactica,* and backstage on the set someone high up in the production pinned her against the wall and started feeling her up. That was her initiation to Hollywood.

"And there was the plane crash, in October 1980, which scared the hell out of us. 'Come on, we're going in a Lear jet and hang out at my ranch in Colorado,' I'd said, or something like that to impress her. I guess the guy had never flown into Aspen before. The plane didn't have reverse thrust, which is desirable for landing in Aspen. He came in too high, meaning altitude not brain, and too fast, and burned out the brake pads. We went sailing off the end of the runway at about sixty miles an hour, went through a cow pasture, a couple of barbed-wire fences, which helped to slow the plane down. Rocks ripped the entire bottom of the plane off. I was afraid the plane was going to explode. I had the presence of mind to try to get the emergency door open. Maren thought we were going to die. She looked over at me, gripped my hand, and said 'I love you.' I thought to myself, 'Shit, if I can just get through this, *the girl loves me. . . .'*

"I grabbed the emergency door and ripped it off while the plane was still rolling. We were slowing down to a speed that wasn't lethal. Still, one spark from one rock and the entire plane would have exploded. I threw Maren out of the plane. I looked up through the cockpit, and through the front window [I could see] the fucking copilot running in the field. The pilot, to his credit, was flipping overhead toggle switches off as the fire trucks were coming.

"Maren landed on a huge boulder, on her stomach and face. She was black and blue all over. I jumped out behind her, and we started running as fast as we could, over barbed wire and rocks. Two days later I saw them lifting the wreckage with a crane, hanging there like a fish. The funny part is the plane company sent me a seven-thousand-dollar bill for the flight. Irving sent it back with a note scrawled across the front — 'We do not pay for crash landings.'

"Shortly after that, Maren got a part in this hideous movie, *Deadly Blessing,* produced by Jon Peters, which was being shot in Dallas, of all places. She had to take her top off and do a love scene with some hunky guy, and that was hard for the both of us. Maren, bless her heart, wasn't aggressive enough and driven to be a star. She was too gentle. Her lineage is Danish and Hawaiian, and she was just not a tough girl. I wasn't cut out for it, either, to be the boyfriend of an actress who had to do this kind of stuff. Even though it was acting, I didn't like seeing my girlfriend up on the screen, with everybody else watching, making it with some guy. Maybe I wasn't secure enough as a man, or maybe I was right. Shooting in Dallas stressed her out so much she fell ill on the set, and they put her in the hospital. Because the film had to continue, they took her out and put her back on the set. She finished the film, got back to L.A., and collapsed.

"It took us two or three years to get her properly diagnosed. She had Epstein-Barr, which is now called chronic fatigue syndrome. They didn't know what it was back then, which is why a lot of rumors went around the set that the real reason she was sick was because we were both junkies and she was shooting up. I took Maren to Scripps Institute, in San Diego, to try to find out what was wrong with her. They suggested she see a shrink. Just another crazy actress. We went to several doctors in L.A. before we finally got it properly diagnosed.

"At the time this was all very difficult for me to handle. My group had just broken apart, and I had, in a sense, tried to move on and grow up by dating this beautiful girl, who shortly thereafter practically became an invalid. She was literally in bed for a year. I had to feed her, help her get to the bathroom. It was hard for me to cope, and as a result I began to drink more heavily, and do other stuff.

"Back in L.A. we hibernated. We stayed in my L.A. house, where she moved when the film was done. She couldn't go out, she couldn't be around people, which fueled a whole new rash of rumors about what was going on. Then my mother got breast cancer and had to have a mastectomy.

"I was lost and scared." On top of everything else, he was the victim of a police conspiracy that was the focused attempt by the LAPD and the powers behind them to "clean up" the entertainment business. Rock stars and well-known movie and TV people were being busted all over the place, and many were forced to turn in friends. Plus, a lot of the drug dealers and Hollywood madams were very closely wired into the local political scene. When the shit hit the fan, they were the first to ask for, and receive, protection. Some of it was the coming of the Reagan years. Some of it had to do with an ongoing dislike for those with privilege, power, and youth. Some of it had to do with politics, as it seemed only the most liberal were targeted. He was warned that he was being watched but didn't think much of it. There was one incident where he was definitely set up. "I was stupid and naive, but it was obvious they wanted to hang me and put me away. I was fortunate enough to get out of it relatively unscathed. Except it made me even more of a recluse. Maren, to her credit, sick as she was, stood by me during my own rough time, as I did for her.

"And there was the lunatic brigade. I got death threats from some guy because I wouldn't listen to his tapes, which sounded a little too close to the Charlie Manson scenario of 1969. Maren had stalkers. One was male, one was female. They took over her persona. One managed to get the key to her mailbox and took checks, got her social security number, and *became* her.

"Then John Lennon was killed. That freaked me out. I had an armed guard at my house for a year. It was a bizarre time. Everything was wrong.

"On the one hand I was sick and tired of all the drama and all the fighting that went on with the band. Breaking up was in some ways a horrible relief. I tried to bury the Eagles in the past with as much dignity as I could, saying, 'Oh well, okay, we all need to go our separate ways and do our own thing.' In reality, it scared me to death. I literally did not know what I was going to do with the rest of my life. I was still a shy person, I didn't want to be out front, and I was a collaborator who needed someone to bounce things off of in my writing. The trouble was, I had no one. It was, really, the lowest point of my life."

Everyone else, it seemed, was working and wanted Henley to know it. Randy Meisner was on the road. Joe Walsh had just released a solo album.

Henley had heard that Walsh was performing a couple of Eagles songs on his support tour, including "Life in the Fast Lane." Very funny, as in *not!*

In November 1981, Don Felder released his first solo album, *Heavy Metal.* The headline in the *L.A. Times* entertainment section read, "Felder Flies Without the Eagles," confirming the obvious, that the Eagles had officially broken up. In reply to a question about the status of the band, Felder told the reporter, "The Eagles are on a semi-vacation, in limbo trying to figure out what the next step is."

Six months later, Glenn Frey removed any lingering doubts as to the future of the most popular band of the seventies. "I knew the Eagles were over halfway through 'The Long Run,'" Glenn Frey told the *Los Angeles Times* in May 1982 as part of an interview to promote *his* debut solo album, *No Fun Aloud* — and to make it clear that he was the one who'd broken up the band. He wanted everyone to know that as far as he was concerned he had always been the leader of the band. "I could give you 30 reasons why but let me be concise about it: I started the band, I got tired of it and I quit."

For his debut album, Frey found a collaborator in old friend Jack Tempchin, who'd cowritten several Eagles songs, including "Peaceful Easy Feeling." With *No Fun Aloud,* Frey hoped to achieve the same kind of success. Together they wrote five of the ten songs on the album. Depicted on the album's cover with short hair and without his signature droop mustache, wearing a fashionable white suit and a red tie, Frey was inviting himself into the eighties. To some, he looked foolish, old and tired and absurdly out of fashion. To others, he had performed a miraculous transformation and become the contemporary ultracool, clean-cut *former* Eagle.

Although *No Fun Aloud* ranks among the best and most appealing of Frey's solo work, it failed to catch on with the public in the way he and Asylum had hoped. The album made a steady run up the charts, rising to number thirty-two, then took another seven months to go gold, an agonizingly slow climb to the half-million sales level. It yielded three moderate hits, "I Found Somebody" (number thirty-one), "The One You Love" (number fifteen), and "All Those Lies" (number forty-one).

For anyone else, these numbers would have been proof of a very successful solo debut. For Glenn Frey, they were what one industry observer described as a disaster. Meisner's solo career's going nowhere was one thing. Frey's post-Eagles flop was far more noticeable and, in its way, damaging to the band's reputation.

The professional and personal misfortunes of the individual band members became something of a grim joke among Warner executives, who spoke of "the curse of the Eagles."

No fun allowed? Frey's solo album was a festival of frivolity compared to what Henley intended to bring to the party.

The two things Don Henley needed to get back into music were a new writing partner and a producer, because he had no intention of ever working with "*Glenn Frey*" again. He had heard nothing from Frey since the breakup in Long Beach, which was fine with him. As for Bill Szymczyk, Henley liked his work and had nothing against him personally — the problem was purely geographic. Szymczyk no longer wanted to come to L.A., and the thought of having to travel to Florida each time he wanted to lay down or fix a track did not appeal to Henley.

Indeed, going to the store still seemed like a major journey. In the months following the breakup of the group, Henley had, as he says, become a recluse, preferring to spend his days inside the safety and protection of his house, contacting the outside world by talking on the phone and writing letters. *Lots* of letters. Known for his trigger-happy pen, Henley had always preferred written confrontations to physical ones. Now he found he could hardly stop writing them, to anyone about anything. Friends and associates always looked forward to getting missives from Henley. Whether friendly, hectoring, or angry, they were always long, involved, detailed, highly opinionated, and very entertaining. The subject matter had no boundaries — something someone said that offended him, an incident he'd observed, advice for a politician, an admonition for a friend he felt had wronged him. Recipients considered the letters trophies and took to comparing notes with others who'd received "Henleys" to see whose were more outrageous.

He became so involved with writing letters it seemed at times like an intellectual obsession. Record executive Danny Goldberg, a friend of Henley's, has two "Henleys" framed and hanging in his office alongside several gold records. "One of the best books in the entertainment business would be a collection of Don's letters," recalled Irving Azoff. "I've got a great file." John Boylan refers to Henley as "the mad faxer." One night after a recording session in the midseventies in Szymczyk's Coconut Grove, Florida, studio, Henley wrote what would become his most infamous missive. After he'd spent a long day in the studio followed by some heavy partying back at the hotel, he composed a detailed memo to the maid. He wanted to make sure she understood his preference for the toilet paper coming off the top of the roll rather than the bottom, something she could not seem to get straight. The story goes that part of the memo explained that if the paper had been meant to unroll from the bottom, the pink flowers would have been printed on the inside.

When Henley wasn't passing the day changing the world with his letters and memos, he actually tried to write lyrics. His pattern of work was varied, sometimes writing lines longhand on legal pads while stretched atop his bed, eventually shaping them into lyrics against a recorded click or rhythm track.

He listened to his favorite albums and began to notice a certain sound floating to the surface, particularly in the records of Jackson Browne and James Taylor. He especially liked the approach of Browne's backup band, the core of which was made up of guitarist David Lindley, drummer Russ Kunkel, bassist Lee Sklar, and guitarist-arranger Danny "Kootch" Kortchmar. Henley gradually focused on the contribution of Kortchmar, whose name went to the top of the list of possible collaborators.

Kortchmar grew up with the nickname Happy because, as he later remembered, "I was the most miserable kid you've ever seen in your life. I never smiled. I always wore black. My friends would see me in the summers going to the beach dressed in black. I grew up in Larchmont, which was only twenty minutes out of New York City but still very provincial. I couldn't relate to much that was going on there until I heard rock and roll on the radio when I was seven or eight years old. I especially liked the blues, which is the first music I really got into, folk blues, country blues." Kortchmar had originally been a member of James Taylor's sixties band Flying Machine, which caught the attention of Peter Asher, then the A&R representative for the Beatles' fledgling Apple label. Asher eventually became Taylor's manager and when both were in L.A., introduced the singer and his band to his other major client, Linda Ronstadt, and also good friend Jackson Browne, thus giving them entrée to the select inner circle of Troubadour singers and songwriters.

Henley had met Kortchmar at the Troubadour front bar, known him socially for years, and had recorded with almost everyone Kootch had: Linda Ronstadt, Warren Zevon, and of course Glenn Frey, whom, Henley noticed, Kootch had played with on *No Fun Aloud*. After thinking it over for a couple of days, Henley decided to give Kortchmar a call, knowing he'd have to wrest him away from Frey, Jackson Browne, and his own group, Jo Mama.

As Henley suspected, his and Kortchmar's musical taste meshed, more so than their dark, implosive, somewhat insecure personalities. The former made them the ideal team, the latter made it hard to actually get anything done. They went into the recording studio, where they discovered they both liked to stay high while they worked, these days by sharing a drink. According to Henley, "Kootch and I were just guzzling scotch and vodka; we'd record until three in the morning and then go to my house, sit up with bottles, and tell each other how great we are, just to bolster our confidence." He adds, "He was easy to hang out with. We both had a taste for alcohol and drugs. We were both ravers. We both had fire in our belly. He was just as angry as I was, if not angrier. We hit it off right from the start. I really liked him, and he really understood me. Plus, he was so talented and so versatile. It was fortunate for me, if a bit slow moving."

To move the project along, Kootch suggested to Henley it might be a good idea to hire their mutual friend producer Greg Ladanyi, who was responsible for many of the best recordings of Browne, Ronstadt, Taylor, and Zevon.

Ladanyi recalled, "I was working with Danny [Kortchmar] on something else, and we were a loose sort of team. Danny and I had made a lot of records, starting I guess with Jackson's *Running on Empty,* which we recorded live, and for me, as an engineer, was an amazing education. It's where I figured out how to make records.

"What Kootch and I eventually did was to try to capture an identifiable L.A. sound. What we captured on record with Jackson, James, Linda, and Warren was what everybody meant when they talked about L.A. rock and roll, a group of players who played on everybody else's records and made a very clean sound with great, perfect-sounding harmonies."

It took Henley a year to complete his first solo album. Unlike Frey's *No Fun Aloud*, for which no one at Asylum had been able to muster any real enthusiasm, Henley's *I Can't Stand Still* generated a solid buzz, especially one track, "Johnny Can't Read," which many at the label considered a can't-miss hit single. "My mother was a teacher," Henley comments, "and she used to come home all the time and say she couldn't understand how they passed these kids from one grade to another when they didn't have the basic reading or learning skills. It was appalling then, and they still do it. Randy Newman always said he thought it was a brave song because I blamed the kid. In our liberal society, it was always fashionable to blame the teachers, the schools, the parents, anybody but Johnny himself. I just thought that it was time to blame Johnny for his own failure. Plus, where I grew up football was God, still is, and if you were in the band you were a sissy, looked down upon. You know, it's-good-to-be-stupid anti-intellectualism."

Greg Ladanyi recalls, " 'Johnny Can't Read' was the combination of Kootch and Don — Kootch's sound and Don's lyrics. The song is about a guy who goes to school but never gets the chance to excel. As a result, he grows up stupid. We and the label were so excited about that cut we did it in four languages — French, Italian, English, and Spanish. It was supposed to be the biggest song of the year."

It wasn't. According to Henley, "The song really pissed some people in radio off, I guess because it criticized things like football. There were deejays in the South, particularly in Houston, Atlanta, and Alabama, who were really offended by the song." The single only reached number forty-two on the charts, but nevertheless established Henley's solo music as legitimate and markedly different from the songs he had developed, both as writer and singer, with the Eagles. Layered with a pumping, nervous rhythm section, a piping organ, and a female chorus, the music was startlingly original.

Ladanyi says, "Don's really smart; he knows a lot about what he reads and looks into and what he wants to do. He's also flexible; he lets people do what they want, up to a point, but like anybody else who knows what he wants, Don has the last word, and sometimes that can be frustrating. Still, I enjoyed working with him. I learned a lot about a lot of things.

Songwriting ... patience ... frustration ... patience. Don takes a *very* long time to make a record. The reason being, I think, simply because he can. He's not the kind of person that needs to rush through something to make it happen, whereas today a lot of artists don't have that kind of flexibility, to write a song over three or four months. I mean, they have to do it quickly because there's no money. If one has the time, it means he has the money to take the time, then, if that's what he wants to do, great. I think that's where Don was at. It was his time ... nobody else's, and nobody was about to tell him how to use it, or how fast to go.

"I think he had something to prove, or felt he did, going solo. That first album was really a collaboration among all three of us, Don, Danny, and me. The idea was to make a record that was *not* an Eagle record, that didn't *sound* like an Eagle record. One of the things we did to make it happen was to take Don off the drums. That instantly gave the record another groove pocket that would not be familiar to people listening to it, because Don as the drummer for the Eagles created their groove. When that changes, everything else is going to change.

"Then there is the writing of Danny and Don together as opposed to the writing of Don and Glenn. Completely different. Plus, Danny is a much different guitar player than Glenn is, in both technique and style, maybe a little funkier and more groove-oriented than Glenn, more of a songwriter–guitar player.

"All these things made Don's music change, and also made him sing differently."

Henley described the difference in his singing on the solo album this way: "Kootch and I always tried to put a song in a key that put me in the top of my range, so I had to strain a little to get it. I don't like relaxed vocals. My voice changes a lot while I'm warming up. It confuses recording engineers a lot, who go around trying to fix things."

He recalled the methodology they used for all three albums they would work on together this way: "Kootch would do most of the track in his studio. He either played or programmed every instrument. I wanted to do it that way because of the sound quality, almost like a demo. You lose some of that in a regular studio. I'd been programmed to think you have to record in a big studio for sound quality and fidelity and all that, but I'm not necessarily sure that's true. These recordings Kootch made in his own setup, along with Steve Porcaro, sounded great to me."

Although sales were disappointing for "Johnny Can't Read," executives at the label remained convinced they could break Henley as a solo performer. With the release of the second single, "Dirty Laundry," Henley, with Azoff's encouragement, decided to go out on tour.

To prepare himself for taking front stage by himself, he took dancing lessons. One of the hardest things for him to learn to do was simply stand in front of a microphone and use his hands without looking or feeling foolish. During rehearsals one time, he happened to put his arm around one of the backup dancers and start doing the tango with her. It proved a magical moment and was incorporated into the show.

In 1982, after months of intense preparation, Henley felt ready and gave the okay to start booking venues for the summer. Advance sales started off less than spectacularly. The reason was due less to the music than to Henley and Frey's original vision of the Eagles. They had always insisted that the band remain faceless, both on stage and off, to the point where several of their most successful albums didn't even have the band members on the front cover. So when it came time to promote Henley as a solo artist, relatively few outside the Eagles' immediate circle even knew what he looked like. Unlike his early days with the band, Henley did not open for big-name acts, nor did he have a solid string of solo hit records to draw audiences. However, he was willing to do anything to try to make it on his own, even if it meant going back to the beginning, playing for less-than-full houses, which he did most of the tour, and suffering the growing pains of a far less glamorous life on the road.

All of which changed when "Dirty Laundry" reached number three. At that moment, Henley's career as an "unknown" came to an end. With "Laundry," a denunciation of the press, Henley had returned to more familiar Eagles-like, anticritic turf. It was a song in which Henley alluded to his 1980 legal skirmish. In it, he portrayed himself as the victim of those who make a living airing other people's dirty laundry (sidestepping the question of how the laundry had gotten so dirty in the first place). The way Henley saw things, his victimization was the real crime.

With the success of the song and the album, Henley proved something to himself and the record company — that he didn't need to be a member of the Eagles to be successful.

With "Dirty Laundry" riding high on the charts, *I Can't Stand Still* sold more than 700,000 units, behind which Joe Smith decided to try and capitalize by releasing a second Eagles greatest hits album. It infuriated both Henley and Frey, as had the first one. Moreover, Henley didn't appreciate having any new Eagles product — even a compilation of old songs — out there competing with his solo album. Besides, it was a hastily conceived and sloppy job, with cheap and shoddy cover art, and most of the material taken from *Hotel California* and *The Long Run* with no sense of theme or balance and therefore, to Henley, no artistic integrity.

Shortly thereafter, he decided to end his long association with Warner and Asylum. In this instance, his timing could not have been better. He may not have known it, but already waiting in the wings to shake up anyone and everyone in L.A. all over again was Henley's, and rock and roll's, once and future savior.

FIFTEEN

It was 1980. Four years had passed since David Geffen had moved to New York, where he'd spent his nights buried alive in Studio 54's drug-infested disco scene. He then underwent a lengthy series of tests by a top team of New York doctors, who concluded that he was, in fact, perfectly healthy.

Geffen decided to return to Hollywood. Upon his arrival, he wasted no time in picking up the pieces of his career by forming a new independent record company and signing the biggest available names he believed could most quickly put him back on the big map. The first two were Donna Summer, who had recently left Casablanca Records after a long and bitter contract dispute with that label's owner, and MCA exile Elton John. While neither would prove profitable in the long run, Geffen's third acquisition returned him and John Lennon to the majors.

Unfortunately, Lennon's first album for Geffen would be his last alive for anybody. *Double Fantasy*, with Yoko Ono, released in the immediate aftermath of Lennon's murder, was a smash, the twelfth-biggest-selling album of 1980–81. It sold over three million copies in its initial release, yielded a number three hit, "Starting Over," and reestablished Geffen as a power player in the big-stakes game of rock and roll.

He next set his sights on the one act he wanted more than any other — the one he had once allowed to get away. It wasn't just that Henley was so good; it had as much to do with getting even with or perhaps back at Azoff, who, Geffen believed, had gotten all the glory for the Eagles. For *his* Eagles. What may have prompted Geffen to action was the word on the street that

Azoff was about to take an offer he couldn't refuse, to run the record division of MCA, which had lately fallen into confusion and disarray.

"Why did the Eagles break up?" Azoff replied to the reporter's question, posed in the wake of Henley's successful first solo album, in carefully thought-out phrases. "In my opinion, they broke up because Glenn and Don realized they could both make great solo albums. They realized they don't need the Eagles anymore. That's why you're not going to see them go out and do a farewell tour or a farewell album or a farewell anything. It's over, period."

With his top band officially split up, in 1983, Azoff, looking for something to do, jumped at the chance to become the head of MCA Records. At MCA's insistence, he got out of the management business by turning the day-to-day operation of Front Line over to his partner, Howard Kaufman, and Andy Slater. Azoff did, however, get MCA to agree to let him retain a passive, i.e., financial, interest in Front Line; his wholly owned subsidiary independent label, Full Moon; and Facilities Merchandising, the company he had created to sell T-shirts at venues, which in and of itself had developed into a multimillion-dollar business.

Although Azoff's deal with MCA included an annual base salary of $500,000 and millions more in stock options and bonuses, he told anyone who asked why he would go to work for someone that his decision had nothing to do with money. As he explained to journalist Patrick Goldstein, "There just comes a time when you want to do something else with your life. I've been a manager since I was 19 and I've accomplished everything I set out to do. It's just time for a new challenge."

When pressed by Goldstein to comment on the breakup of the Eagles, Azoff seemed to forget that he had inherited the band after Geffen had put them together and first turned them into hitmakers, and instead put this spin on their history: "I always had a special affinity for the Eagles because we grew up together in the business, going from the bottom to the top. After the group went their separate ways, I think I began to lose my passion for management. After all, how do you top the Eagles?"

Geffen, meanwhile, continued his hot pursuit of Don Henley. While privately telling friends how obnoxious he thought Azoff's obsession with being the next Geffen was, in the press he graciously welcomed Azoff away from

Front Line and into the upper echelons of corporate power. "Irving has to be on anybody's top 10 list of most powerful people in the music business," Geffen told one reporter. "This [deal signing Azoff] means MCA is making a commitment to put 'Music' back into the Music Corporation of America."

Azoff wasted no time. Upon his arrival in Burbank, where MCA Records' (and Universal Pictures') corporate offices were located on the studio complex owned by MCA Corp., the parent company of both, one of the first things he did was to let go forty-one of MCA's forty-six rock acts. Having cleared what he considered to be the accumulated musical debris, he set about revamping the company's black music division by aligning it with Motown. He arranged for MCA to make a distribution deal with the Detroit-based company that included its highly respected and profitable back catalog.

The industry merry-go-round continued as Joe Smith abruptly resigned from Warner, possibly forced out because of his failure to prevent the breakup of the Eagles. Whatever the reason, with Smith gone, there was little if any connection left between the record company and the Eagles. This became painfully and embarrassingly evident when, late in 1983, Glenn Frey delivered the final mix of the tracks for his second LP, *The Allnighter,* and the company passed. The official word that came down was that the tracks sounded too "country" for an eighties rock and roll audience. "What really happened," as one who was in on the decision put it, "[was that] no one at the label was still there who cared about Glenn Frey. He was considered a leftover from the seventies, and not a part of the game plan for the future."

No one could really be blamed for the decision to reject Frey's new album. The Eagles had been the prima donnas of their day, and under Joe Smith's tough if tolerant reign, if they had made more money for Warner than anyone else at the label, they had made more enemies as well. Each of the former Eagles had been given a chance to see what he could do individually, and with the exception of Don Henley, none had really succeeded. As a result, they became victims of their own arrogance as much as their own success.

The founding Eagle took his new material to Irving Azoff, who signed Frey to MCA and immediately released *The Allnighter.* To their delight, the album jumped onto the charts, peaked at number twenty-two, and remained in the top 100 for more than a year. The first single, "Sexy Girl," broke into the top fifteen. For Frey, it meant he had found his way back to the fast lane. For Azoff, it meant he was still a genius. And, perhaps most important, he looked it to the rest of the world.

Geffen closely followed the events surrounding the departure of Joe Smith and Frey's move to MCA, sensing the time might finally be perfect to spring the recalcitrant Henley from WEA. The former Eagle was not getting along with Smith's replacement, Bob Krasnow, a onetime independent record label owner (Blue Thumb Records) now the head of the Warner music empire. Krasnow was from the East and had never been a fan of the Eagles, and both Henley and Geffen knew it. When Henley's first album came out, he had to pay for his own promotion. At one point, Krasnow let it be known that he considered Henley a general pain in the ass, which Geffen took to mean he was expendable. Early in 1984, Geffen made an offer that Henley reluctantly accepted. "I was a little leery about signing with David," recalls Henley. "I still had some hard feelings and unpleasant memories. I was wary of him. On the other hand, I was scared that nobody else wanted me, because I was still largely unproven as a solo artist, and David, with his typical salesmanship, gave me the whole speech about how much he appreciated my talent and how nobody would take care of me like he would; then he signed me to a shitty deal." Not long after Henley signed the new recording contract with Geffen Records, he released his second solo effort, *Building the Perfect Beast*.

For the album's first single, "The Boys of Summer," Henley had crafted one of the most beautiful songs of his oeuvre, with lyrics that memorialized his own youth and the glory days of the Eagles, and recognized that both were over. It was the perfect baby-boomer farewell-to-youth anthem.

This is how Henley described his vision of the song: "The peace-and-love generation has grown up to be coffee achievers. Somewhere in the seventies, people turned from an outward vision ·to an inner vision. Instead of being concerned with social issues, they went inside themselves and said, 'I'm going to put on a coat and tie, go to work, make money and take care of me.' . . . The Cadillac part turns the song into something else. Suddenly, love turns out to be not just between a man and a woman, but the love [of fellowman] . . . in the sixties. Was all that peace-and-love sentiment real or just sloganeering? I'm not sure the '60's were such a great thing. The love we talked about certainly didn't manifest itself in the '70's. In a way, the two elements come together — the one-to-one love and the social love. The song ends up with the guy thinking about the girl when she was back in the '60's and she had daisies around her head. At least I think it does."

"I remember how happy I was when I finished that song," Henley says. "Driving up Pacific Coast Highway, I would park on Zuma Beach and sit there in the driver's seat with my boom box or my Walkman, listening to Mike Campbell's track while writing lyrics on a legal pad. I remember the night we finished recording the song; we had worked all night, and an engineer named Niko Bolas came back to my place about seven in the morning, wired, really excited about it, playing it in the living room. Maren woke up and came in, and there Niko and I were, looking like we were both drunk, dancing around the living room."

Greg Ladanyi remembers the recording of the album this way: "Henley was always writing. When he goes in [to the studio], he is always capable of changing his lyrics, to make them better. Sometimes just by what pops into his head. 'Boys of Summer' is a song I can remember being lyrically pretty much finished [before we started recording]. He wrote that really fast, faster than I remember a lot of the other ones happening. He got that really quickly, while other songs, like 'Dirty Laundry,' I remember that taking a little while to write.

"Another thing to remember is that Don's a great singer, and there were many vocals that were kept that were 'live' vocals. Not in full, but sections of them that were great. Singing with the music as it's going down gives you an energy you can't get when you go back to singing with a track, and that's the way Don always sang."

Off the success of the "Boys of Summer" single, the album exploded onto the charts and into the collective consciousness of the aging-obsessed boomers, for whom the first incarnation of MTV had provided an ongoing, extended visible forum to present rock and roll. "The Boys of Summer" remained in the top ten for months, thanks in large part to the accompanying video Geffen had suggested that the normally reclusive and in this instance particularly unenthusiastic Henley should make. Now Geffen, whose new eponymous movie company was already well on the way to establishing itself as an independent power in Hollywood, used his influence to see to it that a mini movie, rather than a live performance, was built around Henley's great song, a flashy visual that would ensure lots of airplay on MTV.

The video was shot in heavy-contrast, noirish black and white by European director Jean-Baptiste Mondino, who filled it with back projections to evoke the past, jump cuts to evoke the future, and slow motion to suggest an ever-present tension. The scene was set along the beach and in a car, and featured a washed-out, hungover-looking Henley cast in the role of the Greek chorus, haunted by visions of his own youth; a gorgeous, toenail painting, Lolita-type girlfriend; lovers romping on the beach; and, at the end, Henley getting into a car and driving off into the night. "The Boys of Summer" became an MTV favorite and was in heavy rotation for months. It was this video, more than anything else, that finally made Henley's face as immediately recognizable as the distinctive voice that had driven so many of the Eagles' greatest recordings.

"I got lucky," is how Henley characterizes the success of the video. "Andy Slater and Howard Kaufman were my comanagers then. Irving was sort of out of the picture at that point, over at MCA doing his mogul thing. Andy, with the help of Jeff Ayeroff, who was at Virgin at the time, had his finger on the pulse of what was happening with videos. After all, none of us knew anything about them. We hadn't planned on being in movies; we weren't prepared for it. Jean-Baptiste was a still photographer who'd done some work for *Esquire*. He came over to my house, we had a couple of meetings, and I tried to explain to him what I thought the song was about. We were in a time crunch as usual, I was about to go on tour, and so he did a lot of that video without me even being around. Again, it was a return to my grand theme, the loss of innocence.

"He went through several possible scenarios, one about the Vietnam War, which I rejected. That really wasn't the image I wanted portrayed. Then he came up with what became the final video. We had both agreed on one thing, that it should be shot in black and white. Before I left town, during my part of the shooting, I felt very awkward. It was hard for them to get me in a video and keep me from looking like an idiot. They put me on the back of a flatbed truck and drove me around the streets of Van Nuys at two o'clock on a cold November morning. The idea was to make it look as though I was floating, or drifting."

The Henley-Kortchmar-Ladanyi-produced album sold more than two million units in its initial release, went to number thirteen on the charts, and received great reviews from the very same critics who had always put down or dismissed the music of the Eagles. The *Rolling Stone Record Guide* called it "a damn near perfect pop album." Even inveterate Eagle-basher Dave Marsh praised it, if from a distance and at the expense of the rest of the West Coast boys in the band. "How," he asked, "could Don Henley seem so jive as lead vocalist of the Eagles, yet so great on his own? Well, in baseball they call it addition by subtraction; get rid of the mediocrities and let the real talent shine."

The album yielded a string of follow-up hits, including "All She Wants to Do Is Dance" at number nine, the gorgeous "Not Enough Love in the World," number thirty-four, and the melancholic, metaphor-heavy "Sunset Grill," the title the name of a favorite Henley Hollywood hamburger joint, whose hardworking owner reminded him of his own father, number twenty-two.

Kortchmar described "All She Wants to Do Is Dance" as "a song about the ultimate Ugly American couple. All she wants to do is dance, and him, all he wants to do is buy everyone off and throw money at the problem. A nasty, disgusting groove is what I was looking for, and when I found it I almost jumped a mile in the air. It was four in the morning. I called Don and woke him up. Which I've been guilty of doing in the past. 'That's great,' he said, 'Can we go to sleep now?'"

With Henley riding high on the charts, Glenn Frey continued to search not just for success, but for the same kind of impact his former partner was enjoying. As it happened, the impact found him.

It began with the release of a follow-up single, "Smuggler's Blues," off the *Allnighter* album. TV producer-director Michael Mann, whose *Miami Vice* was the hottest series on television at the time, happened to hear the song and thought it might work as a musical narrative for an episode of the heavily sound-tracked show. Borrowing a technique first used twenty years earlier in the feature film *The Graduate,* Mann infused his South Beach–based hip TV detective drama with contemporary rock and roll to establish both the mood and pace of each episode, even if the songs had nothing directly to do with the plot and there was no visible source for the music — no band playing at a bar, no radio or stereo flicked on. The show, sometimes referred to as a dramatic one-hour MTV video, put South

Beach, Don Johnson, rock and roll, and, with the "Smuggler's Blues" episode, Glenn Frey at the top of the eighties' fashionable pop-culture heap.

Mann hired controversial playwright Miguel Piñero to write an episode based on Frey's song, which contained, according to Mann, "some of the most literate lyrics I'd heard this year. The whole theme of the 'politics of contraband' and the trials of being a smuggler fit perfectly into the show. We decided to have our characters, Crockett and Tubbs, go undercover, posing as smugglers, trying to elude both law enforcement and rip-off artists as they try to get a load of contraband back into the country."

Mann began searching for an actor to play a small but key role in the episode as a pilot who ferries the detectives in and out of Columbia. After looking at hundreds of actors, he decided to approach the singer about the possibility of his playing it. Frey jumped at the chance.

By the time the episode aired, he was back on the charts with yet another unexpected hit single, "The Heat Is On," his contribution to the sound track of *Beverly Hills Cop*, which became the surprise hit film of the Christmas season. The Eddie Murphy vehicle sported an all-star sound track, including Frey's version of the Keith Forsey–Harold Faltermeyer song. "The Heat Is On," went to number two, its success helping to drive the sound-track album to the top slot. Both wound up outselling, respectively, Henley's "The Boys of Summer" and *Building the Perfect Beast*.

Miami Vice made Frey's face as familiar to the public as "The Boys of Summer" video had made Henley's. Though the part was originally seen as a onetime appearance, Frey, looking wiped-out and bloodshot — a "spaced-out audiophile-junkie pilot," according to Mann — was so good in the role that the ending of the episode was rewritten to allow his character to make an occasional reappearance on the series. "Smuggler's Blues" was included on the *Miami Vice* sound-track album, was released as a single, went to number twelve, and was followed up with another Frey cut off the sound track, "You Belong to the City," cowritten with Jack Tempchin, which went to number two. *The Allnighter* then jumped back onto the charts and was certified gold.

At the same time, Henley contributed a song to the sound track for the movie *Vision Quest* with the unlikely title of "She's on the Zoom." According to Danny Kortchmar, "There was an album on Folkways Records called

Innerviews, by some old blues cats from Chicago. At one point someone asks someone what happened to Little Walter, the great blues harmonica player, and he says, 'Well, he was kilt "on the zoom," ' which means nobody knows how he was killed. I just loved that expression. I told Don, and it became the title of a song for the *Vision Quest* album."

"She's on the Zoom" reached number eleven and although a legitimate hit, was buried by the airplay Frey's much more popular hit singles received. Henley nevertheless remained the critical favorite, and in March 1986, he won a Grammy for Best Rock Vocal Performance for "The Boys of Summer."

During this time, neither Frey nor Henley kept in direct touch with the other, and neither publicly acknowledged his former partner's success. As far as Frey was concerned, he didn't have to talk to Henley to know everything that was going on with him. "You only need to know two people in Los Angeles to find out what's going on," Frey told one friend in 1985.

"He didn't call," was the deadpan reply Henley gave an interviewer when asked whether or not he had spoken to Frey (since the breakup), and then admitted that the continued silence "hurt a little bit." Privately, Henley told friends that Frey's slick TV-tune hit singles were affecting the image of the Eagles. Whenever anyone asked him if the Eagles might get together again to remind the public just what that image was, his constant reply was "Yeah. Sure. When hell freezes over."

By 1985, Henley had developed an active interest in politics. He became aware from watching CNN of just how serious the problems of American farmers were. Henley told one journalist, "There was a time in my teens when the kids would be hot-rodding around and my dad would make me stay home and work in his field. And I would get really pissed. But the older I get, the more important the land has become to me." Henley quietly arranged for a portion of his profits from *Building the Perfect Beast* to be donated to the American Farmland Trust.

That April, Glenn Frey made a guest appearance on *Late Night with David Letterman.* Henley tuned in. Frey sang "Desperado" and acknowledged Henley's contribution to the song. When it was over, Henley picked up the phone and called his ex-partner. Although he hadn't spoken to Henley in five years, Frey did not act surprised when he heard the familiar voice. Frey told Azoff about the call, and Azoff wasted no time in arranging a meeting between the two former Eagles during the upcoming Christmas holidays. Both Henley and Frey owned houses in Aspen, and Azoff was planning to be there as well.

They met for dinner at Gordon's, and Azoff made sure no business was discussed. The atmosphere at the table remained cool as the two performers talked mostly about their homes and their women, until near the end when, like two former lovers, Henley and Frey lifted their glasses to each other and shook hands. As the evening deepened, they began to reminisce, allowing the bad times to fade into the past even as each pondered what the future implications of this rapprochement might actually be.

It was, after all, a new experience for them — acting like grown men.

SIXTEEN

In spite of Henley and Frey's having broken the ice, the individual members of the Eagles would, throughout much of the eighties and into the nineties, continue to fly solo with, for the most part, less than spectacular results. In 1986, Joe Walsh released an album, *The Confessor,* that failed to hit the charts despite his opening a major tour for Tina Turner. A year later, he released another album, *Got Any Gum?,* which rose only as high as number 113 before fading. Not long after, Walsh's marriage fell apart, and, nearing the bottom, he finally began to deal with his heavy addictions to drugs and alcohol.

Timothy B. Schmit released a solo LP, *Timothy B.* It failed to break the top 100. Two singles, "Boys Night Out" and "Don't Give Up," briefly ticked to number twenty-five and number thirty respectively before disappearing. He spent the rest of the eighties doing mostly sessions and sit-ins.

Randy Meisner made a few live appearances and played on other people's records but remained mostly out of the public eye, as did the increasingly reclusive Don Felder. Bernie Leadon resurfaced as a member of the Nitty Gritty Dirt Band, set out on a national tour, and then receded once more into the ether of his rock anonymity.

Frey, meanwhile, bitten by the acting bug, got his first opportunity to break into theatrical features from film producer Bob Singer. In 1987, Singer, having produced a couple of features, signed on to direct a buddy film set in the old/new West.

Singer remembers that "*Let's Get Harry* was one of those gang-buddy pictures. It had a fine cast — Robert Duvall, Mark Harmon, Gary Busey, and Glenn Frey in a part that had a good deal of screen time.

"When I first approached Glenn to play the role, he read and really turned the charm on. For me, being a big Eagles fan, it was a no-brainer. If he could read his lines in English, I was ready to hire him. We shot the film in Veracruz, Mexico, and it was a nightmare. A lot of the guys got testy and acted with a certain self-importance off-screen, but not Glenn. He was the biggest star among us, and also the most regular guy. He spent most of his time off-screen playing the guitar. It was sort of imbued in his life. Even if the only guys he got to play with those days were other actors and me. The main thing for him, what counted, was to play and party, whenever the opportunity presented itself for either. I thought he was really good in the film. He came off very natural, and fit in well with the others. One of his character's traits was that he had a cocaine problem, which wasn't that much of a stretch for Glenn. He told me once, on the set, matter-of-factly, 'When you blow your nose and your handkerchief looks like the flag of Japan, you know you're doing too much.'

"Glenn set up a mini studio in his hotel room and at one point had Jack Tempchin fly down to hang for a while and work on a new album. A few days later, Glenn decided to rent a car. In Veracruz, the locals drive like lunatics, and it's better to stay off the roads altogether if you can manage it. Anyway, sure enough, the first day, he got into an accident, which was not his fault, but the rule down there is both parties are brought to the jailhouse until the authorities can determine who is at fault. If any damages are to be paid, they have to be settled then and there. Forget about insurance; this is Mexico.

"All I know is I'm standing on the set of the picture when someone comes up to me and says, 'You gotta come right away; Glenn's in the Veracruz constabulary.' I stopped the shoot and went down to see him, and decided for good measure to take one of our Teamsters along. I entered the jailhouse and asked one of the guards if I could talk to Glenn. They were pretty good about everything, very nice, but said he was behind bars and that's where he would have to remain while we talked. I went in, and he jumped up and said, 'Oh, Bob, I'm so glad to see you, oh, God . . .' As he's talking, he grabs my hand and begins to shake it. And slips me two joints.

"After he was released, he couldn't wait to get out of Veracruz. The day the film was finished, Glenn hired a private plane to fly him directly to Aspen, Colorado, to meet his wife and recover from the whole thing."

While decompressing in Aspen, Frey put the finishing touches on his new album, *Soul Searchin'*. Released in 1988, it proved a bust both critically and commercially, yielding one relatively modest hit, "True Love" (number thirteen). *Let's Get Harry,* meanwhile, failed to find a theatrical distributor and was released directly to television, a major disappointment for Frey. Although it received generally poor reviews, it showed off enough of Glenn's work to land him a small but noticeable role as a burned-out record company executive on the TV series *Wiseguy*. After that, Frey had some difficulty finding acting work and eventually wound up doing a series of print ads for a national health club whose slogan was "Hard Rock in the '70's . . . Rock Hard in the '80's." In doing so, he was violating one of the most steadfast rules of the Eagles — to never do personal product endorsements or allow any of their music to be used in commercials. Henley's bemusement at Frey's ads took the form of put-down humor among their mutual friends.

While Frey was in Mexico, Henley was deep into the writing and recording of new songs for his third solo album. The studio door remained generally closed, although at times certain visitors were allowed in. One such invited guest was Axl Rose, of Guns N' Roses. He appeared one night and wound up singing harmony on "I Will Not Go Quietly." One who was present at that session recalls, "A lot of singers showed up, including Peter Wolf from J. Geils, just to see Don, who was the idol of so many other performers. Axl came by, and he can be a real asshole [but] was at least this night on his best behavior. Don invited him to sing on one cut, and Axl was so thrilled, at one point he literally left the studio and dashed over to Tower Records to buy an Eagles album so he could have Don sign it. I remember, though, how surprised Axl was after he laid down his vocal, when Don began playing around with it on the console. 'Oh, my God,' Axl said, somewhat good-naturedly, 'I'm glad you don't make our records.'"

The new album's title track, "The End of the Innocence," would prove to be by far the best solo work yet of any former Eagle. Its critical and popular success removed any lingering doubts about Henley's right to a place in the pantheon of superstar singer-songwriters. At once elegant, menacing, and irresistible, the song opens with a lush piano glissando by Bruce Hornsby, over which Henley's distinctive rasp begins to reminisce about his own youthful days and those of his generation. The song sounds like a combination anthem and eulogy; the opening melody line is virtually that of "America the Beautiful," its minor key imposing a sense of formal melancholia: *"Remember when the days were long. . . ."*

Henley claimed to have come up with the idea for the song during a long drive back from cowriter Bruce Hornsby's house in the summer of 1987. After struggling with the lyrics, Henley had given it to Hornsby to see if he could come up with an approach to recording it. "Bruce had had it for a while and said he couldn't seem to do anything with it," Henley recalled. "I drove out to his house way out in the middle of the San Fernando Valley, on a street called Heart Land, near this big cornfield, which is one of the last pieces of land undeveloped in the valley. It's actually government land, but they let these two Mexican American farmers plant corn on it every year, and they have a corn stand out in the valley, so it was all too perfect."

Out of that bright image came the nightmare of the song. One of the most remarkable aspects of it was the metaphorical abuse of Miss Liberty. Henley wrote it just as his long relationship with Maren Jensen came to a stormy end. They had been through a lot together, including the plane crash and her bout with Epstein-Barr syndrome. Friends who knew both suggested the reason she left was because Henley, forty-one years old and by now apparently a confirmed bachelor, had tired of caring for her and refused to get married.

Another friend added that Henley's heavy gambling habits might have been one of the reasons Maren split from Henley. "Maren was sweet, pretty, everything Don liked in a woman, and I believe he really loved her. By this time, though, he had become a fairly notorious gambler, and anyone who knew Don would tell you that his obsessions usually dominated his behavior. Because of the high-stakes poker games and football betting, his bookie was probably more dear to him than any woman, and eventually that became clear to the both of them. After so many years, [Maren] had simply had enough and broke it up, and Don was bummed about it."

"Maren and I stayed together until 1986," Henley says. "We were engaged, but we just grew apart. We were having some problems, and I just didn't think it felt right. It was hard for her, because her career had been cut short by illness, and by the time of my second solo album I was starting to make it big again. She was supportive of me but very frustrated because she couldn't work. We'd tried to write songs together, and that didn't work. Instead, it fueled the competitive thing between us. Finally, she moved out, partly because of some reprehensible behavior on my part. It just wasn't working for me. I felt a great sense of sadness."

Henley took the breakup hard, and several songs on the *Innocence* album reflect his hurt, none more than "The Heart of the Matter." According to Henley, "I feel like it was another step in my personal growth . . . it took me almost forty-two years to get to that place, to be able to say what I said in that song."

Mike Campbell wrote the musical track, after which J. D. Souther and Henley refined the original lyrics. "I remember the first time I heard that song," recalled a female friend of the boys. "Don wanted to get any girl who was in the studio to come and listen to it. I had tears in my eyes when they finished. It was one of the most beautiful, intelligent, and emotional songs I'd ever heard. What he was actually doing was testing it out on us, especially girls who knew their way around the business, because we had been around and were maybe a little bit harder on the outside and harder to please on the inside. Well, let me tell you, there wasn't one girl who didn't get affected by it. Everyone who heard it that night broke down and cried.

"It was so perfectly Don, because it exemplified the image he liked most about himself, the 'sensitive artist.' I can remember the girls getting together after and talking about how *sensitive* he was, how he was like this perfect guy because he *understood*. That's rock and roll. Don was this great-looking guy, and knew it. He could go out on the town and get literally any woman he wanted. Even girls who were sure they would never go for the kind of stuff he was into always did. Why? Listen to the song: it's there, in all its seductive power, grace, and beauty. The masterful hook of 'The Heart of the Matter' is its notion of forgiveness, 'even if you don't love me anymore.' It is truly an incredible piece of work."

In addition to "The Heart of the Matter," which was a huge hit and remains a perennial on FM adult contemporary stations, *The End of the Innocence* yielded several additional chart singles, including "I Will Not Go Quietly," "New York Minute," and "The Last Worthless Evening."

Still, the price of personal expression continued to take its toll on Henley's friends. Greg Ladanyi recalls, "*The End of the Innocence* is a different-sounding album [than Henley's first two solo efforts]. Part of that I can attribute to my not being there. That mostly had to do with time. Don's time. He was just taking too long with the album. The originally planned length of time that I was prepared to spend on it just kind of came and went. A lot of things were happening in all our personal lives, and at one point, it became a matter of, well, maybe you should go your own way on this. That was Don's response when Danny and I wanted to be paid a little bit more money to continue. He wasn't happy about it. His point of view was that this wasn't about money, it was about the work, and anyway we had points on the record and were going to 'make millions.' All fine and good, we told him, but what do we do now?

"About three days later we got an unofficial call from Irving [Azoff]. Irving said that Don didn't feel he could go on working with Danny and me. Eventually, Danny and Don did get back together to finish the album. I think Danny's involvement in the writing of it was so deep, it was a little too difficult for Don to walk away. But with me, that apparently wasn't the case."

Says Henley: "It had been okay for a while, but again, [with] drugs, drink, and our own personalities . . . after a while there was nobody flying the plane. From the first album, we needed one guy to be straight. By this time, I had for the most part phased drugs out, and making an album became a much more enjoyable experience. I no longer had to depend on drugs or anything else to give me a false confidence. By the time we had gotten halfway through my second album, we had cleaned up the act quite a bit. When I made *The End of the Innocence* I was pretty much drug free."

And alone once more.

In 1988, Henley threw a New Year's Eve party in Aspen. Gary Hart, the Democratic presidential hopeful, had met Henley at several political fundraisers, and the two became friendly. Henley invited Hart to the party. Also there that night was Donna Rice, a former girlfriend of Henley's. Although he has since stated both were there that night, Henley insists he played no part in putting the two together. "Someone introduced them, but it wasn't me. I was off cooking for 60 guests. But I got the credit . . . or the blame, whatever." Hart's association with Rice would prove his downfall. Heavily favored to win the Democratic nomination, he was the one candidate Henley was willing to help in whatever way he could. Hart's affair with the young blond beauty would turn into a major sex-and-politics scandal and help destroy his chance to become president of the United States.

For much of 1989, Henley went back on the road to promote *The End of the Innocence*. These shows had, with one exception, a completely new set of backup performers from those that appeared on the album. Henley proudly and pointedly referred to the new lineup as the "best band I've ever played with." On rhythm and lead guitar were John Corey and Frank Simes; on keyboards, acoustic piano, and synthesizers, Timothy Drury; also on synthesizers, Scott Plunkett; Ian Wallace on drums; Jennifer Condos on bass guitar; and Condos, Dolette McDonald, Lynn Maybrey, and Sheryl Crow on backup vocals.

Crow was the only member of the live show besides Henley who appeared on the album. A talented singer, Crow had become Henley's newest obsession. According to one who was with them on tour, "She had just come off the road with Michael Jackson, for whom she'd sung backup, and was extremely tired, when Don heard about how good she was and decided he wanted her for the album. When he met her, he couldn't get over what a fox she was and began to wine and dine her. The only problem for him was, at the time she was more interested in her solo career than a relationship and just wasn't interested, which of course made him want her all the more. Everybody knew he was going nuts because he couldn't get her. There weren't that many girls at any given party in L.A. that would ever have said no to an offer from Don Henley. The story went around that he wanted to help get her a record deal and that Don even went so far as to get her a lawyer to make sure the deal was the right one. Supposedly he was also going to cowrite at least a couple of songs and maybe even coproduce part or all of her record.

"She sang on his album and agreed to go out on the road with him, but they had no romantic affair. There was some coldness there until she began making noise with her first solo album, on A&M, at which point Henley became very supportive. He even showed up one night when she performed at the Troubadour and sang with her."

The End of the Innocence soured still another relationship for Henley, the always tenuous one between him and David Geffen. Geffen felt that Henley had taken far too long to finish it and told him so. Henley reacted by accusing Geffen of having tried to "nickel-and-dime" the album. The way Henley remembers it, "If I had too many lyrics to put on the cassette card, they didn't want to pay for the extra flap. One extra flap! On the one hand, David was telling me what a great lyricist I was and how it was a really important part of my work and people should be able to read the lyrics; on the other hand, he didn't want to pay the extra penny — *one extra cent* — per cassette so I could have room to print them all. Maddening crap. Eventually I got tired of haggling over stuff like that, over the album-cover budgets, video budgets, promotional money, while other companies were spending fortunes for lousy records to get airplay and to get them to the top of the charts. I could understand to an extent David's theory that you shouldn't have to pay to get a record onto the charts, that it should happen organically, but when everybody else was doing it, I thought I was being handicapped. It struck me that this was the time and place he'd decided to draw the line in the sand; this was when he'd decided to act in a highly moral fashion. At my expense.

"Eventually, I got sick of it, and then David sold the company without really sitting any of us down and telling us he was going to do it. I read it in the paper, just like the last time, with Asylum.

"Which precipitated my leaving, even though my contract said I owed the label more albums. 'Fuck you,' I said, 'I'm outta here.' I got myself a lawyer and got ready to fight all over again. What got me so angry was that when he signed me the second time, when I fell for it again, he was still spouting the same bullshit about this is a family, you're one of my favorite artists, I'll take good care of you, when in fact he was just looking to build up the company so he could sell it for another huge profit. He'd realized he'd sold Asylum way too cheap at seven million bucks, so he was determined to do it again and not get screwed. As a result, I woke up one morning and suddenly I was recording for a Japanese company."

After its release, a reporter who, like everyone else in Hollywood, had heard about the battles between Geffen and Henley, wanted to know if there was bad blood between the two. "There's no blood," Henley replied. Asked if he would ever work for Geffen again, without hesitation, Henley replied, "Absofuckinlutely not."

Ironically, the album's success dissolved into another contentious lawsuit between the two that left Henley feeling bitter and more alone than ever. As the eighties drew to a close, he receded further behind the walls he had built to shield himself from the outside world. For the moment, he had nothing left to say and nobody left not to say it to.

In 1987, with his record sales having tapered off and his acting career on hold, Glenn Frey, looking for a way to pull the parachute chord on his career free fall, decided to pay Irving Azoff a visit, only to find Azoff whizzing past him on the way down.

Azoff's difficulties had begun the day he made the move to MCA, with his insistence on retaining a passive interest in Front Line Management, Full Moon Records, and Facilities Merchandising.

One particularly unhappy about the situation was David Geffen, who'd been down this road with Geffen-Roberts when he'd joined Warner and been forced to surrender *his* active participation in the company. Until then, he'd made little secret of his ongoing involvement with Roberts; he had continued to share office space in the same building and had been part of the decision that led to the Eagles' signing with Azoff. Still, when the news of Azoff's MCA deal was announced, Geffen issued this rather hypocritical statement to the press: "You cannot be in the record business and manage artists on your own label — it's a conflict of interest. How can a manager get the best deal he can for his client if the manager also works for the record company? It's very disturbing. If it's legal, it shouldn't be."

Azoff, unimpressed with and unaffected by Geffen's outcry, at first was delighted with what he saw as the opportunity to leap to the next tier of power. Geffen's successful crossover into movies with the feature *Risky Business,* the film that made Tom Cruise a star, was the talk of Hollywood. Azoff wanted that, and with his beachhead strongly established at MCA, he believed he could easily move into Universal's feature film division.

However, Azoff's reluctance to surrender the passive holdings he'd maintained in his three companies ultimately proved problematic. From 1984, when he joined MCA, Azoff continued to earn significant money from his former companies. That first year he earned $215,000 from his ongoing 25 percent ownership of Facilities and Full Moon, and an additional $70,000 in royalties from Front Line's representation of artists. For the next two years, these dollar amounts continued to steadily rise, until 1987, when Sidney Sheinberg, then MCA's president and chief executive officer, won his long conflict-of-interest legal battle with the government, and with it the right to acquire the outstanding stock in all three of Azoff's companies. He then made Azoff an offer for them he once again couldn't refuse. This time Azoff exchanged his remaining stock for MCA stock, a deal worth more than $15 million, after which Sheinberg consolidated all MCA's record divisions under one new umbrella, MCA Music Entertainment, and appointed Irving Azoff its president.

Unfortunately for Azoff, the acquisitions resulted in new questions being raised rather than old ones being answered. Don Henley, for instance, was under contract to record with David Geffen's record company but was still managed by Front Line, now wholly owned by MCA. The record label could thus conceivably benefit from an unfair advantage when Henley's contract with Geffen expired. Nor was Henley the only major talent caught in this corporate cross fire. Chicago was also a Front Line client that recorded for Warner Brothers. In truth, all of Front Line's clients were put in the position of not being quite sure of who was managing them, who was representing them, who was recording them, who was promoting them, who wanted them, who wanted to be rid of them, and who was going to get them. This had a very familiar ring to many, as somehow Azoff had gotten himself into exactly the same situation Geffen had when he'd joined Warner. However, where Geffen had for a while been able to dance around the detonators, Azoff seemed unable to avoid leaping on them.

In 1988, the delicate situation exploded when reputed mobster Salvatore J. Pisello informed the U.S. government that his professional relationship with MCA, which had begun in 1984, had come about from meetings he had had with Irving Azoff. Pisello was under investigation for income tax evasion having to do with the illegal sale of "cutouts," or unsold and returned record albums for which no royalties are paid to artists. (He has since been cleared of these charges.) To make matters worse, Pisello had a long association with Morris Levy, one of rock and roll's most notorious mob-related figures. Levy's involvement with the 1959–60 payola scandals had marked him in the industry as officially untouchable, forcing him further into the background, from where he continued to run a publishing and independent promotion music empire, using men like Pisello to represent his interests.

From 1988 to 1991, the federal government conducted a formal investigation into the music business, taking an especially close look at one of its favorite long-term targets, MCA. Throughout, Sheinberg and Azoff made it their business to appear publicly united, fiercely determined to repel any attack on their integrity. Although Azoff vehemently denied any involvement (and was never proven to have dealt with Pisello, or any mob figures on any level), the situation behind the scenes was described by one observer as a "shit storm."

Sheinberg couldn't get rid of Azoff when the first so-called link to Pisello had been made because he'd feared that dismissing him might lend credence to the government's investigation. Not only that, but as much as Sheinberg personally disliked what was going down, he couldn't deny that Azoff had done a powerhouse job of overhauling MCA's music division. During his reign, the company's market share had risen from 1.5 percent to more than 11 percent. Indeed, in June 1989, MCA Records, under the supervision of Irving Azoff, had the one, two, and three positions on the *Billboard* top 200 album chart — the Fine Young Cannibals' *The Raw and the Cooked*, Bobby Brown's *Don't Be Cruel*, and Tom Petty's *Full Moon Fever*. Lew Wasserman and Sid Sheinberg publicly lauded Azoff for this achievement with full-page ads in the trades.

Three months later, he resigned.

One record executive reflects on Azoff's departure this way: "I suspect he left at the perfect time. If you could see the books at MCA when Irving resigned, I'm sure there was a lot financially that wouldn't have sat well with the boys upstairs. Irving did it all with mirrors. It's likely that he took money from the corporate account to sign acts, a perfectly legal thing to do. The way someone in Irving's position makes a lot of money in a short amount of time is to spend a lot of money. Believe me, it was Irving who had the last laugh in the whole sordid affair."

Less than two months after leaving MCA, a smiling Azoff announced the formation of Giant, a new country-heavy joint-venture label, publishing, and filmmaking company funded and distributed by Warner. It was a sophisticated and daring move. After all that had taken place during the government's investigation of MCA, this being Hollywood, where the bottom line was not just everything but the only thing, it took Azoff less than a year to get Warner to put up $50 million to launch his new company.

Geffen, whose independent record label was also distributed by Warner, publicly welcomed Azoff to the corporate family. "I started in 1980 with just three employees," Geffen said. "By comparison, [Azoff is] starting with a big company for an independent. Over the years it will grow. Knowing Irving, he'll probably do everything."

Having resurrected his career, Azoff found himself perfectly positioned to pull off one last, great coup — to do what everyone in the business, but no one more than Henley and Frey, believed even for him was absolutely impossible.

With utter confidence and fierce determination, Irving Azoff decided the time had come to bring the boys home. No matter what it took, he was going to reunite the Eagles.

SEVENTEEN

By his midforties, Don Henley had become, according to one friend, "a caricature of himself, somewhere between your grandmother and that chic kind of *GQ* guy he seemed to be when he did the interview and the cover for the August 1991 issue of the magazine." Henley did indeed surprise those who knew him personally by how bachelor cool he looked on the magazine's cover — designer clothes, slicked-back hair, cobalt eyes shining — compared to how pudgily domestic he had become in real life.

He continued to spend inordinate amounts of time inside his L.A. house in the hills, which many considered the ultimate bachelor pad. He would often spend hours a day in his well-organized and highly efficient kitchen, working on his homemade Texas-style chili, in which he took a great deal of pride. It never failed to amuse his guests to see him looking and feeling so totally comfortable with an apron on.

The rest of the house was, in its way, as well laid out as the kitchen. Things might have appeared a bit messy, but everything was placed just as he wanted. Even things that looked cluttered followed a pattern of logic and practicality. To assist him, he always had at least one young secretary in the office part of the house, and there was always a lot for her to do. He was continually writing his letters to editors in response to issues that impassioned him, and to lawyers. He had become involved in several major legal battles that took too much of his time. These included a dispute with a neighbor over landscaping Henley felt was a threat to his privacy, and one with the United Stations Programming Network, a Virginia-based company that had released a compilation of Eagles performances and previously recorded interviews for sale to radio stations. The program was broadcast throughout the United States on May 19, 1989, allegedly without authorization or approval from any of the Eagles or the band's management. This case dragged on for three years before a confidential out-of-court settlement was reached in August 1992.

During this period he experienced a rapid turnover of female assistants. He would often work during the day, and insist his helper be there every morning at nine o'clock. No matter how late he partied, when the sun came up, he was ready to go to work. If a girlfriend stayed the night, he'd arrange for her to leave the next morning through a back-door entrance so she wouldn't have to walk past his assistant.

A few assistants did stay for a relatively longer period, able to adjust to Henley's often cranky narcissism. According to one, "He could wake up with a hangover and be a real shit in the morning and then turn into this totally nice guy by the afternoon. He could brood and need to be alone, and then he'd want to be surrounded by friends. He'd started to get some lines in his face, become a bit paunchy, mostly from the way he cooked and his drinking, all of which hit him in a very sensitive place, because he had always been so gorgeous. He was very concerned with his looks and made no attempt to hide that from us. It was a little bit weird being in his house and seeing him that way, at the same time being his employee."

Henley's major Eagles involvement these days centered on the not-so-easy task of saying no to friend and once-again manager Irving Azoff, who had begun to feel him out about the possibility of a reunion. Henley's reaction was always the same: he thought the idea preposterous. Azoff dangled unbelievable amounts of dollars he said could be made from it, only to have Henley tell him he didn't care how much money it meant, he was not going to work with Frey again.

Not that the two former partners hadn't considered the idea themselves at various times during the past decade. Rumors would quickly spread on the rare occasions they were seen together in public. One time in the mid-eighties, not long after Frey, Henley, and Azoff had met in Aspen, Frey went into the hospital for an attack of diverticulitis, and Henley came to visit. "The weird thing was," one friend recalls, "they lived across the street from each other for a lot of years, and one never acknowledged the other's presence. That's why the hospital thing was so strange, because it almost worked. They tried to bury the hatchet." Frey even consented to appear from his hospital bed via closed-circuit TV at a benefit Henley was producing down South. "Right after, Glenn gave an interview to a newspaper, said something that upset Don, and everything fell apart again for another bunch of years. It didn't take much."

After that, Henley's anger at Frey reverted to a mocking form, and he used every opportunity to gleefully point out to friends what he considered Glenn's post-Eagles failures. As one close to both recalls, "Glenn's songs were . . . well, they weren't 'Eagles'-quality songs, nor anywhere as good as Don's, and [Don] felt the need to let everyone know it. And the physical thing. When Glenn straightened himself out, he got into bodybuilding and, you know, did the ad for the gym. Don, who was not in great physical shape himself, said he looked just so pathetic doing commercials."

Another of Henley's involvements during the nineties was the Walden Woods Project. He had first become aware of the crusade to preserve the land that had inspired Henry David Thoreau in December 1989, after seeing an interview with Tom Blanding, a scholar who'd patterned his life after Thoreau's. Blanding was talking about developers threatening to destroy Walden Woods. The next day, Henley got in touch with Blanding and pledged $10,000 to the cause. Six months later, the two had formed the Walden Woods Project. The goal of the organization was to raise $14 million to buy and preserve the ninety-six acres of forestland that surrounded the famed Walden Pond in Concord, Massachusetts. They also sought to raise the public's awareness of other environmental causes, such as the preservation of the Brazilian rain forests. To do so, Henley, who always considered the press an enemy, granted interviews to any journalist who would talk about his new project. As he told one reporter, "Walden Woods is widely recognized as the cradle of the American environmental movement, and Henry David Thoreau is recognized as the father of that movement. I was appalled when I first heard that the place was in danger. You assume that these places are protected."

He had little else to do, so before long Henley's association with Walden turned personal and obsessive. He sensed in Blanding's campaign a link to his own irretrievable childhood, to those days in Linden when he had to help pick up garbage in front of the house. Blanding himself became something of a father figure to Henley, a living reminder of C. J., a way to revisit the memories of afternoons spent with a man who cared about the land he lived on and kept a garden almost to the end of his days.

With so much either lost or gone with the demise of the band, Henley was able to increase his involvement with the Walden Woods Project that he had founded.

Azoff recognized this and became actively involved with fund-raising and personal donations. His generosity paid off when, in 1990, his heavy participation in the Walden project indirectly led to his putting together what amounted to a onetime and little-noted Eagles reunion.

The possibility first came about when Azoff suggested to the band that it might not be a bad idea to release a third greatest hits package, if for no other reason than to ensure they wouldn't be caught by surprise if the rumors were true and Warner did just that with no warning and no input from the band, as they had when they issued the *Greatest Hits Volume 2* album in 1982. Azoff suggested that Henley and Frey get together and at least talk about writing a couple of new songs for it, with the profits from one or more going to Walden.

No one was more surprised than Frey when Henley said yes. The band had been barraged with Beatles-size reunion offers ever since they'd broken up — as Azoff kept telling Henley, more than one promoter had offered millions for a single live performance — which Henley had always turned down. This time, however, Azoff had tapped into Henley's attachment to the Walden project and managed to convinced him that there was a good reason to at least consider working with his former partner again.

In March 1990, Henley and Frey met for several hours. Some time later, Azoff suggested that Frey join Henley at the Centrum, in Worcester, Massachusetts, for two benefit concerts for Walden. Frey agreed. Henley then contacted Schmit and Walsh and invited them as well. Notably absent from these performances was Don Felder, whose presence would likely have all but guaranteed Frey's refusal to participate.

The two shows were extremely well received, and after, Azoff suggested to Frey that he think about the possibility of doing more. Frey agreed, but a month later, things fell apart again, and he and Henley seemed as distant toward each other as ever. When asked by one friend what had happened, Henley said something about ghosts rearing their ugly heads. One who

knew both insists it was Frey who'd become the reluctant one, "more interested in playing golf than music."

In truth, while the moment may have been fun, it was difficult for either
to build much lasting enthusiasm for working together again. Money was
not a factor; both had invested well and were set for life. Nor was there any
desire to go back out on the road. Although Henley still continued to
tour as a solo act, he now chose to devote much of his time to Walden and
other related causes. Henley had a highly successful post-Eagles career and
couldn't see a real reason to step back into the restrictive confines of the
drum-playing-vocalist role in a band. Especially *that* band. In their brief
reunion, Henley discovered, the same old song kept playing between the
two. Frey had remained as difficult for him to work with as ever, still acting
the leader, still wanting to call the shots. Who needed any of it, Henley concluded, putting for the moment any thoughts of a reunion on a very low-lit
back burner.

And there was something else. Henley had met a woman by the name of
Sharon Summerall, a model out of Texas. He had promised himself he would
give this relationship every opportunity to work, which made the idea of
going back on the road ill timed, to say the least.

Frey had other interests as well. In the fall of 1993, still hoping to make a
name for himself as a serious actor, he'd gotten his best chance to go one
step better than starring with his old *Miami Vice* pal Don Johnson when he
received an offer to appear in a show in which he could *become* him. At the
age of forty-four, Frey went through yet another image makeover and
signed on to star as a fashion-conscious, hip detective in a new CBS prime-
time action-adventure series, *South of Sunset.*

Stan Rogow, the producer of the show, had been impressed by Frey's
work on *Miami Vice* and *Wiseguy* and wanted him to star in a new series
that would combine the attitude of South Beach with the atmospherics of
Sunset Boulevard. The leads would be a black and white team of hip, bend-
the-law-when-necessary types. In Hollywood development lingo, *Miami
Vice* meets *Beverly Hills Cop.*

According to Rogow, "We'd been looking and looking for four months
[to cast the lead]. When we were asked a year ago by CBS if we would be

interested in doing an L.A. private investigator show, the first thing that came to my mind was 'Hotel California' and Glenn's music. We sat down to talk about it with Glenn, he read the script and said, 'I get it. This show is about the tarnished elegance of L.A.' And I said, 'Well yeah!' Glenn, in his persona, is such the embodiment of California for the last 20 years that it was just a perfect match."

For Frey, the show seemed to signal his arrival as a major TV star, something he dearly wanted. "You get into your mid-30's," he told a reporter, "and I don't think it takes a guru or rehab to tell you that you just can't rock like you used to. So I just ultimately made up my mind that I was going to eat a little healthier, live a little healthier and be able to do better work. . . .

"I've been getting up early because I've been lifting weights and I don't do drugs anymore, so my life is kind of in order. It's got some semblance of discipline."

Frey had tried to clean his act up in more ways than one. Having been unhappy for some time, he divorced his first wife and married a dancer he'd met working on one of his videos. Her name was Cindy, and she was a far more down-to-earth, well-adjusted woman than his debutante, and eager to start a family. She quickly became pregnant and gave birth to the first of the two children they would have together. Having settled into the role of father, Frey feared that returning to the road as an Eagle might be too much of a disruption to his new life, if not an out-and-out risk to his sobriety. Besides, he was sure he was going to be a big TV star now and planned on doing nothing in the foreseeable future except work on his series and raise his family.

That is, until *South of Sunset* debuted, on October 27, 1993, and made broadcasting history as one of a notoriously select group of TV shows to be canceled after one episode. The show had been heavily promoted by CBS and scheduled to follow the number one–rated program of the season, the Super Bowl. The network had given Frey's series a golden time slot, guaranteeing one of the largest lead-in audiences of the year, but also one that demanded huge numbers. So many viewers switched channels after the game that CBS decided their highly touted series had no future and the next day pulled the plug.

No one could have been angrier than Frey, who felt he knew enough about TV programming by now to argue with the producers and network executives prior to the show's airing about changing its time slot. He believed it needed a chance to find its audience and would do better with lower expectations. He also knew the pilot episode was not as good as the other eight already in the can. It had taken several for everyone to find the character, pace, and feel of the show.

The cancellation of *South of Sunset* was described by one friend as a source of amusement for Henley. "Well, Glenn's TV career lasted all of fifty-eight minutes," he joked when the news of the show's demise hit the papers.

Henley, meanwhile, continued to have his share of problems, mostly concerning his ongoing contractual dispute with David Geffen. In one more bizarre twist to the corporate game of musical chairs, six months after Azoff's departure from MCA, Geffen sold Geffen Records to MCA for half a billion dollars in stock and used the money to form a partnership with Steven Spielberg and Jeffrey Katzenberg in DreamWorks SKG Studios. Geffen had been looking to sell his label for more than a year, and might have sold it to MCA sooner if Azoff hadn't still been a part of the company. Somehow, the idea of having to answer to his former employee did not appeal to him.

As for the lawsuit with Henley, Geffen recalls, "After I signed Don to Geffen Records, he put out that first album, and it was so successful it recouped his advance. I think in some way that pissed him off, because it turned out to be a really good deal for us and therefore, to his way of thinking, not such a good deal for him. In other words, if we could make that much, he should have made more. So we wound up in litigation again, twenty-five years after the first time. This time, I told him I would never settle."

Henley had in fact renegotiated his contract with Geffen after the first album, and it was that deal, completed and signed in 1988, that became the focus of a fresh round of lawsuits. As far as Geffen was concerned, the new contract Henley had signed meant he was obligated to the label for an additional seven years. Henley's viewpoint was that the seven-year limit applied to the original 1984 contract, which meant that as of 1991 he was, in effect, a free agent. Besides, his contract with Geffen contained a "key-man clause," meaning that if Geffen left the company, so could Henley.

Which is exactly what had happened. Henley and his attorney, Los

Angeles–based entertainment lawyer Don Engel, then countersued, claiming a conspiracy existed among the six major record labels to make sure that if a performer such as Henley chose to leave one label, no one else would sign him. In fact, when Henley, one of the most successful and highly respected performers in rock and roll for more than twenty years, had put out feelers in anticipation of leaving Geffen, he had gotten very little response. It didn't seem to make sense unless there was indeed some sort of hands-off policy, against him and all superstars, to prevent the type of out-of-control escalation of fees that had become a part of the big business of professional sports.

Geffen offered this explanation for Henley's difficulty finding another label: "The Eagles always sold better than Henley solo albums. Besides, he's a thoroughly unpleasant man, he was getting old, and I'm not sure there was that much of a market left open to him. His most valuable asset was his catalog, most of which belonged to Warner, not his future recordings." (Warner Bros. eventually did sign Henley to a new contract.)

It was this series of lawsuits as much as the collapse of his partnership with Kortchmar that had stalled Henley's solo career and gradually made the thought of an Eagles reunion more palatable. For all the tangled legalities, there was nothing in his contract that said he could not continue to perform or record with the Eagles. Frey too wanted out of his solo contract with MCA, which made reviving the Eagles attractive to him as well.

In March 1990, Henley appeared on an episode of *MTV Unplugged,* the music channel's acoustic series, and performed a set of ballads sitting on a stool in front of a microphone. To everyone's surprise, during the sound check, it was rumored that Glenn Frey had showed up and sat in on keyboards, once more sparking hopes of a possible joint appearance, if not a full Eagles reunion. However, by showtime, Frey was nowhere to be found, and none of the sound-check video showed up in the show's final edit. Henley later denied that Frey had been there at all.

In 1991, Henley did a little payback for Patty Smyth, who'd sung backup on the *End of the Innocence* album, by recording a duet with her, "Sometimes Love Just Ain't Enough." The song was released as a single and went to number one on the pop charts, helped by a heavy-rotation MTV video in which Henley and Smyth both appeared. In January 1993, Henley was invited to appear at the inauguration of President Clinton. He performed several of his own songs at the high-fashion ball, highlighted by a sensational interpretation of Leonard Cohen's "Democracy" that was overshadowed by the televised network broadcast of Fleetwood Mac, singing "Don't Stop," the song adopted by the Clinton campaign as its anthem.

And yet, for all of his sustained visibility and obvious ongoing commercial appeal, Warner decided not to go ahead with a new Eagles "best of" set until Henley settled his new dispute with Geffen. Warner's position, which seemed to favor Geffen, infuriated Azoff so much he threatened to resign from Giant Records.

Meanwhile, the other Eagles — Schmit, Walsh, and Felder — waited and hoped things worked out at least to the point where the new greatest hits album could be released. The simple truth was that, in varying degrees, each could use the money. Felder had recently toured with Dan Fogelberg but otherwise continued to keep a low profile, while Walsh's post-Eagles activities included hosting a syndicated radio program in 1990 and a summer '92 tour with Glenn Frey.

One sunny afternoon early in 1993, Timothy B. Schmit sat with a friend of the band at an outdoor café in Hollywood, musing on what life might be like for him if only Henley and Frey would put aside their differences and allow a reunion to take place. And not just for the peaceful, easy feeling of it. He had bills to pay. The difference between an Eagles reunion and no reunion, Schmit estimated that afternoon, was the difference between his being able to get by and becoming an instant millionaire.

The real catalyst to a possible Eagles reunion came, in fact, from the unlikeliest of sources. In 1992, original Eagle Bernie Leadon, now living in Nashville and playing in a country band he rather amusingly called Run C&W, formed an early-Eagles-sounding group he produced but did not play with called Restless Heart. Leadon had pointedly taken the name of his group from the Eagles' "New Kid in Town."

By 1993, Restless Heart had put together a string of crossover hits and a best-selling album, *Big Iron Horses*. Azoff, forever looking to activate the Eagles catalog, decided to go Leadon one better. Rather than having a bunch of Nashville musicians record songs that sounded *like* Eagles songs, he would put together the cream of the new Nashville crop and have them record an album *of* Eagles songs.

Made in Nashville, *Common Thread: The Songs of the Eagles* was released in the fall of 1993, featuring many of country's most popular performers, including Travis Tritt, Little Texas, Clint Black, John Anderson, Alan Jackson, Suzy Bogguss, Vince Gill, Diamond Rio, Trisha Yearwood, Billy Dean, Tanya Tucker, Brooks and Dunn, and Lorrie Morgan.

The first single off *Common Thread* was the familiar Jackson Browne–Glenn Frey seventies anthem "Take It Easy." Henley agreed to appear with Frey in a video for the song. Azoff's carefully timed release of the video, single, and album helped the album cross over from the country charts to the *Billboard* mainstream pop and rock listing, and caused an explosion of renewed interest in the band that one record executive described as "Eaglemania; just about the last thing anyone expected in the nineties world of alternative rock. Anyone, that is, except Irving Azoff."

Common Thread, released on Azoff's Giant Records, sold more than three million copies its first six months of release and went to number one and number three respectively on the country and pop charts. This surprised no one more than Henley, pleased no one more than Frey, and activated no one more than Azoff. As soon as the album went gold, early in February 1994, Azoff invited the former Eagles to join him once again for lunch in Aspen. Walsh was also invited. No matter what their objections, he told the three of them, there was no longer any question that they had to get back together. What could possibly stand in their way now? Their music had stood the test of time, and they were all far enough away from everything that had gone down in the past that they should be able to set their differences aside and seize this last great opportunity to prove the Eagles were the greatest rock and roll band of all time. And, if they listened to him, the richest as well.

Azoff did a masterful selling job. The result of that meeting was a series of phone calls to the other two band members to see if they were willing to go along with a possible reunion. Schmit and Felder immediately agreed. That May, the Eagles performed their first on-the-record live show together in fourteen years.

The official reunion took place at the Warner Brothers soundstage in Hollywood, before a small, enthusiastic audience invited to the session by MTV, which taped it for future broadcast. Beginning with a lush, protracted arrangement on acoustic guitar by Don Felder, the familiar strains of "Hotel California" floated from the stage. After a momentary spill of nerves, the band began a long-awaited, highly anticipated journey through its own musical history. For the next hour and a half they played every song the audience wanted to hear and four new ones, three Henley and Frey collaborations and one written by friends. "Get Over It" was a comical, good-natured nod at the feud between Henley and Frey. "Love Will Keep Us Alive," written by Pete Vale, Jim Capaldi, and Paul Carrack, was a pledge of sorts for the future. "The Girl from Yesterday" was a neonostalgic glimpse at their generation's romantic youth. "Learn to Be Still," besides seeming to be something of an inside joke regarding the Henley rules of stage performance, was a simple acoustic-guitar-based ballad with a straightforward message based, to some degree, on Henley's studies of Thoreau, Gandhi, and other philosophical types. The song, perhaps somewhat ironically, echoed the same message as one of the lines from one of the Eagles' very first hit singles: *"Don't let the sound of your own wheels drive you crazy."* These four quite ordinary songs did nothing so much as underscore to the audience how powerful and lasting the band's classic body of work really was.

With the MTV show under its belt, and no fistfights backstage, the band members agreed to what they now good-naturedly referred to as the "Hell Freezes Over" tour. Its first public performance was scheduled for May 27, 1994, at the Irvine Meadows Amphitheatre, just south of Los Angeles, of which, perhaps not coincidentally, Irving Azoff was part owner. Tickets were priced at a phenomenal $115 apiece, which the band and its management claimed was the best way to eliminate scalpers. Glenn Frey cited the cost of scalped tickets to L.A. Lakers games going for upward of $500. Besides, he told a reporter, the Eagles were throwing in free parking. The band reportedly demanded and received almost 90 percent of the high-priced gate from most of the major venues it played, leaving the promoters with the privilege of having booked the Eagles and the profit from all the beer they could sell. Move enough beer, Azoff seemed to be telling promoters, and you'll actually walk away with a few dollars.

The high price may have had less to do with money than prestige. Filling arenas at those prices would make the Eagles the top-grossing act that year. At Henley's urging, each member earmarked a chosen organization to share in the tour's profits, including the Walden Woods Project; the Grass

Roots Aspen Experience, an AIDS charity; the T. J. Martell Foundation; the project to preserve Caddo Lake, near Henley's hometown; the American Kidney Foundation; and several programs for inner-city-youth retreats in the mountains.

On that cool night in May, the band members nervously shuffled onstage and took their places down front atop stools, acoustic guitars around their shoulders, flannel shirts on their backs, music on their minds. As Felder and Walsh once again opened the show with "Hotel California's" classic dual guitar riff, the people in the audience threw their fists into the air and screamed with joy. The moment was glorious, filled with a sense of victory and conviction. Just before he kicked in, Henley glanced quickly around the stage, caught Frey's eyes for a second, then turned back to stare straight ahead, waiting for his cue.

"Beware of what you set your heart on. For it surely shall be yours."

And then the guitars kicked in and it was back to that dark desert highway. Once more, he found himself staring into the hot white blindness of the arena's forward spots, as if trying to figure out all over again whether this could indeed finally be heaven or the same old familiar hell.

Nothing had really changed, of course. It was still both.

EIGHTEEN

The 1994 "Hell Freezes Over" tour, originally scheduled to play seventy shows across the United States for seven months, through the end of December, lasted more than two years. It took the Eagles around the world and outgrossed all other competing concert acts, taking in more than $75 million in ticket sales. Wherever it played, the band was greeted by enthusiastic sold-out crowds made up as much of teenagers too young to have seen the band in its first go-around as of baby boomers eager to revisit the memories of their youth. At every two-hour-plus show the Eagles played all their hits and a few by individual members. Among the most requested songs were "The Last Resort" and "The Sad Café."

The album *Hell Freezes Over* sold more than seven million copies, stayed on the *Billboard* top 200 for more than two years, and, according to Soundscan, remains solidly among the fifteen most consistent selling "catalog" albums. Although it was supposed to have been a live recording of their MTV reunion show, the album was, in fact, heavily remixed and over-dubbed. The video (and laser disc) of the "Hell Freezes Over" tour taken from the MTV performance stayed on *Billboard*'s Top Music Video chart for nearly two and a half years, with sales approaching 200,000 units, making it one of the better-selling full-length music videos of all time. Two other Eagles albums, *Their Greatest Hits 1971–1974* and *Hotel California*, are among the top-selling albums of all time. *Hits* goes back and forth between number one and number two with Michael Jackson's *Thriller; Hotel* is firmly in the number eight spot.

One of the interesting things about the choice of tracks on *Hell Freezes Over* was what was included and what was left out. The first four cuts on the album were the new songs: "Get Over It," "Love Will Keep Us Alive," "The Girl from Yesterday," and "Learn to Be Still." These were followed by "Tequila Sunrise," "Hotel California," "Wasted Time," "Pretty Maids All in a Row," "I Can't Tell You Why," "New York Minute," "The Last Resort," "Take It Easy," "In the City," "Life in the Fast Lane," and "Desperado."

With the exception of "Pretty Maids All in a Row," written by Joe Walsh and Joe Vitale, "In the City," by Joe Walsh and Barry De Vorzon, and "Love Will Keep Us Alive," by Pete Vale, Jim Capaldi, and Paul Carrack, every song on the album was written wholly or in part by Don Henley and/or Glenn Frey (and, variously, Joe Walsh, Don Felder, Timothy B. Schmit, Jackson Browne, Jack Tempchin, Stan Lynch, Danny Kortchmar, and Jai Winding). Noticeably absent were any songs by Bernie Leadon or Randy Meisner. And because the versions of the old songs included were newly recorded, neither Leadon nor Meisner would share in any of the album's sales, airplay, or performance royalties.

According to Meisner, this was no coincidence. He viewed it as a deliberately vindictive attempt to ensure that he and Leadon would not benefit financially from the album or the accompanying tour, other than royalties on the rerelease of the back catalog. Meisner says, "At one point, when I heard the band was going to get back together, I called Irving and Glenn. I thought it would be a really cool thing if the reunion was, in fact, a *real* Eagles reunion, meaning everyone who had ever been a part of the group. I figured there was no way any of my songs was going to be included in the new album, and I could live with that. I just hoped that even for just one show, maybe opening night, Glenn or Don might bring me and Bernie out, and we could do one of our old songs. Then we'd leave, and they could do the rest of the show. That would have been something. Anyway, when I called Glenn, he seemed friendly enough and said yeah, that might be nice, and Irving said the same thing, and that was the last I heard from either.

"You know, I've listened to *Hell Freezes Over.* Does that version sound like 'Hotel California' to you? It doesn't to me. What was the purpose of redoing the original, besides making money — to go ahead and tamper with such a classic recording? The new one is pretty, sure, the guitar work is nice, the singing is good, but . . . it's *not* 'Hotel California.' And it's not like the original isn't available right next to it in the CD bins. Yeah, I was hurt and I was disappointed by the actions of the Eagles. I found it unfair, insensitive, and petty."

Meisner's comments are wistfully unrealistic. The group had disbanded with a different membership than the one that had included him. The reunion he sought would have been like a Beatles concert with Pete Best. As for the Eagles, they reminded anyone who wanted to know where Meisner was, and there weren't many, that this was a *resumption* tour rather than a *reunion*, and there was no reason to invite former members Meisner and Leadon, since both had long ago been replaced.

Although the Eagles had been known for their carousing and self-abuse in their former incarnation, it was clear to everyone connected to this tour that these Eagles were no bad-boy rockers. All were approaching middle age, and those who had them were often accompanied by wives and children. Schmit's wife brought their daughter (from his previous marriage) and two sons; Felder his wife and two daughters; Frey his second wife, Cindy, and two boys. According to one close to the tour, Walsh was the biggest potential problem, as Frey had laid out a hard-and-fast rule — no drinks and no drugs backstage. Walsh was quietly approached and told to make sure he could handle being straight. He was always the wildest card because of his preference for hanging out with the roadies (to the point where he often packed his own equipment). Walsh assured the others he wouldn't let them down and, true to his word, stayed sober the entire tour. He even invited his ex-wife, Jodi (remarried but still a friend), and their daughter to several performances. Walsh celebrated his sobriety by appearing throughout the tour as a "bubble-headed bleach blond."

In spite of the outward appearance of tranquillity, if not peace, all wasn't what it seemed. Within a month, it was rumored, the Eagles were no longer talking to each other. Separate vehicles once more became the order of the day. In September 1994, the tour was interrupted when Frey came down with a very serious recurrence of diverticulitis requiring surgery. Talk began to circulate that this was without question the last Eagles tour, if not forever, then for a very long time. "It felt like an old pair of shoes that were comfortable, yet a few nails were sticking through the soles," says Henley. "It was comforting for me because it was so familiar. There I was, back behind the drums again. The other guys were out front, and I didn't have to carry the ball by myself. Glenn is a real take-charge kind of guy, and I always appreciated that part. The romance of the road was great too. For the first two or three months. And then all the old, ugly demons came back. Even older and wiser, the animosities, the jealousies, hurt, and resentment were still there. Glenn and I started to have some competitive issues again. Joe, who I thought was going to be the troublemaker, was great. He was straight, clean, and a lot of fun to be with. We had given him the proviso that he had to be straight, and he came through. We were all very proud of him.

"The tour was great fun when we were getting along and everyone was in a good mood, which was . . . once in a while. I loved touring and was so grateful that we got to go back to all those countries and play again, because we were so drugged out in the seventies I didn't remember a lot of it. Now, here I was, nearly fifty years old, selling out Wembley Stadium for four days. I never expected that kind of reaction. I knew we'd be all right, but nothing like what went on."

Upon Frey's recovery, in January 1995, the band resumed its schedule and stayed out on the road for the next six months. They completed the domestic portion in the spring of 1995 and returned to L.A. for a break as final preparations were made for the 1996 international swing.

On May 20, 1995, a week after the winter tour break, Henley surprised everyone outside his immediate circle when he married Sharon Summerall. Over the years, he had been romantically linked to a string of famous women, including actress Dana Delaney, TV commentator and daughter of the former vice president Eleanor Mondale, and actress Cathy Lee Crosby. Henley finally believed he had found the perfect Southern downhome (Dallas, Texas) woman.

What shocked everyone was that although he was always seriously involved with somebody, marriage had never seemed a viable option for Henley. Moreover, his and Summerall's had not been an especially smooth relationship. There were also concerns about the bride's health, as she was suffering from a chronic but nondebilitating form of multiple sclerosis.

The ceremony was held in private at a secluded ranch in the hills above Malibu that had been rented for the occasion. Henley's mother was in attendance. Musical entertainment was provided by Jackson Browne,

Welcome to the Hotel California

Don Felder
(Jeff Mayer/Star File)

Don Felder
(Laurens Van Houten/Star File)

Joe Walsh
(Laurens Van Houten/Star File)

Joe Walsh and Don Henley.
(Laurens Van Houten/Star File)

At the party following the Madison Square Garden performance of *Hotel California,* the Garden's Penn Plaza Club, New York, 1976. L to R: Don Felder, J. D. Souther, Don Henley, unknown, Dudley Moore (standing). (Richard Aaron/ Star File)

Warren Zevon and Jackson Browne. Crystal Zevon is behind the *People* magazine. (Henry Diltz/Rebel Road)

The First End of the Long Run

Glenn Frey and Jann
Wenner shake hands
at the infamous game,
North Hollywood,
May 1978.
(Andrew Kent)

Glenn Frey signing autographs at the game.
(Andrew Kent)

The final tour. L to R: Timothy B. Schmit, Glenn Frey, Joe Walsh.
(Richard E. Aaron/Star File)

L to R: Timothy B. Schmit, Glenn Frey, Don Felder. (Richard E. Aaron/Star File)

Don Felder and Joe Walsh.
(Jeff Mayer/Star File)

Don Henley
(Jeff Mayer/Star File)

A souvenir of Joe Walsh's try for a
second career.
(Collection of Linda Jones)

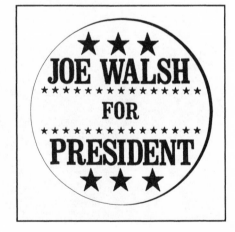

★ ★ ★
JOE WALSH
★ ★ ★ ★ ★ ★ ★ ★ ★ ★ ★ ★ ★
FOR
★ ★ ★ ★ ★ ★ ★ ★ ★ ★ ★ ★ ★
PRESIDENT
★ ★ ★

One of the last photos taken of the Eagles before the 1980 breakup.
L to R: Joe Walsh, Timothy B. Schmit, Don Henley, Glenn Frey, Don Felder.
(Courtesy of Warner Bros.)

The end of the innocence. Don Henley performing solo, 1986.
(Anne Dowie)

Hell Freezes Over

Hell frozen over. The "continuation" tour, 1994.
L to R: Glenn Frey, Don Henley, Don Felder, Joe Walsh.
(Jeff Mayer/Star File)

Sharon Summerall and Don
Henley on their wedding day, 1994.
(Vincent Zuffante/Star File)

Bruce Springsteen, John Fogarty, Sting, Sheryl Crow, Bill Joel, and J. D. Souther. For a donation of $70,000 to his favorite children's charity, Tony Bennett performed a twenty-minute set of songs.

A revitalized Henley became involved in several new non-Eagles projects, among them the recording of Randy Newman's ambitious rock version of *Faust.* The concept album was produced by Peter Asher and Don Was, and featured performances by Henley, Elton John, Randy Newman, Bonnie Raitt, Linda Ronstadt, and James Taylor. Although sales were disappointing, critical response was so great there was talk of eventually turning it into a movie or a Broadway show. Henley also contributed songs to a number of hit movies, including a version of John Hiatt's "Through Your Hands" for *Michael,* the John Travolta vehicle in which the actor played an angel on earth.

In 1995, Henley and Geffen finally settled their lawsuit. Geffen then released a Henley greatest hits album and the Eagles reunion disc, *Hell Freezes Over. Actual Miles: Henley's Greatest Hits* contained a new song, "The Garden of Allah," a hollow, sermonizing echo of "Hotel California" that neither angered nor amused anyone who heard it. The accompanying video featured a short-haired, scowling Henley at his finger-pointing best. The single and album failed to make a serious dent on the charts. Both hovered in the Top 40 for a couple of weeks before fading.

As far as Henley was concerned, blame for the failure for both could be laid squarely at the feet of his old nemesis. "Of course Geffen completely failed to promote the album and 'Allah,' named, by the way, after an old hotel in Hollywood. It was a very famous place, the site of great debauchery and wild parties during Hollywood's heyday. I thought it was a very interesting song, considering what was going on with the O. J. trial. Radio didn't want anything to do with it because it had talking. I guess they don't like to hear white boys rapping, unless you're Vanilla Ice. I spent a million bucks of my own money to make the video. I'm not thrilled with the way it came out. Video directors have become so fucking egotistical. They've got three or four videos going on at the same time; they've got a drawer full of video treatments they open up like a Chinese menu. They don't really care what the song is about. It's more of their vision of something. This video was based on Orson Welles's movie version of Kafka's *The Trial,* which was a little far afield from what I had in mind.

"The song didn't get a whole lot of play; neither did the video. We edited the single of that song four or five times. I finally edited all the talking out of it; it made no sense whatsoever, but the radio people just wanted the singing parts."

Earnings from the "Hell Freezes Over" tour and album and the re-releases of the entire catalog made the Eagles the highest-paid entertainers of the two-year period ending in September 1996, with pretax earnings of $75 million. The only musical acts of any age, style of music, or size of catalog that outgrossed them were the Beatles, Michael Jackson, and the Rolling Stones. The next highest grossing rock act among the top twenty after the Eagles was R.E.M., with earnings of $44 million.

The band offered no apologies for the money it made. "If you're going to be in the business," according to one Eagle, "if you're going to play with the big boys, then you have to learn the game. If we were money conscious, we still made a hell of a lot more money for the record company than for ourselves. Even at the end, they were getting four bucks to our one. That's the way it works in the record business. And we didn't get nearly that much in the beginning. We were always just trying to get what we felt was ours. We'd seen so many artists, so many of our heroes, particularly from the sixties, end up with nothing, people who had all these hit records and got royally screwed. Irving went to bat for us; he knew the business, he could play in both sides of the arena, and he got us what we deserved. And even then, not always. At times we still got screwed, several times. It took us years to get our publishing back from Warners, for instance. We wanted to come out of all this with something."

Irving Azoff had played his hand superbly. Henley, freed from any remaining contractual ties to Geffen, signed a new solo recording deal with Warner Bros. Records. A solo album was set for release in the fall of 1998.

In 1996, Glenn Frey resumed his acting career. Longtime journalist friend Cameron Crowe, who in 1975 had done the first *Rolling Stone* cover story on the Eagles and remained friends with the boys in the band, had become a successful screenwriter. Looking for someone to play the owner of a sports franchise, Crowe offered the role to Frey, who effectively played the small part in what turned out to be one of the largest-grossing films of the year, the Tom Cruise–driven *Jerry Maguire*.

"Hell Freezes Over" once more significantly boosted sales of the entire Eagles catalog, which ended the "threat," as Azoff called it, from Warner to release yet another greatest hits album.

What had begun as a two-hundred-dollar-a-week, rag-tag, backup, temporary road band out of the L.A. club scene had survived into the nineties as an international phenomenon, a living monument to its own and a generation's long-gone youth, heat, and glory.

In 1971, the Eagles had led the celebrated blossoming of L.A. as modern rock's newest utopia. Twenty-five years later, they had become a band of middle-aged men singing in the emotional past tense songs that had distilled to a single, if profound, theme — survival. Like all the great long-running rock stars and groups that had somehow continued to find a way to keep making music — the Rolling Stones, the Who, Pink Floyd, Aerosmith; the remnants of Led Zeppelin, the Band, and the Grateful Dead — the Eagles had survived by completing the subtle but crucial shift in their concerts from event to homage, an experience in collective memory.

Randy Meisner was right when he'd noted how the elaborate, elongated version of "Hotel California" had supplanted the song's, and the band's, great edge with a luxurious dullness, an expansion that somehow reduced the original's impact. In the end, seeing these Eagles was like watching a nineties production of *Beatlemania* performed by the Beatles themselves. Still, if they were no longer who or what they once were, neither was the land that had spawned them. Although the Eagles had managed a revival of sorts, L.A.'s musical landscape, so much a part of the band's vision, identity, and relevance, had not. Almost everything about the Los Angeles of the seventies was changed or gone, from its marvelous Spanish-Deco architecture to its parking spaces. The once seemingly perfect new rock frontier had been blighted by a series of natural and manmade disasters, each leaving a wrinkle on the ever more ravaged face of the City of Angels. The McMartin case. Earthquakes. Drought. Fires. Floods. South L.A. gang wars. Drive-by shootings. Rodney King. The South Central riots. O. J. Simpson. High-powered bank robberies. El Niño.

The "Fabulous Forum," where the band had played so many of its hometown dates, was no longer so fabulous, having been sold to an energy corporation whose first act was to change the name of the venue to the Gulf and Western Forum. The Troubadour never regained the influence it had once wielded. The Whiskey managed to keep its doors open but, like most clubs on the Strip, had gone through a period where anybody could play if he or she could pay the fee to step onstage. In truth, most of L.A. had, for a time, become a pay-to-play venue, filling the clubs with ascerbic, undernourished, stringy-haired rockers all looking to cash in by sounding just like the bands who'd played in the great proven yesterdays, rather than taking a chance on their own unknown tomorrows. The sound of the acts that did manage to break out seemed as exotically different from that of the Eagles' and L.A.'s glory days as one could imagine. Performers such as Dwight Yoakum and Lone Star redefined the sound, appearance, and attitude of California country-rock.

Despite the opening of two new and major venues, the House of Blues, on Sunset, and Billboard Live, a sense of revitalization failed to emerge. The Grammy Awards, long an icon of L.A.'s entertainment industry, had for several broadcasts in recent years relocated to New York City. Even Las Vegas managed to eclipse L.A., as the hottest shows in the West routinely came out of the Hard Rock Hotel's intimate yet influential Joint. Once an image of youthful rebellion, the streets of L.A. now roiled with the heat of ethnic youth gangs, while the club scene suffered from the drug death of young actor River Phoenix.

For these reasons, and others, Los Angeles lost its position as one of the world's capitals of rock and roll. The receding financial influence of the Japanese, whose late-eighties purchase of Columbia's records division had proven less than economically spectacular, caused the majority of overseas record-company money to start coming from Europe again, a shift away from Asia that in turn summoned the corporate heads of America's major labels back to Manhattan.

As a result, New York and its adjacent turf, including New Jersey, Long Island, Virginia, and Washington D.C., experienced a renaissance of new music, while in the West, the scene migrated north to Seattle, where Nirvana, Pearl Jam, and Soundgarden heralded yet another new region and era of what was now being called "alternative" rock and roll. Other cities continued to compete for their place on rock's historic map: Austin, Texas; Santa Barbara, California; Denver, Colorado; and Cleveland, Ohio (Alan

Freed's original base of operations in the early fifties and the home of the Rock and Roll Hall of Fame); all became key commercial turf to record-company scouts mining the fields of youth, forever in search of music's Next Big Time, Place, and Thing.

Shortly after the 1994 earthquake had destroyed his Los Angeles house, Don Henley saw the cosmic handwriting on the wall. The time had finally come. Or gone. He announced his intention to move with his family back to Texas. "I want my daughter to grow up around all those conservatives so she'll know how to rebel properly," Henley joked to the press. Having purchased a home in Dallas, approximately 150 miles outside of Linden, the once and future Eagle packed their belongings and headed out of L.A.

By evening, the sun fallen behind him, Don Henley drove into the twilight, headed at last for home.

EPILOGUE

On January 12, 1998, the Eagles were inducted into the Rock and Roll Hall of Fame. Reunited once more two years after their "Hell Freezes Over" tour ended, this time with the two original and departed members of the band included, Don Henley, Glenn Frey, Randy Meisner, Bernie Leadon, Don Felder, Joe Walsh, and Timoth B. Schmit — the Eagles — became the one hundredth entrant to the twelve-year-old institution.

Although the hall is located in Cleveland, Ohio, a nod to what some consider the "official" birthplace of rock and roll (it having been disk jockey Alan Freed's radio base when he supposedly first used the phrase to describe the music that made him and it famous), the delayed-cablecast ceremonies were held in the music's financial capital, in the Grand Ballroom of New York's legendary Waldorf-Astoria.

This meant the Eagles had to return to one of their least-favorite cities. They might not have attended at all, as they still had no use for one of the hall's and evening's principal sponsors, Jann Wenner, but their respect for another, Ahmet Ertegun, and his ceaseless efforts on behalf of those performers less fortunate than the Eagles, finally persuaded them to participate in the type of award ceremony they had always avoided in the past. Still, they wondered — and within purposeful earshot of the media — why the ceremonies were held in New York City. More pointedly, they wanted to know why this year, at least, they weren't where they should have been, in the City of Angels that had hatched the Eagles and so much of the Southern California–style rock and roll they had driven.

"Eaglemaniacs" came the responsive word in the air, even louder after the band insisted either they perform last or not at all. However, for all the grumbling and finger-pointing, there was no good reason for the Eagles *not* to close the show. Among the living recipients of the night, which included Carlos Santana, the Mamas and the Papas, and Lloyd Price, only Fleetwood Mac could reasonably and rightfully challenge the Eagles for that coveted spot. This made the night more reminiscent of the seventies than anyone might have expected or wanted — the two biggest L.A. bands of that era once again competing for the top spot.

It was part of the charm of the otherwise problematic Hall of Fame that because its induction policies made a band eligible for entry twenty-five years after the release of its first record, the annual event offered an ongoing chronological history of rock and roll. Thus, 1998 became a celebration of the emergence of "Rock and Roll West." Fittingly, 1999 would see the induction of Bruce Springsteen, whose arrival on the recording scene only one year after the Eagles radically shifted the sound, direction, and style of rock and roll back to the East Coast.

The Eagles denied having threatened to pull out of the ceremonies if they didn't get their way (reportedly refusing to sign autographs during their sound check didn't help), but there were some who felt they demonstrated the same arrogance and blatant nastiness here that had always kept them from the hearts of the kids (and the critics) from the East, who would always consider New York music the sharpest blade of rock and roll's cutting edge.

As far as the Eagles were concerned, the New York rock press could . . . stick it to itself. This was their night, they were there, they were *all* there, and they were going to make the most of the occasion, one made possible by what *they'd* accomplished rather than those intent on putting on a show.

About the awards, Henley says, "There's still this stigma that hangs over the Eagles. No matter how many records we've sold, no matter how successful we've been, we're not considered an 'important' band, and it'll always be that way. It's partially because of the New York critical establishment and partially because we had either the fortune or the misfortune to be the middle child of rock and roll, after all the great sixties artists — Dylan, the Beatles, the Rolling Stones. They were the pioneers, we were sort of an afterthought. It also may have looked to some that we took what others had started — the Byrds, Poco, the Burrito Brothers — and capitalized on it, but it was not because we calculated to do that; we just loved the music. As far as I was concerned, in comparison to all that we'd accomplished in our careers, being inducted into the Rock and Roll Hall of Fame seemed a bit hollow."

Henley was among the first to show up the day of the ceremonies for the afternoon rehearsal. He arrived with J. D. Souther, and as the day rolled on, the rest of the band members appeared in the ballroom and greeted each other with hugs and handshakes. For Randy Meisner and Bernie Leadon, it was a night filled with forgiveness and warmth. These two ex-members of the band looked considerably older than the other Eagles, or, as one observer whispered, "like the first wives of movie stars." Gracefully, or gratefully, it was hard to tell which, both had agreed to rejoin the band this one time, to remember their great flight into the high winds of fame and glory.

It was deep into the night when the final award was presented. The honor of introducing the band went to the Eagles' onetime opening act, Jimmy Buffett. "It's nice to see everybody I can recognize in their tuxedos, and we truly do look like the people our parents warned us about tonight," he began, drawing a sliver of titters from the still-cool crowd. "I've known the Eagles for nearly as long as they've been a band. . . . First, with about a jillion other war babies in America in 1972, I was converted instantly to an Eagles fan when I heard 'Take It Easy' on the radio. . . . They put their thumb on the pulse of popular music, where it remained for nearly twenty-seven years. As performers they came with a straightforward style, no smoke bombs or sacrificial guitars. . . .

"The Eagles created their own style, blending banjos and electric guitars, harmonies from the heartland and cutting-edge lyrics from the fault line, and God knows what they did for the chamber of commerce of Winslow, Arizona. . . .

"The Eagles are going into the Rock and Roll Hall of Fame as one of the signature bands that began in the seventies, still alive and kicking ass as we head for the millennium. They've laughed, frolicked, cried, fought, but most of all they have beaten the odds and are as popular today as they were in that incredible summer back in 1972. *And here I am, still opening for this goddamn band!*"

Amid warm laughter, the Eagles swooped onto the stage, smiling triumphantly and patting one another on the back. Forming a loose semicircle behind the podium, resplendent in tuxedos (except Joe Walsh, who wore a suit that looked like a brick wall), they waited for the applause to die down. Henley approached the microphone and delivered a speech he had written that afternoon. With a face hung between pride and perturbation, he delivered what amounted to part lecture, part sermon, and part confession, with a little bit of what can only be described as expansive humility tossed in for good measure.

Clearing his throat, stooping slightly into the mike, he began. "We are all grateful and honored for the opportunity and good fortune that have brought us all here this evening on this *suspicious* occasion!" Thin laughter scattered throughout the house.

"I've had a lot of mixed emotions about the name 'Hall of Fame.' It's the *fame* part that bothers me a little, here in the waning hours of the twentieth century. In what we call Western culture, in this age of media, friends, fame is just not what it used to be. *It's become an ugly, ugly thing!* Andy Warhol was right; anybody can become famous for fifteen minutes — if you're sufficiently starved for attention and willing to be really obnoxious in public and make a complete fool of yourself, you too can be famous. . . . You know, the line between fame and accomplishment is becoming very blurred. I guess they couldn't call it the Hall of Accomplishment. Accomplishment enriches life, and fame always comes with a price. Fame is a by-product of accomplishment. But when a kid picks up a guitar or a drumstick, it's not really to be famous, it's because that kid wants to fit in somwhere and be accepted. He wants to be understood, even. And so I like to think of this award as acknowledging us not for being famous but for doing the work.

"I appreciate all the work these guys behind me have done. I want to thank Irving Azoff, without whom we wouldn't be here today. . . ." A small but spirited round of cheers floated above the crowd, as Frey shouted from his place at the edge of the stage, "Well, we might still have been here, but we wouldn't have made as much money. . . ."

"Right," Henley said, laughing. "As I've said before, he may be Satan, but he's our Satan!"

Bigger laughs, harder applause.

"I want to thank Bill Szymczyk, who's here this evening, our producer. . . . I want to thank Glyn Johns. . . . *Hell, I'll even thank David Geffen!*

"And I want to thank our good friends and compadres Jackson Browne and J. D. Souther, our crew, the many, many good men in our road crew. . . . It's been a good trip, and we appreciate it.

"Last but not least, I want to thank my family, my mother and my father for believing in me early on, for getting me that drum set and letting me play it in the house. And I want to thank my wonderful wife for being patient and kind and loving and understanding. Thank you all."

After solid but polite applause, it was Timothy B. Schmit's turn to approach the mike. "I'd like to thank whoever's responsible for my induction into this Hall of Fame. On a brief personal note, I'd like to say that I was not in the trenches with this particular band, and so I'd like to thank my predecessor for being there and paving the way for my being here tonight. With him beside me and the rest of these guys, I'm very honored. Thank you very much."

Leadon spoke next and delivered his speech with typically dry humor. "Hi, my name is Bernie Leadon. I'm really honored to be here tonight. Thank you. Really proud to have lived long enough to be *indicted*. I'd like to thank everybody on the grand jury who voted for me. To the people already thanked, I want to add the names of a few less well known. One is John Boylan. He was Linda Ronstadt's manager and producer at the time that we got together and had a lot to do with my being included in the first group of four, and I'd really like to thank him personally tonight. I'd also really like to thank Ahmet Ertegun and Atlantic Records for having funded David Geffen and Elliot Roberts and the starting of Asylum Records. I know that Atlantic did a lot of work behind the scenes of the Eagles' success, and I'd like to thank them again. . . . And also, thanks to my family."

Leadon was followed by a visibly humbled Randy Meisner. "I'd just like to say I'm very honored to be here tonight. Thank you, Timmy. It's just great playing with the guys again. I'd like to thank my mother and my father for supporting me during those years."

Joe Walsh was the next to approach the mike, greeted by the most enthusiastic applause of the night. *"Hey, how ya dooin'?"* he asked in his trademark opener. "I would like to thank the people from Canton, Ohio; Akron, Ohio; and Cleveland, Ohio, for believing in me. I'd like to thank Bill Szymczyk for finding me in the middle of nowhere. I'd like to thank Don and Glenn for writing those songs. It makes my job real easy. I'd also like to thank all the guys that drive this equipment around, that drive the trucks, set it up, tune it up, fix it, put it back in the truck, so we can do what we do. God bless the road crew. Thank you!"

Now it was Don Felder's turn, and under his breath he commented on Walsh's "charming" outfit before turning his attention to the audience. "I'd like to again thank Don Henley and Glenn Frey for writing an incredible body of work that propelled this band through twenty-some-odd years of life. . . . Thank you guys. . . . And I'd like to thank my wife, Susan, who put up with me for twenty-six years while we did this."

Finally, it was Frey's turn. Unlike Henley, he took his shot spontaneously, said exactly what he wanted to, and let the chips fall. He strode to the mike, looked around as if waiting for the barbs to come back, took a deep breath, and, noting he was going last, sighed and began. "Well, I'm doing mop up. . . . There's much I'd like to say tonight. . . . Anybody who's been in a band knows what it's like to go through the changes. . . . A lot has been made tonight about disharmony. The Eagles were a very laid-back band in a high-stress situation." Murmurs and giggles went through the house. "A lot has been made and a lot has been speculated about the last twenty-seven years about whether or not we got along. We got along fine! *We just disagreed a lot!* Tell me one worthwhile relationship that has not had peaks and valleys. That's really what we're talking about here."

From behind, Henley smiled broadly and cheered his friend on, as the applause rose. Over it, Frey continued. "You cannot play music with people for very long if you don't genuinely like them. I guarantee you that over the nine years the Eagles were together during the seventies, over the three years we were together during our reunion, the best of times rank in the ninety-five percent, the worst of times rank in the smallest percentile that obviously everybody but the seven of us has dwelled on for the longest time. *Get over it!*

"On a personal note, you get a lot of free advice when you're coming up in the business. When I was still a kid, Bob Seger told me that if I didn't write my own songs I'd never get out of Detroit. I listened to him and said, Well, what if they're bad? The first few will be really bad, but if you're good they'll get better. The next bit of free advice I got was from David Geffen, who told me I should get in a band and find a songwriting partner. I did both, and we're all here to celebrate the fruits of David's advice."

After thanking everyone, Frey stepped back. The boys in the band looked at each other and for one last time approached the equipment waiting behind them on the stage. They had two songs scheduled, and because Henley had spoken first, the kickoff would be Frey's signature "Take It Easy." The performance was unique, as it was the first time all seven Eagles had ever sung together. The rich harmonies and added instruments filled the room with a ringing, churchlike celebration.

The next and last song the Eagles would sing together in this configuration, and perhaps the last one they would ever perform in any, was the anthemic "Hotel California." They kicked into it, driven as always by the guitars of Felder and Walsh, and Henley's vocals and cannon drums. When they finished, there was an awkward moment of silence followed by applause as they slowly put down their instruments and walked into the shadows of the wings.

The lights came up, and the audience slowly dispersed. The big show was over.

POSTSCRIPT TO
THE DA CAPO EDITION

Part One: The Book

To the Limit was originally intended as the third book of a trilogy
about rock and roll, the first being *Death of a Rebel: Starring Phil
Ochs and a Small Circle of Friends* originally published in 1978. *Rebel*
was my biography of the controversial singer-songwriter who
emerged from the sixties' Greenwich Village music scene that was
spearheaded by Bob Dylan and that produced such seminal influences besides Phil as John Sebastian's Lovin' Spoonful; Peter, Paul
and Mary; Jackson Browne; The Mamas and the Papas; David Blue;
Eric Andersen; Tim Hardin; Judy Collins; Tom Paxton; Patrick Sky;
the Blues Project and dozens of others, all of whom played key
roles in launching the era of modern East Coast, acoustic-based,
blues-tinged, politically aware folk-rock.

I began the second book of the trilogy fifteen years later, after a
chance meeting I had with Mike Appel, the man who discovered and
nurtured Bruce Springsteen through the first and most difficult years
of what would become his most extraordinary career. That encounter
led to *Down Thunder Road: The Making of Bruce Springsteen*, originally
published in 1993.

In the interim, despite my sacred vow to never travel above Fourteenth Street (except to attend classes at Columbia University), the unofficial northern tip of the village where I had lived for nearly twenty years, I eventually headed west to write *Walt Disney: Hollywood's Dark Prince*. For research purposes, I reluctantly relocated from New York City to Los Angeles, and it was while living in Hollywood that I began to realize I had actually written the third part of my music trilogy ahead of the second. *Death of a Rebel* dealt with the New York music scene of the sixties, and *Down Thunder Road* climaxed with the Boss's explosive mid-seventies entry into rock's mainstream which, after a decade's occupation of the left coast, reestablished the east as the cultural epicenter of American rock and roll.

What was missing, I realized, was the story of that occupation, rock's second act, the reason for its shift west, which Papa John Phillips had so sweetly romanticized in his group's 1965 echoey autobiographical folk-rock hit "California Dreamin'—" "*All the leaves are brown (all the leaves are brown), and the sky is gray (and the sky is gray) . . . I'd be safe and warm (I'd be safe and warm), if I was in L.A. (if I was in L.A.) . . .* " During the brief but highly influential run of the Mamas and the Papas, Phillips managed to blend his group's sound into that of the native Californian Beach Boys. By doing so, he set the stage for rock's next identifiable sound and decade, roughly from the mid-surfin' sixties through the 1975 summer of Springsteen. Their clarion sound signaled a ten-year journey, during which rock and roll morphed from the wistfully innocent fantasies of "California Dreamin'" to the paranoid preachings of the Eagles' "Hotel California," a place, they told us, we could check out from any time but we could never leave. From the beaches to the suites of the west coast, the American West Coast–rock dominated the singles and album charts for the next ten years.

Once I realized what was missing from my three-part history, I searched for the right group upon which to hang the middle tale. After eliminating the Byrds (their roots too New York City–Dylan folkish), the Mamas and the Papas (Peter, Paul and Mary ditto), the

Grateful Dead (too peripheral, having never significantly entered or affected the singles charts), and the Jefferson Airplane (too culturally monotonic), my short list included the Beach Boys, The Doors, and Crosby, Stills & Nash (and sometimes Young). I had to eliminate the Beach Boys once I realized their music really represented the last vestige of fifties harmonies, chord progressions, and overall teen-idol cheeriness, a sandy bleach-blond version of greasy New York doo-wop infused with an exciting but ultimately unsatisfying surfing sensibility. I might have chosen The Doors if others hadn't beaten me to it. As for Crosby, Stills, Nash & Young, their music just didn't knock me out the way I wanted and needed it to.

And then I hit upon the Eagles, a group everyone knew of but no one thought about all that much . It happened one day when I was cruising in my convertible (natch), headed west down Sunset Boulevard when on the car radio came a whiny sob story about another tequila sunrise. What can I say? It grabbed me and wouldn't let go. I must have heard the song a hundred times before, but on this day, with my BMW caressing the curves of the boulevard as if they were the slopes of a beautiful honey's body, with the top down and the warm Catalina winds blowing through my hair, I suddenly "got it."

Although the Eagles received almost no airplay in New York City, at least not on the stations I'd listened to when I lived there, mostly WNEW and PLJ, and were never taken very seriously by the so-called intelligentsia of the rock press (despite or perhaps because of their reputation as rock's ultimate hedonists, a fact that, unlike Led Zeppelin, did not seem a vital component to their music), I suddenly realized I was indeed listening to primal seventies rock, and that the boys making it were the perfect subjects for the connective middle of my saga.

As I began to gather background material, my writing career took some weird turns. Following on the heels of a front-page controversy over my Disney biography, brought about by the family's vehement denial of certain incontrovertible facts I had uncovered about dear old Uncle Walt, came the OJ Simpson case. I wound up not only writing about the murder (*The Whole Truth* improbably stayed near the top of the *New York Times* bestseller list the entire summer of 1995), I also had somehow become personally involved in it (don't ask, read the book if you must know, if you can find it).

The result of that misadventure was newfound wealth, professional disarray, personal break-ups, living on the run in New York City hotel rooms, and hiding from subpoenas from Marcia Clark, in the midst of which I became personally involved with Crystal Zevon, ex-wife of legendary singer-songwriter Warren Zevon, who happened to be one of the major contributors to L.A. rock of the seventies. Although our relationship would prove to be short-lived, it lasted long enough for me to begin to learn from her, firsthand, about the side of the L.A. music scene that never made it into the standard rock press. In a bizarre example of six-degrees of separation, I quickly discovered that Warren Zevon's best friend and earliest supporter was Jackson Browne, whose roommate was J. D. Souther, whose pal was Glenn Frey, whose Troubadour compadre was Don Henley, whose manager was Irving Azoff, whose mentor was David Geffen, whose partner was Elliott Roberts, whose teenage best friend was my late older brother.

I began *To the Limit* the Tuesday after Labor Day 1995, and spent the next two-and-a-half years researching and writing about nothing but the Eagles. Early on I sent letters to Don Henley and Irving Azoff informing them that I was working on the book and asking for their cooperation in the form of a series of interviews. I emphasized that this was not to be a "tell-all," that I believed my previously published work spoke for itself, and that I was giving them the opportunity to challenge and dispute any material I might uncover in my research and provide properly documented corrective material. In other words, I offered no editorial control, but the opportunity to have a say.

Their response was to tell me to go fuck myself. Not in so many words, of course. In fact, neither Henley nor Azoff answered any of my written or verbal requests. Fine, I thought, I'd been down this road before, I knew how to do my job, I could write the book without them. For the most part, public figures live with their heads in the clouds when it comes to the ability of a professional biographer to gather his material. Often it is the people they believe to be the most loyal, i.e., the least likely to talk, who become the best sources. For the next two years I spent winters in L.A, gathering my story, and summers in Woodstock, New York putting it all together. By the end of August 1997, the book was finished and moving along the production trail to galleys (bound proofs) for advance distribution to the press. And then the fun really began.

It started one day late that August. While I was working at my desk, a fax arrived from my publisher, Lawrence Kirshbaum, the head of Warner Books, with a copy of a letter from Don Henley's attorney and a request that I call Kirshbaum as soon as possible. Now, I knew Kirshbaum, which is to say I knew who he was; I had never actually met him, and technically he was not my publisher at all; Little, Brown was—a smallish, literary house that bore the undeniable stamp of its longtime editor Michael Pietsch. It was Pietsch who had originally signed the Eagles book, before the house "merged" with Warner Books. The reality was that Little, Brown had been bought up by the big Time-Warner media machine, an event that had made me wonder how it might affect me in the long run. I had a meeting with Michael shortly after the merger and reminded him that at the top of our new corporate pyramid was the CEO Gerald Levin, who now controlled Little, Brown, Warner Books, *and Warner music*, whose biggest moneymaker was none other than the Eagles. What, I wondered, would be the reaction to my "unauthorized" biography of their most commercially successful client? Not to worry, Michael said, Little, Brown was going to remain an independently-operated subsidiary, and no one at Warner would even *think* of interfering with my book. So, passionately reassured by Michael, I put all worries aside, or at least buried them so far back I'd forgotten about them until the day I received that fax from Kirshbaum.

I called him and we talked. Ever the charmer, Larry (as he insisted I call him) told me that Henley was making all kinds of noise about my book, noise that couldn't be ignored because it had made it all the way to Gerald Levin's office, which meant, Kirshbaum said, that he was going to have to step in.

Step in? To what? And, for that matter, how had Henley gotten a copy of my book, prior to galleys? In fact, this was not the first serious leak that had occurred with *To the Limit*. A few months earlier, I had received a call from David Geffen, who had gotten a hold of an early draft of the manuscript and, despite the fact that when I had first started writing *To the Limit* I had contacted his office and been informed he was "unavailable," now apparently he had all the time in the world to talk to me about his depiction in my book. To my pleasant surprise, he had a lot of good stuff to add and a perspective that I had not gotten from anyone else. Yes, he and Henley were enemies, and they had had their share of battles, often in the form of major lawsuits, all stemming from Geffen's "original sin" of having sold Asylum, and the Eagles along with it, to Warner, as I describe in the book. On several occasions during interviews, I asked Geffen how he had gotten a copy of the book, and never received a straight answer. He laughed, he sighed, and he told me that that was how life in the "real" world operated. For the rest of our time we talked and I taped, and his contributions proved invaluable.

It also prompted Henley to action but only with Azoff. (None of the other Eagles ever expressed any editorial reaction to me, in public or private, either before or after the publication of *To the Limit*). Henley was livid about what he had read, and expressed as much, through his lawyer, to Kirshbaum. Kirshbaum reassured me that everything would be all right, but would it be possible for me to come into his office and to be prepared to show him where I got some of my information? No problem. The next day I drove into the city, met with him and brought as much of my primary source material as I could carry, mostly tapes and transcripts of the many interviews I had conducted. This physical evidence seemed to ease

Kirshbaum's concerns. He tried to reassure me again, telling me this happened "all the time," that celebrities always overreact, oh and by the way he was leaving later that day for the coast, to take a meeting with Azoff and Henley (and presumably their lawyers), and he hoped that would settle things.

The next time I heard from him was during that trip to L.A. He was at the Beverly Hills Hotel, had just come from his meeting, and called to say he needed to see me right away. I flew out on his nickel, met with him in his suite, and over coffee Kirshbaum told me Azoff and Henley and their "legal reps" had gone over the first hundred pages of the book with him and pointed out "numerous" mistakes.

Mistakes? Such as, I asked. Kirshbaum took out his galley and showed it to me, marked up with Xs on every page. "The changes are numerous," he said, and then proceeded to quiz me on each and every fact that they had disputed, everything, of course, that was the least bit negative to the band. This went on for hours, until by the end of it, I had convinced Kirshbaum that this was really a whole lot about nothing. Kirshbaum seemed to agree, we shook hands, and I told myself, this has to be the end.

I was wrong. Henley, as it turned out, had audio-taped his entire meeting with Kirshbaum, during which he had given his version of many of the stories he called "mistakes" in the manuscript. Kirshbaum, not the most knowledgeable person when it came to rock and roll (and he's the first person who will tell you that), had made little notations next to paragraphs indicating where Henley had said there was a problem, but had not actually written down any of what he had had to say in response.

The next day, Kirshbaum called and said that Henley had offered to meet with me, over the phone, to see if there was any way to work out what was now being described as an impasse over certain "controversial" passages, before he took legal action against Warner Books, Kirshbaum, Levin, and me. Kirshbaum said he didn't want to pressure me in any way, and that if I were sued the company would of course defend me, but if there was any way I could work this thing out without lawsuits by talking to Henley, would I please do so.

As the book had already been accepted by the editorial department, legally vetted, and gone to printed galleys, there was little Warner could do, except decide to not publish it and lose the considerable advance they had already paid me. By contract, I had final approval on the manuscript and was not under any further contractual obligation to make additional changes or do any further work of any kind. The book had been scheduled for release that fall, to coincide with the lucrative Christmas season, the biggest season in publishing. According to my contract, if Warner didn't publish it, after a certain amount of time I could take it across the street to, say, Simon and Schuster, where I had published *Down Thunder Road* and where I, Kirshbaum, and Henley knew it would be picked up in a second. Henley, as it turned out, had already figured on that possibility and to prevent it from happening knew he had no real alternative than to come to the table to see if some sort of deal could be worked out. He knew that if the book stayed at Warner, he might be able to have some input; if it went to Simon and Schuster he would have none.

The big phone meeting was set for that Friday. I wanted Kirshbaum to be in the conversation, and Henley insisted that Azoff be allowed to participate as well. During the subsequent four-way conference call, Henley was polite and subdued, and offered to hand over a tape of the conversation of corrections he had had with Kirshbaum if I were willing to remove the one brief passage from the book he most objected to (not on the grounds that it was wrong, he admitted, but because his eighty-two-year-old mother was still alive and he didn't want it to upset her). My response was immediate. I wanted an interview with Henley, one-on-one, and to be able to ask him anything connected to the Eagles. Further, I was to maintain full editorial control, and I wanted that original tape of the meeting with Kirshbaum. Azoff jumped into the conversation and said I could interview him and could have the tape as well. Thanks, I said, I would take him up on his offer, but I had to have Henley as well.

After a few seconds of awkward silence, Henley said he would go along with everything I wanted, including agreeing to meet with me if I would agree to remove that passage. I said I would, but only after all my conditions were satisfactorily met. I figured the trade-off was a fair one; if Henley could give me relevant material that no one else had ever received, from the inside of this most private of bands, I could lose a 'graph or two dealing with an incident that had taken place some eighteen years before, during Henley's lowest emotional period, and that had already been written about extensively at the time. Was it really big news that Henley, primo L.A. rock and roll hedonist, had had a sexcapade run-in with the law?

Henley said okay, but that he wanted a written confidentiality agreement that ensured no one would know he had been interviewed. I told him that was unacceptable, that I had to be able to say that he had been interviewed, otherwise I would have no source for the material he was going to give me, and he could then deny he had talked to me and ultimately put me in a position where I couldn't defend my own work. It was an obvious trap and I wasn't going to step into it. Okay, he said, he would think it over.

Thus began months of stalling and excuses from Henley and Azoff, with the immediate result being my book pushed off the Christmas list and after that continually postponed. Whenever Kirshbaum called Azoff, he was told that Henley was going to agree to all the terms, that he was willing to talk and hand over the tape, but he just couldn't find the time. He was too busy. Or his secretary was still transcribing the tapes. Or he wasn't feeling well. Or he was in the studio recording his new album. Finally, after nearly a half-year of this, I told Kirshbaum that the time for a decision was at hand. If Warner didn't want to publish my book, I was prepared to take the manuscript and walk. The next day I received a direct phone call from Irving Azoff who, in a soft and gentle voice, told me that Henley was now ready to be interviewed, and so was he. The tape? I would get a transcript of it, and all the "corrections" Henley wanted me to make, if I wanted to make them, of course

And that is how, on a cool March evening in 1997, Don Henley and I finally came face to face, in Irving Azoff's office complex conference room in the Beverly Hills district of Wilshire Boulevard, over a catered Southern fried chicken dinner from The Ivy and two tape recorders—one mine and one Henley's—that both ran the entire time we were together. We began by going over every page of the manuscript. At the end of the first session, Henley had fully and specifically answered all my questions, and I also had in my possession the transcripts of the Kirshbaum meeting that I wanted.

Somewhere during our subsequent conversations Henley began to show a spark of real interest in what we were doing, perhaps sensing that the book was for real and not going away, and he decided that I needed talk to many of the key people that he had long blocked from me, most significantly J. D. Souther, John Boylan, and Joe Walsh (who did respond, through his manager, to several submitted queries from me). I wouldn't say Henley and I became friends, but we did go out for an occasional drink at night after a session and talk about everything that wasn't on the record: women, cars, booze, drugs, and Los Angeles in the seventies. We'd usually start with a vodka or two at the Formosa, a legendary Polynesian restaurant on Santa Monica Boulevard opposite Warner Studios, one of the few places still standing from the L.A. of the seventies, and from there we'd drive up to the Troubadour. One time we walked through the entrance to the empty front bar. (It was still early in the night for the legendary club that, since founder Doug Weston's death, had turned from being the Mecca of California country-folk-rock to the first refuge for metal hair bands and the L.A. post-punk music scene.) There a young, buxom blond bartender in tight, short cut-offs approached us. Watching her own hand use a rag to wipe the dry counter, she asked us what he wanted. Henley smiled tightly and said "I want it to be like it was twenty-five years ago."

I eventually finished the rewrite, handed it in, and thought that finally, this whole thing was over. Wrong again. No sooner did the book come out than Henley, despite his agreement to neither promote nor criticize it in any way (he told Kirshbaum he was hoping it would just go away quietly) went on what I can only describe as a rampage. He was furious that while I had eliminated the offending passages, I had still referred, in the most general way and without any details or incriminating material, to the episode he had so vehemently objected to. I reminded him, Azoff, and Kirshbaum that I had retained editorial control, and to leave out all references to the incident would tarnish the book's credibility. Henley's lawyers screamed back that they were going to sue, that I had violated "the confidentiality agreement" (that didn't exist).

Warner had booked a fairly hefty publicity tour that finally kicked off in New York City on October 14, 1998. After a few appearances, I flew to Chicago for some additional local print and broadcast media and then headed south, where I was scheduled to begin a series of extensive interviews, TV and radio appearances, and book-signings. On the evening of October 16, I was scheduled to sign at a major record/CD/book retail store in the heart of Nashville. The appearance was well-publicized in the press and on local TV and a large crowd was anticipated. Just before I went on, I was taken aside by the store's manager, who said he wanted to apologize to me, that "incredible pressure" had been put on him to cancel the event. By whom, I asked. Don Henley, he answered. The manager then handed me a copy of that morning's *Tennessean*, one of the most respected and influential Southern daily newspapers. On the front page of the entertainment section was this story:

"HENLY TAKES IT TO LIMIT TO STOP BOOK SIGNINGS"

by Brad Schmit

How controversial is this new Eagles book, *To the Limit: The Untold Story of the Eagles*? So controversial that drummer/vocalist/songwriter Don Henley himself called Tower Records on West End Avenue to ask that tonight's book-signing be canceled. Apparently, Don called and even visited a couple of other stores around the country to try to stop book signings by author Marc Eliot. But that won't work here. The show will go on, and Marc will sign at 7 tonight at Tower Records. "There was really pressure to cancel," said one Tower exec. "But [Henley's] no choirboy."

Henley's strategy had backfired, but the article did not stop his efforts. A week later, in Austin, the same thing happened, and again, without my knowledge or involvement, a story appeared in the *Austin American Statesman*:

"HEY DON, JUST TURN THE PAGE"

by Michael Corcoran

Writer Marc Eliot's book-signing Friday evening at Book People had the benefit of a crack advance promo man Don Henley. Citing distortions, half-truths and lies in "To the Limit," the former Eagles drummer/singer came to town recently to try to convince B'People honcho Abe Zimmerman to cancel Eliot's appearance. Henley, who put the "don" in hedonism if only twenty percent of the book is true, has been calling that percentage high and he took Zimmerman to lunch at Cuero's October 4 to plead his case. Like a poster boy for too much free time, Henley has protested several of Eliot's publicity stops and in doing so it makes you wonder whether he's got a cut of the profits . . . the upshot of all this was that Eliot's signing went on as planned, but the author's name was conspicuously missing from the marquees outside B'People and there was little advertising of the appearance.

Needless to say, I was becoming increasingly incensed, not just by Henley's tactics, but by the accusations he was making about the book's inaccuracies, after he had gone over every sentence of the book with me prior to publication, and despite my insistence that he have no editorial say, submitting daily "corrections" to Kirshbaum, who, in turn, pressured me to make nearly all of them. At one point, I spent a half-day arguing with Kirshbaum about a description of Henley's perm'd hair-style he wore in the mid-seventies, a kind of White-boy Southern Afro. Henley had vehemently objected to my use of the word "perm," insisting he had never done any such thing to his hair. I merely showed Kirshbaum the pictures of straight-haired Henley from the '80s and '90s and compared them to the uber-curls he'd donned in the '70s. Despite the evidence, one entire day of my life was wasted defending the use of the word "perm."

As the tour progressed, Henley, to my mind, turned into a modern-day Captain Ahab, so obsessed with my whale of a book that he lost all sense of reason and fairness. His heavy-handed, thuggish tactics with booksellers and record stores was explained to me by one of them this way: Henley's standing offer to any bookstore was that if they cancelled me, he would do a free in-store signing for them whenever his next solo CD was released.

Things got even worse in Dallas, the heart of Texas-born-and-raised Henley. I showed up one Saturday afternoon at a major chain store but could not find any copies of my book to sign. (Bookstores normally love it when an author drops by and signs books that they can then put on display and usually sell out.) I asked the manager if he had received his shipment yet, and his response was to summarily throw me out of the place, along with my local tour handler. No explanation was given, the manager of the store steadfastly refused to talk to us, and we were threatened with a call to the police on charges of trespassing and harassment if we didn't leave the parking lot immediately, even though these were normal business hours in an establishment that was open to the public.

That was enough for me. I called Kirshbaum at his home that very afternoon, told him what was going on, and threatened to leave the tour. He sounded genuinely upset, and told me to stay

273

where I was until he called me back. He then got Azoff on the phone and threatened him with a lawsuit for a number of things, including contract interference (stemming from Henley's continual attempts to get my manuscript edited without my knowledge or approval over certain other "controversial" passages) and unlawful restraint-of-trade. Azoff, Kirshbaum assured me when he called back, had promised that Henley would visit no more bookstores, and not interfere in any way with my remaining appearances.

I only had one or two more stops left in Los Angeles. While there, during the day I went around to the local bookstores and found that in one, on Ventura Boulevard, there was, again, not a single copy of my book. When I asked the manager if he had gotten his order, he checked the computer and said there should be thirty books "around here someplace." I then went back to the section I was supposed to be in and after failing to find it, was almost ready to believe that they might have actually sold them all—this was, after all, ground zero Eagles turf. Then I spotted a small shelf on the floor, where a bunch of books were lined up. On instinct, I went down on my knees, reached in, pulled these books out, and found behind them, completely hidden from view, all thirty copies of *To the Limit*. The manager apologized, denied having had anything to do with it, and promised he would put them on display "immediately."

That evening, I went to a major retail chain outlet on Sunset Boulevard (not Tower), and found, to my pleasure, an entire table in the book section displaying one hundred neatly stacked copies. All right! I told myself. The next night I returned with a friend to show her the display and discovered that it was gone. I asked the manager what happened, and she said, with an I-swallowed-the-canary smirk on her face, that maybe it had sold out. Fine, I said, could you check that on your computer (which managers can do with a single click)? No, she said, that was against store policy. Well, I said, did you personally sell any copies? Instead of answering, she simply turned and walked away without saying another word.

And that's how it ended. I never saw a single ad for *To the Limit* despite the considerable advance they had paid for my work. Despite generally excellent reviews, *To the Limit* eventually faded from sight.

Two postscripts. First, whenever presented with the opportunity, Henley would rail about all the "lies" I had written in my book. One of the things that seemed to irk him the most was my dissection of "New Kid in Town," the J. D. Souther-penned song that I had said was at least in part about the night in 1975 when Springsteen had played the Roxy, stolen the Eagles' thunder, and taken the focus of rock and roll with him back to the east coast. Nevertheless, years later, when it was commercially convenient for Henley to give "personal" interviews to the press to promote his long overdue solo album, here is what he told Cameron Crowe about that very song: ". . . ['New Kid in Town'] is about the fleeting, fickle nature of love and romance. *It's also about the fleeting nature of fame, especially in the music business. We were already chronicling our own demise, saying basically, look, we know we're red-hot now, but we know that someone is going to come along and replace us—both in music and love. We were always doing that double-entendre thing between the music business and personal relationships* . . . "(Emphasis mine.)

The second happened in June 2002. Again, to support his solo album, Henley granted an interview to reporter Jane Stevenson of the *Toronto Sun*. When she mentioned my book, Henley responded: "Marc Eliot is not only a bad writer but an evil person. He was a sick person who had some kind of axe to grind." What can I say? I wear criticism from Don Henley as a badge of honor. As for bad, sick, and evil? One of us was arrested in 1980 for being caught with an underage girl who had overdosed on cocaine and Quaaludes, brought before a judge, and offered probation. The judge strongly recommended that the offender do community service, which he refused. Hint: It wasn't me.

I am, finally, reminded by all of Henley's millionaire posturing in working-class jeans and hollow liberalism of something Bob Dylan once told audiences about the trap of idolizing such "artists" and turning them into culturally heroic icons: "Don't follow leaders, watch the parking meters . . ." That, to me, remains very good advice.

Part Two: The Band

It is not all that unusual for celebrities to be outraged by books written about them. One recalls infamous dust-ups between authors and such volatile subjects as Frank Sinatra and Elizabeth Taylor. However, the difference with Henley was, simply, the difference between Sinatra and the Eagles. The infamous crooner had made his lifestyle of babes, chicks, booze, cigarettes, and lost loves the basis for an image that smacked of sleazy, sexist arrogance redeemed by a genius ability to sing to my father's generation the way Dylan did to mine. Henley, separate and apart from the Eagles, after his 1980 underage sex and drugs bust set, was out on a course of image self-rehabilitation. More than anything, he wanted to recast himself as a Lennonesque working-class hero, a spokesman for freedom, liberty, and the American Way (apparently for everybody but biographers), perfectly personifying what Phil Ochs once said about "liberals," that they were twenty degrees to the left when an issue affected someone else, and twenty degrees to the right when it affected them personally). Toward the end of the eighties, Henley became deeply immersed in his Walden Woods Project. Having spearheaded the drive to save the pond from the grubby hands of developers, he then raised several million dollars to help buy the land back and preserve it. Out of this came his Thoreau Society, located in, of all things, a Tudor-style mansion built just out of sight of the famous pond. In June 1998, while attending the opening ceremonies, Henley took a private walk along the new grounds, accompanied by no less than the President of the United States Bill Clinton and First Lady Hillary, heady company to be sure for one of the former occupants of the mirrors-on-the-ceiling "Hotel California."

By the turn of the new century, downloading music by trading songs on the Web had become the favorite pastime of the college-age set, our little brothers and sisters who had not grown up in the grip of the marketing jungle of must-have record covers, CD "remasters," and other gimmicks meant to sell us the same music over and over again. The whole switchover to CDs was a mother lode for the record companies and their artists, with "remastering" often meaning nothing more than transferring masters to a digital format from an analog at a fraction of what it cost to originally make an album, and releasing it on CD at approximately three hundred percent of what most rock albums in the sixties had been priced on vinyl (and most of the time with far less fidelity, especially in the early, tinny days of the digital revolution). Nevertheless, by 2001, it was clear the new generation of age-ready music customers from 14 to 25, normally the peak buying demographic, were by and large skipping these overpriced reissues and simply downloading for free the songs they wanted. Napster became a part of that generation's cultural vernacular.

All of this was old news, of course, to boomers who grew up with free (pre–subscription satellite) music on something called FM radio and who had libraries of their favorite songs on cassettes they had "burned" from either their own or borrowed records and CDs. Once the industry got past its initial panic over audiences actually listening to their "product" for free, radio and home-compilation cassettes became the best sales devices they could ever have dreamed up. Give it away, get the listener hooked, then watch them go down to the store to buy a better copy. It was during these years that the music business grew into a billion-dollar industry.

Nonetheless, newly socially-conscious Don Henley decided it was up to him to save the record industry from all those teenage thieves and cutthroats out there. He formed something called RAC—Recording Artists Coalition—to fight for truth, justice, and royalties forever to rock artists in danger of going broke by the downloading craze, even as his solo album *Actual Miles: Don Henley's Greatest Hits* went platinum (one million units sold), and his 1990 *The End of the Innocence* album passed the six–million units sales mark.

In 1991, Henley filed a lawsuit against Paramount Pictures for the studio's having failed to make good on their promise to use his

"Taking You Home," in the film *Double Jeopardy*. Upon the song's release, it immediately entered the Top 40, and the following February it won three Grammys (Best Male Pop Vocal Performance, Best Pop Vocal Album, Best Male Rock Performance). At the time, Henley, based on comparable rock fortunes, was worth in my estimation fifty to seventy million dollars.

While his career, both in music and lobbying remained in active overdrive, the Eagles, after a brief 1994 reunion tour to promote *Hell Freezes Over*, seemed to finally have faded into that good L.A. That is until one night late in the fall of 2000, when rumors began swirling throughout the industry that in the wake of the great Boomer band revivals led by massive shed concerts by (and subsequent impressive CD sales of) the Rolling Stones, Bruce Springsteen, and the never-ending commercial phenomenon of the Beatles, the Eagles were indeed planning to reunite, release a new album and return triumphantly to the profitable glory of the live-rock road.

On the heels of all this came word of a startling development in the Eagles camp. Apparently without any advance warning, in February 2001, the band fired longtime member Don Felder, who quickly responded with two lawsuits, the first for "Breach of Contract," the second for "Wrongful Termination." According to sources, the basis of the firing was money. The remaining Eagles insisted that Felder's salary was too high. Felder, who had been asked to join the band for 1974's *On the Border* album, when they were looking for a harder rock sound, and who became a permanent Eagle and one of the co-writers of the single "Hotel California," for which he shared the Grammy, was taken completely by surprise, and, in the words of his attorney (who contacted me about the possibility of my testifying for Felder if the case went to trial), the firing "left my client without a career."

Whatever the particulars, the framework seemed all too familiar. The band was squabbling over the only thing that, away from the bittersweet romance of their music, ever seemed to really matter to them—the green stuff, and I don't mean the environment.

With Felder out, a hired hand could play his parts for a relative pittance during what was now shaping up to be one of the biggest tours of 2003.

Of course, an excess of money was the reason Glenn Frey had "retired," even more than the animosity that had grown increasingly bitter between him and Henley. When he had had enough of both money and Henley, Frey turned to the golf course, where he eased his way into middle age comfortably heavier and noticeably softer than he had kept himself during his rock and roll prime. Indeed, Frey's last moment of solo significance had come back in the eighties, during the heyday of *Miami Vice* when he had his biggest non-Eagles hit, "The Heat Is On." As for Walsh, Felder, and Timothy Schmit, they all recorded post-Eagle solo albums that were immediately consigned to the oblivion bin. None was capable of selling enough tickets to support a major tour, and all were more or less living off their Eagles earnings, waiting for Henley and Frey to agree to go back on the road. It was something that was bandied about from time to time between the boys but never seemed to get very far.

It almost happened in 1998, when the Eagles played a surprise concert to benefit Tiger Woods's foundation. Frey and Woods had become friends, and Frey agreed to do the fundraiser, held, appropriately enough, at the Universal Amphitheater, with Hootie and the Blowfish and Babyface opening. In many ways it appeared the show was a litmus test of sorts, to see if the Eagles could still sell out the "Hotel California."

This was the first official concert the Eagles played after the publication of *To the Limit*, and they performed like they had something to prove. In truth, the audience that night, of which I was a part, went legitimately crazy as soon as the familiar opening guitar riff of "Hotel California" clanged through the concert halls, reminding me and everyone else all over again of just how maddeningly essential this band really was.

After the success of the Woods benefit, the Eagles began to talk more opening among themselves about going back on the road and even the possibly of recording a new album. Of course, nothing ever happens quickly with this band, and while they tried to pull things together as a group Henley released *Inside Job*, telling one reporter it had been festering inside of him for eight years before he officially began to lay down some tracks in 1997 with co-producer Stan Lynch, the drummer for Tom Petty's Heartbreakers. One reason for all this "festering" was Henley's long battle with Geffen to win his contractual release, which he finally did that year, after which he quickly signed a solo contract with Warner, the Eagles longtime recording and publishing home. He then apparently stopped festering and got down to business, in a comparatively short time composing most of his new material in the car while driving between the Malibu studio and home. Three years later, in 2000, and with great fanfare (and no new Eagles music in sight), Henley finally released *Inside Job*.

On it, Henley, the so-called uber-hedonist whose most famous songs had celebrated wasted time, broken hearts, fast cars, and faster women, sang about, of all things, the soft-around-the-middle-eight joys of post-rock mellowing. It was hard to believe, but true, that a Don Henley song with as provocative a title as "Taking You Home" was actually about a father picking up his newborn child from the hospital. Another song, "For My Wedding," was one Henley hoped would become a ceremonial standard, alongside such white-gown Boomer staples as the Carpenters's "We've Only Just Begun," and The Four Seasons's "You're Just Too Good To Be True." It didn't and it isn't.

Not that *Inside Job* was a flop. Despite the fact that Henley hadn't released a solo album in more than a decade, or any new material with the Eagles in six years (the four forgettable songs included in *Hell Freezes Over*), *Inside Job*, released in May 2000, did extremely well. With guest appearances on the album by Stevie Wonder, Randy Newman, and even Glenn Frey, and "Taking You Home" used on the soundtrack of Julianna Margulies's final appearance on TV's enormously popular *ER*, the album rode the pop and country charts for months. It eventually went platinum, selling well over a million units, and became a mainstay of "easy listening," "adult contemporary," and "soft country" FM radio. Henley did a brief tour of midsize venues to support the album and "Taking You Home," eventually broke onto the singles charts.

In the end, *Inside Job* remained outside the consciousness of its listeners the way Rod Stewart's neo-Sinatra efforts would, but its success apparently was enough to once again push the Eagles into the studio and eventually back on the road. The summer of Henley's solo album's release, the band had, in fact, reconvened in L.A. and quietly recorded a few songs, mostly covers, as a way of reacquainting themselves with each other and rediscovering the close harmonies that had been so much a part of their sound. Henley expressed disappointment with the results and nothing further happened with the Eagles.

Until Felder's abrupt dismissal and Henley's impressive solo showing. The four remaining Eagles returned once more to the studio with the intention of recording enough new material to release a new Eagles album. The question was, could they come back as a group as successfully as Henley had going solo? Was there any way these middle aged men could still find relevance in their role as L.A.'s primo post-teen rebels? According to Henley, in an interview he gave to a reporter while promoting *Inside Job*, there was an immediate, familiar tension in the studio between the Eagles. He talked about old and acrimonious ghosts that seemed to haunt the band whenever they tried to make new music and suggested that jealousy (over his solo success) may have played a part in it.

Still, they were willing to test the reunion waters with a Europe-only summer 2001 tour, playing several countries they had never appeared in before, including Russia, Finland, and Italy, apparently figuring that if they bombed, they were far enough away to be beyond the reach of even *Rolling Stone*.

The international tour ended in August, Henley's solo album was riding high on the charts, and the rest of the band was now convinced a return to relevance (and royalties) was possible. They immediately booked studio time to try to record a new album. The planned date for their return to the studio was September 11, 2001.

The catastrophic events of that day put a temporary halt to their studio gig. That same night, alone in L.A., Henley stayed home and sat at his piano where he put the first chords together for something he called "Hole in the World."

Many months went by before Henley felt ready to show Frey what he had, and it was Frey who then wrote the song's second verse. At this typically crawling Eagles' pace, however, there was no way a new album was going to be ready any time in the immediate future. Somewhere along the way, the Eagles and their management got the idea to re-release both *Greatest Hits* albums— *Volume One*, which continued to do battle with Michael Jackson's *Thriller* for the honor of holding the title of bestselling album of all time, somewhere north of twenty-eight million units, and *Volume Two*, which had sold nearly fifteen million units.

The obvious question remained: Was there anybody left who by now did not already own some version of all this Eagles music, either or both *Greatest Hits* albums, or the originals from which they were compiled? How many times did the Eagles expect their fans to buy the same music? Whatever the rationale, the aim was clear enough, to reclaim, without question, the all-time single album sales record. With Jackson entering into what increasingly looks like permanent career decline, it now seemed possible to eclipse the gloved one forever.

In 2003, with both *Greatest Hits* albums combined into one sixteen track album, the last track being "Hole in the World," the only new Eagles song on it, *Eagles—Very Best Of* was released. To support it, the band went back out on the road, this time playing dates in the United States.

For the first leg of the summer/fall 2003 tour, the band's guarantee—the amount of money they had to be paid before a single ticket went on sale, even if no one bought any—was $750,000. The album then took off, and to everyone's amazement, except perhaps the Eagles, it debuted on the *Billboard* Top Two Hundred Albums at number *two* (its eligibility due to the inclusion of the one new song), and stayed on the charts for months, hovering just inside the top thirty and racking up astonishing sales figures for the seventies band. The album's success confirmed once and for all that the Eagles would be the sole owners of the greatest selling album of all time.

Eagles—Very Best Of made back its relatively inexpensive production costs even before the first leg of the tour ended, while the album and the tour began to promote each other—the more it sold, the more demand there was for the band to appear, the more the band toured, the more the album sold (and along with it the sales of all previous eleven Eagles albums, and Henley's solo efforts). By the time the second phase of their American tour was announced for late 2003 into 2004, the band had earned an additional $10 million in album sales, and their guarantee had risen twenty-five percent to an all-time high of a million dollars a performance. Even before 2003 ended, the Eagles had grossed $62 million from the tour, album sales, and, for Henley and Frey, J. D. Souther, Jackson Browne, Timothy B. Schmit, Joe Walsh, Jack Temchin, Felder and the rest of the writers who had at one time or another contributed to the Eagles catalogue, $5 million dollars in royalties. "Hole in the World" was released on CD and became 2003's seventh highest selling single, helped by an in-studio video that played in heavy rotation on VH–1. These numbers were good enough to make the Eagles the third highest grossing band of 2003, behind the Rolling Stones (whose earnings reached an astonishing $84 million in 2003), and Bruce Springsteen and the E Street Band, whose *The Rising* tour earned $81 million. And, finally, for the summer 2004, the top Eagles ticket price was $252.50, the third highest among major shed acts, behind only Simon and Garfunkel ($354.50) and Madonna ($300), and, on a dollar-for-dollar basis, the highest-priced ticket-to-profit ratio. That's taking it easy, but not cheaply.

And so it went, and so it goes. The Eagles are once more perched atop the platinum rock and roll mountaintop. If their goal had been to extend their continuing relevance, they succeeded in doing just that. If the goal had been to increase their financial legacies, they hit a grand-slam there as well. In the end, they proved themselves the ultimate seventies band; the acquisition of great sums of money was not merely the measure of their art, but the actual art itself.

In that sense, then, they were and will always be rock and roll premiere desperadoes.

SELECTED BIBLIOGRAPHY

BOOKS

Bego, Mark. *Linda Ronstadt: It's So Easy.* Austin, Texas: Eakin Press, 1990.

Bruck, Connie. *Master of the Game: Steve Ross and the Creation of Time Warner.* New York: Penguin Books USA, Inc., 1995.

Clarke, Donald, ed. *The Penguin Encyclopedia of Popular Music.* New York: Viking Penguin, 1989.

Crosby, David, and Carl Gottlieb. *Long Time Gone: The Autobiography of David Crosby.* New York: Doubleday, 1988.

Dannen, Fredric. *Hit Men: Power Brokers and Fast Money Inside the Music Business.* New York: Vintage Books, 1990.

Draper, Robert. *Rolling Stone Magazine: The Uncensored History.* New York: HarperCollins, 1990.

Farr, Jory. *Moguls and Madmen: Pop Music's Big-Time Operators.* New York: Simon & Schuster, 1994.

Fawcett, Anthony and Henry Diltz. *California Rock, California Sound.* Los Angeles: Reed Books, 1978.

Frame, Pete. *The Complete Rock Family Trees.* New York: Omnibus Press, 1993.

Goodman, Fred. *The Mansion on the Hill.* New York: Random House, 1997.

Haring, Bruce. *Off the Charts: Ruthless Days and Reckless Nights Inside the Music Industry.* New York: Birch Lane Press, 1996.

Hendler, Herb. *Year by Year in the Rock Era.* New York: Praeger Publishers, 1987.

Knoedelseder, William. *Stiffed: A True Story of MCA, the Music Business and the Mafia.* New York: HarperCollins, 1993.

Ladd, Jim. *Radio Waves: Life and Revolution on the FM Dial.* New York: St. Martins, 1991.

Marsh, Dave and John Swenson, eds. *The Rolling Stone Record Guide.* New York: Random House/Rolling Stone Press, 1979.

Newman, Rayce. *The Hollywood Connection: The Drug Supplier to the Stars Tells All.* New York: S.P.I. Books, 1984.

Pareles, Jon and Patricia Romanowski, eds. *The Rolling Stone Encyclopedia of Rock & Roll.* New York: Simon & Schuster/Rolling Stone Press, 1983.

Phillips, Julia. *You'll Never Eat Lunch In This Town Again.* New York: NAL-Dutton, 1992.

Pollack, Bruce. *Hipper Than Our Kids.* New York: Macmillan Publishing Company, 1993.

Ribowsky, Mark. *He's a Rebel: The Truth About Phil Spector — Rock and Roll's Legendary Madman.* New York: Dutton, 1989.

Rolling Stone Staff. *The Rolling Stone Interviews, 1967–1980.* New York: St. Martin's Press/Rolling Stone Press, 1981.

Rose, Frank. *The Agency: William Morris and the Hidden History of Show Business.* New York: HarperCollins, 1995.

Ryan, Thomas. *American Hit Radio: A History of Popular Singles 1955–Present.* Rocklin, CA: Prima Publishing, 1996.

Selvin, Joel. *Ricky Nelson: Idol for a Generation.* Chicago: Contemporary Books, 1990.

Schipper, Henry. *Broken Record: The Inside Story of the Grammy Awards.* New York: Birch Lane Press, 1992.

Shapiro, Mark. *The Long Run: The Story of the Eagles.* London: Omnibus Press, 1995.

Smith, Joe. *Off the Record: An Oral History of Popular Music.* New York: Warner Books, 1988.

Stambler, Irwin. *The Encyclopedia of Pop, Rock and Soul,* Revised Edition. New York: St. Martin's Press, 1989.

Stokes, Geoffrey, Ed Ward, and Ken Tucker. *Rock of Ages.* New York: Summit Books, 1986.

Wexler, Jerry and David Ritz. *Rhythm and the Blues: A Life in American Music.* New York: Knopf, 1993.

Whitburn, Joel. *Billboard Top 1000 Singles, 1955–1986.* Milwaukee: Records Research/Hal Leonard Books, 1986.

———. *The Billboard Book of Top 40 Albums,* Revised and Enlarged Third Edition. New York: Billboard Books, 1995.

White, Timothy. *The Nearest Faraway Place.* New York: Henry Holt, 1994.

———. *Rock Lives: Profiles and Interviews.* New York: Henry Holt, 1990.

Wiley, Mason and Damien Bona. *Inside Oscar: The Unofficial History of the Academy Awards.* New York: Ballantine Books, 1986.

NEWSPAPERS AND PERIODICALS

(Specific issues cited in Notes and Sources)

Billboard	*New York Times*
Crawdaddy!	*New York Times Magazine*
Entertainment Weekly	*The New Yorker*
Fortune	*Rolling Stone*
Goldmine	*Vanity Fair*
GQ	*Village Voice*
Los Angeles Times	*The Washington Star*
Musician	*Zigzag 67*
The Nation	

NOTES AND SOURCES

INTRODUCTION: THE ROOTS OF THE AVOCADO MAFIA

p. 4. Crosby, Stills, Nash and Young — Besides Neil Young, the original members of Crosby, Stills and Nash included Dallas Taylor on drums and Greg Reeves on bass. According to Stephen Stills, the group was one of the happy accidents of casual harmonizing with friends: "Atlantic Records was supporting me, and waiting for me to think of something to do [after the demise of Buffalo Springfield in the late sixties]. I was sitting around experimenting on some songs with David Crosby. We were all up at John Sebastian's house one day and Willie [Nash] came over, because the Hollies were in town. Well, Willie tried joining in on a couple of songs — and Crosby and me just looked at each other. It was one of those moments" (Stephen Stills, quoted in Frame, Pete, *The Complete Rock Family Trees* [New York: Omnibus Press, 1993].)

Neil Young, having just left Buffalo Springfield, was invited to sing live with C, S and N on several club gigs prior to Woodstock. When he was formally asked to join, at the urging of Ahmet Ertegun, he decided instead to pursue a solo career. Young was one of the producers of the group's successful follow-up album, and received equal billing. Through the years, he occasionally joined the group on record and stage.

PART ONE — DESPERADOES

ONE

p. 9. "The car is a nice little capsule . . ." — Don Henley, interviewed by White, Timothy, as part of a syndicated radio series, *Timothy White's Rock Stars*. This interview is from the 1987 episode "Don Henley: I Will Not Go Quietly."

p. 10. "My father and . . ." — Henley, interview with Eliot. Unless otherwise noted, all Henley quotes in this chapter are from Henley/Eliot.

pp. 10–11. Cucumbers — This anecdote, related by Henley, is expanded upon in White, Timothy, *Rock Lives: Profiles and Interviews* (New York: Henry Holt, 1990). The quote "pure hell" comes from "Don Henley: I Will Not Go Quietly."

p. 11. **Mail-order go-cart and "Rat Fink" T-shirt** — From White, Timothy, *The Nearest Faraway Place* (New York: Henry Holt, 1994).

p. 11. **"a forty-eight Dodge . . ."** — Henley, from "Don Henley: I Will Not Go Quietly."

p. 12. **"In some ways he never did leave . . ."** — Anon., interview with Eliot.

p. 13. **"Mrs. Henley was a real fine lady . . ."** — Richard Bowden, quoted in Young, Charles M., "Hell Is for Heroes," *Rolling Stone,* November 29, 1979.

p. 13. **"It was a small town . . ."** — Anon., interview with Eliot.

p. 14. **"We eventually realized . . ."** — Bowden, quoted in Young.

pp. 14–15. **"When I was fourteen . . ."** — Michael Bowden, interview with Eliot. Unless otherwise noted, all Michael Bowden quotes in this chapter are from M. Bowden/Eliot.

p. 15. **"[My father] saved . . ."** — Henley, quoted in Young.

p. 16. **"all you can do . . ."** — Henley, quoted in Rhulmann, William, "The Birdmen of Southern California," *Goldmine,* #338.

pp. 17–18. **"I bought the album . . ."** — Henley, quoted in Ladd, Jim, *Radio Waves* (New York: St. Martin's Press, 1991).

p. 18. **"Emerson's essay on self-reliance . . ."** — Henley, from an interview with Danny Kortchmar and Timothy White, part of a radio network special broadcast, July 9, 1989.

p. 21. **Taking Michael Bowden . . .** — Information on the drive west is from White, *The Nearest Faraway Place.*

p. 22. **"the Baptists and . . ."** — Henley, quoted in Young.

TWO

p. 25. **"Seger was cool . . ."** — Glenn Frey, quoted in Stambler, Irwin, *The Encyclopedia of Pop, Rock and Soul* (New York: St. Martin's Press, 1989).

p. 25. **"I remember telling . . ."** — Nellie Frey, quoted in Crowe, Cameron, "Chips Off the Old Buffalo. . . ," *Rolling Stone,* September 25, 1975.

p. 27. **"I was from the East . . ."** — Frey, quoted in Frame.

THREE

p. 28. **"Playing was the only thing . . ."** — Randy Meisner, interview with Eliot. Unless otherwise noted, all Meisner quotes in this chapter are from Meisner/Eliot.

p. 28. **The Soul Survivors** — Not the group of the same name that had the hit recording "Expressway to Your Heart." Meisner's Soul Survivors was a local Denver band that featured Gene Chalk and Allen Kemp on guitars, and drummer Pat Shanahan, who would later reteam with Meisner in Rick Nelson's Stone Canyon band.

p. 30. The Poor and Boenzee Cryque — The Poor recorded two singles, "Once Again," in November 1966, and "She's Got the Time, She's Got the Changes," in February 1967. Boenzee Cryque was George Grantham on drums/vocals, Rusty Young on pedal steel, Sam Bush on bass/vocals, Mort Mitchell on guitar/vocals, and Jed Neddo on guitar/vocals. The band recorded a few singles in Colorado and is noted for two things: a song called "Sidewalk Street" on the sound track of a 1968 pre–*Easy Rider* Jack Nicholson film, *Psyche Out*, and the eventual teaming of Young and Meisner in Poco.

p. 30. Rusty Young "owned that sound" — Frame.

p. 31. Buffalo Springfield — The band was originally formed in March 1966, with Bruce Palmer on bass, Stephen Stills on guitar/vocals, Dewey Martin on drums/vocals, Richie Furay on guitar/vocals, and Neil Young on guitar/vocals. Furay and Stills had played together before, in a New York folkie band called The Au Go Go Singers. According to Frame, Stills quit the band and headed west after seeing *A Hard Days' Night*. The group had constant personnel problems, among them Bruce Palmer's chronic immigration problems (he was Canadian) and Neil Young's reluctance to make an exclusive commitment to the group. The second incarnation of the group included Doug Hastings on guitar/vocals, Jim Fielder on bass, Ken Koblun on bass, Bruce Palmer on bass, Ken Forssi on bass (all regularly substituted for one another during live shows), Stephen Stills on guitar/vocals, Dewey Martin on drums/vocals, Richie Furay on guitar/vocals, Neil Young on guitar/vocals. The third and final incarnation was Stephen Stills on guitar/vocals, Dewey Martin on drums/vocals, Jim Messina on bass/vocals, Richie Furay on guitar/vocals, and Neil Young on guitar/vocals.

p. 33. "The Troubador was everybody's . . ." — Anon., interview with Eliot.

p. 34. "Strange combinations . . ." — Babitz, Eve, "Honky-Tonk Nights," *Rolling Stone*, August 23, 1979.

p. 34. "Like more than one . . ." — Ibid.

p. 35. Epic — Epic Records, a subsidiary of Columbia, was the second label the band auditioned for. The first was Apple, the Beatles' label, which, while enthusiastic about the band, was having organizational problems and was unable to close the deal.

p. 35. — *The Ozzie and Harriet Show* began as a radio program in 1948. Rick and Dave Nelson joined in 1949. A film was made in 1952 based on the radio version, called *Here Come the Nelsons.* The network TV series *The Adventures of Ozzie and Harriet* followed, and ran until 1966.

p. 36. — Chart information on "Poor Little Fool" and "Stood Up" is from Whitburn, Joel, *Billboard Top 1000 Singles, 1955–1986* (Milwaukee: Records Research/Hal Leonard Books, 1986).

p. 36. "After the series ended . . ." — Rick Nelson, to the *New York Times* (1972), quoted in Selvin, Joel, *Ricky Nelson: Idol for a Generation* (Chicago: Contemporary Books, 1990).

p. 36. Rick Nelson's deal with Decca was groundbreaking, and helped pave the way for all rock and roll contracts. Rick originally signed a five-year deal with Imperial, but Ozzie Nelson, who supervised every move of his son's career, wanted a major label, rather than an independent, to ensure the continued growth of Rick's musical career. They chose Decca because the company was represented by Mickey Rockford, whose partner, Sonny Werblin, represented Ozzie Nelson's TV dealings. In 1962, Rick Nelson signed a twenty-year deal with Decca for a million dollars up front, unheard of at a time when rock and roll, in the years before the Beatles, was considered by the East Coast record industry, where the majors were still located and controlled, to be fading.

p. 36. John Boylan — "Born in New York City and raised in Buffalo, the hip, urbane Boylan went to the fashionably leftist Bard College, where he roomed with comic Chevy Chase, who was dating actress Blythe Danner, and used to play in bands with Walter Becker and Donald Fagen, later of Steely Dan. From this hotbed of hipsterism, Boylan graduated directly into the offices of Koppelman and Rubin, and his trip to produce Rick was his first big-time assignment in the music business" (Selvin).

p. 38. Timothy Schmit did not immediately join Poco. He was attending Sacramento State College, majoring in psychology and afraid that if he quit to play full-time, he would be drafted. In addition, he had joined a band called Glad, which had signed with ABC Records, produced by Terry Melcher, who had also produced the Byrds and Paul Revere and the Raiders. Poco actively pursued Schmit, and he eventually joined the band, replacing Meisner on bass. Schmit was replaced in Glad by Andrew Samuels, after which the band changed its name to Redwing, signed with Fantasy, and quickly faded from sight. His full name is Timothy Bruce Schmit. During the eighties, he decided to add his middle initial as part of his stage name, and became Timothy B. Schmit.

p. 38. Tom Brumley, who had joined Owens's backup band, the Buckaroos, was unsatisfied with the financial arrangements the country music legend offered his players. Brumley was actually Boylan's second choice, after Sneaky Pete Kleinow of the Flying Burrito Brothers, who declined to make a full-time commitment to the band.

FOUR

p. 39. "awestruck" — Henley, to *Rolling Stone*, 1985, quoted in Selvin.

p. 39. "California represented the dream . . ." — Henley, from "Eagles Family Tree Special," VH1, 1994.

p. 39. "After about two weeks . . ." — Ibid.

p. 40. "The Troubadour was the first . . ." — Henley, quoted in Smith, Joe, *Off the Record: An Oral History of Popular Music* (New York: Warner Books, 1988).

p. 40. "I'd come here . . ." — J. D. Souther, interview with Eliot. Unless otherwise noted, all Souther quotes in this chapter are from Souther/Eliot.

p. 41. "It wasn't so much . . ." — Souther, from transcript of interview with *Oui*, February 1977.

p. 42. "Soon after . . ." — Frey, quoted in Crowe.

p. 43. "The deal from the publishers' . . ." — Souther, from "Eagles Family Tree Special."

p. 43. "We were playing . . ." — Frey, from "Eagles Family Tree Special."

p. 43. "a lot of . . ." — John Boylan, interview with Eliot.

pp. 43–44. Jackson Browne's five-hundred-dollar advance — Publishing deals were the route to survival. In those days, publishers invested what was in effect very little money in anyone who showed any potential, correctly believing that in the world of rock and roll, anyone could write a hit, and that the long-term profits associated with any copyright were well worth the up-front gamble.

p. 44. "Tim Buckley was in . . ." — Jackson Browne, from "Eagles Family Tree Special."

p. 44. Soft White Underbelly — After Jackson Browne left, the band changed its name to Blue Oyster Cult, whose biggest hit was the 1976 single "Don't Fear the Reaper," which went to number twelve on the national charts.

p. 44. "Jackson was always the kid . . ." — Babitz.

p. 45. "The Troubadour was the big thing . . ." — Browne, quoted in Smith.

p. 45. "The Troubadour, man . . ." — Frey, quoted in Crowe.

pp. 46–47. "David Crosby is responsible . . ." — Elliot Roberts, quoted in Crosby, David and Carl Gottlieb, *Long Time Gone: The Autobiography of David Crosby* (New York: Doubleday, 1988).

p. 47. "Everyone knew David . . ." — Ibid.

p. 47. "a model environment . . ." — Crosby.

p. 48. Neil Young had a nonexclusive, ongoing solo recording contract on Reprise, a Warner subsidiary.

p. 49. Geffen's high school record — Information on Geffen's high school record is from Weinraub, Bernard, "Still Hungry," *New York Times Magazine*, May 2, 1993, and Seabrook, John, "The Many Lives of David Geffen," *The New Yorker*. February 23 and March 2, 1998.

p. 49. Geffen and William Morris — Background and additional information for this chapter is found in Rose, Frank, *The Agency: William Morris and the Hidden History of Show Business* (New York: HarperCollins, 1995).

p. 49. "The way he . . ." — Roberts, quoted in Crosby.

p. 50. "*Schmuck* . . ." — Brandt, Jerry, quoted in Rose.

p. 50. **Ashley Famous agency** — Formerly Ashley-Steiner, the agency underwent a name change after being bought out by Kinney Car Rental heir Steve Ross, on his way to acquiring Warner Brothers.

pp. 50–51. **"The band made that decision . . ."** — David Geffen, interview with Eliot.

p. 51. **Geffen and the signing of C, S, N and Y** — According to Carl Gottlieb, "From its inception, the association of Crosby, Stills, Nash and Young struggled to achieve an ideal: an ongoing commitment to combining talents without submerging identities or sublimating individual aspirations. The contracts reflected that, and each member of the group was free to record and tour as an individual or with other musicians" (Crosby).

p. 52. **"As we were going across the street . . ."** — Roberts, quoted in Crosby. The handshake deal proved more than just a gesture of friendship. California law prohibits agents from also being managers. Geffen had recently switched agencies again, this time moving with his roster of clients to Creative Management Associates, where he'd opened an office that he would use almost exclusively to book Lookout Management artists prior to the formation of Geffen-Roberts. Although it has always been reported that the split was 75/25 in favor of Geffen, both he and Roberts confirm it was an even deal. Additional information from Elliot Roberts, interview with Eliot.

p. 52. **"After a year . . ."** — Geffen, interview with Eliot.

p. 52. **"I went back . . ."** — Ibid.

FIVE

p. 54. **"Then our two . . ."** — Henley, interview with Eliot. Unless otherwise noted, all Henley quotes in this chapter are from Henley/Eliot.

p. 54. **"Kenny was at . . ."** — Michael Bowden interview with Eliot. Unless otherwise noted, all Michael Bowden quotes in this chapter are from M. Bowden/Eliot.

p. 55. **"It was more of a personal thing . . ."** — Norman, interview with Eliot. After Shiloh, Norman quit performing and went to work in a local Wherehouse record store. About a year later, he joined a new group, Uncle Jim's Music, formed by a friend from Texas. He then went into producing and arranging, worked on several Eagles albums and later solo efforts by individual members of the band (see discography) and is today the head of Warner's country music division. He is credited with making Randy Travis a star.

p. 56. **"I hated that album . . ."** — Linda Ronstadt, quoted in Bego, Mark, *Linda Ronstadt: It's So Easy* (Austin, Texas: Eakin Press, 1990).

p. 56. "They just didn't . . ." — John Boylan, interview with Eliot. Unless otherwise noted, all Boylan quotes in this chapter are from Boylan/Eliot.

p. 56. "I wasn't quite sure . . ." — Ibid.

p. 57. "One night I heard . . ." — Ibid.

p. 57. "started out to be . . ." — Ibid. Ronstadt stayed with Boylan until 1993, when Peter Asher finally agreed to take her on. Prior to this he had been reluctant because Kate Taylor, his client, was seen as too similar.

p. 58. "The two hundred a week . . ." — Frey, quoted in Frame.

p. 58. "Glenn was really charming . . ." — Henley, quoted in Connelly.

p. 60. "It's no secret . . ." — Souther, interview with Eliot. Unless otherwise noted, all Souther quotes in this chapter are from Souther/Eliot.

p. 62. "how a seventeen . . ." — Paul Rothchild, quoted in Fawcett.

p. 63. "I looked at the glossy . . ." — Geffen, interview with Eliot.

p. 63. "I went to everybody . . ." — Geffen, quoted in *Playboy*, September 1994.

SIX

p. 67. "A lot of people . . ." — Boylan, quoted in "The 25 Best-Selling Albums of All Time," *Entertainment Weekly,* May 3, 1996. *Linda Ronstadt* in some ways could be considered the first Eagles album, as all the original members of the band appear in various configurations on every cut. Henley plays drums on five cuts, including "Rock Me" and "Crazy Arms," Frey plays on "Rock Me" (which he also arranged) and four other cuts, Bernie Leadon on three, and Randy Meisner on two. Meisner also sings harmony, as do Henley and Frey, on three cuts.

p. 67. "Atlantic didn't really disagree . . ." — Geffen, interview with Eliot.

p. 67. Jackson Browne's first album — Browne was backed up by Russ Kunkel on drums, Leland Sklar on bass, Jim Gordon on organ, Sneaky Pete on pedal steel, Jim Fadden on mouth harp, David Campbell on viola, Clarence White on acoustic guitar ("Jamaica"), Craig Doerge on piano ("Rock Me on the Water," "My Opening Farewell," and "From Silver Lake"), David Jackson on piano ("Under Falling Sky"), Albert Lee on electric guitar ("A Child in These Hills," "Under the Falling Sky"), Jesse Davis on electric guitar ("Doctor My Eyes"), Leah Kunkel vocal harmony ("From Silver Lake"), and additional harmonies by David Crosby.

p. 67. "Boylan was a great guy . . ." — Henley, interview with Eliot. Unless otherwise noted, all Henley quotes in this chapter are from Henley/Eliot.

pp. 67–68. "Glenn was already . . ." — Boylan, interview with Eliot.

p. 68. "Right after I . . ." — Geffen, interview with Eliot.

p. 68. There is some question regarding the resolution of Shiloh's contract. Boylan and Henley remember Henley, on his own, approaching Kenny Rogers, who had a piece of Shiloh's publishing as well, asking for it back, and getting it, while Geffen dealt with Boylan.

p. 68. "it was nothing . . ." — John Hartmann, quoted in Goodman, Fred, *The Mansion on the Hill* (New York: Random House, 1997).

p. 68. "That was the combination . . ." — Geffen, interview with Eliot.

p. 69. "At one point . . ." — Meisner, interview with Eliot. Unless otherwise noted, all Meisner quotes in this chapter are from Meisner/Eliot.

p. 69. "The fact of the matter . . ." — Anon., interview with Eliot.

p. 69. "I was signed . . ." — Souther, interview with Eliot.

p. 70. "Money . . ." — Ibid.

p. 70. "We all wanted . . ." — Bernie Leadon, quoted in Fawcett.

p. 72. Glyn Johns — Among the albums he has produced are *December's Children, Get Yer Ya-Ya's Out, Their Satanic Majesties Request, Let It Bleed, Exile on Main Street,* the Rolling Stones; *Real Live,* Bob Dylan; *Combat Rock,* the Clash; *Slowhand, Backless,* Eric Clapton; *Who's Next,* the Who; *Rough Mix,* Pete Townshend; *Ooh-La-La, A Nod's as Good as a Wink,* Faces; *Rock On,* Humble Pie; and albums by Boz Scaggs, Fairport Convention, John Hiatt, and more than seventy others.

pp. 72–73. "I personally didn't think . . ." — Glyn Johns, quoted in Flanagan, Bill, "Glyn Johns Produces," *Musician,* July 1983.

p. 73. "He didn't think . . ." — Henley, quoted in Crowe.

p. 73. "[Geffen] kept after me . . ." — Johns, quoted in Flanagan.

p. 73. "Now, Glyn thought . . ." — Henley, from a 1975 interview with David Rensin that appeared in *Crawdaddy!*.

p. 73. "[Glyn Johns] was the key . . ."—Frey, quoted in Flanagan.

pp. 74–75. Glyn Johns and the recording of *Eagles* — According to Randy Meisner, "As a gesture of friendship, Glyn had these solid-gold medallions made for each of us, after which they threw away the mold. It had an Eagle on the front, and our names on the back. Proof that I was an original Eagle" (Meisner, interview with Eliot).

p. 75. "The sound he was creating . . ." — Henley, quoted in Shapiro, Mark, *The Long Run: The Story of the Eagles* (London: Omnibus Press, 1995).

p. 76. "Take It Easy" — Jackson Browne had originally intended to use the song on his own album but was never quite satisfied with it and eventually gave it to Frey. Glenn

295

added the crucial second "Winslow, Arizona" verse, which gave the song its strong visual sense, a couple of young guys trying to pick up girls while driving around a typical American town with the radio up and the top down. It was also Frey who stretched the "e" in *easy* to make the chorus scan better, and laid the whole thing down with a standard R&B arrangement. When Johns heard it, he reworked it into the pop version that eventually appeared on the Eagles' album. Browne recorded the song on his second album.

p. 76. "Witchy Woman" — According to Henley, "Witchy Woman" was written while he had the flu and was reading a biography of Zelda Fitzgerald. "The fever that I had helped me conjure up some of those images, similar to the ones Zelda was having toward the end of her life. Like all songs, it's a combination of things. The rest of it is about the girls we used to meet at the Whiskey" (Henley/Eliot).

p. 76. Jack Tempchin — Tempchin was yet another member of the Troubadour scene. One who was close to the action referred to him as the third "unofficial Eagle" (along with Jackson Browne and J. D. Souther). Another dubbed him "the poor man's David Blue," an ironic reference to the similarities of their individual quests for fame. While neither became a household name, Blue did achieve a certain cult status, particularly among Dylan fans, after his appearance as the pinball-playing narrator in *Renaldo and Clara*. Blue died in 1982. Tempchin collaborated on several Eagles songs, and today can still be seen playing the folk-rock club circuit, mostly in Los Angeles. According to one friend, "Jack kind of gave up on the fame thing when the money he made from the Eagles' albums his songs appeared on kept rolling in. It freed him to do exactly what he does, which is play his guitar in clubs, and not have to worry about paying his bills" (Anon., interview with Eliot).

pp. 76–77. "We met at the Troubadour . . ." — Leadon, quoted in Fawcett. According to Henley, "If you see an early copy of the foldout version of the album cover, before the record company changed it — they like to do that after you've sold a few copies; to increase their profit margin they'll turn a foldout double-cover album into a single cover and not even tell you — you clearly see we were all smashed on peyote. We had a road manager at the time named John Barrick, who's dead now. We met him when he was sweeping floors at the Troubadour. He'd worked for the Byrds at one point, your basic hippie but intellectual in a charming sort of way, and into all of that" (Henley/Eliot).

p. 77. Eagles tour — Geffen came from an agency background and believed that touring was the best way to sell records. There are two theories regarding band promotion. One says that record sales will fill houses; the other says that full houses will sell records. Geffen, like Azoff later on, believed a successful band was one that played live. Both managers kept the Eagles on the road as much as possible.

p. 77. "I remember them standing . . ." — Anon., interview with Eliot.

pp. 77–78. Eagles/Jethro Tull tour — The Eagles took more than a lesson in discretion from touring with Jethro Tull. Not long after that summer, the Eagles would write and record "Tequila Sunrise," which bore some musical resemblance to the title track of Tull's *Thick as a Brick*. Later on, some British critics swore they heard the unmistakable strains of "Locomotive Breath" echoed in the guitar solos that opened and closed the single "Hotel California."

pp. 78–79. "For the whole nightmare" — Bob Sterne, interview with Eliot.

p. 79. "We didn't go in . . ." — Henley, quoted in Rensin.

p. 79. "The Eagles wanted . . ." — Ken Graham, interview with Eliot.

pp. 79–80. " 'The Eagles' [sic] . . ." — Scoppa, Bud, *Rolling Stone*, June 22, 1972.

p. 80. "Take It Easy" — The single returned to the charts in 1975 for an additional four-month run.

p. 81. "product . . ." — Robert Christgau, writing for the *Village Voice*, quoted in *Goldmine*, #133.

SEVEN

pp. 83–84. "There was a basketball game . . ." — Anon., interview with Eliot.

p. 84. "the Kirkwood Casino and Health Club" — Ibid.

p. 84. "At four-thirty or five . . ." — Ibid.

p. 84. "It was pretty loose . . ." — Paul Ahern, interview with Eliot. Unless otherwise noted, all Ahern quotes in this chapter are from Ahern/Eliot. It was Ahern whom the Eagles thanked "for leaving town" in the liner notes of their third album, *On the Border*. While it has widely assumed this was a put-down by the band, in fact it was an affectionate inside joke noting the party-hearty atmosphere that had prevailed at Frey's house during the three years Ahern had been his roommate. The meaning of the mention was twofold. First, the Eagles liked to thank everyone on the record, so to speak, as a way of acknowledging friends and associates, and, as one close to the band noted, "instead of paying anything." Second, it was their way of thanking Ahern for getting lost so Frey could do some serious work.

Later on, after Ahern went to work for Azoff's Full Moon Records, Dan Fogelberg added in his liner notes for *Souvenirs*, "Thanks to Paul Ahern for coming back to town." The dig was aimed at Geffen, a belated nod to Ahern's somewhat thankless job of field promotion while with the pre-Azoff Eagles.

p. 85. "I lived . . ." — Henley, interview with Eliot. Unless otherwise noted, all Henley quotes in this chapter are from Henley/Eliot.

p. 86. "Mine was Chipmunk . . ." — Meisner, interview with Eliot. Unless otherwise noted, all Meisner quotes in this chapter are from Meisner/Eliot.

297

p. 88. "We're the Oakland A's . . ." — Frey, quoted in Crowe.

p. 89. David Blue — Blue was actually the second act Geffen signed to Asylum, although his first album, *Stories,* was released ahead of Jackson Browne's because of the speed with which David recorded it. Blue, as David Cohen, formed part of the performing clique of what one member close to the music scene described as the "power base of New York to L.A. Jews." The comment was not meant to be derogatory, but rather a description of an aspect of the Avocado Mafia as distinct as the black power presence at Motown. Geffen and Roberts were also Jewish.

p. 89. "We didn't manage . . ." — Geffen, interview with Eliot.

p. 89. Geffen's stable of artists — There was a sense of inbreeding that continued within the Geffen roster. Souther was a lover of Linda Ronstadt, Joni Mitchell had an affair with David Blue (which she chronicled in the album she is said to have named after him, *Blue,* one of the signature works of her career), and there was the constant "sitting in" of virtually every member of Asylum's roster on everyone else's albums.

p. 92. "Our first album . . ." — Henley, interviewed by DeCurtis, Anthony, for "VH1 to One," 1996.

p. 93. "Glenn, Ned Doheny, J. D., and Henley . . ." — Anon., interview with Eliot.

p. 94. "Glenn and I . . ." — Henley, quoted in Crowe.

p. 94. Eagles copyrights — At the same time, provisions were made for The Eagles, a California company that decreed that Eagles Ltd. owned the exclusive right to the name "the Eagles," a move made to prevent any members from splitting and going out on the road with any other group of musicians calling themselves "the Eagles."

p. 94. Future Eagles Don Felder, Joe Walsh, and Timothy B. Schmit all had their own publishing companies as well. Felder's was Fingers Music, Walsh's was Wow and Flutter Music, Schmit's was Jeddrah Music.

p. 95. Randy Meisner's request for a "sit-down" with Johns — from Flanagan.

p. 95. "It was not . . ." — Johns, quoted in Flanagan.

p. 95. Jim Ed Norman — Like J. D. Souther, Jack Tempchin, and Jackson Browne, Norman continued to play a role in the recording of the Eagles. First listed in the credits of *Desperado,* Norman worked on every subsequent album the band released. He is currently the head of Warner's country music division.

p. 96. "A magical day . . ." — Anon., interview with Eliot.

pp. 96–97. "It was shot . . ." — Frey, interviewed by Ladd, Jim, "Innerview" syndicated radio special, 1977.

p. 97. Release of *Desperado* — Not long after its release, there was some talk of turning the concept album into movie and, when that failed to happen, a Broadway show, an idea Henley did not go for. In a radio interview Henley said, "They're trying to take it and make a Broadway play out of it like they did *Tommy*. I personally can't see a bunch of guys in cowboy suits dancing around singing 'Desperado,' choreographed. . . . I just [couldn't] see it" (Ladd).

p. 98. "That day . . ." — Roberts, quoted in Crosby.

EIGHT

p. 99. Joe Walsh — To this day, Joe Walsh credits Pete Townshend (and Elvis) as his primary musical influences.

p. 101. "I hired Irving . . ." — Geffen, interview with Eliot. Unless otherwise noted, all Geffen quotes in this chapter are from Geffen/Eliot.

p. 101. "Tell them to get . . ." — Irving Azoff, interview with Eliot. Unless otherwise noted, all Azoff quotes in this chapter are from Azoff/Eliot.

p. 102. "We couldn't think . . ." — Henley, interview with Eliot. Unless otherwise noted, all Henley quotes in this chapter are from Henley/Eliot.

p. 102. "You can't settle . . ." — Meisner, interview with Eliot.

p. 102. "The six weeks . . ." — Johns, quoted in Flanagan.

pp. 102–103. "Glyn recorded them . . ." — Richard Fernandez, interview with Eliot. Unless otherwise noted, all Fernandez quotes in this chapter are from Fernandez/Eliot.

p. 104. "The first night we met Irving . . ." — Frey, quoted in Crowe.

pp. 106–107. "Make that . . ." — Bob Buziak, interview with Eliot.

p. 107. "bunker mentality . . ." — Ahern, interview with Eliot.

p. 108. "Everyone on that side of the line . . ." — Irving Azoff, quoted in Knoedelseder, William, *Stiffed: A True Story of MCA, the Music Business, and the Mafia* (New York: HarperCollins, 1993).

p. 108. "Napoleon with a heart . . ." — Henley, quoted in Crowe.

p. 108. Ronstadt, J. D. Souther — Two singles were released from *Don't Cry Now*. They were "Love Has No Pride," which went to number fifty-one, and "Silver Threads and Golden Needles," which went to number sixty-seven. At the same time, Capitol Records released a "best of" compilation, which went to number ninety-two. The timing of Capitol's reissue probably hurt both albums.

Most likely, Elektra/Asylum signed the Souther-Hillman-Furay Band to keep Souther and the Eagles happy and together in what Geffen still thought of as one big happy family of artists. The label's publicity machine was cranked so high for Souther, Hillman (ex

Byrds), and Furay (ex Poco) that it shipped gold (500,000 units). However, it still failed to establish the band as one of the "supergroups" of Southern California. After one more album, released in 1975, the group disbanded, proving Geffen's theory of Souther's inability to function in a band correct.

There was talk among the Eagles after Azoff took over that one of the reasons *Desperado* hadn't done as well as it should have was that the band had not gotten enough of a promotional push. The blame was put squarely on Geffen, whose pursuit of Dylan had seemed to overtake all other priorities. When Geffen then poured so much money into the Souther-Hillman-Furay Band, an unknown entity in spite of its elite personnel, the distance between Geffen and the Eagles inevitably grew wider.

p. 109. "Bernie was always . . ." — Anon., interview with Eliot.

p. 110. "When I first walked in . . ." — Don Felder, quoted in Hilburn, Robert, "Tensions in the Eagles' Nest," *Los Angeles Times,* February 17, 1980.

p. 110. "We had more . . ." — Frey, quoted in Rensin. Part of this quote was quoted in Hilburn, Robert, *Los Angeles Times,* January 12, 1998.

p. 111. "Frey adds the grease . . ." — Henley, quoted in Rensin.

p. 113. "I must say . . ." — Johns, quoted in Flanagan.

p. 114. "no matter what . . ." — Joe Berry, interview with Eliot.

p. 114. "It's simple . . ." — Sterne, interview with Eliot.

pp. 114–115. "The quintessential Irving . . ." — Dannen, Fredric, *Hit Men* (New York: Vintage Books, 1991).

p. 116. "Someone looked up . . ." — Buziak, interview with Eliot.

p. 117. "that . . . was exactly what . . ." — Anon., interview with Eliot.

p. 117. "Nobody else . . ." — Henley, quoted in Flanagan.

pp. 118–119. "some 850,000 people . . ." — *Time,* August 18, 1975.

p. 119. Descriptions of the individual members of the band — Ibid.

PART TWO — LIFE IN THE FAST LANE

NINE

p. 124. Henley and fidelity — Loree Rodkin, interviewed by Christopher Connelly for his 1991 profile of Henley in *GQ* magazine, is quoted thusly: "'I think probably Don was more prone to having a girlfriend at the time, whether that had parameters for him or not.' Parameters such as? 'Fidelity,' says Rodkin, laughing" (Connelly).

p. 125. "They could make any woman . . ." — Anon., interview with Eliot.

p. 126. "Tagamet was his best friend . . ." — Anon., interview with Eliot.

p. 126. "need to argue . . ." — Anon., interview with Eliot.

p. 126. "Rodkin did teach . . ." — Anon., interview with Eliot.

p. 127. "Glenn and I would . . ." — Henley, quoted in Smith.

pp. 127–128. "Or we'd have . . ." — Henley, interview with Eliot. Unless otherwise noted, all Henley quotes in this chapter are from Henley/Eliot.

pp. 128–129. "When Lindsey and I . . ." — Stevie Nicks, quoted in Love, Courtney, "Blonde on Blonde." *Spin*, October 1997.

p. 129. "[Stevie had] named the . . ." — Henley, quoted in Connelly.

p. 131. Frey's reduced album time — He sang solo lead on one song for *Hotel California* ("New Kid in Town") and one on *The Long Run* ("Heartache Tonight").

p. 131. "[Glenn] was generous . . ." — Henley, quoted in Flanagan.

p. 131. Meisner's version of the Leadon walkout — Meisner, interview with Eliot.

p. 132. "I believed in him . . ." — Joe Walsh, quoted in Isenberg, Barbara, "Putting Stars in Their Places," *Los Angeles Times*, June 27, 1996. The second part of the quote, beginning with "being with an established group . . ." is from Meijers, Constant, *Zigzag 67*, December, 1976.

p. 133. "When we brought Joe in . . ." — Henley, quoted in Flanagan.

p. 133. "Joe Walsh came to me . . ." — Bowden, Richard, quoted in Young.

p. 134. "Well, [Walsh's addition is] . . ." — Frey, quoted in Meijers.

pp. 134–135. Joe Walsh chain-saw story — Anon., interview with Eliot.

p. 135. Joe Walsh defacing painting — Young.

p. 135. "The good news . . ." — Hilburn, Robert, *Los Angeles Times*, May 4, 1976.

p. 135. The Eagles fail to appear at the New England Folk Festival — From the *New York Times*, June 14, 1976.

p. 136. "drive us all a little crazy . . ." — Steve Wax, quoted in the *Los Angeles Times*, June 26, 1976.

p. 137. "I had already left . . ." — Geffen, interview with Eliot.

p. 137. "He had worn . . ." — Anon., interview with Eliot.

pp. 137–138. Eagles lawsuit against Geffen — "Glen [sic] Frey, Randy Meisner, Bernie Leadon, Don Henley and Don Felder v. Warner Bros. Inc., WB Music Corp., David Geffen, Companion Music, Benchmark Music, et al, Case #C199570. Filed 9/8/77 in Superior Court of the State of California, County of Los Angeles." The announcement of the lawsuit came several months before its actual filing, and the actual settlement years after it was "dropped."

p. 138. "Bullshit . . ." — Geffen, interview with Eliot.

p. 138. "There's no question . . ." — Joe Smith, interview with Eliot. Unless otherwise noted, all Smith quotes in this chapter are from Smith/Eliot.

p. 138. "Whenever I'd call . . ." — Azoff, interview with Eliot.

p. 140. Greatest hits album — *Their Greatest Hits 1971–1975* has been on the charts for 133 weeks, and to date has sold more than 24 million copies. In 1997, it temporarily passed Michael Jackson's *Thriller* to become the biggest-selling album of all time. According to *Billboard,* it still sells an average of five thousand copies a week. See discography for songs.

TEN

pp. 144–145. "The Eagles thought . . ." — Anon., interview with Eliot.

p. 145. "Zevon is on Asylum . . ." — Marcus, Greil, "Warren Zevon's Red Harvest," *Village Voice,* March 6, 1978.

p. 145. "Greil Marcus is . . ." — Henley, interview with Eliot. Unless otherwise noted, all Henley quotes in this chapter are from Henley/Eliot.

p. 146. "His method was simple . . ." — Anon., interview with Eliot.

p. 147. "We were [all] . . ." — Meisner, interview with Eliot.

p. 148. "Hotel California" — According to Henley, "There's a little bit of Latin feel to the song, and a reggae sound that nobody ever notices, except they always want to know what *colitas* means. I think Richie Fernandez's father gave me that word. It's supposedly Spanish for bud. I was looking for a way to describe the smell of lit weed" (Henley, interview with Eliot).

p. 148. "A lot of the best lines . . ." — Anon., interview with Eliot.

pp. 148–149. "New Kid in Town" — Although also credited on the album to Henley and Frey, it is generally considered among those who were there during its creation to be J. D. Souther's composition.

p. 149. "Everybody's got cocaine . . ." — Henley, quoted in Flanagan.

p. 150. "People tend to think . . ." — Henley, quoted in "The 25 Best-Selling Albums of All Time."

p. 152. "All of us . . ." — Souther, interview with Eliot.

p. 153. "'Hotel California' showcases both . . ." — Walters, Charley, *Rolling Stone.*

ELEVEN

p. 154. The inside cover of *Hotel California* was photographed in the lobby of the Lido apartments, in Hollywood.

p. 154. "I was flown . . ." — Graham, interview with Eliot.

p. 156. "We rehearsed intensely . . ." — Joe Berry, interview with Eliot.

p. 156. Firing of Richard Fernandez — Fernandez, interview with Eliot.

p. 157. "gave him . . ." — Azoff, interview with Eliot.

p. 157. "Richard's a good guy . . ." — Henley, interview with Eliot. Unless otherwise noted, all Henley quotes in this chapter are from Henley/Eliot.

pp. 157–158. "One time in Japan . . ." — Berry, interview with Eliot.

p. 158. "At some point . . ." — Meisner, interview with Eliot. Unless otherwise noted, all Meisner quotes in this chapter are from Meisner/Eliot.

p. 159. "like a king . . ." — Bob Sterne, interview with Eliot.

p. 160. "The Eagles' show . . ." — Azoff, interview with Eliot.

p. 162. Schmit's joining the Eagles — Meisner left Poco in February, 1970, Schmit officially became a member in November.

p. 163. "He couldn't get . . ." — Anon., interview with Eliot.

p. 164. "Everything's changed." — Boyd Elder, interview with Eliot.

TWELVE

p. 167. "Because of our stature . . ." — Henley, quoted in Meijers.

p. 167. "People seem to be lost . . ." — Henley, from an interview with the Eagles by Jim Ladd, syndicated on FM radio, 1976.

p. 168. "When I met her . . ." — Henley, interview with Eliot.

pp. 168–170. The Grammys — None of the Eagles, or Azoff, had expected the band to win the award for best single, one of the reasons he decided against having them show up and look like losers. The word in the industry was that either Debby Boone ("You Light Up My Life") or Barbra Streisand ("Love Theme from 'A Star Is Born' [Evergreen])" would win. The Bee Gees won out over both Fleetwood Mac (*Rumors*) and the Eagles (*Hotel California*) for Best Pop Vocal Performance by a Duo, Group, or Chorus on an Album (*Saturday Night Fever*).

p. 169. "tightening up some tracks . . ." — Azoff, quoted in Fong-Torres, Ben, *Rolling Stone*, April 6, 1978.

p. 170. "I never indicated . . ." — Ibid.

p. 171. "The *Rolling Stone* critics . . ." — Draper, Robert, *Rolling Stone Magazine: The Uncensored History* (New York: HarperCollins, 1990).

p. 171. "As a short, brash . . ." — Ibid.

pp. 173–174. *FM* — Although the film proved a box-office dud, the double-album sound track reached number five on the charts and went double platinum (one million units of a two-record set). It produced a huge hit single, Joe Walsh's "Life's Been Good," which became one of his signature pieces. This would not be Azoff's only involvement with the film business. In 1980 he coproduced *Urban Cowboy* at Paramount with Bob Evans, and produced the hit sound track. He also produced the sound track for 1982's *Fast Times at Ridgemont High*.

At the time of *FM*'s sound track release, Randy Meisner's first full-length solo album was released. *Randy Meisner* received little airplay, failed to chart, and caused the singer to give up music and leave L.A., this time for Colorado, where he decided to try ranching. Still another ex-Eagle, Bernie Leadon, was working on a concept album about the Civil War called *White Mansions*. The project was envisioned to be a more contemporary version of *Jesus Christ Superstar* and had the participation of Jessi Colter and Waylon Jennings for "authentic" Southern flavor, and Eric Clapton. The producer was Glyn Johns. The album failed to chart.

p. 173. "No one except . . ." — Anon., interview with Eliot.

p. 174. "You don't hate music . . ." — Julia Phillips, interview with Eliot.

p. 175. Frey and Henley taking coke during meeting — Ibid.

pp. 175–176. "She's a liar . . ." — Henley, interview with Eliot. Unless otherwise noted, all Henley quotes in this chapter are from Henley/Eliot.

p. 176. "They really didn't want . . ." — Anon., interview with Eliot.

pp. 176–177. "Henley and Irving had . . ." — Anon., interview with Eliot.

p. 177. "Then, of course, the marriage . . ." — Anon., interview with Eliot.

p. 177. "Irving soon made it clear . . ." — Anon., interview with Eliot.

p. 177. "Glenn Frey is the best . . ." — Ronstadt, quoted in Herbst, Peter, "The Rolling Stone Interview: Linda Ronstadt," *Rolling Stone,* October 19, 1978.

THIRTEEN

p. 180. Eagles lawsuit — The Eagles' copyrights were returned to the band. Warner Bros. retained overseas administration rights.

p. 180. "Our motto . . ." — Azoff, quoted in Young.

p. 181. "I Can't Tell You Why" — Writing credit is given to Schmit, Henley, and Frey.

pp. 181–182. "Our friendship . . ." — Henley, interview with Eliot.

p. 182. "When we finished 'Hotel California' . . ." — Walsh, quoted in Hilburn, "Tensions in the Eagles' Nest."

p. 183. "The creative stalemate . . ." — Ibid.

p. 183. "The Long Run" — Officially listed as a Henley-Frey composition, it is generally believed to be Henley's composition.

p. 184. "Glenn and I . . ." — Souther, interview with Eliot.

pp. 184–185. "I heard 'Teenage Jail' . . ." — Henley, quoted in Flanagan.

p. 186. "By and large . . ."—Ibid.

p. 186. *The Long Run* competition — In the top ten the week the Eagles landed with *The Long Run* were such other mainstream rock and roll icons as Led Zeppelin (*In Through the Out Door*), Bob Dylan (*Slow Train Coming*), Foreigner (*Head Games*), the Knack (*Get the Knack*), Cheap Trick (*Dream Police*), Neil Young (*Rust Never Sleeps*), and the Commodores (*Midnight Magic*). Creeping up the list were a curious mix of the old and the new, including Jethro Tull, Michael Jackson, Blondie (two albums: *Eat to the Beat* and *Parallel Lines*), Talking Heads, Karla Bonoff, the Cars, the Kinks, Nick Lowe, Santana, the Who, the Doobie Brothers, David Johansen, and Dire Straits.

pp. 186–187. "A chilling and altogether . . ." — White, Timothy, *Rolling Stone*, November 15, 1979.

p. 187. Robert Hilburn's review of *The Long Run* — *Los Angeles Times*, September 30, 1979.

p. 187. *Tusk* — Fleetwood Mac's double-album *Tusk* retailed at $15.98, nearly double the price of *The Long Run*.

p. 188. J. D. Souther's *You're Only Lonely* — The single from the album of the same name hit the top ten list in November 1979.

pp. 188–189. "The recording of 'Long Run' . . ." — Azoff, quoted in Hilburn, "Tensions in the Eagles' Nest."

p. 189. "What I think I'd really like to do . . ." — Henley, quoted in Hilburn, "Tensions in the Eagles' Nest."

p. 189. "It just isn't . . ." — Anon., interview with Eliot.

pp. 190–191. "I spent a year . . ." — Smith, interview with Eliot.

p. 191. "They wanted to do . . ." — Graham, interview with Eliot.

p. 192. "The decision to do . . ." — Henley, interview with Eliot.

p. 193. "Bull . . ." — Anon., interview with Eliot.

p. 193. "Am I getting . . ." — Anon., interview with Eliot.

p. 194. "If looks could kill . . ." — Anon., interview with Eliot.

p. 195. "We started . . ." — Henley, interview with Eliot.

p. 195. "When we were doing fixes . . ." — Bill Szymczyk, quoted in Connelly.

p. 196. "Jesus . . ." — Anon., interview with Eliot.

PART THREE — THE END OF THE INNOCENCE

pp. 199–203. "The group's splitting . . ." — Henley, interview with Eliot. Unless otherwise noted, all Henley quotes in this chapter are from Henley/Eliot.

p. 202. The LAPD's "conspiracy" — The LAPD did indeed declare a war of sorts on the entertainment industry in 1981. Highly publicized drug-related arrests were made against Flip Wilson, Louise Lasser, Robert Evans, director Stan Dragoti, and John Phillips. In April 1981, five months after Henley's skirmish, *People* magazine ran a story with the following headline: "Amid Cries of Witch-Hunt and Whispers of Blacklisting, Congress Probes the Hollywood Drug Scene." According to the article, leading the attack were Illinois representative Tom Railsback and California congressman Robert Dornan.

p. 203. "Felder Flies Without the Eagles" — Manna, Sal, "Felder Flies Without the Eagles," *Los Angeles Times*, November 15, 1981.

p. 203. "The Eagles are on a semi-vacation . . ." — Felder, quoted in Manna.

p. 205. "One of the best . . ." — Azoff, quoted in Connelly.

p. 205. "the mad faxer . . ." — Boylan, quoted in Connelly.

p. 205. Toilet paper memo — Young.

pp. 205–206. "I was the most miserable . . ." — Danny Kortchmar, from syndicated radio special, "Don Henley: The End of the Innocence," Timothy White, producer-host, July 8, 1989.

p. 206. "Kootch and I . . ." — Henley, quoted in Connelly.

pp. 206–207. "I was working . . ." — Greg Ladanyi, interview with Eliot.

p. 207. "'Johnny Can't Read' was the combination . . ." — Ibid.

p. 207. "Don's really smart . . ." — Ibid.

p. 208. "Kootch and I . . ." — Henley, from "Don Henley: The End of the Innocence."

pp. 208–209. "Kootch would do the entire . . ." — Ibid.

p. 209. "Dirty Laundry" — Apparently there was an actual "bubble-headed bleach-blond" Henley was referring to in the song's lyrics. On L.A.'s local ABC TV outlet, there was a blond anchorwoman on the six P.M. newscast. Although Henley did not identify her by name, he referred to her in an article by Howard Rosenberg in the *Los Angeles Times* this way: "She doesn't come on at five, she comes on at six, but I couldn't get six to rhyme [with the lyric of the song]." It was generally believed he was referring to Christine Lund, who was the only local blond newscaster on at that time.

"The certain woman broadcaster," Henley said, reflects the "emotionless, remorseless, robotic-like way in which news is reported. I don't want tears from these people," he said, "but there should be some dignity."

FIFTEEN

p. 212. "In my opinion . . ." — Azoff, quoted in Hilburn, Robert, "The Eagles — A Long Run Is Over," *Los Angeles Times*, May 23, 1982.

p. 212. Full Moon — Joe Walsh and Dan Fogelberg recorded for Full Moon and were managed by Front Line.

p. 212. Azoff on the Eagles — Patrick Goldstein, interview with Eliot. Also, Goldstein, "Challenge Draws Azoff to MCA Post," *Los Angeles Times*, April 29, 1983.

p. 213. "Irving has to be . . ." — Geffen, quoted in the *New York Times*, April 27, 1983.

p. 213. "What really happened . . ." — Anon., interview with Eliot.

p. 214. "I was a little . . ." — Henley, interview with Eliot. Unless otherwise noted, all Henley quotes in this chapter are from Henley/Eliot.

pp. 214–215. "The peace-and-love generation . . ." — Henley, quoted in Hilburn, "Don Henley Taking Life Literally," *Los Angeles Times*, December 2, 1984.

p. 215. "Henley was always . . ." — Ladanyi, interview with Eliot.

p. 217. "a damn near perfect pop album . . ." — Marsh, Dave and John Swenson, eds., *The Rolling Stone Record Guide* (New York: Random House/Rolling Stone Press, 1979).

p. 217. "a song about . . ." — Kortchmar, from "Don Henley: The End of the Innocence."

p. 218. "some of the most . . ." — Michael Mann, quoted in Goldstein, Patrick, "Frey Cops Out in New Episode of His Career," *Los Angeles Times*, January 20, 1985.

p. 218. "spaced-out audiophile-junkie . . ." — Mann, quoted in Goldstein.

pp. 218–219. "There was an album . . ." — Kortchmar, from "Don Henley: The End of the Innocence."

p. 219. "He didn't call . . ." — Henley, quoted in Connelly, Christopher, "Don Henley: The Former Eagle Has Landed," *Rolling Stone*, April 25, 1985.

p. 219. "There was a time . . ." — Henley, quoted in Connelly.

SIXTEEN

p. 221. "*Let's Get Harry* . . ." — Bob Singer, interview with Eliot.

p. 223. Frey and commercials — Frey also licensed "You Belong to the Night" to Pepsi, which reportedly further outraged Don Henley.

p. 223. "A lot of singers . . ." — Anon., interview with Eliot.

p. 224. "Bruce had had it . . ." — Henley, quoted in White, syndicated FM radio broadcast, July 8, 1989.

p. 224. "Maren was . . ." — Anon., interview with Eliot.

pp. 224–225. "Maren and I . . ." — Henley, interview with Eliot. Unless otherwise noted, all Henley quotes in this chapter are from Henley/Eliot.

p. 225. "I feel like it was . . ." — Henley, quoted in White (radio), July 8, 1989.

p. 225. "I remember . . ." — Anon., interview with Eliot.

pp. 225–226. *The End of the Innocence* . . ." — Ladanyi, interview with Eliot.

pp. 226–227. Henley, Hart, and Donna Rice — It is widely believed that Henley's song "Little Tin God" (from *The End of the Innocence*) is about this incident. According to Henley, "The song is not about Donna Rice . . . but Donna put me through quite a lot of aggravation. . . . My role in the thing was so blown out of proportion that I was fairly indignant about it. . . .

   "I mean, I knew this girl, I dated her three or four times. She was at my house. He was at my house. I don't know who introduced them. But I got credit for it. . . . Another case of the American news media as proctologists, as America stares up its own asshole" (Flanagan).

p. 226. "Someone introduced them . . ." — Henley, quoted in Flanagan.

p. 227. "the best band I've ever played with . . ." — Henley, quoted in White (radio), July 8, 1989.

p. 227. "She had just come off . . ." — Anon., interview with Eliot.

p. 229. "You cannot be . . ." — Geffen, quoted in Knoedelseder, Wm. K. Jr., "MCA to Acquire 3 Companies Partly Owned by Azoff," *Los Angeles Times*, May 7, 1986.

pp. 230–231. MCA and the federal government — The studio successfully battled antitrust charges stemming from its original inception as a talent agency for nearly forty years.

p. 231. "shit storm . . ." — Anon., interview with Eliot.

p. 231. "I suspect . . ." — Anon., interview with Eliot.

p. 232. "I started in 1980 . . ." — Geffen, quoted in Hochman, Steve, "Former MCA Chief Azoff Gets New Warner Bros. Label," *Los Angeles Times*, November 1, 1989.

SEVENTEEN

p. 233. "a caricature of himself . . ." — Anon., interview with Eliot.

p. 234. "He could wake up . . ." — Anon., interview with Eliot.

pp. 234–235. "The weird thing . . ." — Anon., interview with Eliot.

p. 235. "Glenn's songs . . ." — Ibid.

p. 235. "Walden Woods is widely . . ." — Henley, quoted in Verna, Paul, "Henley-Led Walden Woods Project on Course to Goal," *Billboard*, December 28, 1996. Today, fully 75 percent of Walden Woods is protected and preserved. Henley's organization has so far raised more than $18 million.

p. 237. "more interested . . ." — Anon., interview with Eliot.

pp. 237–238. "We'd been looking . . ." — Stan Rogow, quoted in Willman, Chris, "He's Got a Peaceful TV Feeling," *Los Angeles Times*, October 24, 1993.

p. 238. "You get into your mid-30's . . ." — Frey, quoted in Willman.

p. 239. "Well, Glenn's TV career . . ." — Anon., interview with Eliot.

p. 239. "After I signed Don . . ." — Geffen, interview with Eliot.

p. 240. "The Eagles always sold . . ." — Ibid.

p. 241. Schmit comments — Anon., interview with Eliot.

p. 242. "Eaglemania . . ." — Anon., interview with Eliot.

EIGHTEEN

p. 245. **Eagles earnings** — These figures are from the September 1996 issue of *Forbes* magazine, in which it listed the highest-paid entertainers in show business. The magazine compiled its list by combining income from the two previous years.

The issue's complete list of the top twenty (in millions of dollars) show-business earners: Oprah Winfrey (171), Steven Spielberg (150), Beatles (130), Michael Jackson (90), Rolling Stones (77), **Eagles (75)**, Arnold Schwarzenegger (74), David Copperfield (74), Jim Carrey (63), Michael Crichton (59), Jerry Seinfeld (59), Stephen King (56), Garth Brooks (51), Andrew Lloyd Webber (50), Tom Hanks (50), Siegfried and Roy (48), Tom Cruise (46), Harrison Ford (44), Clint Eastwood (44), R.E.M. (44). Michael Jackson did not tour during this tracking period.

p. 245. **Soundscan and *Billboard*** — Catalog albums are at least two-year-old titles that have fallen below 100 on the *Billboard* top 200, or reissues, that continue to sell. Figures are calculated by Soundscan from national retail store and rack sales.

pp. 246–247. "At one point . . ." — Meisner, interview with Eliot.

pp. 247–248. "It felt like . . ." — Henley, interview with Eliot.

pp. 249–250. "Of course, Geffen . . ." — Ibid. Henley's legal bills in the case against Geffen totaled a million dollars.

p. 250. "If you're going . . ." — Anon., interview with Eliot.

p. 250. Azoff's Giant Records — Although Azoff's ironically named Giant failed to break into the movie business, it did its share of nineties rock pioneering, giving the world Big Head Todd, Clay Walker, and the biggest act Azoff has broken since the Eagles, the heavy-metal band Metallica. When Azoff formed Revolution Records, Giant became a more exclusively country-oriented label. In 1998 Revolution signed Brian Wilson to a solo recording contract.

EPILOGUE

p. 254. Rock and Roll Hall of Fame — The nominees for 1998 were the Eagles, Fleetwood Mac, the Stooges, Santana, the Mamas and the Papas, Dusty Springfield, Del Shannon, Gene Vincent, Joe Tex, Gene Pitney, the Moonglows, Solomon Burke, Lloyd Price, Billy Joel, and Earth, Wind and Fire. Of these, the most notable name not admitted was inveterate East Coast rocker Billy Joel. The rules for induction state that acts become eligible for the hall twenty-five years after their first recording is released. Along with the Eagles, rock acts inducted in January 1998 were Fleetwood Mac, Santana, the Mamas and the Papas, Lloyd Price, and Gene Vincent. Songwriter and producer Allen Toussaint and jazz composer Jelly Roll Morton were also admitted. One hundred tickets to the ceremony were offered to the public, with prices ranging from $1,200 to $2,000 per person, which included cocktails and dinner.

All speeches quoted were obtained from an unedited videotape of the Eagles' acceptance speeches, provided to the author by the Eagles and Irving Azoff.

pp. 255–256. "There's still . . ." — Henley, interview with Eliot.

DISCOGRAPHY

Compiled by Marc Eliot

Primary source materials include author's (Eliot's) record, tape, and CD collection, *The Rolling Stone Record Guide*, A-1 Record Finders, Tower computers, Virgin computers, *Wasted Times* (Eagles fan club newsletter), Record Surplus, *The Schwann Guide to Rock, All Music Guide to Rock* (Miller Freeman Books, 1995 edition), *Encyclopedia of Rock Stars* (Dafydd Rees Luke Crampton 1996), the *All Music Guide* on the Internet, "The Last Resort" Eagles home page, *Desperado* home page, plus other related artist and information home pages. Although I have attempted to be as complete as possible, there are some catalog and serial numbers that proved unattainable. Also, I have chosen to highlight and detail those recordings by the individual members of the Eagles I determined were noteworthy because of their importance, entertainment value, commercial success, accessibility, and relevance to the overall body of work. All code numbers and release dates are for the original recordings and original formats, either 45 rpm, LP, cassette, or CD, unless, in certain instances, otherwise noted.

ALBUMS RECORDED BY THE EAGLES

EAGLES
Original Release Date: June 1, 1972
Elektra / Asylum Records (WEA International)
Produced and Engineered by Glyn Johns at Olympic Sound Studios, London
Direction: The Geffen Roberts Co.
Mastering: The Mastering Lab, Los Angeles
(CD version mastering by Barry Diament, Atlantic Studios)

Songs
Take It Easy
Written by Jackson Browne, Glenn Frey
Witchy Woman
Written by Don Henley, Bernie Leadon

Chug All Night
> Written by Glenn Frey

Most of Us Are Sad
> Written by Glenn Frey

Nightingale
> Written by Jackson Browne

Train Leaves Here This Morning
> Written by Gene Clark, Bernie Leadon

Take the Devil
> Written by Randy Meisner

Earlybird
> Written by Bernie Leadon and Randy Meisner

Peaceful Easy Feeling
> Written by Jack Tempchin

Tryin'
> Written by Randy Meisner

DESPERADO

Original release date: April 17, 1973
Elektra / Asylum Records, a Division of Warner Communications, Inc.
Produced by Glyn Johns
Recorded at Island Studios, London
Engineer: Glyn Johns. Assistant: Howard Kilgour
LP mastered at: The Mastering Lab, Hollywood
CD mastering by Barry Diament, Atlantic Studios
String Arrangements: Jim Ed Norman

Songs

Doolin-Dalton
> Written by Glenn Frey, J. D. Souther, Don Henley, Jackson Browne

Twenty-One
> Written by Bernie Leadon

Out of Control
> Written by Don Henley, Glenn Frey, Tom Nixon

Tequila Sunrise
> Written by Don Henley, Glenn Frey

Desperado
> Written by Don Henley, Glenn Frey

Certain Kind of Fool
> Written by Randy Meisner, Don Henley, Glenn Frey

Doolin-Dalton (instrumental)
> Written by Glenn Frey, J. D. Souther, Don Henley, Jackson Browne

Outlaw Man
    Written by David Blue
Saturday Night
    Written by Randy Meisner, Don Henley, Glenn Frey, Bernie Leadon
Bitter Creek
    Written by Bernie Leadon
Doolin-Dalton / Desperado (Reprise)
    Written by Glenn Frey, J. D. Souther, Don Henley, Jackson Browne

ON THE BORDER
Original Release Date: March 22, 1974
Elektra / Asylum Records, a Division of Warner Communications, Inc.
Produced and Engineered by Bill Szymczyk for Pandora Productions Ltd.
Assisted by Allan Blazek and Gary Ladinsky
Recorded at The Record Plant, Los Angeles
"You Never Cry Like a Lover" and "Best of My Love" produced and engineered by
Glyn Johns, assisted by Rod Thaer, recorded at Olympic Studios, London
Remix Engineer: Bill Szymczyk

Songs
Already Gone
    Written by Jack Tempchin and Bob Strandlund
    Lead vocal: Glenn Frey
    Solo guitars: Glenn Frey and Don Felder
You Never Cry Like a Lover
    Written by J. D. Souther and Don Henley
    Lead vocal: Don Henley
Midnight Flyer
    Written by P. Craft
    Lead vocal: Randy Meisner
    Slide guitar: Glenn Frey
My Man
    Written by Bernie Leadon
    Lead vocal: Bernie Leadon
    Pedal steel guitar: Bernie Leadon
On the Border
    Written by Don Henley, Bernie Leadon and Glenn Frey
    Lead vocal: Don Henley
James Dean
    Written by Jackson Browne, Glenn Frey, J. D. Souther and Don Henley
    Lead vocal: Glenn Frey
    Solo guitars: Bernie Leadon

313

Ol' 55
> Written by Tom Waits
> Lead vocals: Glenn Frey and Don Henley
> Pedal steel guitar: Al Perkins

Is It True?
> Written by Randy Meisner
> Lead vocal: Randy Meisner
> Slide guitar: Glenn Frey

Good Day in Hell
> Written by Don Henley and Glenn Frey
> Lead vocals: Glenn Frey and Don Henley
> Slide guitar: Don Felder

The Best of My Love
> Written by Don Henley, Glenn Frey, J. D. Souther
> Lead vocal: Don Henley
> Pedal steel guitar: Bernie Leadon

ONE OF THESE NIGHTS

Origin release date: June 28, 1975
Asylum 7E 1039
Produced by Bill Szymczyk for Pandora Productions Ltd.
Engineered by Bill Szymczyk and Allan Blazek with Ed Mashal, Don Wood, Michael Braunstein and Michael Verdick
Recorded at Mac Emmerman's Criteria Studios, Miami, and The Record Plant, Los Angeles
Strings arranged and conducted by Jim Ed Norman

Songs

One of These Nights
> Written by Don Henley and Glenn Frey
> Lead vocal: Don Henley
> Lead guitar: Don Felder

Too Many Hands
> Written by Randy Meisner and Don Felder
> Lead vocal: Randy Meisner
> Lead guitars: Don Felder and Glenn Frey
> Tablas: Don Henley

Hollywood Waltz
> Written by Bernie Leadon, Tom Leadon, Don Henley and Glenn Frey
> Lead vocal: Don Henley
> Mandolin and steel: Bernie Leadon
> Harmonium: Glenn Frey
> Synthesizer: Albhy Galuten

Journey of the Sorcerer
>Written by Bernie Leadon
>Fiddles: David Bromberg
>Strings by The Royal Martian Orchestra
>Recorded "In Root"

Lyin' Eyes
>Written by Don Henley and Glenn Frey
>Lead vocal: Glenn Frey
>Lead guitar: Bernie Leadon
>Piano: Jim Ed Norman

Take It to the Limit
>Written by Randy Meisner, Don Henley and Glenn Frey
>Lead vocal: Randy Meisner
>Piano: Jim Ed Norman

Visions
>Written by Don Felder and Don Henley
>Lead vocal: Don Felder
>Lead guitar: Don Felder

After the Thrill Is Gone
>Written by Don Henley and Glenn Frey
>Lead vocals: Glenn Frey and Don Henley
>Lead guitar: Don Felder

I Wish You Peace
>Written by Patti Davis and Bernie Leadon
>Lead vocal: Bernie Leadon
>Lead guitar: Bernie Leadon

EAGLES — THEIR GREATEST HITS 1971–1975
Original release date March 6, 1976
Elektra / Asylum / Nonesuch Records, 6E-1052
A division of Warner Communications, Inc.
Some songs produced by Glyn Johns for Interglobal Records, all other songs produced by
Bill Szymczyk for Pandora Productions Ltd.

Songs
Take It Easy
>Written by Jackson Brown and Glenn Frey
>Produced by Glyn Johns

Witchy Woman
>Written by Don Henley and Bernie Leadon
>Produced by Glyn Johns

Lyin' Eyes
> Written by Don Henley and Glenn Frey
> Produced by Bill Szymczyk

Already Gone
> Written by Jack Tempchin and R. Strandlund
> Produced by Bill Szymczyk

Desperado
> Written by Don Henley and Glenn Frey
> Produced by Glyn Johns

One of These Nights
> Written by Don Henley and Glenn Frey
> Produced by Bill Szymczyk

Tequila Sunrise
> Written by Don Henley and Glenn Frey
> Produced by Glyn Johns

Take It to the Limit
> Written by Randy Meisner, Don Henley and Glenn Frey
> Produced by Glyn Johns

Peaceful Easy Feeling
> Written by Jack Tempchin
> Produced by Glyn Johns

The Best of My Love
> Written by Don Henley, Glenn Frey and J. D. Souther
> Produced by Glyn Johns

HOTEL CALIFORNIA

Original release date: December 25, 1976
Asylum Records — 6E103
1976 Elektra / Asylum / Nonesuch Records, Los Angeles, California. A division of Warner Communications, Inc.
Produced by Bill Szymczyk for Pandora Productions Ltd.
Engineered by Bill Szymczyk, Allan Blazek, Ed Mashal and Bruce Hensal
Recorded at Criteria Studios, Miami and the Record Plant, Los Angeles
Mixed by Bill Szymczyk in Miami
Mastered at Sterling Graphics by Kosh

Songs

Hotel California
> Written by Don Felder, Don Henley and Glenn Frey
> Lead vocals: Don Henley
> Guitar solos: Don Felder and Joe Walsh
> Percussion: Don Henley

New Kid in Town
> Written by John David Souther, Don Henley and Glenn Frey
> Lead vocal: Glenn Frey
> Guitar one: Randy Meisner
> Electric guitars: Don Felder
> Electric piano and organ: Joe Walsh

Life in the Fast Lane
> Written by Joe Walsh, Don Henley and Glenn Frey
> Lead vocal: Don Henley
> Lead guitar: Joe Walsh
> Clavinet: Glenn Frey

Wasted Time
> Written by Don Henley and Glenn Frey
> Lead vocal: Don Henley
> Piano: Glenn Frey
> Organ: Joe Walsh
> Guitar: Don Felder

Wasted Time (Reprise)
> Written by Don Henley, Glenn Frey and Jim Ed Norman
> Strings arranged and conducted by Jim Ed Norman

Victim of Love
> Written by Don Felder, John David Souther, Don Henley and Glenn Frey
> Lead vocal: Don Henley
> Slide guitar: Joe Walsh
> Lead guitar: Don Felder

Pretty Maids All in a Row
> Written by Joe Walsh and Joe Vitale
> Lead vocal: Joe Walsh
> Piano: Joe Walsh
> Synthesizer: Joe Walsh and Glenn Frey

Try and Love Again
> Written by Randy Meisner
> Lead vocal: Randy Meisner
> Lead guitar: Glenn Frey
> Gretsch guitar: Joe Walsh

The Last Resort
> Written by Don Henley and Glenn Frey
> Lead vocal: Don Henley
> Synthesizer: Joe Walsh and Don Henley
> Pedal steel guitar: Don Felder

THE LONG RUN
Original release date: October 20, 1979
Asylum 5E-508
Elektra / Asylum Records. A Division of Warner Communications
Produced by Bill Szymczyk for Pandora Productions Ltd.
Engineered by Bill Szymczyk and Ed "Radar" Mashal
Recorded at Bayshore Recording Studio, Coconut Grove, Florida
Engineering assistants: Dave Crowther and John Swain

Additional recording at: One Step Up Recording Studio, Los Angeles, CA
Engineering assistants: Mark Curry, Bob Stringer, Dan Everhart
Love 'n' Comfort Recording Studio, Los Angeles, California
Assistant Engineer: Bob Winder
Brittania Recording Studio, Los Angeles, California
The Record Plant, Los Angeles, California
Assistant Engineer: Phil Jamtass

Mixed at Bayshore Recording by Bill Szymczyk
Disc mastering by Ted Jensen, Sterling Sound, New York City

Songs
The Long Run
> (Cass County Music / Red Cloud Music ASCAP)
> Written by Don Henley and Glen Frey
> Lead vocal by Don Henley
> Slide guitar by Joe Walsh
> Organ by Don Felder

I Can't Tell You Why
> (Jeddrah Music / Cass County Music / Red Cloud Music — ASCAP)
> Written by Timothy B. Schmit, Don Henley and Glenn Frey
> Lead vocal by Timothy B. Schmit
> Guitar solos by Glenn Frey

In the City
> (Wow & Flutter Music — ASCAP)
> Written by Joe Walsh and Barry De Vorzon
> Lead vocal by Joe Walsh
> Slide guitar by Joe Walsh

The Disco Strangler
> (Fingers Music / Cass County Music / Red Cloud Music — ASCAP)
> Written by Don Felder, Don Henley and Glenn Frey
> Lead vocal by Don Henley

King of Hollywood

  (Cass County Music / Red Cloud Music — ASCAP)

  Written by Don Henley and Glenn Frey

  Lead vocals by Don Henley and Glenn Frey

  First guitar solo by Glenn Frey

  Second guitar solo by Don Felder

  End guitar solo by Joe Walsh

Heartache Tonight

  (Cass County Music / Red Cloud Music / Gear Publishing Co. / Ice Age Music)

  Written by Don Henley, Glenn Frey, Bob Seger and J. D. Souther

  Lead vocal by Glenn Frey

  Slide guitar by Joe Walsh

Those Shoes

  (Fingers Music / Cass County Music / Red Cloud Music — ASCAP)

  Written by Don Felder, Don Henley and Glenn Frey

  Lead vocal by Don Henley

  Talk box guitars by Joe Walsh and Don Felder

  Solo by Joe Walsh

Teenage Jail

  (Cass County Music / Red Cloud Music / Ice Age Music)

  Written by Don Henley, Glenn Frey and J. D. Souther

  Lead vocals by Glenn Frey and Don Henley

  Synthesizer solo by Glenn Frey

  Guitar solo by Don Felder

The Greeks Don't Want No Freaks

  (Cass County Music / Red Cloud Music — ASCAP)

  Written by Don Henley and Glenn Frey

  Lead vocal by Don Henley

  Background vocals by "The Monstertones" featuring Jimmy Buffett

The Sad Café

  (Cass County Music / Red Cloud Music / Wow & Flutter Music / Ice Age Music — ASCAP)

  Written by Don Henley, Glenn Frey, Joe Walsh and J. D. Souther

  Lead vocal by Don Henley

  Guitar solo by Don Felder

  Alto saxophone by David Sanborn

  (This song is dedicated to the memory of John Barrick) [on liner notes]

EAGLES LIVE

Original release date: November 29, 1980

Elektra / Asylum Records. BB-705. A division of Warner Communications, Inc.

Produced by Bill Szymczyk for Pandora Productions Ltd. Engineered by Bill Szymczyk,

319

Allan Blazek, Billy Youdelman, Buddy Thornton, Biff Dawes and Kelly Kotera
Assistant Engineers: Jay Parti, Phil MacConnell, Dennis Mays and Jimmy Patterson
Strings arranged and conducted by Jim Ed Norman
Remote Recording at the Santa Monica Civic Auditorium and Long Beach Arena by
Wally Heider Recording and at The Forum by The Record Plant, LA
Mixed by Bill Szymczyk at Bayshore Recording Studio, Coconut Grove, Florida
Mastering by Ted Jensen, Sterling Sound, NYC
Engineering note: The close-out groove on Side Four is not effective

Additional musicians:
J. D. Souther — Vocals and acoustic guitar
Joe Vitale — Piano, organ, drums and percussion
Phil Kenzie — Saxophone
Vince Melamed — Electric piano
Jage Jackson — Rhythm guitar, percussion

Songs
Hotel California
    Recorded July 29, 1980 at the Santa Monica Civic Auditorium
Heartache Tonight
    July 27, 1980, Santa Monica Civic
I Can't Tell You Why
    July 28, 1980, Santa Monica Civic
The Long Run
    July 27, Santa Monica Civic
New Kid in Town
    October 22, 1976, The Forum, Los Angeles
Life's Been Good
    July 29, Santa Monica Civic
Seven Bridges Road
    July 28, Santa Monica Civic
Wasted Time
    October 22, 1976, The Forum
Take It to the Limit
    October 20, 1976, The Forum
Doolin-Dalton (Reprise II)
    October 21, 1976, The Forum
Desperado
    October 21, The Forum
Saturday Night
    July 28, 1980, Santa Monica Civic

Life in the Fast Lane
    July 27, 1980, Santa Monica Civic
All Night Long
    July 31, 1980, Long Beach Arena
Take It Easy
    July 27, Santa Monica Civic

EAGLES GREATEST HITS VOLUME 2
Original release date: December 1, 1982
Asylum 960205-1.
Various producers, all cuts previously released.

Songs
Hotel California
Heartache Tonight
Seven Bridges Road
Victim of Love
The Sad Café
Life in the Fast Lane
I Can't Tell You Why
New Kid in Town
The Long Run
After the Thrill Is Gone

HELL FREEZES OVER
Original release date: November 1, 1994
Copyright 1994 Eagles Recording Co. Copyright 1994 Geffen Records, Inc.
Produced by the Eagles with Elliot Scheiner and Rob Jacobs
"Learn to Be Still" produced by the Eagles with Stan Lynch and Rob Jacobs
Live tracks recorded and mixed by Elliot Scheiner
Studio tracks recorded and mixed by Rob Jacobs
Horn and string arrangements by the Eagles, Jay Oliver and Don Davis
Second Engineers: Tom Winslow, Barry Goldberg, Ken Villeneuve, Carl Glanville, Andy Grassi, Charlie Bouis, Tom Trafalski
Studio tracks recorded at The Village Recorder, Los Angeles; Sounds Interchange, Toronto
Mixed at The Village Recorder and A&M Recording Studios, Los Angeles; Hit Factory, New York City
Live Recording Coordinator: David Hewitt
Guitar Techs: Chris Buttleman, Mike Harlow, Tony LaCroix, Todd Bowie
Drum Tech: Gary Grimm
Keyboard Techs: Bill Lanham, Mike Rodriguez

Live tracks recorded at Warner Burbank Studios with Le Mobile
House mixer at Warner Burbank: Dave Kob
Monitor mixer at Warner Burbank: Dave Reynolds
Edited and mastered by Ted Jensen at Sterling Sound, New York City

Executive producer: Joel Stillerman
Program producer: Carol Donovan
Program director: Beth McCarthy
Program line producer: Audrey Johns
An MTV Production

Don Felder: guitars, vocals
Glenn Frey: guitars, piano, keyboards, vocals
Don Henley: drums, percussion, vocals
Timothy B. Schmit: bass, vocals
Joe Walsh: guitars, organ, vocals

Additional musicians:
John Corey: keyboards, guitar, vocals
Scott Crago: percussion, drums
Timothy Drury: keyboards, vocals
Stan Lynch: percussion
Jay Oliver: keyboards
Paulinho DaCosta: percussion
Gary Grimm: percussion

Songs
Get Over It
    Written by Don Henley and Glenn Frey in 1994
Love Will Keep Us Alive
    Written by Pete Vale, Jim Capaldi and Paul Carrack in 1994
The Girl From Yesterday
    Written by Glenn Frey and Jack Tempchin in 1994
Learn to Be Still
    Written by Don Henley and Stan Lynch in 1994
Tequila Sunrise
    Written by Don Henley and Glenn Frey in 1973
Hotel California
    Written by Don Henley, Glenn Frey and Don Felder in 1976
Wasted Time
    Written by Don Henley and Glenn Frey in 1976
Pretty Maids All in a Row
    Written by Joe Walsh and Joe Vitale in 1976

I Can't Tell You Why
Written by Don Henley, Glenn Frey, and Timothy B. Schmit in 1979
New York Minute
Written by Don Henley, Danny Kortchmar and Jai Winding in 1989
The Last Resort
Written by Don Henley and Glenn Frey in 1976
Take It Easy
Written by Jackson Browne and Glenn Frey in 1972
In the City
Written by Joe Walsh and Barry DeVorzon in 1979
Life in the Fast Lane
Written by Don Henley, Glenn Frey and Joe Walsh in 1976
Desperado
Written by Don Henley and Glenn Frey in 1973

SINGLES RELEASED BY THE EAGLES

(Asterisk denotes number one single)

Take It Easy b/w *Get You in the Mood*
Release date: June 24, 1972
Peak position: 12
Weeks originally charted (in *Billboard*'s Top 40): 8
Asylum 11005
Witchy Woman b/w *Early Bird*
Release date: September 30, 1972
Peak position: 9
Weeks originally charted: 10
Asylum 11008
Peaceful Easy Feeling b/w *Tryin'*
Release date: February 3, 1973
Peak position: 22
Weeks originally charted: 6
Asylum 11013
Tequlia Sunrise b/w *Twenty-One*
Release date: April 17, 1973
Asylum
Outlaw Man b/w *Certain Kind of Fool*
Release date: August 6, 1973
Asylum
James Dean b/w *Good Day in Hell*
Release date: August 14, 1974
Asylum

323

Already Gone b / w *Is It True?*
    Release date: June 22, 1974
    Peak position: 32
    Weeks originally charted: 3
    Asylum 11036
*Best of My Love b / w *Ol' 55*
    Release date: December 28, 1974
    Peak position: 1
    Weeks originally charted: 14
    Asylum 45218
*One of These Nights b / w *Visions*
    Release date: June 14, 1975
    Peak positlon: 1
    Weeks originally charted: 14
    Asylum 45257
Lyin' Eyes b / w *Too Many Hands*
    Release date: September 27, 1975
    Peak position: 2
    Weeks originally charted: 11
    Asylum 45279
Take It to the Limit b / w *After the Thrill Is Gone*
    Release date: January 17, 1976
    Peak position: 4
    Weeks originally charted: 14
    Asylum 45293
*New Kid in Town b / w *Victim of Love*
    Release date: December 25, 1976
    Peak position: 1
    Weeks originally charted: 13
    Asylum 45373
*Hotel California b / w *Pretty Maids All in a Row*
    Release date: March 12, 1977
    Peak position: 1
    Weeks originally charted: 15
    Asylum 45286
Life in the Fast Lane b / w *The Last Resort*
    Release date: May 28, 1977
    Peak position: 11
    Weeks originally charted: 11
    Asylum 45403
Please Come Home for Christmas b / w *Funky New Year*
    Release date: December 23, 1978

Peak position: 18
Weeks originally charted: 5
Asylum 45555

Heartache Tonight b/w *Teenage Jail*
Release date: October 13, 1979
Peak position: 1
Weeks originally charted: 13
Asylum 46545

The Long Run b/w *The Disco Strangler*
Release date: December 8, 1979
Peak position: 8
Weeks originally charted: 12
Asylum 46569

I Can't Tell You Why b/w *The Greeks Don't Want No Freaks*
Release date: March 1, 1980
Peak position: 8
Weeks originally charted: 12
Asylum 46608

Lyin' Eyes b/w *Lookin' for Love* by Johnny Lee
Urban Cowboy sound track version
Released October 13, 1980
Asylum 47073

Seven Bridges Road b/w *The Long Run*
Release date: January 1, 1981
Peak position: 21
Weeks originally charted: 7
Asylum 47100

Get Over It b/w *Get Over It* (Live)
Release date: November, 1994
Geffen 21966

Learn to Be Still b/w *Hotel California* (Live) and *Wasted Time* (Live)
Release date: 1995
Geffen 21980

Love Will Keep Us Alive b/w *New York Minute* (Live) b/w *Help Me Through The Night* (Live)
Release date: 1985
Geffen 21980

Hotel California b/w *New Kid in Town*
Rerelease 1996
Elektra "CD Backtrax" series #45085-2

SOLO ALBUMS AND OTHER NON-EAGLES RECORDINGS

DON HENLEY — SOLO ALBUMS

I CAN'T STAND STILL
Asylum E1 60048 (CD 960048-2) — 1982
Produced by Don Henley, Danny Kortchmar and Greg Ladanyi
Recorded and mixed by Greg Ladanyi
Engineering assistants: Jamie Ledner, Niko Bolas, Wayne Tanouye
Additional engineering: Niko Bolas, Jim Nipar
Recorded and mixed at Record One, Sherman Oaks, California
Disc mastering by Doug Sax and Mike Reese of the Mastering Lab, Los Angeles

Songs
I Can't Stand Still
> Written by Don Henley and Danny Kortchmar
> Danny Kortchmar: Guitars and keyboards
> Rob Glaub: Bass
> Don Henley: Drums
> Max Gronenthal, Timothy B. Schmit, Don Henley: Harmony vocals

You Better Hang Up
> Written by Danny Kortchmar
> Danny Kortchmar: Electric guitar
> Steve Lukather: Electric guitar
> Bob Glaub: Bass
> Don Henley: Drums
> Jeff Porcaro: Drums and maracas
> John David Souther and Timothy B. Schmit: Harmony vocals

Long Way Home
> Written by Don Henley and Danny Kortchrnar
> Ben Tench: Keyboards
> Danny Kortchmar: Baritone guitar
> John David Souther: Acoustic guitar
> Lee Sklar: Bass
> Jeff Porcaro: Drums
> Steve Foreman: Percussion
> Don Henley, Timothy B. Schmit: Background vocals

Nobody's Business
> Written by Don Henley, Bob Seger and John David Souther
> Danny Kortchmar: Electric guitar
> Waddy Wachtel: Electric guitar
> Ben Tench: Keyboards

Timothy B. Schmit: Bass

Russ Kunkel: Drums

John David Souther: Acoustic guitar

Talking to the Moon

Written by Don Henley and John David Souther

Ben Tench: Piano

Garth Hudson: Synthesizer

Steve Porcaro: Synthesizer

Danny Kortchmar: Electric guitar

Steve Lukather: Acoustic guitar

Kenny Edwards: Bass

Jeff Porcaro: Drums

Dirty Laundry

Written by Don Henley and Danny Kortchmar

Steve Porcaro: Keyboards, special keyboard effects

Danny Kortchmar: Rhythm guitar

Joe Walsh: 1st guitar solo

Steve Lukather: 2nd guitar solo

Jeff Porcaro: Drums

Roger Linn: Special effects

George Gruel, Timothy B. Schmit, Danny Kortchmar and Don Henley:
Background vocals

Johnny Can't Read

Written by Don Henley and Danny Kortchmar

Andrew Gold: Keyboards

Kenny Edwards: Electric guitar

Danny Kortchmar: Baritone guitar

Bob Glaub: Bass

Mark T. Williams: Drums

Maren Jensen and Louise Goffin: Harmony vocals

Them and Us

Written by Don Henley and Danny Kortchmar

Danny Kortchmar: Electric guitar

Kenny Edwards: Bass

Don Henley: Drums

Warren Zevon: Harmony vocals

La Eile

Original arrangement by Paddy Maloney

Paddy Maloney: Tin whistle

Derek Bell: Harp

(*La Eile* is Gaelic for "Another Day")

Lilah

> Written by Don Henley and Danny Kortchmar
> Danny Kortchmar: Electric guitar
> John David Souther: Acoustic guitar
> WaddyWachtel: Slide guitar
> Paddy Maloney: Uilleann pipes
> Ben Tench: Piano
> Lee Sklar: Bass
> Don Henley: Drums

The Unclouded Day

> Written by J. K. Alwood and J. F. Kinsey
> Arranged by Don Henley and Danny Kortchmar
> Waddy Wachtel: Electric guitar
> Danny Kortchmar: Baritone guitar
> Ben Tench: Keyboards
> Bob Glaub: Bass
> Ian Wallace: Drums
> Ras Baboo: Timbales and percussion
> Bill Withers: Harmony vocals

BUILDING THE PERFECT BEAST

Geffen 24026 — 1984 (original vinyl release)
Produced by Don Henley, Danny Kortchmar and Greg Ladanyi
Recorded and mixed by Greg Ladanyi and Niko Bolas
Additional mixing by Niko Bolas
Additional engineering: Niko Bolas, Richard Bosworth and Tom Knox
Engineering assistants: Richard Bosworth, Duane Seykora, David Schober and Dan Garcia
Recorded at Record One, Sherman Oaks, California

Songs

The Boys of Summer

> Words and music by Don Henley and Mike Campbell
> Guitars, synthesizer and percussion: Mike Campbell
> Synthesizer: Steve Porcaro
> Synthesizer guitar: Danny Kortchmar

You Can't Make Love

> Words and music by Don Henley and Danny Kortchmar
> Guitar: Danny Kortchmar
> Guitar: Lindsey Buckingham
> Keyboards: Ben Tench
> Bass: Pino Palladino

Drums: Don Henley
Harmony vocals: Don Henley, Lindsey Buckingham
Man with a Mission
Words and music by Don Henley, Danny Kortchmar, J. D. Souther
Guitar: Charlie Sexton
Guitar, synthesizer horns: Danny Kortchmar
Drums: Don Henley
Harmony vocals: Belinda Carlisle
You're Not Drinking Enough
Words and music by Danny Kortchmar
Organ, omnichord, guitar: Danny Kortchmar
Piano: David Paich
Synthesizer: Steve Porcaro
Bass: Tim Drummond
Drums: Don Henley
Harmony vocals: Sam Moore
Not Enough Love in the World
Words and music by Don Henley, Danny Kortchmar and Ben Tench
Guitars: Danny Kortchmar
Keyboards: Ben Tench
Keyboards, harmony vocals, percussion: Don Henley
Bass: Tim Drummond
Drums: Ian Wallace
Building the Perfect Beast
Words and music by Don Henley and Danny Kortchmar
Guitars, synthesizer, percussion: Danny Kortchmar
Synthesizer, percussion: Don Henley
Synclavier: Albhy Galuten
Programming and sequencing: Mike Boddicker
African drums: Kevin McCormick
Harmony vocals: Patty Smyth
Chants: The Occasionally Perfect Beasts (Martha Davis, Don Henley, Michael
O'Donahue, Carla Olson, Danny Kortchmar, Patty Smyth, John David Souther,
Waddy Wachtel)
All She Wants to Do Is Dance
Words and music by Danny Kortchmar
Synthesizer: David Paich
Guitar: Danny Kortchmar
Drums: Don Henley
Programming: Steve Porcaro
Harmony vocals: Martha Davis, Patty Smyth, Don Henley

329

Sunset Grill
  Words and music by Don Henley, Danny Kortchmar and Ben Tench
  Synthesizers and emulator: Mike Boddicker
  Synthesizers: Ben Tench
  Guitar, synthesizer, guitar (horn) solos: Danny Kortchmar
  Piano solo: David Paich
  Bass: Pino Palladino
  Harmony vocals: Patty Smyth
  Synthesizers arranged by Randy Newman with Mike Boddicker, Ben Tench,
  Don Henley and Danny Kortchmar
  Horns arranged by Jerry Hey
  Horns recorded at Ocean Way Recording Studios by Allen Sides; assisted by Mark Ettel
Drivin' with Your Eyes Closed
  Written by Don Henley, Danny Kortchmar and Stan Lynch
  Guitars, keyboards, bass, percussion: Danny Kortchmar
  Percussion: Don Henley
  "The French Girls": Dominique Mancinelli and Merle Pascale Elfman
Land of the Living
  Words and music by Don Henley and Danny Kortchmar
  Synthesizers, percussion programming: Bill Cuomo
  Guitar, percussion arrangement: Danny Kortchmar
  Bass: Pino Palladino
  Harmony vocals: Patty Smyth, Don Henley

THE END OF THE INNOCENCE:
Geffen 24217 — 1989
Produced by Don Henley and Danny Kortchmar (except "The End of the Innocence" pro-
duced by Don Henley and Bruce Hornsby, "The Last Worthless Evening" produced by Don
Henley, John Corey and Stan Lynch, "Gimme What You Got" produced by Don Henley,
Stan Lynch and John Corey and "The Heart Of The Matter" produced by Mike Campbell,
Don Henley and Danny Kortchmar)
Mixed by Shelly Yakus and Rob Jacobs
Engineered by Shelly Yakus
Assistant Engineer: Brian Scheuble
Additional Engineers: Brian Scheuble, Rob Jacobs, Mark McKenna, Bob Vogt,
Marc Desisto, Eddie King
Additional Assistants: Tom Banghart, Ed Goodreau, Ranall Wine, Randy Staub,
Greg Goldman
Mixing Assistant: Robert "R. J." Jackzko
A&M Tech Squad: Mike Morengell, Jonathan Little, Gary Myerberg, Dale Asamoto,
Fred Bova, Steve Barncard, Gary Mannon, Mark Opie, Lars Lyons, Bob Borbonus

Songs

The End of the Innocence
> Written by Don Henley and B. R. Hornsby
> Bruce Hornsby: Piano, additional keyboards
> Jai Winding: Keyboard bass
> Michael Fisher: Percussion
> Wayne Shorter: Soprano sax solo

How Bad Do You Want It?
> Written by Danny Kortchmar and Stan Lynch
> Danny Kortchmar: Basic track
> Patty Smyth, Valerie Carter: Background harmony vocals

I Will Not Go Quietly
> Written by Don Henley and Danny Kortchmar
> Danny Kortchmar: Basic track, solo guitar
> Waddy Wachtel: Acoustic guitar
> W. Axl Rose: Harmony vocals

The Last Worthless Evening
> Written by Don Henley, John Corey, Stan Lynch
> John Corey: Guitars, keyboards
> Bob Glaub: Bass
> Stan Lynch: Percussion
> Mike Campbell: Additional guitar

New York Minute
> Written by Don Henley, Danny Kortchmar and Jai Winding
> Danny Kortchmar: Keyboards, guitars
> Jai Winding: Keyboards
> Pino Paladino: Bass
> Jeff Porcaro: Drums
> Steve Madaio: Trumpet solo
> David Paich: Piano and strings
> Take 6: Background harmony vocals
> Basic track recorded by Greg Ladanyi at The Complex

Shangri-La
> Written by Danny Kortchmar, Steve Jordan and Don Henley
> Danny Kortchmar: Guitar, keyboards
> Steve Jordan: Wah-wah guitar and drums
> Pino Palladino: Bass
> Jai Winding: Additional keyboard
> Jim Keltner: Additional percussion
> Don Henley: Three-part harmony gospel licks
> Take 6 (background harmony vocals): Don Henley, Ivan Neville, Steve Jordan, Charlie Drayden

Little Tin God
> Written by Don Henley, Danny Kortchmar and J. D. Souther
> Danny Kortchmar: Basic track
> Pino Palladino: Bass
> David Paich: Additional keyboard
> Don Henley: Harmony vocals
> Basic track recorded by Greg Ladanyi at The Complex

Gimme What You Got
> Written by Don Henley, Stan Lynch and John Corey
> John Corey, Stan Lynch: Basic track
> Danny Kortchmar: Lead guitar
> Melissa Etheridge, Edie Brickell: Background harmony vocals

If Dirt Were Dollars
> Written by Don Henley, Danny Kortchmar and J. D. Souther
> Danny Kortchmar: Basic track
> Stan Lynch: Additional percussion
> Sheryl Crow, Don Henley, J. D. Souther: Background vocals
> Basic track recorded by Greg Ladanyi at The Complex

The Heart of the Matter
> Written by Mike Campbell, Don Henley and J. D. Souther
> Mike Campbell: Guitars and keyboards
> Larry Klein: Bass
> Stan Lynch: Drums and percussion
> Julia Waters, Maxine Waters, Carmen Twillie: Background harmony vocals

ACTUAL MILES: HENLEY'S GREATEST HITS
Geffen Records 24834 — 1995
(Production credits for contents same as original releases, except where noted.)

Songs
Dirty Laundry
> from I Can't Stand Still

The Boys of Summer
> from Building the Perfect Beast

All She Wants to Do Is Dance
> from Building the Perfect Beast

Not Enough Love In The World
> from Building the Perfect Beast

Sunset Grill
> from Building the Perfect Beast

The End of the Innocence
> from The End of the Innocence

The Last Worthless Evening
    from **The End of the Innocence**
New York Minute
    from **The End of the Innocence**
I Will Not Go Quietly
    from **The End of the Innocence**
The Heart of the Matter
    from **The End of the Innocence**
The Garden of Allah
    "(A tale in which the Devil visits a large Western city and finds that he has become obsolete)"
    Written by Don Henley, Stan Lynch, John Corey and Paul Gurian, copyright 1995
    Wisteria Music / WB Music Corp / Matanzas Music / Grey Hare Music
    Produced by Don Henley, Stan Lynch and John Corey
    Engineered and mixed by Rob Jacobs
    Additional Engineer: Roger Sommers
    Assistant Engineers: Chad Munsey and Jim Labinski
    Musicians: Vinnie Colaiuta, John Corey, Sheryl Crow, Don Henley, Danny Kortchmar, Stan Lynch, Neil Stubenhaus
You Don't Know Me At All
    Written by Don Henley, Stan Lynch and John Corey, copyright 1995 Wisteria Music / WB Music Corp / Matanzas Music / Grey Hare Music
    Produced by Don Henley, Stan Lynch and John Corey
    Engineered and mixed by Rob Jacobs
    Additional engineering: Roger Sommers
    Assistant Engineer: Krish Sharma
    Musicians: Vinnie Colaiuta, John Corey, Don Henley, Stan Lynch, Timothy B. Schmit, Frank Simes, Mindy Stein, Neil Stubenhaus
Everybody Knows
    Written by Leonard Cohen and Sharon Robinson, copyright 1987 Leonard Cohen
    Stranger Music, Inc., a division of MCA Inc. / Geffen Music, Robinhill Music
    Produced by Don Henley and Stan Lynch
    Recorded and mixed by Rob Jacobs
    Additional engineering: Bill Dooley
    Assistant Engineers: Chad Munsey, Michael W. Douglass, John Aguto and Barry Goldberg
    Production Coordinator: Julie Larson
    Musicians: Scott Crago, Don Henley, Scott Plunkett, Jimmy Rip, Neil Stubenhaus, Ben Tench, Carmen Twillie, Julia Waters, Maxine Waters (Also appeared as part of *Tower of Song*, a compilation tribute album to Leonard Cohen.)

SINGLES

Johnny Can't Read b/w *Long Way Home*
    Asylum 699717 — 1982
Nobody's Business b/w *Long Way Home*
    Asylum 69831 — 1982
Dirty Laundry b/w *Lilah*
    Asylum 69894 — 1982
I Can't Stand Still b/w *Them and Us*
    Asylum 69931 — 1982
The Boys of Summer b/w *A Month of Sundays*
    Geffen 29141 — 1984
All She Wants to Do is Dance
    Geffen 29065 — 1985
Not Enough Love in the World
    Geffen 29012 — 1985
Sunset Grill
    Geffen 28906 — 1985
The End of the Innocence
    Geffen — 1989
The Last Worthless Evening
    Geffen — 1989
How Bad Do You Want It?
    Geffen — 1989
New York Minute
    Geffen — 1989.
New York Minute / Sunset Grill (Live) / *Gimme What You Got*
    Geffen mini-CD — 1989

ADDITIONAL NON-EAGLES RECORDINGS

SHILOH — SHILOH

Amos Records AAS7015 — 1970
Henley's recording debut. Appears with the band. Does lead vocals, plays drums. Michael Bowden: bass, Richard Bowden: guitars, Jim Ed Norman: guitar and keyboards, Al Perkins: guitar, steel guitar.
(Currently out of print, sometimes available on the collector's market in vinyl only.)

Songs

Simple Little Down-Home Rock & Roll Love Song for Rosie
I'm Gone
Left My Gal in the Mountains
It's About Time

Swamp River Country
Railroad Song
Same Old Story
Du Raison
Down on the Farm
God Is Where You Find Him
Jennie (Also released as a single)

Linda Ronstadt — Linda Ronstadt
    Capitol / EMI 80127 — 1972
    Drums and harmonies (as part of "pre-Eagles" Linda Ronstadt backup group)
Windfalls — Rick Roberts
    A&M 4372 — 1972
    Drum, vocals, choir, chorus, harmony
For Everyman — Jackson Browne
    Asylum 5067 — 1973
    Background vocals: "Colors of the Sun"
She Is a Song — Firefall
    1973
    Vocals
Souvenirs — Dan Fogelberg
    Epic EK33137 — 1974
    Vocals and drums: "Better Change"
Late for the Sky — Jackson Browne
    Elektra Entertainment 1017 — 1974
    Harmonies (with Joyce Everson, J. D. Souther, Beth Fitchet, Dan Fogelberg,
    Terry Reid, Doug Haywood and Perry Lindley)
Good Old Boys — Randy Newman
    Reprise MS4-2193 — 1974
    Vocals, vocal backgrounds
So Long, Harry Truman — Danny O'Keefe
    Atlantic / Atco 18125 — 1974
    Vocals: "So Long, Harry Truman," "Covered Wagon"
    Drums: "Steel Guitar"
Heart Like a Wheel — Linda Ronstadt
    Capitol / EMI SW-11358 — 1974
    Drums: "You Can Close Your Eyes"
So What — Joe Walsh
    Dunhill 50171 — 1974
    Background vocals: "Falling Down," "Time Out," "Turn to Stone," "Help Me Through
    the Night"

Trouble in Paradise — Souther-Hillman-Furay Band
    Elektra / Asylum 7E-1036 — 1975
    Background vocals (as part of "The Sons of the Desert" — Henley, Glenn Frey, and
    J. D. Souther): "Somebody Must Be Wrong"
The Pretender — Jackson Browne
    Asylum 107 — 1976
    Vocal harmony: "The Only Child"
Hasten Down the Wind — Linda Ronstadt
    Asylum 7E-1072 — 1976
    Vocal (background): "Hasten Down the Wind"
    Drums
Black Rose — J. D. Souther
    Asylum 7E-1059 — 1976
    Background vocals: "Black Rose"
You Can't Argue with a Sick Mind — Joe Walsh
    ABC 932 — 1976
    Vocals (same cut as 1975, above): "Help Me Through the Night"
Warren Zevon — Warren Zevon
    Asylum 7E-1060 — 1976
    Vocals: "The French Inhaler"
Hard Candy — Ned Doheny
    Columbia 34259 — 1976
    Background vocals
Terence Boylan — Terence Boylan
    Elektra 7E-1091 — 1977
    Vocals: "Where Are You Hiding?"
Nether Lands — Dan Fogelberg
    Full Moon / Epic 34185 — 1977
    Vocals: "Once Upon a Time," "Loose Ends," "Love Gone By"
Little Criminals — Randy Newman
    Warner Bros. K-3079 — 1977
    Vocals: "Rider in the Rain"
Simple Dreams — Linda Ronstadt
    Asylum 7E-1072 — 1977
    Vocals (background): "Blue Bayou"
Twin Sons of Different Mothers — Dan Fogelberg
    Epic EK35339 — 1978
    Vocals: "Tell Me to My Face," "The Power of Gold"
But Seriously Folks . . . — Joe Walsh
    Elektra 141 — 1978
    Vocals: "Tomorrow"

Excitable Boy — Warren Zevon
   Asylum — 1978
   Vocals
Restless Nights — Karla Bonoff
   Columbia CK35799 — 1979
   Vocal backgrounds: "Restless Hearts"
Christopher Cross — Christopher Cross
   Warner Bros. 2-3383 — 1979
   Harmony vocals: "The Light Is On"
You're Only Lonely — John David Souther
   Legacy 36093 — 1979
   Background harmonies
Kid Blue — Louise Goffin
   Asylum 203 — 1979
   Vocals
Suzy — Terence Boylan
   Asylum 6E-201 — 1980
   Vocals: "Ice and Snow," "Did She Finally Get to You?"
21 at 33 — Elton John
   MCA MCAD 31054 — 1980
   Vocals: "White Lady White Powder"
One More Song — Randy Meisner
   Epic 36748 — 1980
   Background vocals
Against the Wind — Bob Seger
   Capitol / EMI 4X-12041 — 1980
   Vocals: "Fire Lake"
For the Working Girl — Melissa Manchester
   Arista 9533 — 1980
   Vocals
Bad Luck Streak in Dancing School — Warren Zevon
   Elektra 60561-2 — 1980
   Background harmonies (with Jackson Browne, J. D. Souther): "Gorilla, You're a Desperado"
   Harmonies (with Glenn Frey): "Wild Age"
Nothing But Time — Blue Steel
   Asylum 308 — 1981
   Vocals: "Nothing But Time"
   (Blue Steel was Richard Bowden's group, in which he played guitar. He gave the band its name, Texan slang for an erection that refuses to go down, based on the stories that followed Bowden on the road.)

The Innocent Age — Dan Fogelberg
Full Moon / Epic E2K-37393 — 1981
Vocals: "The Lion's Share"
Bella Donna — Stevie Nicks
Modern 38193 — 1981
Vocal (duets): "Leather and Lace," "The Highwayman"
Fast Times at Ridgemont High — Sound track
Full Moon 60158 — 1982
Lead vocal, writer with Danny Kortchmar: "Love Rules"
Wild Heart of the Young — Karla Bonoff
Columbia 37444 — 1982
Vocal background: "Personally"
The Envoy — Warren Zevon
Asylum 60159 — 1982
Background vocals
Another Page — Christopher Cross
Warner Bros. 23757 — 1983
Vocals: "Deal 'Em Again," "Nature of the Game"
Trouble in Paradise — Randy Newman
Warner Bros. 23755 — 1983
Vocal backgrounds and harmonies
Tell Me the Truth — Timothy B. Schmit
MCA MCAD 6420 — 1983 (released in 1990)
Producer, background vocals: "Tell Me the Truth"
You Bought It, You Name It — Joe Walsh
Warner Bros. 23884 — 1983
Vocals
Home by Dawn — J. D. Souther
Warner Bros. 25081 — 1984
Vocals, vocal background: "Bad News Travels Fast"
Playing It Cool — Timothy B. Schmit
Asylum 9603591 — 1984
Percussion, drums, vocals, background vocals: "Something's Wrong"
Dog Eat Dog — Joni Mitchell
Geffen 24074 — 1985
Vocals: "Tax Free," "Dog Eat Dog," "Shiny Toys"
That's Why I'm Here — James Taylor
Columbia 40052 — 1985
Vocals
Color of Money — Sound track
MCA MCAD 6189 — 1986
Lead vocal, producer: "Who Owns This Place?"

Like a Rock — Bob Seger
Capitol / EMI 46195 — 1986
Vocal: "Miami"
Vision Quest — Sound track
MCA 6189 — 1986
Producer: "She's on the Zoom"
A Quiet Normal Life: The Best of Warren Zevon — Warren Zevon
Asylum 60503-2 — 1986
Background vocals: "The Envoy"
Sentimental Hygiene — Warren Zevon
Virgin 86012 — 1987
Vocals: "Trouble Waiting to Happen," "Reconsider Me"
Chalk Mark in a Rain Storm — Joni Mitchell
Geffen 24172 — 1988
Vocals: "Lakota," "Snakes and Ladders"
Tell Me the Truth — Timothy B. Schmit
MCA 6420 — 1990 (see 1983)
Timespace: The Best of Stevie Nicks — Stevie Nicks
Modern 91711-2 — 1991
Vocals (duet): "Leather and Lace"
Leap of Faith — Sound track
MCA MCAD 10617 — 1992
Lead vocal: "Sit Down You're Rockin' the Boat"
Patty Smyth — Patty Smyth
MCA 10633 — 1992
Vocals (duet): "Sometimes Love Just Ain't Enough"
Hearts in Armor — Trisha Yearwood
MCA MCAD 10641 — 1992
Vocals (duet): "Walkaway Joe"
Songs for a Dying Planet — Joe Walsh
Epic Associated 4891 — 1992
Vocals
Amused to Death — Roger Waters
Columbia CK-47127 — 1992
Vocals
Get a Grip — Aerosmith
Geffen 24455 — 1993
Vocals: "Amazing"
I'm Alive — Jackson Browne
Elektra Entertainment 61524 — 1993
Backing vocals (with David Crosby): "All Good Things"

Duets — Elton John
    MCA 10926 — 1993
    Vocals: "Shaky Ground"
Suspending Disbelief — Jimmy Webb
    1993
    Vocals
Bluest Eyes — Storyville
    November 1107 — 1994
    Background vocals
Leaving Las Vegas — Sound track
    Pangea 72438 3607129 — 1994
    Lead vocal: "Come Rain or Come Shine"
The MTV Unplugged Collection: Volume One
    Warner Bros. 9 45774-2 — 1994
    "Come Rain or Come Shine" (same as *Leaving Las Vegas*)
Kermit Unpigged
    Jim Henson (label) 15004 — 1995
    Lead vocal: "Being Green"
    (Henley, Linda Ronstadt, Vince Gill and Jimmy Buffett are joined in song by various
    Muppets.)
Dane Donohue — Dane Donohue
    Columbia 34278 — 1995
    Vocal backgrounds
Glenda Griffith — Glenda Griffith
    Ariola 50018 — 1995
    Percussion, drums, vocals, producer
Wave of the Hand — Carla Olson
    Watermelon 1046 — 1995
    Vocal backgrounds, harmonies
Randy Newman's Faust — Randy Newman
    Reprise 9 45672-2 — 1995
    Lead vocal: "Bless the Children of the World," "The Man"
    (Theme album. Cast: Devil: Randy Newman; Lord: James Taylor; Faust: Don Henley;
    Angel Rick: Elton John; Margaret: Linda Ronstadt; Martha: Bonnie Raitt.)
Michael — Sound track
    1996
    Lead vocal: "Through Your Hands" (written by John Hiatt)

GLENN FREY — SOLO ALBUMS

NO FUN ALOUD
Elektra / Asylum E1-60129 — 1982
Produced by Glenn Frey, Allan Blazek and Jim Ed Norman
Engineered by Allan Blazek and Steve Melton
Mixed by Allan Blazek
Recorded at Wilder Bros. Studios and Rudy Records, Los Angeles, Muscle Shoals Sound,
Sheffield, Alabama
Bayshore Recording Studio, Miami
Mixed at Bayshore Recording Studio
Assistant Engineers: Ray Blair, Jay Parti, Mary Beth McLemore, Ben King, George Gomez
and Glenn Frey
Concept by Glenn Frey and Allan Blazek

Songs
I Found Somebody
> Glenn Frey / Jack Tempchin
> Drums: Michael Huey
> Bass: Bryan Garofalo
> Guitar: Josh Leo
> Lead guitar and organ: Glenn Frey
> Synthesizer: David "Hawk" Wolinski
> Tenor sax: Al Garth

The One You Love
> Glenn Frey / Jack Tempchin
> Guitars, electric piano and bass: Glenn Frey
> Saxophone: Ernie Watts, Jim Horn
> Strings arranged by: Jim Ed Norman

Partytown
> Glenn Frey / Jack Tempchin
> Drums: Michael Huey
> Bass: Bob Glaub
> Guitars: Josh Leo
> Lead guitar and piano: Glenn Frey
> Background vocals by the Monstertones, featuring Duane Monstertone, Leon Blazek,
> Freddy Buffett, Urban Azoff, Pee Wee Solters, Marion Kinde, Buckley Wideface,
> Tommy Obnozzio, Jingles Squirrel Heart, Floyd Tempchin, Ollie Blair, Hugh Gotteny,
> Peter Rennert, John McEnroe and Peter Fleming

I Volunteer
> Jack Tempchin / Bill Bodine
> Drums: Michael Huey

Bass: Roberto Piñon
Organ: Hawk
Guitar: Dan Kortchmar
Lead guitar: Glenn Frey
Background vocals: Marcy Levy, Tom Kelly, Bill Champlin and Glenn Frey

I've Been Born Again
Don Davis / James Dean
Drums: Michael Huey
Drums: John Robinson
Bass: Bob Glaub
Guitars and electric piano: Glenn Frey
Percussion: Steve Forman
Horns by: The Heart Attack Horns
Trumpets: Lee Thornburg, John Berry
Saxophones: Bill Bergman, Jim Coile
Baritone: Greg Smith
Horns arranged by: Lee Thomburg and Jim Ed Norman

Sea Cruise
Huey Smith / John Vincent
Drums: Roger Hawkins
Bass: David Hood
Guitar: Duncan Cameron
Piano: Clayton Ivey
Organ: Hawk
Saxophones: Harvey Thompson, Ronnie Eades

That Girl
Glenn Frey / Bob Seger
Drums and bells: Roger Hawkins
Bass: David Hood
Organ: Hawk
Electric guitar: Duncan Cameron
Acoustic guitar: Wayne Perkins
Electric piano: Glenn Frey
Strings arranged by: Jim Ed Norman

All Those Lies
Glenn Frey
Drums: Roger Hawkins
Bass: David Hood
Guitar: Duncan Cameron
Organ and synthesizer: Hawk
Lead guitar and electric piano: Glenn Frey
Background vocals: Oren Waters, Julia Waters and Maxine Waters

She Can't Let Go
    Glenn Frey / Jack Tempchin
    Percussion: Steve Forman
    All other instruments: Glenn Frey
Don't Give Up
    Glenn Frey / Jack Tempchin
    Drums: Michael Huey
    Bass: Bob Glaub
    Synthesizers: Hawk
    Guitars, clavinet, synthesizers: Glenn Frey
    Additional keyboards: Allan Blazek
    Background vocals: Oren Waters, Julia Waters, Maxine Waters and Glenn Frey

THE ALLNIGHTER
MCA 31158 — 1984
Produced by Glenn Frey, Allan Blazek and Barry Beckett
Engineered by Allan Blazak

Songs
The Allnighter
    Glenn Frey / Jack Tempchin
Sexy Girl
    Jack Tempchin / Glenn Frey
I Got Love
    Glenn Frey / Jack Tempchin
Somebody Else
    Hawk Wolinski / Glenn Frey / Jack Tempchin
Lover's Moon
    Jack Tempchin / Glenn Frey
Smuggler's Blues
    Glenn Frey / Jack Tempchin
Let's Go Home
    Glenn Frey / Jack Tempchin
Better in the U.S.A.
    Glenn Frey / Jack Tempchin
Living in Darkness
    Glenn Frey / Jack Tempchin / Hawk Wolinski
New Love
    Jack Tempchin / Glenn Frey

Barry Beckett — Synthesizer, piano: "I Got Love," "Sexy Girl," "Better in the U.S.A."
William Bergman — Saxophone: "Living in Darkness"

Duncan Cameron — Guitars, background vocals

Nick DeCaro — Accordian: "Lover's Moon"

Victor Feldman — Vibes: "Let's Go Home"

Steve Forman — Percussion: "Smuggler's Blues," "Living in Darkness," "The Allnighter"

Glenn Frey — Synthesizer, bass, guitar, piano, drums, keyboards, vocals: various

Roy Galloway — Vocals: "Better in the U.S.A.," "Let's Go Home," "Living in Darkness," "New Love," "Sexy Girl," "Somebody Else"

Bryan Garofalo — Bass: "Let's Go Home," "Living in Darkness," "New Love," "Smuggler's Blues," "The Allnighter"

Al Garth — Saxophone: "Let's Go Home," "Somebody Else"

The Heart Attack Horns — "I Got Love," "Let's Go Home," "Living in Darkness"

David Hood — Bass: "Better in the U.S.A.," "I Got Love"

Michael Huey — Drums: "Let's Go Home," "New Love," "Smuggler's Blues"

Josh Leo — Guitar: "Let's Go Home," "New Love," "Smuggler's Blues"

Larrie Londin — Drums: "Better in the U.S.A.," "I Got Love," "Sexy Girl"

Vince Melamed — Electric piano: "Let's Go Home"

John "J. R." Robinson — Drums: "Somebody Else," "The Allnighter"

Jack Tempchin — Vocals: "Better in the U.S.A.," "Sexy Girl"; Guitar: "Lover's Moon"

Lee Thornburg — Flugelhorns: "New Love"

Luther Waters — Vocals: "Better in the U.S.A.," "Sexy Girl"

Oren Waters — Vocals: "Better in the U.S.A.," "Let's Go Home," "Living in Darkness," "New Love," "Sexy Girl," "Somebody Else"

Hawk Wolinski — Organ: "Let's Go Home," "New Love"; Keyboards: "The Allnighter," "Somebody Else"; Fuzzy guitar: "Somebody Else"; Synthesizer programs: "Living in Darkness," "Somebody Else"

SOUL SEARCHIN'

MCA 6239 — 1988

Produced by Barry Beckett, Glenn Frey, Elliot Scheiner, Hawk Wolinski, James Newton Howard

Engineered by Elliot Scheiner, Ray Blair, Jack Joseph Puig, Dan Garcia, Alec Head, Glen Holguin

Songs

Livin' Right
    Glenn Frey / Jack Tempchin
Some Kind of Blue
    Glenn Frey / Jack Tempchin
True Love
    Glenn Frey / Jack Tempchin
Can't Put Out This Fire
    Glenn Frey / Jack Tempchin

I Did It for Your Love
    Glenn Frey / Jack Tempchin
Let's Pretend We're Still In Love
    Glenn Frey / Jack Tempchin
Soul Searchin'
    Glenn Frey / Jack Tempchin / Duncan Cameron
Working Man
    Glenn Frey / Jack Tempchin
Two Hearts
    Hawk Wolinski / James Newton Howard
It's Your Life
    Glenn Frey / Steven Thoma

Barry Becket — Synthesizer, piano: "Soul Searchin'," "True Love"

William Bergman — Saxophone: "Livin' Right"

Robbie Buchanan — Keyboards: "True Love," "Two Hearts"

Duncan Cameron — Guitar, background vocals: "Soul Searchin'"

Max Carl — Vocals

Dave Chamberlain — Bass: "It's Your Life"

Steve Forman — Percussion: "Can't Put Out This Fire," "I Did It for Your Love," "Livin' Right," "Working Man"

Glenn Frey — Synthesizer, bass, guitar, piano, drums, keyboards, vocals: various

Bruce Gaitsch — Guitar: "Two Hearts"

Roy Galloway — Background vocals: "Let's Pretend We're Still in Love," "Some Kind of Blue," "Soul Searchin'"

Al Garth — Saxophone: "Some Kind of Blue"

Roger Hawkins — Drums: "Soul Searchin'"

The Heart Attack Horns — Horns: various

David Hood — Bass: "Soul Searchin'"

The Institutional Radio Choir — Background vocals: "Soul Searchin'"

Paul Jackson, Jr. — Guitar: "Two Hearts"

Russ Kunkel — Drums: "I Did It for Your Love," "Livin' Right"

Michael Landau — Guitar: "It's Your Life," "Let's Pretend We're Still in Love," "Some Kind of Blue"

Ralph MacDonald — Percussion: "It's Your Life," "Let's Pretend We're Still in Love," "Soul Searchin'," "True Love," "Two Hearts"

Christian Mostert — Saxophone: "True Love," "It's Your Life"

Steve Nathan — Keyboards: "Soul Searchin'"

Prairie Prince — Drums: "It's Your Life"

John "J. R." Robinson — Drums: "Can't Put Out This Fire," "Let's Pretend We're Still in Love," "Some Kind of Blue," "Two Hearts"

Timothy B. Schmit — Background vocals: "Let's Pretend We're Still in Love," "Some Kind of Blue"

Ron Skies — Keyboards: "Can't Put Out This Fire," "I Did It for Your Love," "It's Your Life," "Some Kind of Blue," "Working Man"

Neil Stubenhaus — Bass: "Two Hearts"

Steve Thoma — Keyboards: "It's Your Life," "Soul Searchin'," "Working Man," "Can't Put Out This Fire"

Maxine Willard Waters — Background vocals: "Can't Put Out This Fire," "Soul Searchin'," "True Love"

Julia Tillman Waters — Background vocals: "Can't Put Out This Fire," "Soul Searchin'," "True Love"

Oren Waters — Background vocals: "Soul Searchin' "

Hawk Wolinski — Keyboards: "I Did It for Your Love," "Livin' Right," "Two Hearts," "Working Man"

STRANGE WEATHER — LIVE IN DUBLIN

MCA3P-2469 — 1992 (CD only)
Audio produced by Elliot Scheiner and Glenn Frey
Edited by Denny Diante and Paul Elmore at MCA Recording Studios
(Studio versions of "Strange Weather," "River of Dreams," and "Love in the 21st Century" appear on the Glenn Frey album *Strange Weather* — MCAC-10599 — 1993 — see below.)
All songs taken from Glenn Frey's *Strange Weather — Live in Dublin* MCA Home Video MCAV-10676

Songs

Strange Weather
    Glenn Frey, Jack Tempchin and Jay Oliver
Peaceful Easy Feeling
    Jack Tempchin
New Kid in Town
    J. D. Souther
    (Note individual credit given to Souther, whereas original credit on *Hotel California* is given to Souther, Frey, and Henley.)
River of Dreams
    Glenn Frey and Jack Tempchin
Love in the 21st Century
    Glenn Frey, Jack Tempchin and Danny Kortchmar
The Heat Is On
    Glenn Frey (Listed elsewhere as cowritten by Keith Farsey and Harold Faltermeyer. Frey given solo credit on this CD.)

STRANGE WEATHER
MCA CD 10599 — 1993
Produced by Elliot Scheiner and Glenn Frey
Engineered by Elliot Scheiner and Mike Harlow

Songs
Silent Spring
    Jay Oliver / Glenn Frey
Long Hot Summer
    Glenn Frey / Jack Tempchin / Hawk Wolinski
Strange Weather
    Glenn Frey / Jack Tempchin / Jay Oliver
Aqua Tranquillo
    Glenn Frey
Love in the 21st Century
    Glenn Frey / Jack Tempchin / Danny Kortchmar
He Took Advantage
    Glenn Frey / Jack Tempchin
River of Dreams
    Glenn Frey / Jack Tempchin
I've Got Mine
    Glenn Frey / Jack Tempchin
Rising Sun
    Jay Oliver / Glenn Frey
Brave New World
    Glenn Frey / Jack Tempchin
Delicious
    Glenn Frey / Jack Tempchin
A Walk in the Dark
    Glenn Frey / Jay Oliver
Before the Ship Goes Down
    Glenn Frey / Jack Tempchin
Big Life
    Glenn Frey / Jack Tempchin
Part of Me, Part of You
    Glenn Frey / Jack Tempchin

*Japanese release includes "Ain't It Love"

Kenny Aronoff — Drums: "Part of Me, Part of You"
Rosemary Butler — Background vocals
Valerie Carter — Background vocals

Lenny Castro — Additional percussion
Glenn Frey — Vocals, guitars
Al Garth — Saxophone: "River of Dreams"
Mark Goldenberg — Guitar: "Part of Me, Part of You"
Mike Harlow — Additional programming
The Heart Attack Horns
Robby Kilgore — Additional keyboards
Robert Martin — Background vocals
Chris Mostert — Saxophone: "I've Got Mine"
Jay Oliver
Jerry Scheff — Bass: "Part of Me, Part of You"
Ben Tench — Organ: "Part of Me, Part of You"
Scott Thurston — Piano: "Part of Me, Part of You"

LIVE
MCA CD 10826 — 1993
Produced by Elliot Scheiner and Glenn Frey
Recorded at The Stadium, Dublin, Ireland, July 8, 1992
Engineer: Elliot Scheiner

Songs
Peaceful Easy Feeling
　　Jack Tempchin
New Kid in Town
　　J. D. Souther / Glenn Frey / Don Henley
The One You Love
　　Glenn Frey / Jack Tempchin
Wild Mountain Thyme
　　Bert Jansch
Strange Weather
　　Glenn Frey / Jack Tempchin / Jay Oliver
I've Got Mine
　　Glenn Frey / Jack Tempchin
Lyin' Eyes — Take It Easy (Medley)
　　Don Henley / Glenn Frey & Jackson Browne / Glenn Frey
River of Dreams
　　Glenn Frey / Jack Tempchin
True Love
　　Glenn Frey / Jack Tempchin
Love in the 21st Century
　　Glenn Frey / Jack Tempchin / Danny Kortchmar

Smuggler's Blues
    Glenn Frey / Jack Tempchin
The Heat Is On
    Keith Forsey / Harold Faltermeyer
Heartache Tonight
    Don Henley / Bob Seger / J. D. Souther / Glenn Frey
Desperado
    Don Henley / Glenn Frey

Glenn Frey — Guitars, vocals
Martin Fera — Drums
Bryan Garofalo — Bass, vocals
Al Garth — Saxophone, violin
Danny Grenier — Guitar, vocals
Darrel Leonard — Trumpet
Chris Mostert — Saxophone, percussion
Jay Oliver — Keyboards
Michito Sanchez — Percussion
Barry Sarna — Keyboards, vocals
Duane Sciacqua — Guitar, vocals
Greg Smith — Baritone sax

SOLO COLLECTION (COMPILATION)

MCA CD 11227 — 1995
Producers: Glenn Frey, Elliot Scheiner, Jim Ed Norman, Allan Blazek, Barry Beckett, Keith Forsey, Harold Faltermeyer, Don Was

Songs

(All previously recorded; writing credits as above, except where noted.)
This Way to Happiness
    Glenn Frey / Jay Oliver / Jack Tempchin
Who's Been Sleeping in My Bed
    Bobby Whitlock / Jack Tempchin
Common Ground
    Glenn Frey / Jack Tempchin
Call On Me (Theme from *South of Sunset*)
    Glenn Frey / Jack Tempchin
The One You Love
Sexy Girl
Smuggler's Blues
The Heat Is On

349

You Belong to the City
True Love
Soul Searchin'
Part of Me, Part of You
I've Got Mine
River of Dreams
Rising Sun
Brave New World

Bill Bergman — Horns: "This Way to Happiness," "Who's Been Sleepin' in My Bed"
Scott Crago — Drums: "This Way to Happiness," "Who's Been Sleepin' in My Bed," "Common Ground"
Laura Creamer — Background vocals: "This Way to Happiness"
Glenn Frey — Vocals, guitars, keyboards: "Common Ground"; Bass on "Who's Been Sleepin' in My Bed," "Common Ground," "Call on Me"
Danny Greiner — Guitar: "This Way to Happiness"
Darrell Leonard — Horns: "This Way to Happiness," "Who's Been Sleepin' in My Bed"
Donna McDaniels — Background vocals: "This Way to Happiness"
Chris Mostert — Horns: "This Way to Happiness," "Who's Been Sleepin' in My Bed"
Jay Oliver — Keyboards: "This Way to Happiness"; Drums: "Who's Been Sleepin' in My Bed," "Call Me"
Greg Smith — Horns: "This Way to Happiness," "Who's Been Sleepin' in My Bed"

SINGLES
I Found Somebody b/w *She Can't Let Go*
    Asylum 47466 — 1982
The One You Love
    Asylum 69974 — 1982
All Those Lies
    Asylum — 1982
Sexy Girl
    MCA 52413 — 1984
The Allnighter
    MCA — 1984
The Heat Is On b/w *Shoot Out* (by Harold Faltermeyer)
    MCA 52512 — 1984
Smuggler's Blues
    MCA 52546 — 1985
You Belong to the City
    MCA 52651 — 1985
True Love
    MCA 53363 — 1988

Soul Searchin' b / w *It's Cold in Here*
MCA — 1988
Livin' Right
MCA — 1988
Part of Me, Part of You
MCA — 1991
I've Got Mine
MCA — 1992
River of Dreams
MCA — 1992

ADDITIONAL NON-EAGLES RECORDINGS

LONGBRANCH PENNYWHISTLE — LONGBRANCH PENNYWHISTLE
Amos AAS 7007 — 1969
Buddy Emmons: steel guitar; Doug Kershaw: guitar, vocals; Ry Cooder: guitar;
James Burton: guitar; Glenn Frey: guitar, vocals; Larry Knechtel: piano; Joe Osborn:
bass; J. D. Souther: guitar, vocals

Songs
Jubilee Anne
J. D. Souther
Run Boy, Run
Glenn Frey
Rebecca
Glenn Frey
Lucky Love
J. D. Souther
Kite Woman
J. D. Souther
Bring Back Funky Women
Frey, Souther
Star-Spangled Bus
Mister, Mister
Don't Talk Now
Never Had Enough

(Credits for the last four songs unclear.)

Ramblin' Gamblin' Man — Bob Seger
Capitol ST-172 — 1968
Guitar
Linda Ronstadt — Linda Ronstadt
Capitol / EMI 80172 — 1972

Guitars and occasional harmonies (as part of "pre-Eagles" Linda Ronstadt backup group)

John David Souther — John David Souther
 Asylum 5055 — 1972
 Guitar: "The Fast One"

Nice Baby and the Angel — David Blue
 Asylum — 1973
 Harmony: "Lady 'O Lady"

For Everyman — Jackson Browne
 Asylum 5067 — 1973
 Cowriter: "Take It Easy"
 Harmony: "Red Neck Friend"

Don't Cry Now — Linda Ronstadt
 Asylum 5064 — 1973
 Guitar, cowriter: "Desperado"
 Guitar: "The Fast One"

So What — Joe Walsh
 Dunhill 50171 — 1974
 Background vocals: "Help Me Through the Night," "Turn to Stone"

Souvenirs — Dan Fogelberg
 Epic EK-33137 — 1974
 Vocals: "Someone's Been Telling You Stories"

Good Old Boys — Randy Newman
 Reprise 2193 — 1974
 Vocals, background vocals, guitar: various (unspecified) songs

So Long, Harry Truman — Danny O'Keefe
 Atlantic / Atco 18125 — 1974
 Guitar: "Steel Guitar"

Common Sense — John Prine
 Atlantic 18127 — 1975
 Vocal, vocal backgrounds

Trouble in Paradise — Souther-Hillman-Furay Band
 Elektra / Asylum 7E-1036 — 1975
 Background vocals (as part of "The Sons of the Desert" — Frey, Don Henley, and J. D. Souther): "Somebody Must Be Wrong"

Fool's Gold — Fool's Gold (former backup band for Dan Fogelberg)
 Col PC-34828 — 1976
 Coproducer

Another Passage — Carly Simon
 Elektra 2 1064 — 1976
 Guitar: "Libby"

Black Rose — John David Souther
   Asylum 7E-1059 — 1976
   Guitar: "If You Have Crying Eyes"
   Background vocals: "Black Rose"
You Can't Argue with a Sick Mind — Joe Walsh
   ABC-932 — 1976 (rereleased on MCA CD MCAD 31120)
   Vocals: "Help Me Make It Through the Night"
Warren Zevon — Warren Zevon
   Asylum 7E-1060 — 1976
   Background vocals: "The French Inhaler," "Carmelita"
Karla Bonoff — Karla Bonoff
   Columbia 34672 — 1977
   Vocals: "If He's Ever Near"
Don Juan's Reckless Daughter — Joni Mitchell
   Asylum BB-701 — 1977
   Vocals: "Off Night Back Street"
Little Criminals — Randy Newman
   Warner Bros. K-3079 — 1977
   Guitar, vocals, background vocals: "Short People," "Little Criminals," "Baltimore,"
   "Rider in the Rain"
Randy Meisner — Randy Meisner
   Elektra / Asylum 140 — 1978
   Cowriter (with J. D. Souther): "Bad Man"
   Cowriter (with Randy Meisner and Don Henley), vocals: "Take It to the Limit"
Stranger in Town — Bob Seger
   Digital Compact Classics 1055 — 1978
   Guitar solo: "Til It Shines"
But Seriously Folks . . . — Joe Walsh
   Asylum 6E-141 — 1978
   Harmonies: "Tomorrow," "Theme from Boat Weirdos," "Endless Seas"
You're Only Lonely — John David Souther
   Legacy 36093 — 1979
   Cowriter: "Last in Love"
   Vocal harmonies: "Till the Bars Burn Down"
21 at 33 — Elton John
   MCA 31054 — 1980
   Background vocals: "White Lady White Powder"
Hits! — Boz Scaggs
   Columbia 36841 — 1980
   Background vocals: "Look What You've Done to Me" (Also appears on *Urban Cowboy*
   original sound track — Elektra 60690)

Against the Wind — Bob Seger
 Capitol / EMI 4X-12041 — 1980
 Background vocals: "Fire Lake," "Against the Wind"
Bad Luck Streak in Dancing School — Warren Zevon
 Elektra 60561-2 — 1980
 Harmonies: "Bill Lee"
 Background vocals (with Don Henley): "Wild Age"
Old Enough — Lou Ann Barton
 Antone's 21 — 1982
 Producer, guitar, vocals
The Distance — Bob Seger
 Capitol / EMI C2-46005 — 1982
 Harmonies, guitar: "Shame on the Moon"
Last Mango in Paris — Jimmy Buffett
 MCA MCAD 31157 — 1985
 Guitar, vocal backgrounds
Miami Vice — Sound track
 MCA 6150 — 1985
 Songs: "You Belong to the City," "Smuggler's Blues"
Ghostbusters 2 — Sound track
 MCA MCAD 6306 — 1989
 Producer: "Flip City"
Beverly Hills Cop — Sound track
 MCA 10239 — 1991
 Song: "The Heat Is On"
Thelma and Louise — Sound track
 MCA 10239 — 1991
 Song: "Part of You, Part of Me"
Reminiscing: The Little River Band — The Little River Band
 CEMA 9530 — 1992
 Vocal: "Lonesome Loser"
Great Days: John Prine Anthology — John Prine
 Rhino 71400 — 1993
 Vocals: various
After the Rain (Also known as *Lonely Midnight*) — Jack Tempchin
 Night River 1001 — 1993
 (Participation undefined)
Billboard Top Hits '85
 Rhino R2-71640 — 1994
 Song: "The Heat Is On"

Billboard Top Hits '86
    Rhino R271641 — 1994
    Song: "Addicted to Love"
Frat Rock 80's
    Rhino 72133 — 1995
    Song: "The Heat Is On"
Soundtrack Smashes — The '80s
    MCA 6330 — 1995
    Song: "The Heat Is On"
Look What I Did! — Joe Walsh
    MCA 11233 — 1995
    Vocals: "Ordinary Average Guy"

RANDY MEISNER — SOLO ALBUMS

RANDY MEISNER
Elektra / Asylum
Elektra LP 140 — 1978. Rerelease on CD 4142 (Japan only)
Produced by Alan Brackett

Songs
Bad Man
    J. D. Souther / Glenn Frey
Daughter of the Sky
    Bill Lamb
It Hurts to Be in Love
    R. Toombs / J. Dixon
Save the Last Dance for Me
    Doc Pomus / M. Shuman
Please Be with Me
    S. Boyer
Take It to the Limit
    Randy Meisner / Don Henley / Frey
Lonesome Cowgirl
    Alan Brackett / J. Merrill
Too Many Lovers
    Lamb
If You Wanna Be Happy
    F. Guida / C. Guida / J. Royster
I Really Want You Here Tonight
    Brackett

Every Other Day
    Lamb
Heartsong
    B. Martin

Additional musicians: Byron Berline: fiddle; Alan Brackett: background vocals, Marxaphone; David Cassidy: background vocals; Steve Edwards: guitars, dobro; Victor Felman: percussion; Joh Hobbs: piano, organ, electric piano; Tita Kerpan: background vocals; Bill Lamp: background vocals; Geoffrey Leib: piano; Kerry Morris: bass; Steven Scharf: background vocals; Kelly Shanahan: drums; Scott Shelley: string synthesizer; J. D. Souther: background vocals; Jerry Swallow: guitars; Donny Ullstrom: background vocals; Richie Walker: background vocals; Ernie Watts: saxophone; Jayne Zinsmaster: background vocals

ONE MORE SONG
Epic / Legacy Records 36748 — 1978
CD (Japan only)
Produced by Val Garay

Songs
Hearts on Fire
    Randy Meisner / Eric Kaz
Gotta Get Away
    Meisner / Kaz / Wendy Waldman
Come on Back to Me
    Meisner / Kaz / Waldman
Deep Inside My Heart
    Meisner / Kaz
I Need You Bad
    Meisner / Kaz / Waldman
One More Song
    Jack Tempchin
Trouble Ahead
    Meisner / Kaz / Waldman
White Shoes
    Tempchin
Anyway Bye Bye
    Richie Furay

Additional musicians: The Silverados: percussion; Don Francisco: background vocals; Bryan Garofalo: bass; Craig Hull: guitars and pedal steel; Sterling Smith: keyboards; Wendy Waldman: background vocals, acoustic guitar; Kim Carnes: background vocals; Bill

Cuomo: synthesizer strings; Glenn Frey: background vocals; Don Henley: background vocals; Michael Jacobson: saxophone

RANDY MEISNER

Epic 38121 — 1982
Elektra CD rerelease (Japan only)
Produced by Mike Flicker

Songs

Never Been in Love
    Craig Bickhardt
Darkness of the Heart
    David Palmer
Jealousy
    Randy Meisner / Dixon House / Howard Leese
Tonight
    Bryan Adams / Jim Vallance
Playin' in the Deep End
    Meisner / House
Strangers
    Elton John / Gary Osborne
Still Runnin'
    House / Leese
Nothing Is Said ('Til the Artist Is Dead)
    Meisner / House
Doin' It for Delilah
    John Corey

Additional musicians: Denny Carmassi: drums; John Corey: piano, backing vocals, guitar; Tom Erak: bass; Mitchell Froom: synthesizer; Nicy Hopkins: piano; Dixon House: piano, organ, backing vocals; Phil Kenzie: sax solos; Howard Leese: electric guitar, backing vocals, synthesizer; Marcy Levy: backing vocals; Brian Smith: guitar; Sterling Smith: piano, organ, synthesizer; Ann Wilson: vocals; Nancy Wilson: backing vocals; Tower of Power Horns

SINGLES

Once Again — The Poor
    1966
She's Got the Time, She's Got the Changes — The Poor
    1967
Deep Inside My Heart
    Epic — 1980

357

Hearts on Fire
  Epic — 1980
Gotta Get Away
  Epic — 1980
Never Been in Love
  Epic — 1982

ADDITIONAL NON-EAGLES RECORDINGS

Pickin' Up the Pieces — Poco
  Legacy Records 66227 — 1969
Long Vacation — Rick Nelson
  Imperial LP 9244 — 1963
  Bass, vocals: all songs
Sweet Baby James — James Taylor
  Warner Bros. 2-1843 — 1970
  Bass: all songs
Linda Ronstadt — Linda Ronstadt
  Capitol / EMI 80172 — 1972
  Bass, vocals
Garden Party — Rick Nelson
  MCA 31364 — 1972
  Bass, vocals
In Concert — *Troubadour 1969* — Rick Nelson
  MCA 25983 — 1973
Souvenirs — Dan Fogelberg
  Epic EK-33137 — 1974
  Vocals
So Long, Harry Truman — Danny O'Keefe
  Atlantic SD 18125 — 1974
  Bass
So What — Joe Walsh
  Dunhill 50171 — 1974
  Vocals, bass
Hymn to the Seeker — Mac Gayden
  ABC 960 — 1976
  Vocals
FM — Sound track
  MCA 6900 — 1978
  "Life in the Fast Lane"

Man Overboard — Bob Welch
    Capitol 12107 — 1980
    Vocals
I Still Have Dreams — Richie Furay
    Asylum 213 — 1981
    Vocals
Richard Marx — Richard Marx
    Capitol / EMI 46760 — 1987
    Vocals
Get into the Greed — Compilation
    Sony 66392 — 1995
    Song: "Hearts on Fire"
In California — Compton and Batteau
    Columbia 30039 (date unknown)
    Bass

BERNIE LEADON — ALBUMS

NATURAL PROGRESSIONS — THE BERNIE LEADON–MICHAEL GEORGIADES BAND
Asylum 1107 — 1977

Songs
Callin' for Your Love
How Can You Live Without Love?
Breath
Rotation
You're the Singer
Tropical Winter
As Time Goes On
The Sparrows
At Love Again
Glass Off

EVER CALL READY
A&M — 1985
With Chris Hillman, Al Perskins, Jerry Scheff, and Dave Mansfield

ADDITIONAL NON-EAGLES RECORDINGS

Bluegrass Favorites — The Scottsville Squirrel Barkers
    Crown CST 346 — 1963

Of Horses, Kids and Forgotten Women — Hearts and Flowers
    Capitol ST 2868 — 1968
The Fantastic Expedition — Dillard and Clark
    A&M SD-4158 — 1968
Through the Morning, Through the Night — Dillard and Clark
    A&M SD-4248 — 1969
The Banjo Album — Doug Dillard
    A&M — 1969
The Flying Burrito Brothers — The Flying Burrito Brothers
    A&M SD-4295 — 1971
Linda Ronstadt — Linda Ronstadt
    Capitol / EMI 80172 — 1971
    Guitars and vocals
Last of the Red Hot Burritos — The Flying Burrito Brothers
    A&M 4343 — 1972
Windfalls — Rick Roberts
    A&M 4372 — 1972
    Banjo, guitar, vocals
Good Old Boys — Randy Newman
    Reprise MS4-2193 — 1974
    Vocal backgrounds
So Long, Harry Truman — Danny O'Keefe
    Atlantic / Atco 18125 — 1974
    Song: "So Long, Harry Truman"
Sleepless Nights — The Flying Burrito Brothers
    A&M 4578 — 1976
Honky Tonk Heaven — The Flying Burrito Brothers
    A&M — 1976
Greatest Hits — Linda Ronstadt
    Asylum 6E-106 — 1976
    Song: "Different Drum" (Acoustic guitars — originally released by Stone Poneys)
Morning Sky — Chris Hillman
    Sugar Hill 3729 — 1982
Workin' Band — The Nitty Gritty Dirt Band
    Warner 25722 — 1988
It's All About to Change — Travis Tritt
    Warner — 1989
Big Iron Horses — Restless Hearts
    1992
    Producer
Street Angel — Stevie Nicks
    Warner — 1994

Row vs. Wade — Run C&W
    1994

DON FELDER — SOLO ALBUM

AIRBORNE
Elektra / Asylum 60295 — 1983

ADDITIONAL NON-EAGLES RECORDINGS

Flow — Flow
    CTI 1003 — 1970
Pretender — Michael Dinner
    Fantasy 944454 — 1974
    Guitar
Comin' Back for More — David Blue
    Asylum 7E-1043 — 1975
    Guitars
Two Lane Highway — Pure Prairie League
    RCA APLI-0933 — 1975
A Rumor in His Own Time — Jeffrey Comanor
    Epic PE 34080 — 1976
Fool's Gold — Fool's Gold
    Col PC 34828 — 1976
    Guitar: "I Will Run," "Rain, Oh, Rain"
You Can't Argue with a Sick Mind — Joe Walsh
    MCA 31120 — 1976
    Guitar
Mr. Lucky — Fool's Gold
    CBS 34828 — 1977
Stranger in Town — Bob Seger
    Capitol / EMI CZ-46074 — 1978
    Guitar: "Ain't Got No Money"
You're Only Lonely — J. D. Souther
    Legacy 36093 — 1979
    Guitar
Suzy — Terence Boylan
    Asylum 6E-201 — 1980
    Electric guitar: "Going Home"
Hits — Boz Scaggs
    Columbia CK 36841 — 1980
    Guitar

Plantation Harbor — Joe Vitale
  Asylum 529 — 1980
  Guitar
Bad Luck Streak in Dancing School — Warren Zevon
  Elektra 9 60561-2 — 1980
  Song: "A Certain Girl"
Living Eyes — Bee Gees
  RSO 13098 — 1981
Bella Donna — Stevie Nicks
  Modern 38193 — 1981
  Guitar: "The Highwayman"
Alive Alone — Mickey Thomas
  Elektra 530 — 1981
Heavy Metal — Sound track
  Asylum 90004 — 1981
  Songs: "Heavy Metal (Takin' a Ride)," "All of You"
Fast Times at Ridgemont High — Sound track
  Full Moon 60158 — 1982
  Song: "Never Surrender"
The Distance — Bob Seger
  Capitol / EMI CZ 46005 — 1982
  Songs: "Even Now," "Boomtown Blues"
Secret Admirer — Sound track
  MCA 5116 — 1985
  Song: "She's Got a Part of Me"
Slugger's Wife — Sound track
  MCA MCAC 5578 — 1985
  Song: "Wild Life"

TIMOTHY B. SCHMIT — SOLO ALBUMS

TELL ME THE TRUTH
MCA (MCAD — 1990) 6420 — 1983

PLAYIN' IT COOL
Asylum 960539 — 1984

TIMOTHY B.
MCA 42049 — 1987

SINGLES

So Much in Love b/w *She's My Baby* ("So Much in Love" from sound track of *Fast Times at Ridgemont High*)
　　　Asylum 60539 — 1982
Boys Night Out b/w *Don't Give Up*
　　　MCA MCAC 6420 (cassette only) — 1987

ALBUMS WITH POCO

Poco
　　　Epic E-26522 — 1970
From the Inside
　　　Legacy 30753 — 1971
A Good Feelin' to Know
　　　Epic PE-31601 — 1972
Crazy Eyes
　　　Legacy 66968 — 1973
Seven
　　　Legacy 66985 — 1974
Head Over Heels
　　　MCA 31327 — 1975
Rose of Cimarron
　　　One Way 22076 — 1976
The Very Best of Poco
　　　Epic PEG-33537 — 1976
Indian Summer
　　　MCA 31353 — 1977
Inamorata
　　　Atlantic 80148 — 1984

ADDITIONAL NON-EAGLES RECORDINGS

Glad — Glad
　　　ABC 60158 — 1970
Mary Called Jeanie Greene — Jeanie Greene
　　　Elektra 74103 — 1971
No Other — Gene Clark
　　　Asylum 1016 — 1974
Pretzel Logic — Steely Dan
　　　MCA MCAD 31165 — 1974

First Grade — Thomas Jefferson Kaye
    Dunhill 50142 — 1974
Bob Neuwirth — Bob Neuwirth
    Asylum 1008 — 1974
Heart Like a Wheel — Linda Ronstadt
    Capitol C2-46073 — 1974
Sweet Surprise — Eric Andersen
    Arista 4075 — 1976
Night After Night — Steve Cropper
    Epic 34080 — 1976
Royal Scam — Steely Dan
    MCA MCAD 31193 — 1976
Slippin' Away — Chris Hillman
    Asylum 1062 — 1976
Cardiff Rose — Roger McGuinn
    Columbia CK-34154 — 1976
Clear Sailin' — Chris Hillman
    Asylum 1104 — 1977
Cate Brothers Band — Cate Brothers
    Asylum 1116 — 1977
Aja — Steely Dan
    MCA MCAD — 1977
Luna Sea — Firefall
    Atlantic 19101 — 1977
Little Criminals — Randy Newman
    Reprise 3079 — 1977
Greatest Hits — Steely Dan
    MCA MCAD2 6008 — 1978
Dance a Little — Richie Furay
    Asylum 115 — 1978
Jack Tempchin — Jack Tempchin
    Arista 4193 — 1978
Peaks, Valleys, Honky Tonks and Alleys — Michael Murphy
    Epic 35742 — 1979
Suzy — Terence Boylan
    Elektra 201 — 1980
21 at 33 — Elton John
    MCA MCAB 31054 — 1980
Hits! — Boz Scaggs
    Columbia CK-36841 — 1980
Plantation Harbor — Joe Vitale
    Asylum 529 — 1980

There Goes the Neighborhood — Joe Walsh
    Asylum 523-2 — 1981
Right Place — Gary Wright
    Warner Bros. 3511 — 1981
Wild Heart of the Young — Karla Bonoff
    Columbia 37444 — 1982
Rumor in His Own Time — Jeffrey Comanor
    Epic 5340 — 1982
Daylight Again — Crosby, Stills, Nash and Young
    Atlantic 19360-2 — 1982
Eye to Eye — Eye to Eye
    Warner Bros. 3570 — 1982
Fast Times at Ridgemont High — Sound track
    Full Moon 60158 — 1982
    "So Much in Love"
I Can't Stand Still — Don Henley
    Asylum 2-60048 — 1982
Quarterflash — Quarterflash
    Geffen 2-2003 — 1982
Toto IV — Toto
    Columbia CK 37728 — 1982
Perfect Stranger — Jesse Colin Young
    Elektra 60151 — 1982
Airborne — Don Felder
    Elektra / Asylum 60295 — 1983
Dirty Looks — Juice Newton
    Capitol 12294 — 1993
Take Another Picture — Quarterflash
    Geffen 4011 — 1983
Windows and Walls — Dan Fogelberg
    Full Moon EK 39004 — 1984
Home by Dawn — J. D. Souther
    Warner Bros. 25081 — 1984
Youngblood — Carl Wilson
    Caribou 37970 — 1984
Secret Admirer — Sound track
    MCA 5611 — 1985
    "Leaving It Up to You"
Against the Wind — Bob Seger
    Capitol C2-46060 — 1985
Confessor — Joe Walsh
    Full Moon 2-25281 — 1985

Allman and Woman: Two the Hard Way — Greg Allman
    Warner Bros. 3120 — 1986
Like a Rock — Bob Seger
    Capitol C2 46195 — 1986
Little America — Little America
    Geffen 2-24113 — 1987
Richard Marx — Richard Marx
    Capitol C2-46760 — 1987
Hot Water — Jimmy Buffett
    MCA MCAD 42093 — 1988
Soul Searchin' — Glenn Frey
    MCA 6239 — 1988
Other Roads — Boz Scaggs
    Columbia CK 40463 — 1988
Off to See the Lizard — Jimmy Buffett
    MCA 6314 — 1989
Mr. Jordan — Julian Lennon
    Atlantic 81928-2 — 1989
Back from Rio — Roger McGuinn
    Arista ARCD 8648 — 1990
Don't Tell Mom the Babysitter's Dead — Sound track
    Giant 2-24428 — 1991
    "I Only Have Eyes for You"
Born to Rock and Roll — Roger McGuinn
    Columbia CK 47494 — 1992
Vol. 2: Live from Montreaux — Ringo Starr
    Rykodisk 20264 — 1993
    Live version of "I Can't Tell You Why"
Bye Bye Love — Sound track
    Warner Bros. 24609-2 — 1995
    "Let It Be Me" (with Jackson Browne)
Actual Miles — Henley's Greatest Hits
    Geffen 24834 — 1995

JOE WALSH — SOLO ALBUMS

BARNSTORM
Dunhill 50130 — 1972
Produced by Bill Szymczyk

THE SMOKER YOU DRINK, THE PLAYER YOU GET
MCA 31121 — 1973 (rereleased in a "gold disc" version, MCA Masterdisc 11170 — 1994)
Produced by Joe Walsh and Bill Szymczyk

Songs

Rocky Mountain Way
  Walsh / Joe Vitale / Kenny Passarelli
Book Ends
  Vitale
Wolf
  Walsh
Midnight Moodies
  Rocke Grace
Happy Ways
  Passarelli
Meadows
  Walsh
Dreams
  Walsh
Days Gone By
  Vitale
Day Dream Prayer
  Walsh

Additional musicians: Joe Vitale: drums, flute, vocals, keyboards, synthesizer; Rocke Grace: keyboards, vocals; Kenny Passarelli: bass, vocals; Joe Lala: percussion; Clydie King: background vocals; Venetta Fields: background vocals

SO WHAT?
Dunhill 50171 — 1974
Produced by Joe Walsh and John Stronach
Guest artists: Glenn Frey, Don Henley, J. D. Souther, Dan Fogelberg

Songs

Welcome to the Club
  Walsh
Falling Down
  Walsh / Don Henley
Pavanne
  Maurice Ravel
Time Out
  Walsh
All Night Laundry Mat Blues
  Walsh
Turn to Stone
  Walsh

Help Me Through the Night
    Walsh
County Fair
    Walsh
Song for Emma
    Walsh

Additional musicians: James Bond: acoustic bass; Jody Boyer: background vocals; Dan Fogelberg: guitar, snarks and misc.; Glenn Frey: background vocals; Guille Garcia: congas; Bryan Garofalo: background vocals, bass; Ron Grinel: drums; Don Henley: background vocals; Russ Kunkel: drums; Randy Meisner: background vocals; Kenny Passarelli: bass; J. D. Souther: background vocals; Leonard Stephenson: organ; John Stronach: misc.; Joe Vitale: drums

YOU CAN'T ARGUE WITH A SICK MIND
ABC LP 932 — 1976
(Release of previously recorded songs.)

Songs
Walk Away
    Walsh
Meadows
    Walsh / Patrick Cullie
Rocky Mountain Way
    Walsh / Joe Vitale / Ken Passarelli / Rocke Grace
Time Out
    Walsh
Help Me Through the Night
    Walsh
Turn to Stone
    Walsh / Terry Trebandt

BUT SERIOUSLY FOLKS . . .
Elektra Entertainment 141 — 1978
Produced by Bill Szymczyk

Songs
Over and Over
    Walsh
Second Hand Store
    Walsh / Mike Murphy

Indian Summer
    Walsh
At the Station
    Walsh / Joe Vitale
Tomorrow
    Walsh
Inner Tube
    Walsh
Theme from Boat Weirdos
    Walsh / Vitale / Jay Ferguson / Willie Weeks / Bill Szymczyk
Life's Been Good
    Walsh

Additional musicians: Jay Ferguson: keyboards; Joey Murcia: guitar; Joe Vitale: drums, percussion, flute, synthesizer, background vocals; Willie Weeks: bass; Jody Boyer: background vocals; Don Felder: pedal steel guitar, guitar; Glenn Frey: background vocals; Don Henley: background vocals; Timothy B. Schmit: background vocals; Bill Szymczyk: tambourine, background vocals

BEST OF JOE WALSH
MCA 1601 — 1978

Songs
Turn to Stone
Mother Says
Help Me Through the Night
Rocky Mountain Way
Meadows
County Fair
Funk #49
Time Out
Walk Away

Additional musicians on "Funk #49" and "Walk Away": Jim Fox: drums, percussion; Dale Peters: bass, percussion; Bill Szymczyk: percussion

ADDITIONAL SOLO ALBUMS (POST-EAGLES)

THERE GOES THE NEIGHBORHOOD
Elektra 441 (and Elektra 523) — 1981
Produced by Joe Walsh

YOU BOUGHT IT, YOU NAME IT
Warner Bros. 23884-1 — 1983
Produced by Bill Szymczyk

THE CONFESSOR
Warner Bros. 25281 — 1985
Produced by Keith Olsen
Appearance by Timothy B. Schmit

GOT ANY GUM?
Warner Bros. 25606 — 1987
Produced by Terry Manning

JUMP THE BLUES AWAY (WITH ALBERT COLLINS AND ETTA JAMES)
Verve 841287

ORDINARY AVERAGE GUY
Epic Associated 47384 — 1991
Produced by Joe Walsh and Joe Vitale

SONGS FOR A DYING PLANET
Epic Associated 48916 — 1992
Produced by Bill Szymczyk

LOOK WHAT I DID! THE JOE WALSH ANTHOLOGY
MCA CD2-11233 — 1995
Glenn Frey: vocals, "Ordinary Average Guy"

SINGLES

Rocky Mountain Way
    Dunhill 4361 — 1973
Life's Been Good
    Asylum 45493 — 1973
All Night Long
    Asylum 46639 — 1980
A Life of Illusion
    Asylum 47144 — 1981
The Waffle Stomp b/w *Things*
    Full Moon 29611 — 1983
Space Age Whiz Kids b/w *Theme from Island Weirdos*
    Full Moon 29672 — 1983
The Radio Song b/w *How Ya Doin?*
    Warner Bros. 28304 — 1987

ALBUMS WITH THE JAMES GANG

Yer Album
    One Way 22052 — 1969
The James Gang Rides Again
    ABC X-711 — 1970
Thirds
    ABC 721 — 1971
Live in Concert
    ABC X-733 — 1972

ADDITIONAL NON-EAGLES RECORDINGS

Indianola Mississippi Seeds — B. B. King
    MCA 31343 — 1970
    Guitars
All American Boy — Rick Derringer
    Blue Sky ZK-32481 — 1973
She Is a Song — Rick Roberts
    A&M-4404 — 1973
Souvenirs — Dan Fogelberg
    Epic EK-33137 — 1974
    Produced by Joe Walsh
    "Part of the Plan" (guitars, keyboards, vocals); "Changing Hearts" (guitars); "Illinois"
    (12 string); "Better Change" (guitars); "Souvenirs" (harp bass); "The Long Way" (elec-
    tric slide, background vocals); "As the Raven Flies" (guitars); "Morning Sky" (guitars);
    "(Someone's Been) Telling You Stories" (guitars, vocals); "There's a Place in the World
    for a Gambler" (guitars)
Kids and Me — Billy Preston
    A&M 3645 — 1974
Two Sides of the Moon — Keith Moon
    MCA 2136 — 1975
Rollercoaster Weekend — Joe Vitale
    Atlantic 18114 — 1975
All Alone in the End Zone — Jay Ferguson
    Asylum 7E-1063 — 1976
Firefall — Firefall
    Atlantic 4-19125 — 1976
Mr. Lucky — Fool's Gold
    Arista 5500 — 1976
    Song: "Coming Out of Hiding"
A Night on the Town — Rod Stewart
    Warner Bros. 3116 — 1976

Black Rose — J. D. Souther
    Asylum 1059 — 1976
    Slide guitar: "Baby Come Home"
Stone Alone — Bill Wyman
    Rolling Stones QD-79103 — 1976
Works, Volume 1 — Emerson, Lake and Palmer
    Atlantic 2 7000 — 1977
    Slide, talk box, and scat vocals: "L.A. Nights"
Nether Lands — Dan Fogelberg
    Full Moon / Epic 34185 — 1977
    Guitars: "Loose Ends"
Little Criminals — Randy Newman
    Warner Bros. 3079 — 1977
FM — Sound track
    MCA 12000 — 1978
    Song: "Life's Been Good"
Warriors — Sound track
    A&M SP-4761 — 1978
    Song: "In the City" (prior to inclusion in a different version on
    The Long Run)
Thunder Island — Jay Ferguson
    Asylum 111 — 1978
Urban Cowboy — Sound track
    Asylum 90002 — 1980
    Song: "All Night Long"
Bad Luck Streak in Dancing School — Warren Zevon
    Elektra 60561-2 — 1980
    Lead guitar: "Jungle Work"
    Solo guitar: "Jeannie Needs a Shooter"
Earth and Sky — Graham Nash
    EMI / Capitol 12014 — 1980
Terms and Conditions — Jay Ferguson
    Capitol 12083 — 1980
Too Late the Hero — John Entwistle
    Atco 38142 — 1981
    Producer, guitar
Fast Times at Ridgemont High — Sound track
    Full Moon 60158 — 1982
    Song: "Waffle Stomp"
Greatest Hits — Dan Fogelberg
    Epic 38381 — 1982
    Producer: "Part of the Plan"

I Can't Stand Still — Don Henley
    Asylum E160048 — 1982
    Guitar: "Dirty Laundry"
Lionel Richie — Lionel Richie
    Motown 6007-2 — 1982
Wild Heart of the Young — Karla Bonoff
    Columbia 37444 — 1982
    Electric guitar: "It Just Takes One"
White Noise — Jay Ferguson
    Capitol 12196 — 1982
Old Wave — Ringo Starr
    Capitol 29675 — 1983
    Producer, guitar
Take Another Picture — Quarterflash
    Geffen 4011 — 1983
Playin' It Cool — Timothy B. Schmit
    Asylum 960539 — 1984
No Lookin' Back — Michael McDonald
    Warner Bros. 2-25291 — 1985
Back in the High Life — Steve Winwood
    Island 422-830148-2 — 1986
Richard Marx — Richard Marx
    Capitol / EMI CZ-46760 — 1987
Great Outdoors — Sound track
    Atlantic 81859-1 — 1988
    Song: "Big Country"
Heavy Metal Memories
    Rhino R215-70986 — 1991
    Song: "Rocky Mountain Way"
The Fire Inside — Bob Seger
    Capitol / EMI 91134 — 1991
Beverly Hillbillies — Sound track
    MCA 66313 — 1993
    Song: "Honey Don't" (with Steve Earle)
Vol. 2: Live from Montreux — Ringo Starr
    Rykodisc 20264 — 1993
Earthrise: The Rainforest Album
    1995
    Song: "Look at Us Now"
Frat Rock: More of the 70's
    Rhino 72132 — 1995
    Song: "Life's Been Good"

Actual Miles — Henley's Greatest Hits — Don Henley
    Geffen GEFD 2834 — 1995
    Guitar: "Dirty Laundry"
Robocop: The Series — Sound track
    Pyramid 71888 — 1995
    Songs: "A Future to This Life," "Guilty of the Crime," "Fire and Brimstone," "A Future to This Life" (with Lita Ford), "Guilty of the Crime" (with Frankie Miller, Nicky Hopkins)
Finer Things — Steve Winwood
    Island 314-516860 — 1995

In addition, previously recorded songs of Joe Walsh appear on the following CD compilations: *70's Greatest Hits, Vol. 1, Rock of the 70's, Vol. 3, Best of King Biscuit Live, Vol. 1, Reeling in the Years, Vol. 3, Classic Rock, Classic Rock, Vol. 1, All Rock and Roll* (KCBS) (KKRW) (WARW) (KRRW) (WAKS) (KKRO) (WGFX)

EAGLES GRAMMY AWARDS

1975
Best Pop Vocal Performance by a Duo, Group or Chorus: "Lyin' Eyes"

1977
Record of the Year: "Hotel California" (single)
Best Arrangement for Voices: "New Kid in Town"

1979
Best Rock Vocal Performance by a Duo or Group: "Heartache Tonight"

1986 (Individual)
Don Henley — Best Rock Vocal Performance, Male: "The Boys of Summer"

1990 (Individual)
Don Henley — Best Rock Vocal Performance, Male: "The End of the Innocence" (single)

Note: In 1995, *Hell Freezes Over* was nominated for Best Pop Performance by a Duo or Group with Vocal: "Love Will Keep Us Alive," Best Pop Album, Best Rock Performance by a Duo or Group with Vocal: "Hotel California," Best Engineered Album, Non-Classical. The album failed to win in any of its categories.

COMPILATION ALBUM OF EAGLES SONGS
BY NON-EAGLES

COMMON THREAD: THE SONGS OF THE EAGLES
Giant Records 9-24531-2 — 1993
Executive producer: James Stroud
Mastered by Bernie Grundman at Bernie Grundman Mastering Studio, Hollywood, CA
Creative Consultant: Ralph Sall

Songs
Take It Easy
>Performed by Travis Tritt
>Produced by James Stroud

Peaceful Easy Feeling
>Performed by Little Texas
>Produced by Christy DiNapoli and Doug Grau

Desperado
>Performed by Clint Black
>Produced by James Stroud

Heartache Tonight
>Performed by John Anderson
>Produced by James Stroud

Tequila Sunrise
>Performed by Alan Jackson
>Produced by Keith Stegall

Take It to the Limit
>Performed by Suzy Bogguss
>Produced by Suzy Bogguss

I Can't Tell You Why
>Performed by Vince Gill
>Produced by Tony Brown

Lyin' Eyes
>Performed by Diamond Rio
>Produced by Monty Powell

New Kid in Town
>Performed by Trisha Yearwood
>Produced by Garth Fundis

Saturday Night
>Performed by Billy Dean
>Produced by Lynn Peterzell and Billy Dean

Already Gone
  Performed by Tanya Tucker
  Produced by Jerry Crutchfield
Best of My Love
  Performed by Brooks and Dunn
  Produced by Don Cook and Scott Hendricks
The Sad Café
  Performed by Lorrie Morgan
  Produced by Richard Landis

"A portion of the royalties from the sales of this collection will go to the Walden Woods Project, a nonprofit organization founded in 1990. The purpose of the Walden Woods Project is to purchase, and thereby preserve, environmentally sensitive and historically significant forestland located near Henry David Thoreau's famed retreat at Walden Pond."

ACKNOWLEDGMENTS

I've always loved the music of the Eagles. For me, their great harmonies, richly textured arrangements, clanging guitars, and smart lyrics grace rock's endless highway with beauty, wit, intelligence, and majesty. This is a band whose imagined vision of lush, edgy Left Coast beauties with restless, sweet hearts and lovely, if lying, eyes; of excess and emptiness, meaning and meaninglessness, and the meaning *of* that meaninglessness, has landscaped so many of the shared hopes, heartbreaks, desires, and dreams of one generation and surely countless more to come.

As the premier American band of the seventies, the Eagles provided the essential musical link between the classic rock and roll of the fifties and sixties and the progressive sound that formed the eighties and nineties. As such, they occupy one of the key positions in the history of American pop culture.

My interest in becoming the biographer of the Eagles certainly stems in part from my admiration of their body of work and, in a broader sense, out of my love for rock and roll. I am often asked if I know my subjects personally when I first begin to gather the stories of their lives. The answer is sometimes I do, sometimes I don't, and sometimes I get to know them in the course of my research and writing. Phil Ochs was one of my best friends. I began writing his biography (*Death of a Rebel*) in 1976 shortly after his death. I did not know Bruce Springsteen when I wrote *Down Thunder Road,* although I did become very good friends with Mike Appel, the man who discovered and managed Bruce for the first five years of his career, up to and including *Born to Run.* Beyond that, the question of "knowing" becomes more philosophical than journalistic. My two mentors at Columbia University's Graduate School of the Arts were the noted biographer Frank McShane and the great American film historian and critic Andrew Sarris, neither of whom understood, appreciated, encouraged, or condoned my life-long obsession with rock music. Still, in response to the question of my qualifications, and my personal knowledge of the Eagles, I quote from Sarris's *You Ain't Heard Nothin' Yet*. He describes being asked by a reporter in 1986 to comment on the death of Cary Grant, specifically as to whether he had ever known the man. Sarris writes: "I said no very quickly. But having seen sixty-nine of his seventy-two movies, and having witnessed his marvelously gracious performances at several public occasions, can I be said to have 'known' him less intimately than I would have if I had peppered him with journalistic queries at some marathon interview or other? Very probably, I 'knew' much the best part of him, a part that I suspect he would have wanted me to know if he had had any inkling of how much I respected and admired all that he was, all that he had achieved, and all that he had overcome." *Amen, brother! Praise the Lord and pass the Eagles albums!*

Still, I determined early on to get as many of the Eagles as possible to come to the table and be "peppered with journalistic queries." This proved no easy task. At first they steadfastly refused, and went so far as to put up barriers they felt would be as impenetrable as the wall that once divided Berlin. However, walls of restriction inevitably fall, and so too did these. It was always the Eagles' right to choose to remain private, and it was always mine to choose to examine the lives of public figures who occupy a major place in the panorama of our pop culture. I find it intriguing when artists whose most revealing work provides such a personal and revealing side of them blanch at the thought of anyone actually wanting to *know* anything about them. As I see it, the more we learn about those we idolize, the better off we are. When *any* rock star or band of elitist millionaires dresses in blue jeans and sings about the heartbreak of working-class teens, I think it is valid, if not crucial, for the youngsters who identify with and idealize these guitar-slung heroes to want to know just who and what it is they are believing in and trying to emulate.

Having said that, I wish to thank the following people who were willing to talk about the Eagles with me:

After nearly two years of abject refusal, Don Henley agreed to be interviewed, first in writing and then in person. It is to Henley's credit that after reading an early version of this book, he decided it was important to make sure I got the story right. Once we did get together, mostly in Irving Azoff's headquarters, Henley was forthcoming, contemplative, witty, articulate, critical, confrontational, genteel, personal, and charming. He answered every question I had, corrected much of the chronology of the early part of the book, and I firmly believe made it possible for me to take it to a whole other level. I must emphasize that *To the Limit* is and always was intended to be a completely unauthorized book. Neither Don Henley nor anyone else interviewed had any editorial control. Those who chose to talk were encouraged to make suggestions and provide factual, provable corrections. Don Henley is a gentleman and a man of his word. I know it was difficult for him to talk to me about the Eagles and his private life, and I thank him for it.

Irving Azoff, who at first led the charge against me, was also the one who eventually helped turn the spigot of information back on. When we finally met, he was gracious, generous, and spirited. We talked quite often, and he proved a great help in opening doors that otherwise would surely have remained shut. To paraphrase something Henley said at his Rock and Roll Hall of Fame induction, Azoff may be Satan, but when he's your Satan, *hot damn!* Thank you, Irving.

Former Eagle Randy Meisner was an invaluable contributor to this book. I remain impressed by his candor, manner, and talent, and appreciative of his cooperation and support.

Also crucial was David Geffen. When I first called his office and asked for an interview, I passed through a chain of command that, even for a Hollywood mogul, was quite impressive. I left my message with a fourth- or fifth-tier voice, and a few days later, at eight o'clock in the morning, my phone rang, and when I picked it up, I heard, "Hold for David Geffen, please." We talked for quite a while, and I was struck by his clairty, openness, detail of observation, and brilliant understanding of both the business and the nature of rock and roll. I thank him for sharing some of it with me.

Joe Smith made himself available in his home, letting me fire away with all I had. I love people like this: powerful, smart, tough, and willing to keep the record straight.

John Boylan was remarkable in his vast recollection of the early days of the Eagles. He was articulate and vividly illuminating as he patiently reviewed the events of his participation in the formative period of the band. I thank him for his information, his encouragement, his enthusiasm, and his effort.

J. D. Souther was informative, friendly, cooperative, and great fun to interview.

Others who were remarkably generous with their time and knowledge and to whom I remain grateful include Joe Walsh, Jim Ed Norman, Michael Bowden, Elliot Roberts, Barry De Vorzon, Mark Volman, Don Engel, Linda Jones, Greg Ladanyi, Paul Ahern, Richie Fernandez, Larry Solters, Judi Ricor, Bob Singer, Joe Berry, Bob Sterne, John Vanderslice, Bonnie Covelli, Fred Walacki, Peter Golden, Chris Charlesworth, David Rensin, and Bob Spitz.

I have known Elliot Roberts since I was ten years old. We were both born and raised in the Bronx, where Elliot was my late older brother Jeffrey's best friend. As New York City teenagers, they were intensely devoted to nickel bags, great-looking chicks, and the music of the Temptations. It took a while, but Elliot did lend his inimitable touch to this book, for which I thank him.

Jackson Browne called me one night at home to "set the record straight" about something. Jackson and I ran into each other socially a few times during the time it took for me to write *To the Limit*, once at a Bruce Springsteen concert, once at a Christmas party, maybe another time or two. We had a long, fascinating conversation that night on the phone about the right of free expression, the obsessive nature of biography, the price of fame, and the music of, among other people, Phil Ochs.

Many others I interviewed willingly opened up their hearts and minds and, understandably, for a variety of reasons did not wish to be named in the text or listed here. I shall, of course, honor these requests. Detailed records of what was said and by whom remain in my possession.

Laurence Kirshbaum, the head of Warner Trade Publishing, is a truly amazing man. I cannot sufficiently acknowledge how much his extraordinary support of my effort to keep the integrity of this biography intact means to me. He was unswerving, unfailingly enthusiastic, and compassionate about the nature of my journalistic responsibilities.

I wish to thank my editor, Michael Pietsch. I have known Michael a long time and consider it both a professional and personal privilege to work with him. To be an editor, I believe, is to be born with great talent and incredible patience. He has an abundance of both, much to my good fortune. I also wish to thank the editorial team of Nora Krug, David Gibbs, and Betsy Uhrig.

I wish to thank my agent, Eric Simonoff, of the Janklow-Nesbit Literary Agency.

Personally, I wish to thank the following:

My oldest and dearest friend in the whole wide world, the Chairman of the Board, Mr. Dennis Klein.

My uncle Duane. They say you can choose your friends but not your relatives. Don't be so sure. Thanks, Unc.

Lenard, who never minded when I turned his living room in St. Croix into what seemed to me a quite good place to spread out my stuff, turn up the volume, and write.

The late Karen Hubert Allison, my dear friend for twenty-seven years, who remained unfailingly supportive and close through so many of the best and worst of both our times. I shall dearly and deeply miss her.

My beautiful, funny, and supportive Chi-Li, so special, precious, and inspiring.

Also, Phil Ochs, who first introduced me to the idea of living in Los Angeles; David Blue, who ran with me when I finally made my move; and these magnificent women of the Left Coast: Donna Ted from Lafayette, Liz from Beechwood, Debbie from Beverly Hills below Wilshire, Jenny from Beverly Hills above, Hollywood, and Hampstead, Christine from the valley, Bon-Bon from Burbank, Carol Anne from New Zealand, Kathy from Santa Monica, Karen from Santa Monica, Karen from the valley, Cyndy from Sunset, Kim from Hollywood and Ocean, Nicole from Mojacar, Caroline from the Avenue of the Americas, Elizabeth from the West Side . . . and 'Mona — some were lovers, some were friends, all shared a little time and space with me during the years I spent living it up at the Hotel California.

·

INDEX

Evans, Robert, 168
Everly Brothers, 34, 42, 55, 87, 185

Facilities Merchandising, 212, 229
Faltermeyer, Harold, 218
Felder, Don, 236 (*see also* Eagles, the)
  Hall of Fame speech, 259
  joins the Eagles, 109–111, 113
  marriage, 247, 259
  solo career, 203, 221, 241
  songwriting credits, 148, 149, 183–184,
    246
Felicity (band), 15
Fenton, David, 192
Fernandez, Richard (Richie), 97, 102–103,
  110, 114, 154–158
Fields, Verna, 173
films. *See* movies
Fine Young Cannibals, the, 231
First Edition, 18
Flack, Roberta, 80
Fleetwood, Mick, 34, 84, 128
Fleetwood Mac, 168, 170, 187, 241, 255
Fleetwood Mac (album), 128
Flo and Eddie, 146
Flying Burrito Brothers, the, 21, 60, 85,
  255
FM (film), 173–174, 280*n*
Fogarty, John, 249
Fogelberg, Dan, 98, 101, 104, 106, 115,
  241
Forsey, Keith, 218
Four Speeds, the, 13–14
Frame, Peter, 30
Frampton, Peter, 168
Freed, Alan, 252–253, 254
Frey, Glenn, 5 (*see also* Eagles)
  acting career, 217–218, 221–223,
    237–239, 250–251
  arrest, 222
  childhood/youth, 23–27
  early musical career, 23–27, 40–43, 45
  as group's leader, 68–70, 95, 248
  Hall of Fame speech, 259–260
  health, 130, 156, 234, 247–248

Henley, relationship with, 69, 87–88,
  93–95, 111, 127–128, 130–131,
  146–147, 150, 155–156, 158, 181–182,
  188, 189, 208, 219–220, 234–235,
  240, 248
  marriages, 238, 247
  musical style, 72, 73, 87–88, 118, 178
  nickname, 86
  publishing rights, 93–94
  romances, 129–130
  Ronstadt, association with, 57–61, 66, 67
  solo career, 203–204, 206, 213–214,
    217–218, 223, 240, 241
  songwriting credits, 40–43, 76, 92, 96,
    102, 112, 131, 149, 178, 183–184, 243,
    246, 258–259
  substance abuse, 26, 27, 43, 130–131,
    222, 238
  TV appearances, 219–220
Frey, Nellie, 23, 25, 26, 40
Front Line Management, 98, 106, 132, 134,
  173, 212, 229–230
Full Moon Records (company), 212, 229
Furay, Richie, 29, 31–32, 37, 108–109

"Garden of Allah, The" (song), 249–250
Geffen, David, 5, 46, 258, 259 (*see also*
  Asylum Records)
  Azoff and, 101, 229, 232
  Azoff lawsuit, 137–140, 174–175, 180
  C, S, N and Y, contract dispute, 49–53
  health, 136–137, 211
  Henley and, 104–105, 214–216,
    227–228, 239–241, 249–250, 257
  as record producer, 63–69, 83, 88–92,
    96–97, 104–109, 135–138, 140,
    211–216, 274*n*
Geffen-Roberts Company, 52–53, 63, 68,
  90–91, 101, 229, 269*n*
George, Lowell, 36
"Get Over It" (song), 243, 246
Giant Records (company), 231–232, 241,
  286*n*
Gill, Vince, 242
"Girl from Yesterday, The" (song), 243, 246

387

391